Mourning Remains

Mourning Remains

State Atrocity, Exhumations, and
Governing the Disappeared in Peru's Postwar Andes

Isaias Rojas-Perez

Stanford University Press

Stanford, California

Stanford University Press
Stanford, California

Printed in the United States of America on acid-free, archival-quality paper

Library of Congress Cataloging-in-Publication Data

Names: Rojas-Perez, Isaias, author.
Title: Mourning remains : state atrocity, exhumations, and governing the
    disappeared in Peru's postwar Andes / Isaias Rojas-Perez.
Description: Stanford, California : Stanford University Press, 2017. | Includes
    bibliographical references and index.
Identifiers: LCCN 2016049918 (print) | LCCN 2016051528 (ebook) |
    ISBN 9781503600881 (cloth : alk. paper) | ISBN 9781503602625 (pbk. : alk.
    paper) | ISBN 9781503602632 (e-book)
Subjects: LCSH: Disappeared persons—Peru. | Disappeared persons' families—
    Peru. | Quechua Indians—Crimes against—Peru. | State-sponsored
    terrorism—Peru. | Exhumation—Political aspects—Peru. | Transitional
    justice—Peru.
Classification: LCC HV6322.3.P4 R65 2017 (print) | LCC HV6322.3.P4 (ebook) |
    DDC 362.870985—dc23
LC record available at https://lccn.loc.gov/2016049918

Typeset by Newgen in 11/13.5 Adobe Garamond Pro

Chinkaqkuna mamankunapaq
To the Mothers of the Disappeared

Contents

Illustrations

Maps

Figures

Acknowledgments

MANY PEOPLE HAVE made this book possible. In the years it took me to complete it, I have accumulated profound debts. My greatest is to the Quechua-speaking survivors and relatives of victims of the campaign of state terror in Peru's central southern Andes, who generously shared with me their personal and collective stories of suffering as well as resilience in the face of adversity. I hope that this book somehow contributes to their ongoing struggle for justice.

I am particularly indebted to the Ayacuchano mothers of the disappeared. As the pages of this book make abundantly clear, without their voices this project would not have seen the light of day, and I cherish the moments of pain, indignation, resolve, hope, and laughter that we shared as we observed together the forensic procedures that were meant to cast light upon the fate of their missing relatives. I am also deeply indebted to the survivors of the 1985 massacre of Accomarca, who opened the doors to their homes and their lives to let me in, generously tolerated my presence in their community, and sympathetically engaged with my inquiries into their past and present. Rarely have I met people with such a love for life. In this book, I have offered just a glimpse of the history of their struggle for justice, and I hope to offer a more complete account of it in the near future. I am particularly thankful to Cesareo Gamboa and Benita Medina, who made me feel that I was at home in Accomarca. Sadly, Cesareo died in a car accident in 2011. Benita passed away months later. The last time we met, Cesareo asked me not to forget them. And, Cesareo, I never will.

My fieldwork would not have gotten off the ground without the help of several professionals, institutions, and organizations in Peru. To begin with, I am grateful to the legal and forensic personnel of the Ministerio Público and the Instituto de Medicina Legal in Ayacucho, Peru, for allowing me to participate in and observe their work in a very difficult political context. In particular, I thank Cristina Olazábal, the courageous prosecutor who at the time was in charge of investigating major cases of human rights crimes carried out during the internal war in the region. I also thank the personnel of the forensic archaeology team, whose professionalism I deeply respect and admire. Special thanks go to the human rights attorneys from the Asociación Pro Derechos Humanos (APRODEH), the most prestigious civilian organization of human rights in Peru, and particularly to Gloria Cano, in Lima, and Yuber Alarcón and Ernesto Andia, in Ayacucho. Their courageous, compassionate, and efficacious work in defense of human rights is exemplary. I cannot thank them enough for their support during my fieldwork. Heartfelt thanks to my former colleagues at the Instituto de Defensa Legal (IDL). In the more than twelve years I worked with them, I learned everything I know about what it takes to defend human rights in a context of mass violence, death, and political instability. I also extend my thanks to the Equipo Peruano de Antropología Forense del Perú (EPAF) for insightful conversations. Finally, my thanks to Rocío Quispe, whose help as research assistant was invaluable during the last stage of my fieldwork.

At the New School for Social Research first and then at Johns Hopkins University, I was fortunate to have Deborah Poole as my advisor. Without her teaching, dedication, generosity, and active engagement with my work at every stage of my academic training I could not have brought my project to fruition. I also thank Veena Das, at Johns Hopkins, for her teaching and her generous and insightful response to my work. Clara Han accompanied me as a generous reader and friend during the early writing stage of this project and as a member of my committee. I am also grateful to the other two members of my committee, Jennifer Culbert and Ali Khan.

The Department of Anthropology at Johns Hopkins was the best intellectual community I could have asked for to develop this project during its initial stages. At various times I benefited from the support of professors Jane Guyer, Niloofar Haeri, and Pamela Reynolds. A special thanks to Professor Paula Marrati, who, despite the fact that she wasn't a faculty member in my department, was always supportive of my work through her teaching and friendship. I also express my gratitude to the many friends and colleagues with whom I shared precious moments of intellectual camaraderie throughout the years of graduate studies. First of all, to my cohort—Sylvain Perdigon, Bhrigupati Singh, Anila Dalautzi, Rasna Dillon, and Christopher Kolb. Special thanks to other colleagues, such as Citlalli Reyes-Kipp, whose friendship and support was inexhaustible; and Sameena Mulla and Aaron Goodfellow, whose generous guidance was invaluable. My gratitude also to my colleagues Valeria Procupez, Richard Barxtom, Todd Meyers, Maya Ratnam, James Williams, Juan Felipe Moreno, Gabika Bockaj, Hester Betlem, Andrew Bush, Sidharthan Maunaguru, and Michael McCarthy for their friendship and support.

At Rutgers-Newark I found the perfect institutional environment to write, rewrite, and eventually complete this book. I am privileged to have an incredibly supportive group of colleagues in the Department of Sociology and Anthropology. Brian Ferguson, Alex Hinton, Genese Sodikoff, Sean Mitchell, and Aldo Civico, in anthropology, and Jamie Lew, Ira Cohen, Kurt Shock, Sherri-Ann Butterfield, and Clayton Hartjen, in sociology, were always ready to respond to my work and generously supported me in any way they could as I completed this writing project.

For their advice, commentary, and conversation over the years about the material in this book, I am also grateful to numerous people who read early chapters or fragments of chapters, especially Richard Kernaghan, Citlalli Reyes, Daniella Gandolfo, Patrick Dixon, Victoria Sanford, and friends and colleagues from the SAR seminar "Disturbing Bodies," particularly Zoe Crossland, Rosemary Joyce, and Tim Thompson. My thanks also go to my many friends and colleagues who heard presentations and offered comments in the many panels we shared at conferences, professional meetings, workshops, and talks: Sharika Thiranagama, Finn Stepputat, Kimberly Theidon, Valerie Robin, Sandra Rozental, Francisco Ferrandiz, Pilar Rau, Serra Hakyemez, Jo Marie Burt, Coletta Youngers, Olga Gonzáles, Nathalie Koc, and Annabel Pinker, among many other brilliant colleagues. My deep thanks also to Rasna Dhillon for her editorial insights during the final stages of the manuscript, which made my nonnative English more understandable than it initially was. Thanks also to Kelly Beseck for copyediting earlier versions of some chapters.

At Stanford University Press, I have been fortunate to work with Michelle Lipinski, and I thank her for her support and faith in this project. Without her skillful, intelligent, and sensitive guidance and editorial vision I would not have been able to bring this project to fruition. My gratitude also goes to the anonymous reviewers who provided insightful comments and suggestions to strengthen this book. Many of the insights offered here are the result of their generous responses.

In Peru, I extend my gratitude to many friends and colleagues whose support has been crucial for me at various moments of my academic training. In particular, I thank my friends Jaime Márquez, Carlos Rivera, and Gaby Joo. I cherish our friendship that was born during the times of uncertainty and despair brought about by the internal war in Peru. In the United States, many thanks to Lisa, Kathi, Antonio, and Daniella, friends who at various times not only offered me their unconditional support, but also gave generously of their time.

Funding for the fieldwork from which this book draws came from the Jennings Randolph Peace Scholarship Dissertation Program at the United States Institute of Peace (USIP) and the Law and Social Sciences Program at the National Science Foundation (NSF). Additional funding for short summer trips came from the Program for Latin American Studies (PLAS), the Women and Gender Studies (WGS) program, and the Department of Anthropology at the Johns Hopkins University. My gratitude also goes to Rutgers-Newark for granting me a sabbatical semester that allowed me to make significant progress in completing the manuscript of this book.

Parts of Chapter 1 originally appeared in the edited volume *Necropolitics: Mass Graves and Exhumations in the Age of Human Rights* (ed. Ferrandiz and Robben, 2015). Parts of Chapter 3 originally appeared in the edited volume *Disturbing Bodies: Perspectives on Forensic Anthropology* (ed. Crossland and Joyce, 2015).

Last, I thank my family. My greatest debt goes to my parents, Raúl and Esperanza, and my daughters, Angela Lucía and Andrea Alejandra. Their love is my inexhaustible inspiration, and my love for them as their son and father, respectively, has been a major driving force behind this work.

Abbreviations

ANFASEP Asociación Nacional de Familiares de Detenidos y Desaparecidos en Perú (National Association of the Families of the Detained and Disappeared in Peru)

APRODEH Asociación Pro Derechos Humanos (Association for Human Rights in Peru)

CVR Comisión de la Verdad y Reconciliación (Truth and Reconciliation Commission)

IACHR Inter-American Commission of Human Rights

IACourtHR Inter-American Court of Human Rights

IML Instituto de Medicina Legal (Legal Medicine Institute)

MRTA Movimiento Revolucionario Tupac Amaru

NGO nongovernmental organization

Mourning Remains

MAP 1. Map of Ayacucho, Peru.

Introduction

"There must have been three thousand of them," he murmured.
"What?"
"The dead," he clarified. "It must have been all of the people who were at the station."
The woman measured him with a pitying look. "There haven't been any dead here," she said.
    —Gabriel García Márquez, *One Hundred Years of Solitude*

¿Y cuándo vuelve el desaparecido?
Cada vez que lo trae el pensamiento.
¿Cómo se le habla al desaparecido?
Con la emoción apretando por dentro.
    —"Desapariciones" (Disappearances), Rubén Blades[1]

ON JUNE 29, 2011, the foggy winter evening in southern Lima was lit up with the bright colors of a magnificent spectacle of lights and fireworks celebrating the official birth of the Cristo del Pacífico—a gigantic statue of Christ erected to look over Peru's capital from the historic hill to the south known as Morro Solar, just as the world-famous Christ the Redeemer statue overlooks Rio de Janeiro in Brazil. From the rooftop of the building where I had rented a room in the adjacent district of Surco, some thirteen kilometers from Morro Solar, I could see the dazzling display and hear the fireworks, and even the background music, with perfect clarity. Some neighbors in contiguous buildings were also watching, as were limeños throughout the southern part of the city. It was a highly anticipated event, not only because of the direct involvement of then-President Alan García, who had donated the statue, and the controversy surrounding the project from the start, but also because many limeños thought that this imposing Cristo del Pacífico would bring their city the same esteem as Rio de Janeiro.[2]

Media covered the event extensively, and that night, in the intimacy of their homes, Peruvians all over the country watched on television the details of how the limeño ruling elites had inaugurated their Cristo del Pacífico. The ceremony was not an official act of state, but all the same pageantry was on display. It began with the national anthem performed by a military band and solemnly sung by President García, his ministers of government, Catholic bishops, leading businesspeople, local authorities, and a crowd of political followers. The evening's climactic moment came after speeches by local and ecclesiastical authorities, when García declared that the Cristo del Pacífico would protect the country in its march toward future prosperity and harmony and would guide Peru in becoming a model nation in the world. He ended his speech by reading the Beatitudes and calling for unity among Peruvians. The papal nuncio then blessed the statue on behalf of Pope Benedict XVI, after which the height of the ceremony—the spectacle of lights, fireworks, and music—unfolded before the enraptured gaze of those attending.

García wanted this to be the last major public act of his second term (2006–2011), which would come to an end in three weeks. He said he wanted to offer this "gift" to Lima and Peru as a gesture of thanksgiving and as praise to God for the country's sustained economic growth in recent history, including during his second term. García had pulled off a stunning political resurrection after his populist but disastrous first tenure (1985–1990), which had brought Peru to the brink of collapse. When he returned to office in 2006, like a newly converted zealot he devotedly abided by the neoliberal consensus that had set in among Peruvian ruling elites in the early 1990s during President Alberto Fujimori's regime (1990–2000). Since then, following severe neoliberal reforms and the defeat of two guerrilla groups (the Communist Party of Peru, also known as the Shining Path, and the Movimiento Revolucionario Tupac Amaru [MRTA]), Peru's economy had been steadily growing and seemed to be improving according to many indicators of "development." The ruling elites thus had cause for celebration, despite ever-increasing inequality and widespread popular protest against the new economic model.

Opponents accused the president of a conflict of interest because he was funding the statue with the help of big firms that held contracts with the Peruvian state, particularly the Brazilian conglomerate Oderbrecht, which had carried out billion-dollar construction projects such as Lima's metro system and an international highway connecting Brazil and Peru.[3] In contrast, García's friends and allies rallied behind his plans. Most notable among these allies was Cardinal Juan Luis Cipriani, a prominent figure of the Opus Dei in Peru, who, in a preinaugural consecration of the statue, read a letter of blessing sent by the pope and asked Peruvians to worship this new image of Christ. Cipriani scorned the critics, praised the donors, and said he was convinced that the Cristo del Pacífico would soon become a site of pilgrimage. He went on to say that he actually hoped that, on every single hill or mountain in the country, there was a Christ blessing the Peruvian population, who loves God so much.[4]

This incident, striking though it was, did not lead me to ask how events of this kind could still take place in a country that claims to be secular and to abide by the constitutional separation of church and state. Nor was I particularly struck by the fact that, in defending García's project, the Catholic religious elites evoked images of the colonial evangelization of Andean peoples. As a Peruvian, I knew only too well the duplicitous political culture in which rulers allow themselves to desecularize modern liberal politics when necessary for the tasks of governance, as long as they restrict their use of religion in the public sphere to addressing the public's "moral conscience" by means of persuasion and not institutional coercion.[5] I was indeed familiar with the fact that religion in Peru is yet another "vehicular language" of the state, seeking to shape the life of the community as much as, say, bureaucratic languages.[6] What intrigued me about the inauguration of the Cristo del Pacífico was that this gesture of national optimism encapsulated an act of memory, or more accurately, an act of "nonmemory."

García's gift was concerned with progress and the nation's future. In his view, the path to becoming a player in the global arena had been successfully tested, and Peruvians could confidently envision individual and national prosperity as long as they did not abandon that path and instead took the risk of walking it to completion. Suppressed from this gesture of national optimism was any reference to the violence, mass death, and atrocity that had ravaged the country during the previous quarter century, in which García himself had played a major role. In 2003 the Peruvian Truth and Reconciliation Commission (Comisión de la Verdad y Reconciliación, CVR) had concluded that the internal war from 1980 to 2000 between the

Peruvian military, the Shining Path, and the MRTA was "the most intense, extensive and prolonged episode of violence in the entire history of the [Peruvian] Republic" and had resulted in the deaths of sixty-nine thousand Peruvians (Comisión de la Verdad y Reconciliación 2004, 433). The Cristo del Pacífico was intended to announce a brilliant future of prosperity and well-being, a future that could not accommodate the memory of such brutal times. With their "gift," the ruling elites were inviting Peruvians to become pilgrims to a future without a (particular) past in the constitution of their body politic. The Cristo del Pacífico was thus blessing a particular political temporality meant not so much to abstractly prioritize the future at the expense of the past, as to foreclose those areas of the past that did not serve the purposes of that future. As a kind of affective lighthouse in the landscape of time that would orient Peruvians toward the future as a strong and unified society, García's "gift" embodied a careful selection of the past.

Just two weeks after the splendid inauguration of the Cristo del Pacífico in Lima, on July 16, I attended the modest inauguration of La Cruz de la Hoyada in the Andean city of Ayacucho. This was a plain cement cross, three meters high, that a group of elderly, illiterate Quechua-speaking mothers of the *desaparecidos* (the disappeared) had managed to erect on La Hoyada—a former training and shooting field adjacent to the military fortress of Los Cabitos, the regional headquarters of the counterinsurgency in the Peruvian central southern Andes during the 1980s and 1990s. The CVR concluded that Los Cabitos had been a major center of detention, torture, and disappearance of suspected "terrorists" during Peru's "war on terror." In early 2009, the Public Prosecutor's Office completed a six-year forensic investigation at La Hoyada that uncovered dozens of clandestine mass graves containing the remains of an unknown number of the disappeared.[7] The authorities also uncovered the foundations of industrial-style furnaces where the bodies of the victims presumably had been incinerated so no trace of them could ever be found.

I had been following the investigation at Los Cabitos closely since late 2005, when I started my fieldwork on postconflict exhumations in Peru, and I was familiar with the public silence that encircled the case from the start. In several respects, it resembled one of those "public secrets" that everybody knows but nobody wants to talk about.[8] In fact, the opening of the trial on the case in a national court in Lima on May 26, 2011— that is, just weeks before the inauguration of both the Cristo del Pacífico and La Cruz de la Hoyada—had gone unnoticed in the national media despite the fact that it was allegedly one of the most important legal cases in modern Peruvian history. It thus was not surprising for me to see no national authority attending the inauguration ceremony at La Hoyada and no national press coverage. Only two local authorities, the mayor of the city and the regional director of the Ombudsman Office, had accepted the mothers' invitation. Yet, the mothers did not seem concerned by the absence of national authorities. What mattered to them was that, despite the military's opposition, they were finally inaugurating this symbol on behalf of their missing relatives, who had presumably been killed and disposed of without a trace at this site. La Cruz de la Hoyada unveiled the "public secret" of the atrocities that had occurred at Los Cabitos, and as such, a certain air of achievement circulated in the event's atmosphere, mingling with its mournful character.

At the ceremony's central moment Mama Angélica, the founder and leader of the organization of mothers of the disappeared (ANFASEP), spoke. Expressing herself partly in Quechua and partly in broken Spanish, she uttered the inaugural words in the name of the disappeared:

[*In Quechua*] This cross is in the name of so many of our dead and disappeared. It is their presence so we can respect them, so we can see them. It is the presence of the more than eight hundred people disappeared here. [*Shifting to Spanish*] It must be respected; we must be watchful about it, always; it cannot be left just like that, because we could never find our children. In this wasteland, many corpses, men and women, were thrown in [unmarked] pits. [. . .] This wasteland [witnessed] so much pain and sorrow, so many disappeared. This wasteland is their memory. It [the cross] must be respected; we must be watchful about it; we must not just leave it here and that's it, we do not come back anymore; that cannot do; we must always walk here; that is respect for the Holy Cross [*Señor Cruz*]. Of all the disappeared, of all those killed, this cross is the glory.

Uttered in the context of the inauguration of the Cristo del Pacífico and the silencing of the violence and atrocity of the recent past, these words unravel the political temporality that the Peruvian elites attempt to fabricate.[9] They bring back into the public sphere the presence of those about whom the nation does not want to speak and whose atrocious deaths at the hands of the state it wants to forget. Like a nightmarish apparition that comes out of nowhere to haunt the nation's celebration of its well-being, La Cruz de la Hoyada emerges to disrupt the dream that a society can march toward a future of prosperity without facing its recent past and mourning the unmournable.

Both the Cristo del Pacífico and La Cruz de la Hoyada are entries into the public sphere; both make claims about political community in languages that secular modern politics would look at with suspicion; they share symbols, vocabulary, and even the same genealogy. But the similarities end there: each evokes a different political temporality and hence a different image of political community—a difference grounded in how this political community relates to its recent past of mass death and atrocity. While the rulers' words gesture toward the economic health of the nation, taking for granted the political community, the mothers' words interrogate the nature of the political community itself. These words do not just reiterate the well-known saying that a country that does not learn from its past is doomed to repeat it. Nor are they a call for recognition, reparation, and reconciliation. Rather, they articulate a critique of violence and call for a specific kind of political becoming that a postconflict society would need to prevent the repetition of atrocity in the future.

The Cristo del Pacífico and La Cruz de la Hoyada emerged into the public sphere almost at once, more than two decades after the official end of the internal war and more than a decade after the beginning of a large project of transitional justice in Peru (see Chapter 1). They present strikingly different, even contradictory, visions of political community and temporality, and their simultaneous emergence is a remarkable reflection of the fact that for Peruvians the question of how to reckon with the recent past of violence and atrocity is far from settled. This book takes the perspective of a group of elderly and illiterate Quechua-speaking mothers of the disappeared from Ayacucho—the region most heavily affected by the war—to tell the story of how this struggle over political community happens within and outside of the state's vehicular languages. This struggle centrally revolves around what it would take for Peruvians to remake their relationships with those who were killed and disappeared by the state during the war.

Counting and Accounting for the Dead

Several years before these vastly different inaugurations, an important segment of the Peruvian Spanish-speaking elite had articulated the idea that the kind of political community that would emerge after the internal war would be largely determined by the kind of relations Peruvians were able to establish with their war dead. This was perhaps one of the most moving parts of the speech by the CVR chairman, Salomon Lerner, during the official presentation of the CVR's final report on August 28, 2003. Following the revelation that more than sixty-nine thousand Peruvians had died as a result of the twenty-year war, Lerner emphasized that these new figures nearly doubled prior estimates of thirty-five thousand deaths and disappearances. He then asked how so many deaths could have gone unaccounted for and, much worse, unnoticed. "In effect," he said, "we Peruvians used to say in our previous worst-case scenarios that political violence caused 35,000 casualties. What does it reveal about our political community to know now that 35,000 more people are missing, our brothers and sisters, and nobody missed them?" (Lerner 2003).[10]

The CVR's epidemiology of violence offered a partial answer to Lerner's question. Of the total number of victims reported to the commission, 79 percent lived in rural areas, 56 percent were engaged in farming or livestock activities, and 75 percent spoke Quechua or other native languages as their mother tongue. These figures are salient in the context of a national population in which only 16 percent speak these native languages and only 29 percent live in rural areas. Educational level offered another statistical marker; although more than 60 percent of Peruvians have obtained a high school degree, nearly 70 percent of the victims had only primary education. "Of every four victims of the violence," Lerner summarized, "three were peasants whose native tongue was Quechua— that significant segment of the population that has historically been neglected, and on occasions disparaged, by both state and urban society—the [other] segment which does enjoy the benefits of the political community" (Lerner 2003).[11]

In addition to distributing victimhood, this epidemiology of violence also allowed the CVR to distribute moral and political responsibilities. The commission concluded that the Shining Path was responsible for about 54 percent of the deaths and accused the Maoists of having committed crimes against humanity and of attempting to incite genocide by provoking the state. The CVR also accused the MRTA of criminal acts, although to a much lesser extent. Finally, the commission concluded that at "some places and moments in the conflict," the response of the armed forces to the insurgency entailed not only individual excesses, but also "generalized and/or systematic practices of human rights violations" that constituted crimes against humanity as well as transgressions of international humanitarian law (Comisión de la Verdad y Reconciliación 2004, 442).

For the CVR, however, responsibility lay not only with the direct perpetrators of atrocity, but ultimately with Peruvian society at large. That tens of thousands of Peruvians were killed without anyone in mainstream society becoming concerned demonstrated a deep malaise in Peruvian society—namely, that exclusion in Peru was still "absolute," as Lerner put it. This picture of "absolute exclusion," as illustrated in the idea of mainstream Peruvians failing to take note of what was happening to their less fortunate compatriots, led the CVR to draw one major conclusion: in a broad historical context, the worst episode of violence in modern Peru had to be understood not *just* as the result of the political will of terrorist groups, but ultimately as a product of persisting unjust structural conditions in Peruvian society *as a whole*. The racism, economic inequality, and social and cultural discrimination that continue to structure Peru's social order made some Peruvians more "killable" than others. This conclusion suggests, in other words, that violence expanded lethally because it operated within a broader "biopolitics of neglect."[12]

The CVR was the most visible component of a broad project of transitional justice initiated by the interim government of Valentín Paniagua in 2001 after the dramatic collapse of Fujimori's regime in late 2000. In addition to the establishment of the CVR, this project included the forensic exhumation and reburial of victims of the internal war, whose bodies lied hidden in mass graves scattered in former war-torn areas in rural Peru, and the prosecution of human rights crimes carried out during the internal war—both initiatives animated by Peruvian legal institutions. The CVR's specific task was to write a report casting light on the process, facts, and responsibilities for political violence and human rights crimes imputable to both terrorist organizations and state officials between 1980 and 2000.

But the CVR did not stop at being just a commission of inquiry whose work would document violence and supplement the work of the law. Rather, modeling itself after the South African Truth and Reconciliation Commission, the CVR became an active agent of postconflict nation-making and embodied the project of transitional justice that it heralded.[13] The history books on Peru were full of episodes of violence in which the events of mass death were rarely if ever problematized in their aftermath at the state level, but this time the story would be different. Mass death was made an object of both inquiry and intervention. It was counted, dissected, categorized, measured, totaled, historicized, moralized, and linked to chains of causality connecting individual agency, institutional failure, and historical patterns in terms of preventing its repetition in the future. Moreover, while the dead in the episodes of violence recounted in history books were always unknown and unaccounted for—except for leaders and historical protagonists—this time the dead would be identified and accounted for as much as possible.[14]

To this end, the CVR went so far as to encounter the material reality of dead bodies and remnants of atrocity by inserting itself into the project of excavating mass graves in former war-torn areas that the legal institutions initiated in 2001 (see Chapter 1). The commission drafted an initial list of forty-six hundred burial sites, conducted preliminary investigations at twenty-two hundred of them; developed a long-term exhumation plan; and participated in three excavations. Furthermore, perhaps uniquely among similar bodies of inquiry in the world, the CVR performed high-profile ceremonies of reburial to officially dignify and present the recovered victims to that larger and less attentive sector of the nation for whom the war had imposed less tragic and immediate consequences. In doing this, the CVR sought to elicit compassion and recognition for the forgotten Quechua-speaking victims of violence as fallen fellow nationals and to bring them back into mainstream society as legal subjects (victims), cultural subjects (people to be properly buried and mourned), and moral subjects (people to be properly recognized as fellow human beings).

Thus, for the first time in a history marked by bloody chapters of political violence since colonial times, the dead in these episodes of mass killing in Peru were not simply to be counted but also accounted for and recognized as deceased members of the political community. In direct opposition to a politics of impunity and oblivion characteristic of the previous two decades of internal war, in the democratic transition happening at the dawn of the new century, the Peruvian liberal elites adopted a broad project of memory, accountability, justice, recognition, reparation, and institutional reform in which the specific project of governing dead bodies had a central role.[15] If Peruvians abided by this project, they would eventually be able to bridge the lethal gulf that had historically separated the elites from the neglected communities and to realize the promise of Peru's birth as a liberal republic—to become, in Lerner's words, "a political community of human beings equal in dignity, in which *the death of each citizen counts as our own misfortune*; and in which every human casualty resulting from either arbitrariness, or crime or abuse of power, sets into motion the wheels of justice to compensate for the loss and to punish the perpetrators" (Lerner 2003; emphasis added).[16]

Desecularizing Transitional Justice

The CVR's intervention in exhumations and reburials has been largely ignored in academic studies of violence, memory, and transitional justice in Peru. In one example among many, Hayner (2011), in her oft-cited work on truth commissions, lists the CVR as one of the five strongest commissions in history, and yet her account only briefly mentions the commission's work on exhumations and says nothing about the ceremonies of reburial it performed.[17] This absence reflects a tendency in mainstream transitional justice theories to focus primarily on the problem of how to prevent the repetition of mass violence in the future rather than the problem of how to properly dispatch the dead. These theories study the viability and impact of technologies such as prosecution, truth-telling, reconciliation, institutional reform, and/or reparation in terms of "breaking the cycles of violence," as Minow (1998) put it, but rarely examine what societies do with the dead and their bodies in terms of rebuilding political communities in the aftermath of the killing.[18]

The absence also reflects the privileging of secular languages of modern politics in the discussion of how societies reckon with recent mass atrocity. The assumption is that languages of numbers, evidence, rights, the rule of law, exclusion, recognition, trauma, and other related notions have a privileged grasp of reality compared with, say, the language of ritual. Moreover, because these languages are intelligible in the always already constituted public sphere, they are seen as de facto vehicles for eliciting a response to questions concerning the protection of the life and personal integrity of individuals as well as the viability of the body politic. The implication is that questions of funerary rites or forms of mourning belong to the private sphere, or to the realm of cultural or religious beliefs, whose political efficacy, if any, is largely symbolic.

Perhaps the most compelling evidence of this secularist impulse is the centrality of the CVR's final report in much of this literature. Despite the fact that the report was one element among others in a broader official project of reckoning with past atrocity, as mentioned previously, it has over time become the most ambitious, comprehensive, and lasting legacy of this project because, no doubt, it is seen as a document that sets the terms of the rational debate concerning the most tragic episode of violence in Peru's modern history. No academic publication on violence, human rights, or contemporary history or politics in Peru fails to mention it.[19] I contend that this focus on the written text and its ability or inability to shape the rational discussion of the violence of the past eludes the central question of how survivors and relatives of victims reckon with the *material* remnants of atrocity.

It also misses the extent to which the CVR's exhumations and reburials reveal a novel and subtle articulation of power that, by means of governing dead bodies in contexts of mass violence, seeks to shape post-conflict worlds. This form of power operates through material practices that go beyond the text and seeks to address that which exceeds the usual frames and languages of modern secular politics: the sheer excess of suffering and terror that the event of atrocity leaves behind. The event can be read in inscriptions and signs such as bodies shattered beyond recognition, chronic uncertainty, pervasive injustice, forgetting and denial, but there is always an excess that escapes those inscriptions and signs.[20] The CVR's rituals of reburial were meant to symbolically capture and dissipate such excess. The exhumations were not just about recovering the victims' bodies, but also about helping their souls to leave the "misty passage between life and death" where they were thrown, allowing the relatives to finally begin their suspended processes of mourning (Robben 2009, 142). I see the CVR's rituals of reburial as a gesture of desecularizing transitional justice.

I am sympathetic to this gesture of desecularization because it implicitly acknowledges that questions concerning sovereignty, belonging, legitimate violence, and even the sacred (in the sense of limits), which are crucial for the constitution of political communities, are implicated with questions concerning the proper dispatching of the dead in episodes of mass violence. In this sense, this gesture invites us to consider the problem of the political in the aftermath of atrocity in terms of *not only* the usual languages of modern politics—say, rights or the rule of law—but *also* the languages, practices, and technologies of truth and self that exceed the constraining frames of those secular languages. Here, death and its ritualization become a field of engagement with the excess of atrocity and with the question regarding the possibility of people living together again in political community in the aftermath of atrocity, through means that modern politics eyes with skepticism and even suspicion.[21]

However, the CVR's gesture of desecularizing transitional justice simply opened the door to the ritual practices of mainstream Catholicism, which, functioning as another vehicular language of the state, operated as another component of what I below conceptualize as the necro-governmentality of postconflict. In contrast, I consider this gesture of desecularization from a different angle. I look at the ways that Quechua-speaking relatives of victims engage the material remnants of atrocity and mobilize ordinary practices, languages, and technologies of truth and self in an attempt to cope with and domesticate the excess of events of atrocity that have gone beyond the limits within which Andean peoples test what a human form of life is. These are practices, languages, and technologies that modern politics, and even a rationalized religion such as Catholicism, would see as premodern relics and vestiges of "magical" practices and beliefs.

I look at the survivors' mobilization of the ordinary in response to atrocity in the context of the project of forensic excavation of mass graves in former war-torn areas that began in mid-2001. This project has focused mainly, though not exclusively, on the highland department of Ayacucho, the Quechua-speaking region of the Peruvian Andes that was most heavily affected by the internal war. By the CVR's estimates, more than 40 percent of the more than sixty-nine thousand victims lived in this region.[22] In addition to the massive loss of lives, the war was experienced as a "form of cultural revolution," in Theidon's (2006) felicitous expression. In a context of widespread terror waged by both the military and the Shining Path, relatives buried most victims hastily wherever they had fallen. Others did not receive even a hasty burial, as they were thrown into clandestine mass graves or incinerated. By mid-2015, more than eighteen thousand Peruvians remained "disappeared," according to the estimates of the Legal Medicine Institute (Instituto de Medicina Legal, IML).[23]

More than a decade after its launch, the project has not been able to fully realize the promise of bringing the unknown dead and disappeared back to the care of their families. As of August 2015, the legal institutions had recovered the bodies of at least 3,100 victims, identified 1,715 of those victims, and returned 1,599 bodies to their relatives.[24] This means that, after more than a decade, state institutions had recovered only one-fifth (and identified only one-tenth) of the estimated eighteen thousand disappeared. These results indicate the complexity of the problem. Recovering human remains scattered throughout the formidable Andean landscape is a daunting task. But one of the main reasons for the failure is that in many cases the victims' bodies were shattered beyond recognition, making their postmortem individualization and identification impossible.

Such was the case at Los Cabitos. In the legal search for the disappeared, the forensic investigation at the military site uncovered evidence demonstrating that some practices of state terror resulted in something resembling what Hannah Arendt called the "fabrication of corpses," referring to the factory-like production of mass death in Nazi concentration camps.[25] The resemblance lies not just in the fact that mass killing took place on a bureaucratic site, or in the methods used to eliminate human lives. Rather, the primary resemblance lies in the kind of death that the Peruvian military inflicted upon perceived transgressors of the sovereign's rule. At Los Cabitos, as in the Nazi death camps, not only were individuals' lives taken away anonymously, but their deaths and the memory of their deaths were also eliminated. The victims were subjected to forms of asocial death—death without mourning, rituals of remembrance, and even grief—death "robbed of its meaning as the end of a fulfilled life," as Arendt put it.[26]

But, as Presner (2007, 223) notes, Arendt did not limit her reflections on what occurred at the camps to the destruction of the meaning of death; she also asked whether the actions of the perpetrators could be understood and judged within the conventional grids of intelligibility. She asked, "What meaning has the concept of murder when we are confronted with the mass production of corpses?" (Arendt, 1968, 441). The illiterate Quechua-speaking mothers of the disappeared, participating as plaintiffs in the forensic procedures at Los Cabitos, implicitly ask a similar question when they refer to what happened at Los Cabitos as something unnamable—as practices that do not have a name in language and human experience: "no tiene nombre" (that which does not have name for it).

In this book I show how these mothers reclaim death as a human experience in response to the state's practices of the "fabrication of corpses" and how they restore the victims to the human community by weaving together materiality, biography, and nonhuman agency. I explore the implications for political community of this gesture of redrawing the ontological boundaries between life and death, in the context of the official project that seeks to bring the forgotten and neglected victims of atrocity back into the fold of the nation's citizenry as legal subjects, cultural subjects, and moral subjects—but not as political subjects because the nation presumes most of them to be "terrorists." These implications emerge more clearly when, as in the case of Los Cabitos, the promise of official restitution fails because of its inability to produce the missing body. By looking at how, in the face of this failure, the mothers rearrange senses of community, belonging, authority, and the human through ordinary practices and technologies of self and truth, I consider the ways this subaltern response to the long-standing legacy of state terror evokes the figure of the people reemerging from the remnants of atrocity to (re)establish the possibility of political community. A conceptual detour will help us to cast light upon how practices and technologies that modern politics tends to dismiss as "irrational" interrogate the nature of sovereignty itself and encapsulate a political response to both the power that kills and the power that cares.

The Necro-governmentality of Postconflict

The Peruvian project of excavating clandestine mass graves containing the remains of victims of violence is one among many similar cases. These state interventions in response to violent mass death began to proliferate in the mid-1980s. Starting with the well-known case of the disappeared in Argentina, the attempt to recover the remains of unknown victims in order to gain a sense of justice and closure has expanded rapidly on a global scale—from the terrorist attacks on the World Trade Center to the counterinsurgency campaigns in countries such as Guatemala and Chile, from ethnic cleansing in the Balkans or Rwanda to various civil wars (including the long-ended Spanish civil war). An assemblage of cutting-edge technologies of identification including DNA testing and new forensic anthropological techniques has been set in motion in these former war-torn settings to shape postatrocity worlds. Moreover, as practitioners have begun to reflect on the epistemological foundations of their work as well as the ethical and political stakes of their interventions, new subdisciplines have emerged, and some have even started to talk of a "forensic turn."[27]

Questions pertaining to the management of dead bodies and regulation of mortuary practices are certainly not new in the history of the modern state. As Stepputat (2014, 17) notes, with the emergence of the modern state, death becomes an object of intense biopolitical intervention. The development of biomedical science introduces shifts in the treatment of dead bodies, which are now seen as a problem of public health. Extramural cemeteries are introduced to contain the danger of disease and infection from decomposing dead bodies in uncontained burial sites (e.g., houses and churches). New public health regulations introduce a clear separation between the space of the dead and the space of the living. Also, as a new object of power/knowledge, death demands the development of specific technologies of knowledge, such as the registration and codification of the causes of death, which in turn feed public health policies. Finally, forensic science emerges and develops in association with state attempts to enforce criminal law and uphold its monopoly on the legitimate use of violence.

Furthermore, the religious and political colonization of death constituted a cornerstone in the worldwide expansion of the European colonial project. The zeal of colonizers and missionaries particularly targeted native mortuary practices and beliefs that they considered to be not only savage and barbaric and, as such, intolerable, but also sources of idolatry and superstition as well as revolt and political resistance against the colonial project.[28] The "Christianization of death" was a condition sine qua non for both the "conversion" of native peoples and the construction of the colonial order. This campaign involved not only eliminating pagan practices and capturing the indigenous imagination, but also reorganizing sacred space by removing and destroying natives' sites of worship and the remains of their ancestors.[29] As Lomnitz (2005) argues, the colonial state attained a position as mediator between the dead and the living as a result of the work of two antithetical midwives: the brutality and bestializing violence of the conquistador and the disciplinary administration of life and death by means of which the missionary sought to respond to mass death among native peoples.

What is novel in contemporary attempts at governing dead bodies and modulating mortuary practices in response to mass violence and death is that they are articulated at the intersection of three broad global developments: the intensification of biopolitics, the emergence of a new moral economy of suffering, and the proliferation and mutation of international human rights law. I argue that what emerges here is a form of power that moves in the shadows of what Fassin (2011) calls the "politics of life" in his reproblematization of the concept of biopolitics. In order to make my point, let us take a brief look at his argument. Building on the distinction between life as matter (the biological reality of life) and life as meaning (the experience of living), Fassin submits that biopolitics moves in a continuum between these two poles. Life as both *form* and *value* is what is at stake in a "politics of life." He then argues that an anthropology of biopolitics needs to account for both what is being done to living beings through various forms of government and what sort of life is taken for granted in this process.

I retort that anthropology also needs to account for what is being done to dead bodies as part of the global work of the "politics of life," particularly in contexts of mass violence. I thus suggest that the emergent form of power that has death as object moves in the shadows of the "politics of life," as its counterpart, in an attempt to shape postwar or post–mass violence worlds. It is a form of power that moves between two deaths— death as a plain termination of life and death as human experience— seeking to unravel the enduring legacies of mass atrocity and reorder the chaos and disorder that violence and war introduce on a mass scale in life, in the form of fragmented bodies, mass graves, unburied bodies, disappeared persons, and traumatized survivors (see Wagner 2008).

In so doing, this form of power is a counterpart of the "politics of life" in at least three respects. First, not a day goes by when a new threshold is not crossed in the manipulation of the "substance of life," and modern biopolitical technologies have exponentially increased not only the "power to make live," but also the "power to let die" as inequalities of living conditions mediate the access to the perceived benefits of the power to make live. I suggest that these same technologies are paradoxically making possible a more effective disposal of the bodies of those who are either killed or "let die" in the name of protecting the body politic (Foucault 1978; see also Mbembe 2003 and Agamben 1998). As evident in myriad present-day interventions in situations of mass death originating in humanmade or natural catastrophes all over the world, innovative biotechnologies now have a central role in projects of recovering, counting, individualizing, identifying, and disposing properly of unknown dead bodies as part of the contemporary work of "make live."[30]

Second, as Fassin (2011) persuasively argues, humanitarianism has penetrated politics in our contemporary world. Humanitarianism, in his view, has become a category resting on the principle of an ethical approach to human life that is placed above other values. Physical life emerges as a superior value and humanitarian reason as the ethical idea. He argues then that the study of contemporary society invites us to consider not biopower, which is power over life, but "biolegitimacy," which would be the legitimacy of life—in other words, the valuation of being alive as the supreme good. I suggest that the counterpart of this biolegitimacy is the resignification of death as a human value. Part of the experience of living is the experience of dying, or affirming the possibility of a biography. This resignification belongs to a new moral economy of suffering that establishes "a new relationship to time and memory, to mourning and obligations, to misfortune and the misfortunate" (Fassin and Rechtman 2009, 276).

Third, this counterpart to the "politics of life" also finds conditions of possibility in the proliferation and mutation of international human rights law. Informing this evolution is the novel notion of the "right to truth," which protects victims' rights of access to information concerning human rights violations, including information about the whereabouts of the disappeared and their right to a proper burial. Noticeably, the right to truth belongs not only to individual victims, but also to society at large. Knowing the truth of atrocity, this doctrine states, prevents the repetition of mass violence and death in the future (see Chapter 1). Thus, within this framework, while survivors and relatives of victims are now incited to stake their claims in terms of rights rather than in the old languages and categories of religion, state intervention in the recovery and reburial of those killed by mass violence is sanctioned and legitimized as a fulfillment of international obligations on human rights with the purpose of protecting the life of the population.

This form of power stands in opposition term by term to "necropower"—a term Mbembe (2003) coined to argue that biopower ultimately manifests itself in the power to kill or to allow to live, particularly in colonial or colonial-like contexts.[31] This contrast is most visible in the ways these forms of power operate. While the forms of necropower that Mbembe sees at work in contemporary politics operate within frames of sovereignty, the form of power concerned with dead bodies in contexts of mass violence works within a frame of governmentality—that is, it aims at structuring the field of the *possible* action and speech of survivors, relatives, and the population so as to conduct their conduct as free subjects.[32] A complex set of legal and disciplinary technologies of self and truth come together to structure such a field of possible action and speech by producing particular kinds of objects and subjects, as well as narratives of suffering and recovery. While mass graves are located; dead bodies are recovered, examined, identified, and reburied; and surviving relatives are counseled and consoled, the truth that these remnants of atrocity tell is exposed to society at large and translated into specific disciplinary languages that render such atrocity intelligible so as to prevent its repetition in the future. I conceptualize this form of power as the necro-governmentality of postconflict.

This form of governmentality deploys three material strategies. First, at the level of dead bodies:[33] their localization, examination, individualization, identification, and eventual return to the care of their families for proper burial is meant to restore the distinction between the family and the community that is crucial for modern politics and the state. Second, at the level of territory: the forensic excavation of mass graves scattered in former war-torn areas alters the relationship between the geography of violence and that of memory because memory travels with the remains of the dead. By means of the traffic of dead bodies, the state seeks both to reoccupy a territory free from the material traces of the war and to govern the memory of the war. Third, at the level of language: because postatrocity projects of exhumation are articulated within the frames of human rights law and global humanitarianism, they come with specific grammars and vocabularies (such as rights and trauma) that, while "skeletonizing" the reality of violence and suffering (Wilson 1997), are meant to allow for a controlled recovery of the past (see Chapter 3).

The Figure of the Grieving Woman

This global project of necro-governmentality, however, encounters culturally charged terrains in local worlds. Even in ordinary contexts, death is a realm of excess in which a complex set of institutions, practices, and ideas—pertaining to pollution, transgression, body and soul, ancestorship, the human and the animal, grief, and the disposal of the corpse, as well as forms of nonhuman agency such as ghosts, spirits, and even things—is set in motion as soon as death strikes home in order to govern the transition from biological death to cultural death. Not only is this transition usually highly regulated and ritualized, but different forms of political, religious, communal, or moral authority claim the right to govern dead bodies and the means of properly dispatching them, as a way of restoring local worlds in the aftermath of devastating loss.[34] Given that this is also a time during which the modern state manifests an intense presence, the governance of dead bodies frequently becomes a site of political contestation.

But more importantly, this project of necro-governmentality, moving between two deaths, encounters the figure of the grieving woman who also inhabits that space between two deaths.[35] As the anthropological literature shows, in the gendered division of labor in the work of mourning, women are seen as primarily dealing with the loss of the individual life while men are in charge of ritually inscribing such a loss in the collective social order. Women usually embody the polluting and transgressive elements of death, manifesting the excess of pain and giving expression to the voice of kinship—all engagements with loss that are central to the task of symbolically regenerating life in the wake of biological death. But according to a deep-rooted line of interpretation in anthropology, because of their closeness to the event of biological death, grieving women embody everything that needs to be negated (grief, emotions, individual loss, mourning) if the social order and the life of the community are to be symbolically reestablished after an individual death. It is the ritual negation and vanquishment of everything women embody in response to death that allows for the possibility of symbolically regenerating social life in the aftermath of the loss of biological life (see especially Bloch 1982).

It is perhaps this close association between women, mourning, and family and kinship—present in almost every society and culture—that has made the figure of Antigone so persuasive in the analysis of the relationship between violence, dead bodies, and the political community. Her figure emerges most clearly when the dead bodies in question belong to the "internal enemy," those victims of state terror whose death the sovereign declares to be unmournable. As is well known, Antigone disobeys the rule of the sovereign and clandestinely offers some form of proper burial to her brother Polyneices, a transgressive act that leads to her own death. In a reading of the play that has in itself become a kind of vehicular language (see, for instance, Sant Cassia 2005), Hegel (1999) sees here a fundamental opposition between two principles of law: the law of the state and the law of the family. In his view the woman is "pathetically possessed" by the interest of family while the man is concerned with the welfare of the community. In Antigone's protection of the sacred rights of kinship, her dilemma is whether to obey or disobey the law of the sovereign. Voice emerges here in the act of transgression to the law.

In this book I take a different direction in exploring how voice emerges in the act of mourning the unmournable. The issue of obedience or disobedience to the law of the sovereign was also the dilemma the Quechua-speaking mothers of the disappeared faced during the counter-insurgency campaign (see more in Chapters 4 and 5). However, in the context of the forensic exhumation of the remnants of atrocity, their dilemma is entirely different because it occurs in a different temporality: the temporality of the aftermath. This is not the temporality in which corpses of the enemy are left to rot before everyone's eyes as a sign of the sovereign's power, but the temporality in which the sovereign recovers, examines, identifies, and returns those bodies to their relatives for proper burial. In this temporality, the mothers' dilemma is not whether to obey or disobey the sovereign's law, but what to do with the remnants of atrocity when faced with the inability of what I call the necro-governmentality of postconflict to unmake the sovereign's "fabrication of corpses."

Because of the utter destruction of human bodies at Los Cabitos, the forensic project is unable to individualize, rearrange, examine, and identify those remains and bring them to the care of their families for proper burial. Hence, the project is unable to fulfill the promise of bringing those unknown dead and disappeared back into the nation's citizenry as legal, moral, and cultural subjects and finally allow these relatives to return home after many years of searching for their disappeared in vain. The project was meant to restitute the distinction between kinship and community, reorder the geographies of violence and memory, allow the law to do its work of assigning legal responsibilities, rearrange the visibility of suffering to redistribute moral responsibilities, and modulate how to talk about past atrocity. Structuring the field of possible action and speech of survivors and the population thus, this project of governmentality was meant to reconstitute a political community. But the Los Cabitos case reveals the limits of this project.

As for the mothers of the disappeared, not knowing with certainty, despite the exhumations, whether the unidentifiable human remains recovered at Los Cabitos belong to their missing relatives does not paralyze them. The mothers inhabit this limit-experience in the subjunctive mood of the "might be" (see Chapters 6 and 7) to reclaim death as human experience in response to both the state's practices of the "fabrication of corpses" and the inability of necro-governmentality to produce the missing body for justice and mourning. First, they mobilize ordinary languages, practices, and technologies through which Andean people cope with loss in everyday life to resignify the former site of mass killing as a sacred site of memory and commemoration of the "disappeared." Second, in response to the impossibility of individual bodies being identified, these mothers collectively embrace the remains of the unknown dead as theirs, and in so doing make irrelevant the distinction between kinship and community that is central for the efficacy of necro-governmentality. Third, where the postconflict legal and forensic intervention was meant to eventually send the mothers back home after years of vain search, these mothers renew their search, which now focuses not only on finding the individual missing body, but also on reestablishing the conditions of possibility for a life together in society *again* in the aftermath of atrocity. Through this gesture of mourning—in the double sense of mourning what remains and acknowledging that what remains is mourning—the Quechua mothers of the disappeared make a claim, in their own terms, on history and political community.

I argue that this gesture of mourning in response to the state's "fabrication of corpses" evokes the figure of the people reemerging in the aftermath of state atrocity to reclaim the possibility of political community. Here, I find guidance in the distinction Foucault makes between the notions of people and population, and in his notion of "counterconduct." In his brief conceptualization, Foucault (2007, 43–44) conceives of the people as including "those who conduct themselves in relation to the management of the population, at the level of the population, as if they were not part of the population as a collective subject-object, and as if they put themselves outside of it, and consequently the people are those who, refusing to be the population, disrupt the system." The figure of the people emerges when people escape governmentality and conduct themselves. But escape is not the same as dissent or resistance. Nor is it transgression of the law. It is doing things otherwise, arranging things differently from how governmentality arranges things to structure the field of potential action and speech of the subjects of government.

I suggest that in the responses of these relatives there are three major implications for political community—or, put otherwise, three implications for how a people may emerge in the oscillation between the power to kill and the power to make live (see Chapter 8). The first is a rejoinder to mainstream understandings of the relationship between violence and gender. As heirs to Hegel's polar opposition of the family and the state, mainstream political theories assume that the state is an intrinsic source of rationality and preoccupation for the entire body politic, while the state's subjects, particularly women, are possessed by passionate and irrational love for their families and therefore able to think of politics only in terms of their own lineage and descent. By contrast, in "doing things otherwise," the mothers of the disappeared actively engaged the wider political problem of the conditions of possibility for political community in the aftermath of state atrocity.

Second, these conditions of possibility imply redrawing the limits of political action. While liberal views consider violence to be the limit of political action, the mothers of the disappeared define these limits in terms of the degree of violence: violence cannot be so absolute that it even subsumes the rights of the dead. Third, the question the mothers are wrestling with is not only how to reinstate the sacred rights of the dead, but also how to relate to the state's ever-present threat of the "fabrication of corpses." Their answer entails permanent dislocation and movement in relation to the state, as manifested in the Quechua notion of *puriy* (movement) (see Chapter 5). Their gesture of mourning is one of becoming a people as the constituent power, in opposition to sovereignty, which is always a constituted power.

Plan of the Book

This book is based on a two-year period of extensive fieldwork with mothers of the disappeared organized by ANFASEP. In addition, I conducted fieldwork among survivors and relatives of the sixty-nine Quechua-speaking peasants massacred by the Peruvian Army in 1985 in the Andean village of Accomarca, Ayacucho, a story I tell briefly in Chapter 1.[36] These relatives and survivors were participating as plaintiffs in the legal case against perpetrators of the massacre—a case that had been reopened in the context of Peru's project of transitional justice. In contrast to Los Cabitos where unknown victims were murdered behind military walls, Accomarca survivors witnessed the massacre and managed to bury the burned remains of their slaughtered relatives. They thus knew their loved ones' whereabouts from the beginning.

In Chapters 1 and 2 I provide the broader context in which I situate my ethnography of the exhumations at Los Cabitos. Specifically, in Chapter 1 I offer a partial history of how the project of governing dead bodies and the disappeared came into being in postconflict Peru as a result of Peru's international human rights obligations and the influence of global humanitarianism. In particular, I examine the CVR's engagement with the material remnants of atrocity and its performance of official reburial rites for unknown victims of violence as a means of addressing the excess of atrocity and eliciting compassion from mainstream Peruvians for their less fortunate fellow nationals who fell victim to violence. In Chapter 2 I focus on a case of suicide in the rural community of Accomarca to offer an ethnographic account of how Quechua-speaking people cope with tragic death (or "bad death") in ordinary contexts. I trace the relations of specificity and continuity between state and cultural practices to properly dispose of the dead body and address suffering in cases of transgressive death. I explore the gendered division of labor in mourning and highlight the central role of women in ordinary mortuary rituals. Finally, I show how, by contrast, the massacre at the hands of the state cannot be absorbed through these ordinary practices until such killing is first legally, politically, and historically prosecuted.

In Chapter 3 I begin my ethnography of the exhumations at Los Cabitos. I offer an ethnographic account of how the forensic findings that proved the Peruvian state's practices of the "fabrication of corpses" were made possible by the unexpected intrusion at the excavation site of a drunken man who was not part of the legal procedures. I also show how this "fabrication of corpses" rendered the individualization and identification of the exhumed human remains impossible. In the face of this impossibility, I explore the limits of rational technologies of self and truth in dealing with the excess of atrocity within the institutionalized structures of science and the law and ask what kind of object state terror is.

In Chapters 4 through 7 I offer an ethnographic account of the specific ways the Quechua-speaking mothers of the disappeared engage the forensic exhumation at Los Cabitos. In Chapter 4 I focus on the stories of suffering the mothers retell at the excavation site to reflect on the nature of the disappearances as an ongoing event. These stories speak of the disappearance of loved ones in terms of both the specific act of abduction of the body and the various languages and practices of denial through which the disappearance continues in the present. In Chapter 5 I explore the question of what it means to be witness *before* terror as opposed to witness *in* terror by looking at the ways these mothers occupied the male public space in search of their missing children and how, in the context of the state of emergency, they contested the sovereign's declaration that the deaths of transgressors to its rule were unmournable.

In Chapter 6 I offer an ethnographic analysis of the ways the mothers reclaim death as human experience in response to the state's "fabrication of corpses." Because the forensic technologies are unable to produce the individual missing bodies, the mothers mobilize ordinary practices of mourning to both imagine the presence of those bodies at the site of mass killing and mourn them in the subjunctive mood of the "might be." Central to this gesture are the agency Andean people assign to dead bodies and how they see the relationship between body, soul, and the earth. In Chapter 7 I expand on the question of the agency of the dead, and of the earth as impersonal witness to human suffering. I describe the ways in which the dead and the earth make the living listen to their voices through culturally constituted means of communication, such as dreams, ghosts, and rites of propitiation, to demand the transfiguration of the site of mass killing into a site of grief, mourning, and commemoration of all the unknown people who were disappeared and massacred during the counterinsurgency campaign.

In the concluding chapter I return to the ceremony of the inauguration of La Cruz de la Hoyada to elaborate on how the mothers' collective mobilization of the sacred emerges as a radical critique of the sovereign power to kill, and as a call for the transfiguration of the political community in the aftermath of state atrocity. The mothers gesture toward the possibility of a people emerging from a project of governmentality. And yet, this possibility of becoming people is tied to the renewal of the search for their disappeared—a search that, following the legal and forensic failure, is no longer focused only on *finding* the individual missing body, but also on *founding* a new relationship with the body politic.

1

Death in Transition
Reclaiming the (Un)known Dead in Postconflict Peru

AT AROUND 1:30 p.m. on a sunny day in May 2007, in a small courtyard of the IML in Ayacucho, a group of forensic anthropologists start to arrange three small white coffins. These will contain the exhumed remains of three of the sixty-nine Quechua-speaking peasants massacred by the army in the Andean village of Accomarca in August 1985. The human remains are packed in sealed cardboard boxes labeled with the victims' names that have been placed on three stretchers alongside the coffins. In white uniforms and wearing white sanitary masks and gloves, the experts proceed to transfer the remains from the boxes to the coffins, one victim at a time. They start with the bones, which they carefully arrange on a bed of rough cotton in the coffin, attempting to give the remains a human anatomic form. The expert in charge of handing the bones from the cardboard box to his colleague placing them in the coffin recites the name of each piece: "left femur," "right femur," "cranium," "coccyx," he says in a grave, soft voice as if reciting a litany. Once the arranged bones resemble a human form, the experts place on top of them the relevant rugged clothes recovered during the exhumation and proceed to seal the coffin with screws. They repeat the same steps for the other two victims, in a procedure we may call a bureaucratic reconstitution of the human body of victims of state terror.

When the coffins are ready, the official ceremony of restitution of the victims' bodies to their relatives begins. This legal act is not open to the public; it takes place within the premises of the IML and is attended only by the victims' direct relatives, leaders of their association (AFAPVDA),[1] their lawyer, and other supporting professionals, including myself. Besides Ayacucho's high-ranking legal and forensic authorities and the IML personnel who have been summoned to participate in the ceremony, no other local, regional, or national authority is present—not even a Catholic priest, whose presence in this kind of ceremony has become usual. The legal act unfolds in an atmosphere of uncanny intimacy, as if, rather than presenting a public performance of sovereignty, the law would prefer to animate a kind of private, face-to-face encounter between the dead, the survivors, and the state. Were it not for the presence of a local TV news reporter, I would have thought that the legal authorities did not want the public to know about the event.

The speech by the Fiscal Decano Superior of Ayacucho (Ayacucho's district general attorney) makes it strikingly clear that this is not a public—hence political—act, but rather a legal and bureaucratic—hence private—act. Addressing the relatives who stand behind the coffins, the *fiscal* begins a formulaic speech by offering them condolences on behalf of the legal and forensic institutions. He emphasizes the "great responsibility" both institutions have before the nation at large and each of the relatives of people who, like those whose remains they are now returning, have been killed. He says that both institutions have fulfilled their duty because the IML professionals have worked hard to complete the identification of the victims and determine the causes of their deaths. "Now," he says, "they can be offered a *cristiana sepultura* [proper burial]."[2] In this way, he concludes, both institutions "have completed a task the law entrusted us." I note here that the *fiscal* does not make any reference to the massacre, nor does he speak of retribution or reparation. His politically sanitized speech is chiefly concerned with the legal return of the victims' bodies to their relatives for a private *cristiana sepultura*.

Celestino, president of the relatives' association, takes the floor on behalf of the bereaved to thank the authorities and forensic experts for their work.[3] He follows the *fiscal*'s script in saying that now that the work of the legal institutions is complete, the families will finally be able to recover the remains of their slaughtered relatives, even if these are just bones, to offer them a proper burial. But then, his speech resituates the act in the political realm. Visibly moved, Celestino says that the massacre has left a deep wound that the survivors will not be able to forget, ever. The forensic work has demonstrated that this was "genocide" and thus corroborates the claims about the atrocity of the massacre they have made ever since the event.[4] Among the victims, he says, were not only newborns and elders, but also pregnant women. He goes on to say that forensic work is helping to demonstrate the truth in many other cases like Accomarca. He concludes that all this evidence backs the relatives' claims for justice, and if the legal authorities are indeed committed to the truth, the perpetrators must be punished so as to prevent the repetition of this kind of atrocity in the future, anywhere in the country.[5]

We are all noticeably affected by Celestino's speech. A relative's description of the massacre as genocide resonates with the way the fateful event entered into a national narrative of the internal war. On August 14, 1985, four platoons of a special division of the army closed in on the village from four directions and gathered the villagers in an expanse known as Llocllapampa in an adjacent ravine. Since many adult men managed to escape, most of those assembled were elders, women, and children. The soldiers forced them into two contiguous huts and separated some women from the group to rape them. Then, after the orders of two young officers, the soldiers shot at the huts with their automatic rifles and grenade launchers. Following the killing, the military set the huts on fire with the intention of destroying the victims' bodies and proceeded to strip the village of anything remaining that could be of value to the survivors. When the patrols left, the terrified survivors returned to the site of the mass killing to hastily bury the burned remains of their relatives in mass graves in the very place they had been killed.[6]

The massacre took place during the Peruvian Army's scorched-earth campaign in the 1980s, when practically the entire Ayacuchano countryside was considered a "red zone," meaning that the area had been deeply infiltrated by the Shining Path. However, the case was distinctive because it happened at the start of Alan García's first term as president. García had won the election with the promise to change his predecessor's counterinsurgency approach. News of the killing reached Lima, and the recently elected congress responded quickly with the appointment of a commission of inquiry, which concluded that the massacre constituted a case of gross violation of human rights and had to be prosecuted in the civilian courts. García fired the top military commanders for their attempt to cover up the abuses. Because of this swift official acknowledgment, Accomarca became one of those cases that, in the words of Ignatieff (1996, 113), narrows down the "range of permissible lies."

However, the military claimed jurisdiction over the case and handed down lenient sentences, mostly administrative in character. Furthermore, in 1995 the Fujimori regime passed a blanket amnesty law that not only closed the legal case but also rehabilitated the military officers involved in the massacre. The nullification of the amnesty law in 2001 allowed civilian courts to reopen the case in 2003, after nearly two decades of impunity. As part of the new criminal investigation, the court ordered the excavation of the unmarked mass graves where terrified survivors had hastily buried the remains of their slaughtered relatives. A professional team of forensic archaeologists from the IML was in charge of the procedures, which began in May 2006 with the exhumation of three victims whose identification was easier because they were, uncharacteristically, buried in marked individual graves.[7]

Yet despite the prominence of the case in the national narrative of the internal war, on that afternoon of May 2007 at the IML premises in Ayacucho, the remains of the first three legally identified victims of the massacre were returned to their relatives for *cristiana sepultura* in a discreet and low-profile ceremony. Following the speeches by the *fiscal* and Celestino, the staff of the IML offered their condolences to the relatives. Then, bringing the bureaucratic act to an end, a clerk asked the relatives to sign and fingerprint the death certificates and forms acknowledging receipt of the bodies. Once the paperwork was complete, the clerk gave copies to the relatives and, echoing the *fiscal*, told them, "With this you will be able to bury your relatives; you will offer them a '*cristiana sepultura*' [Con esto van a poder enterrar a sus familias; con esto van a darle 'cristiana sepultura']." The relatives thanked the clerk. We then took the coffins and left the IML. We had to wait for a while in the building's entryway because some taxi drivers refused to transport the coffins. Eventually, after offering to pay much more for the ride than usual, we managed to get cabs and take the coffins to the lawyer's assistant's office—where they stayed until the next morning, when we carried them back to the village (Figure 1.1).

By mid-2007, gone were the days when the remains of rural Quechua-speaking victims of violence and atrocity were returned to their relatives in high-profile ceremonies of reburial. For about two decades in Peru, in an arresting manifestation of the unequal impact of the internal war on the body politic, the bodies of victims of violence had lain hastily buried wherever they had fallen or had been thrown in clandestine graves scattered throughout former war-torn rural areas. This situation was meant to

FIGURE 1.1. Survivors of the 1985 Accomarca massacre receiving the remains of their slaughtered relatives, Ayacucho, May 2007.

change with the postconflict project of exhumation and reburial launched in 2001 in the context of the democratic transition that followed the collapse of the Fujimori regime in late 2000. During the first two years of the project, which coincided with the CVR's tenure, the authorities performed three major public ceremonies of reburial to officially dignify victims of violence. But following the end of the CVR's mandate, these high-profile ceremonies were reduced to discreet and formulaic bureaucratic acts, as the scene narrated above shows.

In this chapter I offer a partial history of how the question of recovering the remains of victims of violence for proper burial came to occupy center stage in Peru's postconflict project of nation-making. In contrast to the well-known cases of Argentina, Chile, and Guatemala, in Peru exhumations are not primarily meant to dismantle the long-term effects of years of military dictatorship by recovering the remains of victims of campaigns of state terror. While including victims of state terror, in Peru exhumations also aim at recovering victims of the Shining Path within a broad moral framework that seeks to offer due recognition to *all* forgotten victims of violence—a move that is akin to what Verdery (1999, 47) sees nationalisms typically doing in their projects of nation-building, namely, "repossessing 'our' dead." In Peru, the project of offering recognition to ignored victims of violence through proper burial was born with the notion that it would help to bridge the historical gulf that has separated white/mestizo, Spanish-speaking mainstream Peruvians from indigenous, Quechua-speaking peoples. In the CVR's view, this gulf was, in the end, the ultimate cause of violence and prevents Peruvians from becoming a fully realized political community (see the Introduction).

I begin by tracing the political trajectory that led to the articulation of a broad project of reckoning with past violence, including a truth commission, exhumations, and prosecutions, as a result of the influence of international human rights law and global humanitarianism. I then examine the ways in which a project of forensic exhumation that started with the specific goal of shedding light on the whereabouts of the disappeared by the forces of the state ended up as a project of the exhumation and reburial of forgotten victims of both the Shining Path and the army. I also examine the ways this project of reckoning became a project of postconflict necro-governmentality aimed at structuring the field of possible action and speech of victims and survivors, as well as the population, regarding past violence. Finally, I briefly visit the three ceremonies of reburial the CVR performed to show how Quechua survivors received, deflected, accommodated, and contested this project to put forward their own projects of reckoning.

Internal War and the (First) Postwar Period

One of the peculiarities of Peru's internal war is that it happened under formally elected civilian regimes. The violence broke out in May 1980 with the Shining Path's campaign to overthrow the state, right before the inauguration of Peru's first elected government after twelve years of military rule.[8] The group's initial symbolic act was to burn ballot boxes in Chuschi, a remote village in the Andean Quechua-speaking department of Ayacucho. The insurrection soon spread throughout the region, one of Peru's most impoverished areas. In response, the newly elected regime of Fernando Belaúnde (1980–1985) embarked on a brutal counterinsurgency campaign that made extensive use of the state of emergency and granted the military unrestrained powers to confront the Maoists. Following doctrines of national security, the army targeted rural populations that they accused of supporting the guerrillas and deployed strategic forts in areas they considered "red zones." Under the state of emergency, massacres, torture, and the disappearance of terrorism suspects became standard state practices in these areas, but Belaúnde denied their occurrence—setting the script of denial and silencing that later governments would follow.[9]

This strategy of state terror did not prevent the Maoist insurrection from expanding to other rural areas. Some communities formed government-supported civil patrols to fight the guerrillas and committed state-authorized violence, and the war escalated. The Shining Path retaliated with a terror campaign of its own, targeting local authorities, small landowners, popular leaders, and leftist opponents whom the Maoists accused of being state agents. In 1984 the MRTA entered the internal war, further expanding violence to other rural areas such as the central and southern Andes as well as the central Amazonian basin and the Huallaga region. By the mid-1980s most Peruvians lived under a state of emergency.

In 1985 President Alan García (1985–1990) came into office with the promise of changing his predecessor's human rights policy. However, he soon backpedaled and embraced the military's approach. During his regime, the internal war made its brutal practices visible to the rest of the country, including Lima—which until then had been relatively untouched. In June 1986, the Peruvian military extrajudicially executed more than three hundred incarcerated terrorism suspects as part of the state's response to a prison mutiny that the Shining Path organized in Lima and El Callao to force their political demands upon the government. This event marked the final failure of García's promise and constituted a further escalation of violence in the midst of a grave economic crisis that brought Peru to the brink of collapse by the late 1980s. Also during this period paramilitary groups flourished, killing alleged supporters of the guerrilla groups. At the time, Peru regularly appeared on the annual list compiled by the United Nations Commission on Human Rights of countries with the highest number of political disappearances in the world (Poole and Rénique 1992, 12).

President Alberto Fujimori came to power in 1990 during one of the most difficult periods in Peru's recent history. His regime stabilized the economy through severe structural adjustment policies and the imposition of a neoliberal market economy, following an *autogolpe* (self-imposed coup d'état) with the support of the armed forces in April 1992. Just months later, in September 1992, the Shining Path's top leader, Abimael Guzmán, was captured. This marked the strategic defeat of the Maoists as their organization collapsed. Guzmán was put in a cage and displayed to the press and the public; soon afterwards a faceless military court summarily tried and sentenced him to life in prison. The final coup came when Guzmán called on his followers to lay down their arms, and the government claimed victory.[10]

I suggest that a first postwar period begins at this time. During this first postwar period, Fujimori introduced a new constitution in 1993 to cement the neoliberal order. He also oversaw the return of war-displaced populations to their homes and launched a massive program of road and infrastructure construction in these areas. On the other hand, state terror was rearticulated in a more selective manner. Although massacres and disappearances decreased, the regime passed antiterrorist legislation that stripped away due process guarantees and opened the way for mass detentions, routine torture, and summary conviction of suspects by faceless military and civilian courts. The regime also passed "repentance" laws that reduced the severity of the antiterrorist law for suspects who reported their accomplices to the police. The stamp of this first postwar period was the blanket amnesty law passed by the regime in July 1995 right before the inauguration of Fujimori's second term in office that benefited state officials involved in human rights violations committed during the internal war.

The defeat of the guerrilla groups, the return of economic stability, and Fujimori's tight political control based on the expanded powers of the military and intelligence services allowed Fujimori to mask one of the most corrupt regimes in recent history.[11] The defeat of the Shining Path also enabled him to articulate a "memory of salvation," consolidate a logic of victor's justice, and impose the forgetting and silencing of state atrocity.[12] While the two previous regimes had been able to present themselves only as "victims" of terrorism, Fujimori portrayed himself as Peru's victorious savior. Paradoxically, his regime kept alive the "threat" of terrorism to justify his tight control of power and disregard for human rights. In July 1999, in the name of defending the country against the return of terrorism, Fujimori withdrew Peru from the jurisdiction of the Inter-American Court of Human Rights (IACourtHR) in order to avoid any legal oversight of Peru's international obligations on human rights.[13] Thus, despite the defeat of the guerrillas, Peru was trapped in a strange temporality in which the war was simultaneously over and not over yet.

The (Second) Postwar Period and the
Disappeared as a Legal Problem

The dramatic collapse of Fujimori's regime in November 2000, after the inauguration of his unconstitutional third term, signaled the beginning of Peru's second postwar period, which saw a (re)turn to human rights, a concern with truth, and a sudden preoccupation with the unknown war dead and disappeared. In April 2000, violating the constitution his regime introduced in 1993 prohibiting presidential reelection, Fujimori imposed his second reelection with the support of military and business elites. The electoral fraud was so blatant that the usually complacent Organization of American States (OAS) had no choice but to denounce it. However, the OAS recognized Fujimori's reelection anyway, on the condition that the regime initiate negotiations with the opposition to introduce democratic reforms. In September 2000, in an unexpected turn of events, damaging information about the regime's widespread corruption involving Vladimiro Montesinos, the man behind the power, was leaked to the media. A few months later Fujimori fled the country and gained asylum in Japan, his parents' homeland, from where he sent his resignation via fax.

A caretaker civilian government led by Congressman Valentín Paniagua (November 2000–July 2001) was installed to cope with the national crisis. Committed to reestablishing democratic principles and the rule of law in the country, the Paniagua regime set itself two major tasks: to organize and oversee new general elections and to root out Fujimori's legacy of widespread corruption throughout crucial state institutions. After some initial hesitation, the interim regime also took steps toward human rights accountability as a means of establishing its democratic credentials and setting a clear contrast with its predecessor.[14] In mid-January 2001, Paniagua authorized Peru's return to the jurisdiction of the IACourtHR, manifesting the Peruvian state's commitment to once again abide by its international obligations on human rights. Then, in March 2001, Peru signed friendly settlement agreements with the Inter-American Commission of Human Rights (IACHR) to investigate hundreds of cases of human rights violations pending since the 1980s, the vast majority of which concerned the disappeared.

In another bold move, the Paniagua regime acquiesced to all the terms of the landmark sentence of the IACourtHR in *Peru vs. Barrios Altos*, a case handed down in March 2001 which ruled that Peru's 1995 amnesty law was incompatible with the American Convention on Human Rights and that it was consequently null and had no legal standing.[15] This acquiescence set the character and tone of "postconflict" politics toward the recent violence. The Peruvian judiciary enacted the ruling of the international court, and since the amnesty law no longer applied, the legal obstacles that had thus far prevented the prosecution of past human rights crimes were removed. Peruvian legal institutions thus regained jurisdiction over a problem that Fujimori attempted to resolve through legislation, and the more than one hundred cases pending before the IACHR were immediately reopened for criminal investigation.[16]

More notably perhaps, the Peruvian state pledged to establish victim-oriented repertoires of action and thought around novel legal notions such as the "right to truth." In the hearing on the *Barrios Altos* case before the IACourtHR, state representatives articulated the new regime's strategy in the area of human rights as "recognizing [international] responsibilities, but, above all, . . . proposing integrated procedures for attending to the victims based on three fundamental elements: the *right to truth*, the right to justice and the right to obtain fair reparation" (emphasis added.)[17] Never before in Peru's history of violence had a government made such a commitment to a victim-oriented perspective in its human rights policies, in which the truth about the past held a central place. This project of accountability for human rights violations aimed primarily at determining the victims' whereabouts to allow for the possibility of justice and reparations. In fact, as the notion of "right to truth" suggests, finding victims' remains was in itself an act of justice.

In September 2001, just months after the negotiations with both the IACourtHR and the IACHR, the Fiscalía de la Nación/Ministerio Público issued a comprehensive set of rules and procedures that would henceforth govern the forensic investigation of clandestine mass graves according to international standards.[18] As most of the cases pending before the Inter-American system pertained to people "disappeared" during Peru's "war on terror," determining the whereabouts of these victims was the first and foremost legal task, and because they were presumed dead, such a task had to start with the excavation of clandestine graves and sites of burial scattered throughout rural Peru where the disappeared presumably lay buried. These exhumations thus responded primarily to Peru's obligations to international human rights law.

Yet the Fiscalía's concern with specialization, expertise, training, and compliance with international standards in this kind of investigation also revealed how an emergent global discursive practice concerning mass death in contexts of atrocity had made its way to Peru. The ordinance was a way of receiving and translating to the Peruvian reality an assemblage of disciplinary interventions that Rosenblatt (2015) calls "forensic human rights investigations." Bringing together science and human rights, this assemblage propounds the use of innovative scientific techniques to sort out facts from the painful intricacy of mass atrocity and its aftermath, and to recover the remains of victims to offer them postmortem justice.[19] But, as I show below, by embracing this global discursive practice, the Fiscalía not only inserted a set of technologies of truth and self into the legal task of searching for the disappeared, but also introduced a humanitarian perspective that reshaped the work of the law dealing with state atrocity within a broader articulation of power I conceptualize as the necro-governmentality of postconflict.

The Right to Truth and the "Ignored" Dead

In purely legal terms, the Peruvian state could have complied with its international obligations on human rights for those individual cases without starting a broad campaign of exhumations that ended up including a variety of cases that did not concern, strictly speaking, the forced disappearance of terrorism suspects at the hands of the state. These other cases involved mass graves containing the remains of victims of the Peruvian Army's massacres, as in the Accomarca case, but also the sites where survivors buried the victims of the Shining Path's massacres, as in the Lucanamarca case (see below). In other words, a legal project that started with the purpose of shedding light on the fate of the disappeared, after two decades of official denial, oblivion, and silencing, ended up as a broader moral project of national "repossession" of the ignored war dead. I suggest that the ethos of accountability and transparency that pervaded the political atmosphere after Fujimori's downfall made the new ruling elites receptive to a more comprehensive adoption of the right to truth as a means of reckoning with past violence, beyond legal solutions that they saw as individualistic in nature.

Here, let us take a brief detour into how legal scholars have conceptualized the right to truth. They see it as an evolving concept that draws on the fundamental distinction between legal evidence and the truth of atrocity.[20] It emerged first in humanitarian law as a response to the specific problem of the disappearance of dissenters during internal wars and counterinsurgency campaigns; then it was expanded to address other forms of gross human rights violations beyond the confines of forced disappearance. In this expansion, the right to truth also began to demand forms of accountability that transcend the limitations of the legal field in addressing atrocity. In a further evolution, as the idea that knowing has therapeutic effects started to gain global currency, the right to truth came to be seen as a fundamental social and political mechanism to address traumatic legacies of violence and atrocity. The right to truth started thus to be seen as a right belonging not only to victims, but also to society at large. In the words of the IACHR, "every *society* has the inalienable right to know the truth about past events, as well as the motives and circumstances in which aberrant crimes came to be committed, in order to prevent repetition of such acts in the future. Moreover, the family members of the victims are entitled to information as to what happened to their relatives" (emphasis added).[21]

In this formulation, the right to truth belongs *also* to society at large because it prevents the repetition of mass atrocity in the future. It assumes that nonrepetition is best guaranteed when, in addition to the legal truth, society at large knows the truth of the atrocity perpetrated on its behalf. On one hand, the truth of (past) atrocity allows for the possibility of recognition, coping with trauma, and, eventually, reconciliation and closure. On the other hand, it operates in the present at the level of the population to dissuade the potentiality of atrocity in the future. For such a work, nonlegal mechanisms such as truth commissions are needed to do what the law by itself is unable to—that is, to produce the broader truth of atrocity that is irreducible to legal evidence and that, by definition, cannot be produced within the law's formalistic strictures.[22] I suggest that seen in this way, the right to truth emerges as a kind of political technology that, since it aims at modulating the conduct of populations, has a family resemblance to the technologies of governmentality (see the Introduction).

For my purposes here I consider three registers in which the notion of right to truth, understood as a right belonging to society at large, functioned in Peru as a free-floating signifier that allowed a displacement of the question of the truth of atrocity from the specific problem concerning the disappeared to a broad problem concerning the conduct of survivors, relatives, institutions, and the society at large toward the recent past of violence. The first register is the distinction between the truth of violence and the legal truth or evidence for trial, which enabled the possibility of disengaging the problem of prosecuting perpetrators of atrocities from the circumstances in which those crimes were committed. While the obstacles that prevented criminal investigation as a consequence of the 1995 amnesty had been formally removed, gathering evidence for prosecuting these crimes became a daunting task for prosecutors primarily because of the reluctance of the military institutions to cooperate. In the face of this contingency, the legal institutions emphasized their will to find out the truth about the *circumstances* of the crime as a means of opening the way for the potential healing of bereaved families.

How the notion of right to truth reshaped the ways in which legal institutions conceived of their work on state atrocity became apparent to me in a conversation I had in February 2006 with the former chief prosecutor for human rights in Ayacucho. She articulated the new discursive regime in the following terms:

We are aware that most probably we won't be able to identify the perpetrators in all the cases under investigation. Consequently, we won't be able to prosecute them in every single case; but we want to say to the [victims'] relatives: "Look, we could not make justice, but at least we have recovered the remains of your relatives. This is the way in which the state is trying to reach you." We want to say: "Look, we have sought the truth and the truth is that your relative was killed in these circumstances, this is the place in which he was buried, and now we are restoring him to you for proper burial."[23]

In addition to the distinction between legal evidence and the truth of crime, this picture of the work of the law shows how the Peruvian legal institutions adopted the humanitarian notion that both truth and truth-telling have therapeutic powers and considered that, while retribution could not perhaps be served in all cases, some form of restitution could be attained by both telling the victims' relatives the truth about what happened to their loved ones and officially returning their bodies for proper burial. Not surprisingly, convinced of the therapeutic value of the truth, the legal authorities encouraged survivors and relatives to participate actively in the procedures of forensic exhumation in the hope that such participation would not only guarantee fairness in their work of justice-making, but would also help the latter to gain certain closure to their suffering.[24]

A second reconfiguration in the work of the law that the notion of the right to truth enabled was articulated around the distinction between the rights of the victims and the rights of society, which led to the appointment of a truth commission in Peru in June 2001, despite the fact that it was not part of the country's international obligations on human rights, nor was it a national demand. Taking office on the heels of one of the most secretive and corrupt regimes in Peruvian history, Paniagua was persuaded, as already noted, that the comprehensive project his regime had put in motion with the aim of cleansing the political center and reconstituting moral values in Peru also needed an official body of inquiry into past violence. Peruvians needed to cleanse from their body politic not only corruption, but also the legacy of past atrocity.[25] The truth commission was thus born with the notion that while primarily belonging to the victims, the right to truth also belonged to society at large. The supreme decree creating the commission states this explicitly: "The painful violence Peru experienced in the past two decades must be clarified and not left to oblivion, and the state must guarantee *the right of the society to know the truth*" (emphasis added).[26]

This mandate asked the CVR to shed light on "the process, facts, and responsibilities of terrorist violence and human rights violations," imputable to both terrorist organizations and state officials, and thereby entrusted the commission with tasks of truth-finding at two levels. First, it had to produce a historical truth by analyzing the origins as well as the political, social, and cultural "conditions" and "behaviors" that "contributed to the tragic episode of violence Peru went through." Second, the CVR had to contribute, "when pertinent," to the legal investigation of crimes and human rights violations committed by both terrorist groups and state officials and to attribute as far as possible the responsibilities. Here, the mandate emphasized the problem of the disappeared by asking the commission "to *establish the whereabouts and situation of victims*" (emphasis added).[27]

The distinction between legal truth and historical truth reflected the conceptual double bind by means of which the right to truth is intended to respond to both the plight of victims and the presumed needs of society at large for healing and reconciliation. Yet, while the mandate reconciled unproblematically legal truth and historical truth, in practice the CVR had troubles doing this. Concerned primarily with history, politics, and morals, the commission focused on *patterns* of human rights violations that would provide sociological, institutional, and juridical evidence for claims of truth within a broader narrative of violence and injustice. Only midway through its work did the CVR put together a special team of lawyers in charge of preparing legal cases for prosecution.[28] In addition to problems such as how a nonlegal institution could handle legal evidence in criminal cases, there was the problem of the epistemological status of the legal case in a broad historical and moral account of violence and suffering. The idea of an "emblematic case" (*caso emblemático*) would provide a solution: the legal case would both serve the purposes of prosecution and stand as a paradigmatic illustration of atrocity in a narrative pursuant to shedding light upon past injustice and the moral and political failures behind it.

The transfiguration of the legal case into a paradigmatic illustration of a national narrative of suffering and redemption amounted to a third reconfiguration in the postconflict work of dealing with past atrocity introduced by means of the notion of the right to truth, namely, the problem of the whereabouts of the disappeared and the forensic excavation of clandestine mass graves that the Fiscalía had started to conduct as part of Peru's obligations on human rights. The commissioners showed interest in this problem early in their work, even before defining the CVR's legal strategy, and asked the Fiscalía to conduct these interventions jointly. Both institutions arrived at a working relationship after a series of tense exchanges over attributions, competencies, and jurisdiction.[29] In the end, as the legal authority, the Fiscalía would have control and direction of procedures in their totality—that is, it would *formally* decide on the cases for intervention, appoint personnel, collect evidence for prosecution, return recovered bodies to relatives, and provide legal certifications. However, in a sign of flexibility, the Fiscalía *informally* agreed to allow the CVR to select cases for intervention. The CVR could also suggest the names of independent forensic experts to be included in the official teams.

This power to suggest which cases to investigate turned out to be crucial for the CVR's own project of truth-telling and nation-building. While the Fiscalía was in charge of legal aspects, the CVR selected cases that in the commissioners' view were "emblematic" of the story of national tragedy they wanted to tell. In this version, the dead in these cases, whether killed by the state or by armed groups, were all equal in rank: all were *victims*—first of all, victims of atrocity itself; and second, victims of the negligence and indifference of their more privileged fellow citizens. The CVR thus introduced a subtle but crucial shift in the project of the excavation of clandestine graves, from a focus on the legal search for the disappeared to a focus on the moral acknowledgment of the *ignored* dead—that is, those killed during the war who had not been given due recognition as fellow citizens—by means of offering them a *cristiana sepultura*.

The CVR decided that official reburial ceremonies would be a privileged stage to offer this postmortem recognition to the victims and their surviving relatives. By making visible the suffering of these victims, the ceremonies of reburial would also serve to awaken compassion and thus facilitate the moral project of bridging the historical gulf that separated mainstream Peruvians from their less fortunate Andean compatriots, which in the CVR's view was the ultimate cause of violence. In other words, postconflict exhumations and reburials would work toward structuring the field of possible action and speech of survivors, relatives, and society at large in terms of motivating Peruvians to conduct their conduct toward mutual recognition and reconciliation.

In this sense, within a broader articulation of power I conceptualize as the necro-governmentality of postconflict, there was a shift from a political project of unmaking the long-term effects of state terror to a moral project of unmaking the long-term effects of a broader "biopolitics of neglect." Similarly to other experiences in Latin America, the project of postconflict excavation of clandestine mass graves to shed light on the whereabouts of the disappeared had had, for a long while, the specific aim of dissolving state terror's "necropolitical hold" on society—which would remain in place as long as the bodies of those annihilated on behalf of the body politic were not recovered.[30] But in Peru's second postwar period, this political salience was resignified and subsumed into a broader moral project of the recognition of *all* victims of violence—of those who were killed and those who were "let die" by a mainstream society that did not care.

Reburial in Times of Truth

During the two years of its existence the CVR participated in three excavations and performed high-profile reburial ceremonies of ignored victims of the internal war. These events took place in the Andean villages of Chuschi, Totos, and the district of Lucanamarca in the Ayacuchano provinces of Cangallo and Huancasancos. The first two cases involved massacres by the army, and the third concerned one by the Shining Path. The CVR selected these three cases because they were emblematic of the moral story of suffering and neglect that the commissioners wanted to make visible to the national audience.[31] Nearly two decades after the killings, a modern multidisciplinary task force consisting of commissioners, prosecutors, forensic experts, psychologists, delegates of the Ombudsman

Office, and the Peruvian human rights community arrived in these villages to conduct the highly symbolic acts of (postconflict) state. Catholic priests involved in the CVR's work also traveled with the group to offer the victims the proper rites of a *cristiana sepultura.*

Offering a *cristiana sepultura* to unrecognized victims of violence was meant to replace the trajectory of violence and neglect by a path of state recognition.[32] It would start by locating human remains and recovering them from the place where perpetrators left them. Then, it would take those remains to a laboratory for forensic analysis, rearrange them, individualize them, and identify them. Next, it would bring the remains into the legal realm, to restore the victims' legal status and to collect evidence. Finally, it would bring them before the nation's gaze for the recognition and dignification of victims through the performance of proper burial rites. Only then would the human remains, thus recognized and dignified, be returned to the care of bereaved families, who would finally be able to start the work of mourning that, in the absence of proper burial, had remained suspended. By walking this path of state recognition, mainstream Peruvians would finally be able to acknowledge as fellow citizens those victims who were killed or let die as a result of the moral failures of the Peruvian society at large.

But, as we will see, Quechua-speaking survivors were not passive recipients of this official project of postmortem recognition. They responded in a variety of ways to this manifestation of state power that presented itself before them as a power that cares for them and is opposed to the power that kills or lets people die. In most cases, a key area of contestation revolved around seeing violence fundamentally as a political problem rather than a moral one. The brief account that follows is based on the scant textual and visual material recorded by the CVR about the exhumations and reburials in which it was involved.[33]

Exhumation and Reburial in Chuschi

The first intervention took place in the village of Chuschi in late January 2002. Starting a large project of the exhumation and reburial of victims of violence in the very place where the Shining Path had ignited its revolution was a political statement in itself. The CVR wanted to convey the Peruvian state's commitment to breaking with the violence and neglect of the past and its new disposition toward redeeming the suffering of survivors through the rational means of the law and forensic sciences as well as the moral discourses of recognition and inclusion. In short, it was an act meant to (re)proclaim the civilizing mission of the state.

The human remains to be exhumed and reburied in Chuschi belonged to eight villagers from the neighboring community of Quispillacta who had been kidnapped from their homes and executed by an army squad on May 15, 1983. The fact that the relatives knew where the bodies were buried helped the work of exhumation and identification, which occurred in a single operation and concluded with the placement of the rearranged remains in coffins donated by the CVR.[34] This was followed by a legal ceremony for the official return of the victims' remains to their relatives, presided over by a *fiscal* and a CVR commissioner. One by one, the legal authority called a representative from each bereaved family to receive the remains of their loved one. The official proceeded by asking the relative for photo identification to demonstrate his or her legal relationship to the victim and then asked him or her to sign and fingerprint a log to record the legal restitution of remains. The *fiscal* completed the official act by handing over the corresponding death certificate whereby the state officially pronounced death in that specific case and offered condolences to the bereaved on behalf of the Fiscalía and the CVR.[35]

This legal act of restitution was followed by a Catholic funeral mass in the Quispillacta church presided over by two Catholic priests who were CVR commissioners.[36] In contrast to the legal act, the mass was open to the community at large. The eight coffins were accommodated in the central nave of the church before a packed audience composed of visitors from Lima—CVR staff, legal and forensic personnel, and human rights activists—and villagers. Also, in contrast to the legal act of restitution, this act of moral recognition elicited emotions of bereavement while also becoming a scene of instruction. The CVR's regional chief served as translator for the Spanish-speaking priests who did not speak Quechua. Through him, the priests-commissioners preached consolation to the relatives, now that the remains of their loved ones had finally returned home and their souls had found a place in the "eternal life" beside God, and instructed the bereaved to receive this event as a moment of closure of past suffering.

As I see it, the crucial moment of the ceremony is the point at which the priest asks relatives to share their thoughts with the audience as a means of symbolically breaking the silence that had until then prevented them from speaking of their suffering. In the context of official exhumation and reburial of victims of state terror, a ritual gesture that is ordinary in a Catholic mass becomes an act of interpellation of the (postconflict) state. The relatives are invited to speak the truth not of the state that committed violence against their loved ones, but of the state that has recovered their remains, has reassembled and examined them, has restituted their legal identities, and is now offering them recognition and proper burial. That is, the relatives are asked to speak not of the state that kills and forgets, but of the state that cares and recognizes.

All the speakers thanked the *doctores* in Quechua for having helped them finally recover the remains of their relatives for proper burial.[37] One old woman said that now that her loved one was buried in the village cemetery, she would no longer need to go to the previous burial site to visit him and pay her respects to his memory. Another old woman said that it was as if her son had returned home after a very long trip. "My beloved son is coming back; he will be finally back home [Viajeskanmanta, imayna chayachkamuchkanta; chayna wawachallay qamuchqam; wasillayman chaynacha kutiykurunka]," she said.[38]

These moving statements seemed to fully justify the claim that *cristiana sepultura* in the terms here described leads to closure, redemption, and reconciliation. Insofar as the relatives of the victims seemed to conform to the CVR's "public script," they appeared before the gaze of the nation occupying the subject position intended for them: mourners and citizens responding to the interpellation of a (postconflict) state that cares, repairs, invites speech, and remembers, as opposed to a state that kills, terrorizes, silences, and forgets. For these Quechua survivors, the pendulum of sovereignty seemed to have swung from "threat to guarantee" (Poole 2004).

The symbolic and political efficacy of this performance of sovereignty is based on three crucial presuppositions: first, that the material remains of the dead are available for forensic recovery; second, that these are "tragic" deaths—as opposed to, say, "heroic" deaths—and that consequently the remains correspond to people who have been "victims" of violence—as opposed to, say, militants—with no explicit political agency; and third, that survivors conform to the subject position assigned to them. In the Chuschi case all these three conditions concurred: the bodies could be found; the dead could be presented as "victims" with no political agency; and the survivors' responded to the state's interpellation in the way the CVR expected. The state's procedures aimed to tame and contain the excess of violence

through the performance of proper burial rites seemed to have been efficacious in this case.[39]

As I discuss below, circumstances at Totos and Lucanamarca were
significantly different and did not fulfill all three of these criteria. To the
extent that they diverge from the CVR's script, the exhumations and reburials there did not take on precisely the meaning that the commission
intended. Furthermore, the ceremonies and public acts became opportuni-
ties for relatives and survivors to challenge the depoliticized narrative put
forth by the CVR.

Exhumation and Reburial in Totos

The second joint exhumation and reburial took place in the district
of Totos, in the Ayacuchano province of Cangallo, in late August 2002.[40]
In this intervention, the Fiscalía and the CVR planned to recover the bodies of nineteen Quechua-speaking peasants executed by army squads stationed at the infamous military base of Totos—an outpost in a remote
area that in the early 1980s became a site of gross human rights violations.[41]
The victims were executed in two military operations that took place in
April and May of 1983. In the first, a military squad summarily executed
four peasants from the village of Totos in the nearby area of Ccarpaccasa
and buried the bodies in shallow graves. In the second operation, military
squads detained fifteen villagers from Quispillacta and transported them
to the Totos base. After several days of torture, the military executed these
detainees in Sanccaypata, an isolated area near Totos. Relatives of the four
victims killed in Ccarpaccasa soon found the shallow graves and in two
cases transferred the remains to the Totos cemetery. In the case of the
Sanccaypata massacre, however, relatives were unable to discover the burial
sites until a witness spoke out many years after the killings.[42]

The exhumation and identification of the four victims of Ccarpaccasa
was easy.[43] But in Sanccaypata, much to the relatives' frustration, the forensic team found only parts and isolated bones of just seven of the fifteen
bodies they expected to recover. The experts assumed that the graves had
been broken into and that the human remains had been dispersed beyond
recovery because of erosion, scavenging animals, or both. The identification of one body showed that this was the right site but also suggested that
the remaining bodies were perhaps lost forever.

In this case the CVR did not leave audiovisual records of the reburial
ceremony. From written records we know that for the four Ccarpaccasa

victims the proceedings began with the legal act of the restitution of remains to relatives that was held in the Fiscalía's headquarters in Ayacucho city, on September 6, 2002. The district general attorney presided, and four CVR commissioners from Lima attended the ceremony. Following the legal act, attendants carried the four coffins in a procession through the streets of Ayacucho toward the main square of the city and stopped in front of the cathedral for the last funeral ceremony. After an all-night candlelight vigil, the relatives finally took their loved ones' remains back to Totos for private reburial.

Since the archives are mute about how the Ccarpaccasa relatives received the event, we can only surmise that like the Chuschi families, they conformed to the CVR's public script of *cristiana sepultura*. In contrast, the unavailability of the body in the Sanccaypata case makes the CVR's project of reburial unattainable. The CVR's archives hold a video recording of a tense meeting in which the forensic experts are explaining to relatives why they cannot go on with the search.[44] Resistant to the idea that the remains of their missing family members may never be found, the relatives demand that legal authorities continue the investigation.

We can thus say that in this case the disappeared had returned to haunt the official project of exhumation and reburial itself. Without a body to reveal the forensic truth of the violence inscribed upon it, the legal project of gathering evidence of atrocity falters. Nor can the project of restoring the social order, by returning these dead bodies to the private care of their families, be attained. Furthermore, in the absence of bodies with which to conduct reburial rites, the unstated political project of capturing and taming the excess of violence inscribed upon those bodies comes to a halt. And relatives are not inclined to accept the guidance and consolation of experts, practitioners, and state officials in their work of mourning, since *cristiana sepultura* is not available for their missing loved ones. In short, the missing body blocks the postconflict project of ritually reconstituting the political community through exhumation and reburial.

Exhumation and Reburial in Lucanamarca

The third and final joint exhumation and reburial took place in the district of Lucanamarca, province of Huancasancos, in early November 2002. Unlike Chuschi and Totos, the intervention here focused on atrocities committed by the Shining Path. On April 3, 1983, the Maoist group carried out a punitive strike against the communities of Lucanamarca that had rebelled against the party's rule, killed local guerrilla leaders, and allied with the military. The rebels slaughtered sixty-nine peasants, eighteen of whom were children younger than ten, in a massacre that came to be known as one of the worst attacks by the Maoist guerrilla group against Andean communities.[45]

The case of Lucanamarca marks an inflection in the CVR's exhumation and reburial project in several respects. To begin with, the bodies of victims were not missing. Survivors and relatives knew their exact whereabouts because, following the massacre, they managed to bury them where they had fallen and even arranged these burial sites as sites of commemoration.[46] Nor was evidence needed for prosecution because the major perpetrators—among them Abimael Guzmán—had already been sentenced to life imprisonment for masterminding the carnage.[47] Most importantly, unlike the cases of Chuschi and Totos, the Lucanamarca victims were not suspected of terrorism. On the contrary, they had died defending the state. And yet, for almost two decades they lay buried in the very places where they had fallen. In the CVR's view these victims epitomized the double suffering of those killed by the Shining Path: the failure of the state to protect its citizens, and the indifference and neglect of mainstream Peruvians toward their excluded Andean fellow nationals. Their reburial would thus serve to offer these victims the state recognition they did not enjoy in the past and make visible their ignored deaths in order to elicit social solidarity among Peruvians.

The exhumation unfolded uneventfully and was completed ahead of schedule with the recovery of sixty-two bodies. At this point, the contrasts between this case and those of Chuschi and Totos became more pronounced. To begin with, the CVR and the Fiscalía decided to transport the exhumed remains to Lima for the laboratory work, explaining to the relatives that given the large number of bodies, this was the right thing to do. This was an opportunity for the CVR to perform funeral ceremonies that offered these victims recognition in Lima, the nation's political and symbolic center.

The centerpiece was a funeral mass offered at La Recoleta—one of Lima's symbolically most important Catholic churches—on December 20, 2002, conducted by priests who were also CVR commissioners, as well as other well-known Spanish-speaking clerics. A large crowd of Spanish-speaking coastal politicians, CVR commissioners and staff, forensic experts, members of NGOs and the human rights community, Lima-based associations of Lucanamarca migrants, and nuns, among others, gathered to recognize and pay their last respects to these victims of the Shining Path. At the end of the mass, in a display of public mourning, the CVR commissioners alternated with other attendants in carrying the coffins on their shoulders in a procession around the Plaza Francia—a symbolically significant square in downtown Lima. Finally, after condemning Shining Path's terrorism one more time, the attendants bid farewell to the victims and carried their coffins to the trucks that would transport them back to Lucanamarca.

The contrasts with the two previous interventions did not end there. President Alejandro Toledo traveled to Lucanamarca some weeks later to inaugurate the special mausoleum built by his government in the village cemetery for the victims of the massacre—the only time a Peruvian president ever attended this kind of ceremony. The relatives and survivors organized in an association called Heroes del 3 de Abril (Heroes of April 3) had petitioned the construction of the mausoleum with the argument—significantly at odds with the CVR's discourse of victimhood—that as people who stood against the Shining Path, and to acknowledge their patriotic contribution to the nation, their loved ones should be reburied not in plain soil like any ordinary person, but in a mausoleum.[48] In the ceremony of inauguration, President Toledo offered apologies to the survivors and relatives on behalf of the Peruvian state, for not having been able to protect them from the evil forces of terror, and said that the country would never forget the heroism of those "brave Peruvians" who offered their lives in defense of democracy.[49]

The next day, on January 10, 2003, during the final ceremony of reburial, one of the commissioners attempted to reclaim the meaning these ceremonies had for the CVR. In sharp contrast with President Toledo, he did not praise the victims as heroes nor present their deaths as heroic acts of sacrifice in defense of democracy and the nation. Instead, framing the atrocity in Lucanamarca in terms of tragedy, he noted that similar tragedies had occurred among many other communities in the Peruvian Andean countryside and that what the CVR wanted to accomplish with interventions like this was to confront mainstream Peruvian society with the truth of these tragedies and thus overcome their indifference to the suffering of their fellow nationals. The commissioner also said that the CVR hoped that with these exhumations and ceremonies of reburial a tragic chapter in the life of these communities would come to a close. "What we have done with this exhumation here," he said, "is to fulfill a fundamental duty of any human person toward their fellow humans; that is, to recognize the most fundamental human right, which is the right to life, which is the right to have at least a *cristiana y decente sepultura* [decent Christian burial] if one loses his life tragically."[50]

As this quotation shows, the CVR attempted to avoid a heroic and patriotic reading of the internal war and instead emphasized discourses of victimhood and failure. The recent episode of violence in Peru should be seen through the lens of tragedy rather than heroism, and events such as Lucanamarca should not be counted among those that constitute the nation but among those that demonstrate its failure. If there was a lesson to learn from this episode, it was a lesson of failure as a nation—failure manifested in the indifference of mainstream Peruvians who were not able to see or grasp what was happening to their fellow nationals in Andean and Amazonian rural Peru. If some redress could be offered to these forgotten victims, it should begin by recognizing their dignity as fellow nationals—recognition that required their proper burial. As a basic human right, this proper burial should be offered to every single victim of this tragic episode of violence.

In the Totos case we saw that the CVR's project of exhumation and reburial encountered a limit in the forensic inability to recover all the missing bodies. In the case of Lucanamarca we find another limit: the discourse of nationalism and "heroic death." The CVR's project of state recognition drew on notions of "tragic death" and universal victimhood in an attempt to establish grounds for (renewed) social solidarity among Peruvians. By eliciting sentiments of compassion thought to be a common human response to the experience of tragic death, the performances of reburial attempted to persuade mainstream Peruvians that all those killed in the internal war (whether by the military or by armed groups) were ultimately victims and that all deserved the basic human right of a proper burial. In the CVR's humanitarian nationalism there was no place for hierarchies in death. To fulfill its project, the CVR also implicitly invited Quechua-speaking survivors and relatives to present themselves to the nation as victims to gain recognition.

But survivors and relatives in the case of Lucanamarca misrecognized the CVR's interpellation and did not take on the subject position they were offered. The reburial of their loved ones killed by the Shining Path was an opportunity for them to assert a particular relation to the state, drawing on discourses of heroic nationalism. Their relatives were not "victims" but "heroes," and their deaths thus should be seen as "sacrifices" for the lives of both the community and the nation, and not merely as "tragic." In this sense, relatives felt entitled to claim a public place for their dead in the national pantheon and not merely a private place at home. The Quechua-speaking survivors in Lucanamarca thus gain a voice through the discourse of heroic nationalism, which is unreservedly endorsed by the Spanish-speaking coastal elites. But at the same time they contribute to the reintroduction of a nationalistic hierarchy among the dead, in which the nation can forget those seen as the "internal enemy" without any moral misgivings.

Concluding Comments

In August 2003, following the end of the CVR's mandate, the Fiscalía appointed a team of forensic anthropologists specializing in excavating clandestine mass graves in former war-torn areas of rural Peru. Under the name Equipo Forense Especializado (EFE; Specialized Forensic Team), this team has ever since been in exclusive charge of conducting forensic procedures to locate clandestine mass graves, collect evidence, and recover, identify, and return victims' bodies to their relatives for proper burial. Yet, while exhumations have continued to take place, ceremonies of reburial similar to those the CVR organized have not. As the political climate in Peru's post-CVR era changed, no national authority, politician, intellectual, or religious figure has attended such events again. The legal restitution of exhumed bodies to relatives has become a bureaucratic affair conducted on the premises of the provincial branches of the Fiscalía, as shown above in the Accomarca case, and the reburial of these victims has become almost exclusively a local affair.

In this chapter I have shown the emergence in Peru of a form of power I conceptualize as the necro-governmentality of postconflict. It is a form of state power that stands in opposition term by term to the power that kills or "lets die." It is concerned with the government of dead bodies and it seeks to structure the field of *possible* action and speech of survivors, relatives, and the population by means of a complex set of legal and disciplinary technologies of self and truth, so as to conduct their conduct as free subjects toward redemption and reconciliation. As I have shown in this chapter, during the tenure of the CVR this structuring of the field of potential action and speech concerned primarily the modulation of the languages of violence so Peruvians could conduct themselves as moral subjects of a reconstituted postconflict community. By means of reburial ceremonies of "ignored" victims of violence, the CVR attempted to introduce an all-encompassing and depoliticized notion of "tragic death" to speak and make sense of violence and mass death in terms akin to a "biopolitics of neglect." In the post-CVR era, such modulation of the languages of violence involves the return to subtle forms of silencing by means of bureaucratic practices, the privatization of memory, and encouraging survivors to speak of violence in terms of human rights, humanitarianism, and cultural concerns with the rights of the dead.

Yet in the cases discussed in this chapter we also saw how survivors and victims' relatives variously contest these attempts of the state. The stark divergence in Accomarca between the legal authorities' sanitized speech about the massacre and the survivors' politically charged claim that what happened there was genocide, as well as the survivors' demand in Lucanamarca that their slaughtered relatives be assigned the status of heroes, suggests an ongoing struggle in postconflict Peru over how to address the violence of the recent past—a struggle that the officially sanctioned truth of violence did not settle. This ongoing struggle keeps alive a plurality of trajectories of truth and memory, or forms of relation to the past, as well as forms of inhabiting the geography of violence that are informed by the survivors' lived experience of atrocity rather than the state's singular, encompassing, and abstract narratives and regimes of visibility of suffering. It also reveals how the question of violence cannot be subsumed within a moral language of social failure or tropes of "tragic death" or a language of rights and the rule of law. It needs a specific *political* reckoning. I explore this specificity in the next chapter.

2

Malamuerte
Governing Tragic Death in the Andes

WHY DID SURVIVORS hastily bury the bodies of their slaughtered relatives where they had fallen and not attempt to move those bodies to consecrated ground? In his classic work, Robert Hertz (1960) argues that some types of death are considered so violent and abnormal that they are made objects of special rites rather than the normal funerary and mourning rituals. As examples, Hertz lists violent deaths such as murders, accidents, death in childbirth, drowning, and suicide. These deaths inspire such intense horror that it seems that the transitory period extends indefinitely for the victims and that "their death has no end" (ibid., 85). We can add to this list of victims whose death "has no end" the cases of thousands of Peruvians who were disappeared or killed in massacres committed during campaigns of political terror carried out by both the state security forces and the Shining Path and whose deaths cannot be objects of normal funerary and mourning rituals.

In this chapter I focus ethnographically on a case of suicide in the Andean community of Accomarca to explore how rural Quechua-speaking villagers of the Peruvian central southern Andes cope with tragic death in ordinary contexts. I cast light upon the assemblage of juridico-medical and cultural technologies that is mobilized, engaged, conformed with, and deflected to face *malamuerte*, a form of death that is sudden, untimely, and meaningless, ordinarily resulting from a fatal accident, murder, or suicide—that is, a form a death that is considered to be at odds with a "normal" form of death resulting from the "natural" course of life. As we saw in Chapter 1, Accomarca was the site of a brutal massacre by the Peruvian Army in August 1985 and also was where the legal institutions conducted exhumations several years later. By looking at how villagers cope with tragic death in ordinary contexts, we can begin to understand how, in contrast, villagers dealt with the legacy of state atrocity, and why they did not subsume these political massacres under the category of "tragic death" as the CVR attempted to do during its mandate.

Three questions guide my exploration. First, what kind of ordinary affects, imaginations, material practices, and rituals do Quechua-speaking mourners put in motion when facing *malamuerte* in everyday life—that is, what are the social and cultural practices that are usually left out of the state's public reburials (such as those described in Chapter 1)? Second, what kind of relation do these ordinary practices have with the juridico-medical technologies set in motion by the state to govern tragic death? Third, what is the effect of state atrocity on this assemblage of juridico-medical technologies and ordinary rituals and practices that govern death in everyday life? I suggest that mass death of the kind suffered in Accomarca exceeds the framework of "(good) death" as well as of "bad death" and as such falls outside the realm of the normal ritualization of death. This will remain the case until mass death is legally and politically prosecuted—that is, until the public sphere becomes available for survivors to contest the right of the state to produce such kinds of death in the purported defense of the body politic.

I begin with a brief description of Accomarca and the case of a young man's suicide. I then explore the category of *malamuerte* and the danger that cultural representations attribute to this kind of transgressive death. I provide an ethnographic account of the aftermath of the young man's suicide: the intervention of the state, and the rituals of the wake and the burial. I focus particularly on the central place women have in ordinary funerary rites, which allows them to transform the brute fact of biological death into a meaningful death. I finally analyze how these representations are transformed by the unprecedented form of death the massacre inflicted on villagers. I thereby advance in this chapter crucial analytical elements about the work of the ordinary in everyday contexts that reemerge in extraordinary contexts of the "fabrication of corpses" such as in the Los Cabitos case—an analysis I undertake in the following chapters.

A Tragic Loss

I first overheard news of a death in Accomarca during my return from a short visit to Vilcashuamán, the provincial capital, in early November 2006, when some young commuters in the *combi* (van) exchanged agitated comments about it. I chose not to engage with their conversation about what obviously was a sad event in the village, so I did not know who had died and how he or she had died until I arrived in Accomarca. As usual, I went first to visit Mama Benita to conclude some of the errands she had asked me to run for her in Vilcashuamán. She and César, her husband, had survived the massacre of sixty-nine villagers carried out by the Peruvian Army in August 1985, but two small daughters and her mother had been killed. That fateful event had occurred on their plot of land, which subsequently became the site where the survivors hurriedly buried the victims' burned remains in mass graves. I had become acquainted with them at the start of my fieldwork, and I used to visit them first whenever I arrived in the village. After she greeted me warmly, Mama Benita gave me news of the death in the village:

> Mama Benita: There is a dead person in town now. A young man has met *malamuerte*.
> Isaías: So, it is true then. I overheard that in the *combi*.
> Mama Benita: Yes . . . a young man hanged himself. Some men brought us the news.
> Isaías: I guess they have already notified the Public Prosecutor's Office, right?
> Mama Benita: [*Hesitant*] Mmm . . .
> Isaías: [*Nodding*] . . .
> Mama Benita: It is difficult to imagine what his family is going through. They must be in deep grief.
> Isaías: Mmm.
> Mama Benita: Who knows what they are going through?

This is how I learned that Lucho, the nineteen-year-old son of one of the village's most respected families, had committed suicide the night before I arrived.[1] As an unexpected death, it was certainly distressing for the community, and as glimpsed in the fragment of conversation above, words did not come easily to address it. However, it is not that these Quechua-speaking villagers do not have criteria to gauge what kind of event this is. Mama Benita's use of the notion *malamuerte*—a form of death that is violent, sudden, untimely, and meaningless—shows that they do have words and grammar to categorize and speak of such an event.

While every *malamuerte* is painful and disturbing, Lucho's suicide was particularly so. The young man was the eldest son in a family that had converted to Protestantism not long before. His parents were hardworking, and this family was neither among the poorest in Accomarca nor among the wealthiest. They were prosperous enough to have their plots of land in diverse ecological niches.[2] They regularly attended services in the village's small Protestant church and closely followed the ethics of individuality, self-restraint, and prayer that their religion prescribed. They did not drink alcohol or chew coca and were uninterested in local politics. Nor were they among the villagers affected directly by political violence. If people held any possible grudge against them, it was because, as evangelicals, they tended to avoid participation in communal *faenas* and other events that articulate local authority, such as the Catholic-informed *cargos*.[3]

In many ways Accomarca is a typical Andean village. It lies at the end of a secondary road that departs from Vilcashuamán and that was completed as recently as the late 1980s. Until then, villagers used bridle paths to travel in and out of the community. During my fieldwork between 2006 and 2007, an average of two *combis* per day made the 170-kilometer journey between the capital city of Ayacucho and the village, typically taking seven to eight hours. At the time, around three hundred families lived in one-story mud-brick houses with tile roofs, dispersed along winding and steep dirt streets that connect the three neighborhoods of the village. Most houses have storage rooms for the year's harvest as well as small patios and corrals for herds of sheep and goats. The main square is in the lower part of the village and houses most of the public buildings, such as the town hall, the peace court, and the colonial church. The elementary and high schools and the dispensary are situated in the upper part of the village, where one also finds the remains of the former military garrison stationed on the town's highest hill to closely surveil the villagers after the 1985 army massacre until 1994 (Figure 2.1).

Like most of the villages in the Pampas River valley, Accomarca is just over three thousand meters above sea level, midway between the shores of the Pampas River, at around twenty-five hundred meters, and the rocky peaks of the *puna* that are roughly five thousand meters above sea level. Two eroded ravines flank the village. Water is scarce, and the land is mostly arid and stony. The agrarian production is primarily consumed within the village. Because of this economy of subsistence, villagers, mostly men, migrate seasonally to cities, large-scale agricultural areas on the coast, or the jungle to perform unskilled labor and supplement the domestic income.

Lucho had also migrated seasonally to Lima after finishing high school, with the expectation of making some money to help his family. In

FIGURE 2.1. Village of Accomarca in 2006.

addition, he had become engaged to a girl in the village and needed to save money for the wedding and the material foundations for his future new family. With the help of his parents, Lucho had already built a house and received small plots of land from the family's holdings. In Accomarca, as elsewhere in the Andes, ownership of property in different ecological niches is family-based and transferred through inheritance. Because the kinship system is bilateral, inheritance of land does not make gender distinctions, yet there is always a differentiation based on how well children look after their parents when they age.[4] Those who have been loving and caring, reciprocating the care they received in childhood, receive the best part of the inheritance. Typically, the older siblings assume this role of caring for aging parents and thereby receive the authority to guide their younger siblings. Lucho's family was expecting him to assume this role.

In addition, as mobile subjects, young men accumulate forms of social and symbolic capital that may be beneficial not only to their families, but also to the wider community.[5] In the highly stratified hierarchies of power in Peru, the possibilities of connection with broader power networks and of acquiring knowledge of the ways in which this power is negotiated and made intelligible are highly valued in these Andean villages. In short, Lucho was about to become a full member of the community.

So, at first sight there was no apparent reason for him to take such a drastic step. It was in the register of rumor that villagers started to make sense of it. Like other seasonal migrants, Lucho had returned to Accomarca from Lima during the All Saints' Day holidays in early November for a short visit to his family and fiancée. Rumor had it that upon his return he had found out that she had betrayed him. I never attempted to confirm this; what concerns us here is not the victim's motives, but understanding the complex ways in which people in the Peruvian rural Andes cope with tragic death. In this case, putting into circulation the notion of betrayal to make sense of a young man's decision to take his life is part of that complex set of ideas and practices.

Malamuerte or Bad Death

The notion of *malamuerte* comes from the Spanish words *mala* (bad) and *muerte* (death) and has been integrated into Quechua to denote a kind of death that deviates from culturally informed expectations of what a human form of death should be. Saturated with colonial Catholic prescriptions about how a good life inevitably leads to a good death, these expectations build on the radical distinction Catholic theology makes between the human body and the soul. While the body dies, the soul remains *ad eternum*. In these colonial prescriptions, the task of life for Christians is to prepare their souls for eternal salvation so that, when the inevitable moment of biological death arrives, they are ready for the difficult journey their souls must undertake to reach the presence of God. Death thus should occur as a result of the body's "natural" process of decay so that Christians have enough time to prepare their souls and the surviving relatives are able to accompany the dying in their last moments. The grief such a death brings is in some fashion attenuated by this possibility of accompanying the deceased loved one and of conducting proper funerary rites to help the soul find its way to the afterlife.

By contrast, since it occurs both unexpectedly and violently, *malamuerte* is a kind of death that is "unnatural" and undesirable because it breaks the life cycle abruptly and, as such, impedes the possibility of adequately preparing the soul for its difficult journey into the afterlife. As a consequence, having departed with unfinished business the pitiful soul is unable to leave the world of the living, nor is it able to reach the land of the dead. Thrown into disarray, with no place among the dead or among the living, the roaming soul haunts surviving relatives and brings about calamities for the community until their obligations are fulfilled. While there are different kinds of *malamuerte*, not all of them are morally reprehensible. For instance, death as a result of a traffic accident is a kind of *malamuerte* that is not morally reprehensible.

For Accomarquinos, suicide belongs to the realm of morally reprehensible behaviors. This became clear to me the evening I went back to Mama Benita's house, after stopping by the wake to offer my condolences to the grieving family. As usual, I found Mama Benita in her small kitchen, sitting in front of her *q'oncha* (hearth) preparing the evening meal. She had a visitor—Basilia, a lonely relative of hers and also a Protestant who frequently came over to talk about the day's happenings in the village. Predictably, that evening the only topic of conversation was the suicide and the wake. At a certain point, in the semidarkness of the kitchen, which was barely illuminated by the fire's ashes, Mama Benita said that the night the fateful event happened she heard an unusual howling of the village dogs. Basilia replied that she had heard it too. Mama Benita went on: "It must be that his *animu* walked that night [animucha purimuram miki]," confirming the idea that the unusual howling of dogs is a sign announcing death.

Mama Benita was expressing here the widely held belief in the Peruvian rural Andes that just before death the spirit of a person wanders around tracing the places he or she used to frequent, such as dwellings or workplaces.[6] The word *animu* refers to one of the three souls villagers believe a person has. The *animu* is the deindividualized vital force that resides in every living being and anything that contains the possibility of life. By contrast, *alma* refers indistinctly to two other entities. In one sense, as Mama Benita uses it in the dialogue above, it refers to the dead body (*qunam almapas kashqam*). In another sense, it refers to the spirit that goes directly to face God's judgment as soon as a person dies. This latter sense, alluding to the individual's personality, resembles the Christian idea of a soul.[7] While all three entities are to be taken care of, it is primarily the *animu* that the living must deal with first, at the moment of biological death. A vital force that resists leaving the world, the *animu* seeks to reattach itself to life and becomes dangerous. The living must domesticate this vital force through funerary rites and facilitate its departure to the afterlife so it can subsequently return in beneficial form.

If every death brings with it this moment of danger and fear, when the *animu* that leaves the dead body temporarily wanders in disorientation, trying to seize other living bodies, I asked my interlocutors whether the wandering of the human soul in cases of suicide was more frightening than in "normal" deaths. Both replied affirmatively, but Mama Benita clarified that God does not accept the *alma* of the suicide and returns it to the world of the living: "It is said that our God does not receive the souls of those who kill themselves and that he forces them to return to the world of the living [kutichimunsi]," she said.[8]

This is the *alma* (as moral person) that goes directly to God at the moment of death to face divine judgment. In the case of deaths that do not correspond to the will of God, such as suicide, God returns the souls of the dead to the world of the living, so as to go through a long process of expiation of sins. Here a colonial Catholic-inspired moral injunction about God's sovereignty over human life, which no human agency can challenge, is resonant. Since humans are not sovereigns of their own life, they cannot take it themselves, and suicide is thus seen as self-murder, a usurpation of the power over life and death that God alone has the right to exercise. Returned by God to the world of the living and impeded from finding its way to the afterlife, the suicide's soul roams the land, haunting the living and forcing them to respond to its frightening presence by help-ing it find its way to the afterlife. In this sense, agency and responsibility for the moral transgression of the suicide is reversed. Mama Benita's notion of *kutichimunsi* expresses this moral inversion: what started as an event of individual "failure" ends up as a social "failure," and the responsibility to cope with it falls on the community at large.[9]

The fate of the souls of those who commit suicide, then, resembles that of the *condenados*—those cursed specters that populate the wildest areas of the Andean mountains and prey on the living. *Condenados* are not offered a proper burial because during their lives on earth they commit-ted unforgivable sins and are thus rejected *ad eternum* by God. Their path to the afterlife is blocked because of their moral deviance. Sometimes, it is said, their corpses are further desecrated as punishment (Robin 2008). The sins that sanction such an irredeemable fall from grace are the sins of incest (committed within blood or spiritual kinship), avarice, and violence

of children against their parents. Ansion (1987) suggests that these fragments of myth condemn the rupture of relations of reciprocity at different
levels. In his view, reciprocity is the crucial moral mechanism that holds
Andean communities together, and the circulation of stories about *condenados* aims at protecting and enforcing this moral mechanism in everyday
life.[10] But, as we will see, in the case of Lucho these moral injunctions were
mentioned but never enforced.

Governing *Malamuerte*

"It is sad, doctor," Aurelio, the village's *sanitario* (paramedic) told
me in Spanish, "he was so young. It is an absurd death. This has affected
us." Aurelio used the Spanish word *afectar* in two senses that denoted being emotionally touched and also collectively harmed by the tragic event
of Lucho's death. His words thus suggest that the suicide of one young
member of the community was felt as a communal loss and the response
to the tragedy concerned the community at large. In his view, this was an
absurd event, not an immoral one. Clearly, villagers no longer saw suicide as a crime against the sovereign (celestial or terrestrial) deserving to
be punished with some form of ignominious burial or desecration of the
suicide's body, as prescribed in myth. On the contrary, the community
resisted an autopsy, which they consider a postmortem desecration of the
body, despite the fact that it is legally mandatory in cases of violent death
such as suicide.[11]

The morning I spoke to Aurelio he gave me (unrequested) details
about the death to which he had privileged access because of his position
of authority as the village *sanitario*. For him, this was without doubt a case
of suicide.[12] But he knew that as soon events like this happen, the law immediately intervenes to rule out murder, and its first move is to claim the
victim's body for forensic examination via autopsy. It is the regular procedure. "The *fiscal* [prosecutor] and the *juez de paz* [justice of peace] have yet
to intervene," he noted. "There has to be a criminal investigation. Maybe
it was actually a murder. Who knows? Surely they will order an autopsy."

Aurelio also knew the villagers' strong reluctance to have an autopsy
performed. "Here, people do not like autopsy at all," he told me. "I am
sure this family won't want that autopsy to take place at all," he concluded.
As elsewhere in the Andes, in Accomarca this reluctance relates to a rich
set of cultural representations about the fate of the dead. For instance, in

some versions, the desecration of the dead body is believed to obstruct the journey of the soul to the afterlife. In other accounts, the dead inhabit a new world that is an inverse of the world of the living but that nonetheless preserves the basic features of the social fabric. The dead work the land, they sow, they harvest, they get married, they have families, they hate, they love, they laugh, they get thirsty, they get hungry, they can be happy and sad, and so forth, and they need to keep the images of their bodies in order to maintain their social relationships in the afterlife.[13]

Other local authorities such as the *juez de paz* and the *gobernador*[14] shared with Aurelio this anxiety of being torn between simultaneously being state officials in charge of enforcing the law and being villagers who shared their neighbors' sentiments and views about the dead body. On one hand, as local state officials, they were obliged to follow legal procedures and to enact the criminal law's grammar of suspicion—"maybe it was actually a murder"—that mandates an autopsy to rule out criminal intent. On the other hand, as villagers, they shared the belief that the dead body should not endure further desecration and mutilation, and, insofar as they were certain that this was a case of suicide, they viewed the autopsy as an entirely nonsensical procedure. They thus attended to and supported the relatives' desire to bypass the autopsy altogether.[15]

That same morning I overheard Jorge, the acting *juez de paz,* speaking over the only phone in the village with the office of the Fiscalía in Vilcashuamán and obviously negotiating the issue of the autopsy with the provincial legal authorities.[16] He eventually hung up the phone with an expression of relief on his face. Some minutes later, on our way to the house of the dead man's relatives, Jorge told me that he had persuaded the *fiscal* to skip the autopsy and be "flexible" in this case, given the straightforwardness of the facts. However, since legal certainty still needed to be attained, the *fiscal* had asked Jorge to complete the forensic procedures by means of an external examination of the body called *peritaje de necropsia.*[17] The *fiscal* had then delegated his legal powers to Jorge to perform as an acting *juez de paz* the duty of enforcing the legality of the legal and forensic act. The *fiscal* had also appointed a senior *sanitario* from the nearby community of Huarcas to conduct the *peritaje.* Jorge told me that the *fiscal* had insisted that every legal and forensic procedure had to be scrupulously registered in *actas* and that these documents needed to be sent immediately to his office in Vilcashuamán.[18]

Jorge was thus happy for having negotiated a solution to avoid the autopsy. For him, economic reasons were as important as cultural ones.[19] This political exchange in which the dead body of the young man had become a site for complex transactions between legal claims and cultural claims was just the beginning of a more complex struggle over reclaiming authority to tell the truth of the deceased as well as signifying the event of loss in terms of protecting life in the community. Reclaiming the body is reclaiming the possibility of authoring the story which that body embodied as well as the events that surrounded the death. As I show in the ethnographic scene that follows, the state reclaims the uncontested authority to author that story and to resignify the event by means of the law, forensic science, and languages of trauma.

The *peritaje* was performed in the same room where the wake was taking place—one of the areas of a two-room mud-brick house that opened onto the courtyard of the family's compound. The young man's body had been placed in the middle of the room on a table made of planks. Covered in blankets, the body had been arranged along a west-east axis, with the head toward the west and the feet toward the east, as if looking toward the dawn, and was surrounded by candles and some of Lucho's most intimate belongings, such as his deodorant and colognes. When I first entered the room, many villagers were already there, sitting around the table on makeshift seats of stone or wooden blocks, chewing coca and drinking cane liquor that passed from hand to hand. The soft murmuring in the room was interrupted only by the relatives who came in from time to time, bringing more drinks for those attending the wake.

This atmosphere of grief turned into one of expectation when the local authorities arrived. Rogelio, the *sanitario* of Huarcas appointed to conduct the *peritaje*, began the procedure by introducing himself and explaining in Quechua what he and the authorities were about to do. Then, Rogelio turned to Spanish—the language of the state. He asked the parents to show him their son's photo identification so they could open the *acta* with the legal identification of the victim. In the meantime, he read carefully the *acta de levantamiento del cadáver* that Jorge had prepared during the removal of the corpse. Jorge remarked that they had taken care to register every detail of that earlier procedure. Rogelio responded that everything looked okay, but he still needed to ask some formal questions. Speaking in a grave voice, he addressed his questions to Jorge, the *juez de paz*, rather than the bereaved family. I reproduce their conversation in Spanish at length to show how the law "reads" the body in its work of establishing legal truth and finding criminal intent.

Rogelio began by asking how they found the body, and Jorge replied that they found it hanging from the *machu kullu* (central beam) of the room. "In what position did you find him?" Rogelio asked.

"He was looking to that side," answered Jorge, standing against the door.

"Was he hanging?" Rogelio asked, to reconfirm the fact.

"Yes, of course, he was hanging," Jorge replied.

Rogelio continued: "And on which side of his neck was the knot?"

"It was this side," said Jorge, pointing to the left side.

"Ah, to the right . . . and where is the rope now?" Rogelio asked.

"It is here." One of the victim's younger brothers intervened in a dialogue that until then had taken place only between the *sanitario* and the *juez de paz* before the silent gaze of the villagers in the room. The boy went to the adjacent room and returned with a white rope, saying in Quechua, "He hanged himself with this white rope [Kay yuraq sogawan kurwakuram]."

Rogelio took the rope, examined it, and then returned to his questions to Jorge: "And how was the knot arranged?"

Jorge described in detail how he found the rope tied to the central beam of the room and the victim's neck. The villagers followed this uncanny dialogue in absolute silence, as the two officials reenacted the tragic event through speech in what is known in Peruvian legal parlance as *reconstrucción de los hechos* (crime scene reconstruction).

"Was it a slipknot?" Rogelio asked.

"Yes, it was a slipknot," Jorge replied.

"And his eyes? How were they? Open or closed?"

"They were open," Jorge replied. "He had a sock in his mouth. The other sock was on his bed. His shoes were there as well," he added.

"And at approximately what time did it happen?" Rogelio continued.

"His parents say that he came home around 7:00 p.m., accompanying his dad," Jorge said. He then declared in a forensic tone what the relatives had told him:

He [the young man] looked somehow sad and cheerful at the same time. Then he said: "I'd better go to my own place to sleep." Then, he returned to his parents' house around 11:00 p.m. and started to talk with them. His mother did not want to sleep.

He urged his parents to get sleep, but his mother did not want to. Apparently, she had the premonition that something bad was going to happen to them. He insisted that they should sleep. So, the young man already had intent to kill himself. Then, when his parents eventually went to sleep, it seems that the young man came to this room and hanged himself.

"Then, it must have been around 1:00 a.m., right?" Rogelio asked.

"Yes, something like that," Jorge replied. The forensic dialogue had reached a crucial point here, with the *juez* declaring the existence of intent and attributing it to the victim. The *sanitario* seemed to have gathered all the information he needed, but Jorge continued his report: "We have searched in minute detail through any letter or communication with his relatives, but have found nothing."

"The body was hanging, right?" Rogelio asked once again.

"Yes, the body was hanging. There was *intent*," Jorge reasserted, emphasizing the word intent.

"It is okay," Rogelio concluded, "it was a suicide."

The next stage of the *peritaje* consisted of a physical examination of the body to confirm what oral testimony had established. "I am going to examine him," Rogelio said, as he uncovered the body. First he examined the deceased's hands to check the rigidity of the fingers. He then uncovered the upper portion of the victim's body and seemed surprised to find a Bible on his chest. "Huh, so, he was Evangelical, wasn't he?" he asked. The relatives confirmed that he was.[20] Rogelio continued his examination by looking at the neck and checking the rope marks. "Indeed," he concluded, "he hanged himself." The physical examination of the body established the ultimate forensic and legal truth regarding where criminal intention lay.

In concluding the legal and forensic act, Rogelio said, "Okay, let's proceed to write the *acta*."

"Where are we doing it?" Jorge asked.

"In the municipality," Aurelio, who until then had remained silent, intervened. "There is a typewriter there." The local officials left the wake and went to a state building to type in Spanish, on headed notepaper, the legal *acta* in which the state would officially pronounce that a case of suicide had occurred in Accomarca. The legal and forensic ritual for establishing the truth was thus concluded.

This ethnographic scene shows how the state's legal and forensic performance aims not only at dissipating criminal intention from the social body, by locating it in the individual body, but also at constructing the social meanings of an act such as suicide. The legal and forensic event of *reconstrucción de los hechos* and the corresponding *peritaje* did not seek to establish certainty about the event and locate criminal intent as much as to examine physical and psychological signs through which the deceased's state of mind and soul could be carefully inferred. In this sense, the pains-taking medico-judicial and forensic investigation into the circumstances of death became an occasion for the elaboration of an official story (based on the signs of the body) about how such an unexpected event could have happened and, more importantly, how it must be avoided in the future. This is all too clear in the final reflection that both Rogelio and Jorge addressed to the audience of mourners before leaving the wake. Curiously, despite the fact that the *juez* reported that the victim had spent time talking to his parents before committing suicide, the *sanitario* said that this event would not have happened had he spoken with them. "These things happen when people have severe depression," Rogelio emphasized. "The young man must have been going through a state of severe depression and could not talk to his parents. In these moments it is imperative to talk with somebody else."[21] "Indeed," Jorge added, "had he talked with his parents, probably he would not have hanged himself. He had intention." Jorge concluded by reasserting certainty regarding the presence of *intention* in the suicide.

This impulse toward moral judgment and instruction in the face of a form of transgressive death such as suicide emerges from the state's investment in persecuting unnatural death, that is to say, the kind of death that is at odds with collectively expected forms of death. If death is conceived of as a mode of moral exchange, suicide transgresses the logic and law governing such a moral exchange. As such, it is not only a breach of the norm, but a waste that needs to be collectively persecuted. However, the colonial times when the state tried and condemned successful suicides in criminal trials are long gone, and in the Andes, as elsewhere, the contemporary state seeks to steer individuals away from suicidal impulses toward more controlled behavior. Rather than relying on the prohibitory, punitive model of the law, the state seeks to direct the conduct of individuals away from those situations and activities that may lead to suicide. Ultimately, as seen in the ethnographic scene above, the contemporary state in the Andes sees suicide as a problem of bad shepherding, that is, of not having been able to detect the suicide's intentions in a timely fashion. Thus, any instance of suicide becomes a painful moment of learning how to conduct the conduct of others, particularly the most vulnerable members of the community.

Moral Order and Material Order

The first time I visited the family to offer my condolences I found Doña Eulogia, the young man's grandmother, presiding over the wake while Lucho's parents were away, busy with administrative chores for the burial. I had seen the blind old woman before, walking alone and almost imperceptibly on the uneven dirt paths of the village with a cane as her only help; now she was mourning the loss of her grandson without being able to see him for the last time. Don Leandro, one of Lucho's maternal uncles, was sitting beside Doña Eulogia, trying to comfort her. People in the small wake room spoke in low voices, and their murmurs formed a background for the grandmother's mournful laments. At times Doña Eulogia interrupted her soft litany and asked her relatives to offer food and drinks to the villagers attending the wake. "You all eat; give them food [Mikuychis; mikunata koychis]," she said at various moments, to make sure that the visitors were being adequately served. Her expression of pain oscillated between the poles of lamentation and attention to the cultural norms governing funerary rituals in Accomarca.

Given the morally reprehensible nature of Lucho's death, his funerary rites could have been *waqcha* as punishment for his transgression—that is, he and his family could have been left alone in this tragic moment.[22] But instead, many villagers visited the house to offer their condolences. Most of them brought coca, cigarettes, cane liquor and other drinks, food, and firewood to express their sympathy and help with the family's mourning. In turn, the grieving family reciprocated by sharing with visitors what they received. Coca, cane liquor, and cigarettes are to be circulated to protect mourners from the *qayqa* (breath of the dead), which in some accounts is the *animu* of the dead that resists departing from the world of the living and so seeks to seize other human or nonhuman bodies.[23] The energy, or *animu*, embodied in coca leaves and cane liquor, as well as the smoke of cigarettes, serves to shield the living from the dangerous diminishing *animu* of the dead that takes the form of *qayqa*. While coca, cane liquor, and cigarettes circulated inside the wake room, visitors shared other drinks and food outside. Material consumption was clearly a response to the presence of death in this village.

Interlocked with this picture of intense communal consumption was another of intense communal labor. It resembled a *faena*.[24] In the kitchen and makeshift *q'onchas* in the courtyard, some women and men were busy preparing food and drinks that they then circulated among those attending the wake. Other villagers were putting together the wooden cross that would be placed at the head of the tomb, while the village carpenter and two aides were building a rough wooden coffin that they would eventually paint yellow.[25] In the meantime, other men were busy building a *nicho* (niche) with iron and cement in the village cemetery, a type of tomb few villagers can afford. While most of those involved in these preparations were either cognatic or agnatic relatives, or godchildren or godparents of both parents and siblings of the victim, many other villagers who weren't kin helped with the funeral chores when not sitting in the wake room. Clearly, the community was the main protagonist in this process of disposing of the victim's body.

Some ethnographers have seen the intensive consumption and expenditure of labor as a form of reciprocal exchange among the living, in the form of *ayni* (like for like). However, this focus on exchange among the living emphasizes the *moral* relations among the living and overlooks the *material* exchange between the living and the dead. Whereas the state is primarily interested in the legal and moral exchange among the living, the rural community is dealing with something else that is not restricted to the register of the moral order (moral exchange) but also concerns the register of the *material order*. In the fabric of human society, death alters relations not only between humans but also between humans and the earth. The dead are mediators between the earth and the living, and as Gose (1994) has rightly pointed out, the material consumption and expenditure of communal labor is aimed at reciprocating with the dead. The community *also* needs to restore the material order of the world shaken by the death of one of its members.

To enable the moral and material exchange between the living and the dead, the boundaries between life and death need to be carefully redrawn. The ritual treatment of the dead body allows for such a careful separation to be restored. As elsewhere in the Andes, Accomarquinos believe that consanguine relatives should not be in contact with the deceased's body because they are particularly vulnerable to the dangerous forces death unleashes. Responsibility for preparing the dead body for burial thus should be assumed by spiritual relatives such as the *compadre*, who is close enough to the deceased to take care of him or her as a true relative but far enough away so as not to be directly involved in the atmosphere of suspicion over inheritance that usually emerges among direct relatives following the death of an adult.[26]

In the case of Lucho it was his *madrina* (godmother) who assumed the responsibility of preparing his body for burial and, more generally, of conducting the funerary rites.[27] I first noticed her presence when she entered the room to finish dressing Lucho's body. She put socks and new sneakers on him, as if she were dressing someone who was asleep. She then retreated to a position at the back of the wake room from where she would silently follow the mourning rites as they unfolded and intervene whenever she considered it necessary.

The godmother seemed particularly concerned about Lucho's two little siblings, eleven-year-old Pedro and thirteen-year-old Raymundo. She tactfully tried to send them away from the wake room, asking them to do some other chores in the kitchen or the courtyard, but the children assigned themselves the task of taking care of their brother's body. From time to time they cleaned his face of the blood that continued to seep from his nose. Pedro, the youngest, swung between weeping and playing his dead brother's harmonica. He engaged joyfully with his newly acquired instrument, but then he suddenly broke into tears again and embraced his brother's dead body. Raymundo also repeatedly broke into tears while sprinkling deodorant on the body, perhaps in a vain attempt to keep it fresh. Both children were experiencing death for the first time in their lives; but theirs was a brutal initiation, and they had no criteria for responding to the tragic event that had struck home. But even if they had been initiated into such knowledge, their grief led them to transgress those established norms. For them, Lucho's body was not an inert object; it was not a corpse. It was their brother, and by touching it they expressed their affection for him.

At such times, the community's pedagogical role comes forward to initiate its young members into the difficult task of attaining separation from the dead. One instructional moment occurred when the younger siblings inadvertently tossed the napkins they had used to clean the deceased's face onto the wake room's dirt floor. The godmother reemerged from her discreet position to ask them not to do this: "Kutichimunsi [it is said that it makes the *animu* come back]," she stated. "Put them [those pieces of used tissue paper] in a plastic bag and then you will put the bag in his coffin [Plastico bolsachapi churaychis. Chaymanta cajonchampi churan-quichis]," she instructed the children. They followed her instructions and used a plastic bag that Aurelio, the *sanitario*, gave them for that purpose in agreement with the godmother.

The notion of *kutichimunsi* here articulates the fundamental pre-occupation of the community with the question of pollution. While in Mama Benita's iteration of *kutichimunsi* (see above) it is God who rejects the sinner's soul and makes him or her return to the world of the living as a moral punishment, in the godmother's iteration, *kutichimunsi* refers to the material residues of the body that, if separated from the corpse, cause the return of the dead or prevents their definitive departure to the afterlife. *Kutichimunsi* in the godmother's use of the term stresses the notion that there is a zone of danger around the dead body in the material sense. In Accomarca people think that any bodily remains should be carefully col-lected and buried with the corpse in an effort to contain in a consecrated site the material traces left by the dead in the world. Also, the clothes of the dead are ritually washed by the *compadre* and his aides the day after the burial. Then some clothes are burned, others are donated, and only a few are kept as mementos.

This ethnographic scene shows that whether in the grammar of re-ligion, as articulated by Mama Benita, or that of the funerary ritual, as articulated by Lucho's godmother, the notion of *kutichimunsi* expresses the community's desire to reestablish control over both the material and the moral boundaries between life and death. *Kutichimunsi* is the manifesta-tion of the taboo that needs to be established around the dead body and transgressive death as a condition of the possibility for the regeneration of life in the aftermath of devastating loss. The dead should start their mate-rial and moral journey to the world of the dead, to which they now belong and from which they can continue to positively influence the world of the living. This influence becomes possible if the journey is completed and a home is made for them in their new world. Their homeless moral and material wandering among the living, or their return without completing the journey and settling in their new home, is dangerous for life because it can only mean the spread of death in the world of the living. *Kutichimunsi* thus seeks to affirm the idea of separation in the face of the irreversibility of death, which the community imposes on the grieving relatives through the languages and performance of the funerary rituals.

The Figure of the Grieving Woman

But what does "make a home for the dead" mean? The fact that the suicide's blind grandmother presided over the wake indicated how women in the rural Andes, as elsewhere, have a central role in funerary rites. The wake is a public gendered space where women are vocal and openly demonstrate their grief while men are silent and inhibited. Dispatching the dead properly cannot be just about taboo and prohibition, and women take upon themselves the task of symbolically giving birth to the dead and the bereaved, as it were, into their new state of being following their devastating separation. It is a labor of engaging grief and enduring pain for others in which relations are reevaluated in terms of (re)writing the biography of the deceased and thereby (re)writing the biographies of those whom the departed left behind. Death is thus given its social, cultural, and political meaning by the grieving woman moving between two deaths.

The gendered textures of this concern with grief and pain became clear to me that evening in Mama Benita's kitchen when, along with a subtle moral reproach articulated against suicide, as seen above, in the genres of myth and rumor, Mama Benita and Basilia shifted the conversation and focused on the question of the mother's grief. Mama Benita was then drawn to talk about the mother's pain by associating the loss of the newly bereaved with her own loss of two little daughters killed in the massacre. "I live in such . . . sorrow for my little children, who had not reached the age of reason yet; I cannot even imagine my sorrow if that young man were my son," she said. Mama Benita here invoked a region of the self—that of motherhood—that allowed her to bring her own pain close to that of the young man's mother by establishing an analogy between their experiences of loss. Both had lost children to forms of violent death they never imagined could occur.

However, Mama Benita hinted at the singularity of Lucho's mother's pain by suggesting that perhaps it had gone farther than hers, or inhabited a different region, as the latter was mourning the loss of a young man while she, Mama Benita, was still mourning the loss of two little female children. Here, Mama Benita's comment dwells in two cultural registers: little children do not possess the status of full persons because they have not yet achieved the full use of reason, and having male children is in certain respects preferable to having female children. In any event, her *llaki* (grief) for having lost two little daughters to violent death was the only criterion she had to acknowledge the pain of the suicide's mother. As any reference to the suicide's transgressive form of death was dropped to focus entirely on the sheer pain a mother endures in the face of the tragic loss of her children, Mama Benita's comments suggested then that whether culture adds to the pain of losing a son or a daughter, or whether one chooses to take his or her own life, as opposed to having his or her life taken by others, the crucial question for these Andean women was how to contain the suffering unleashed by such a devastating loss.

What we see here is that for Andean women like Mama Benita, discussions about the moral rule give way at a certain point to the crucial question of how to respond to the suffering of the other. In fact, during our conversation that evening in her kitchen, Mama Benita expressed her desire to visit the bereaved to offer her condolences and take coca for the wake. Given Mama Benita's conversion to Protestantism, one could have expected that coca would not be the ideal means for conveying her sympathy to the family. Not only does her church forbid coca, she does not chew coca herself and knows that, as members of the same church, the grieving relatives do not either.[28] However, coca continues to be a crucial material component of the cultural grammar governing funerary rites in Accomarca, and if grammar dictates that taking coca to the wake is one form of participating in the other's pain, Mama Benita was willing to do it. In the face of the urgency to contain pain and suffering, the moral norm is displaced onto a subsidiary plane.

The wake room is where the gendered division of the labor of mourning was most visible. There, the adult female relatives voiced the pain of the family, speaking at times *of* the victim and at others *to* the victim, while the adult male relatives remained stoically silent. People attending the wake responded with sympathy to the women's expressions of pain. It was a form of antiphony of pain and consolation, between the victim's female relatives and the visitors, manifesting the intensely verbal character of mourning. Here I can offer only a glimpse of a prolonged engagement with grief and pain through the two-day wake during which these women resignified the event of bad death by means of reevaluating their relations with their dead. I focus on the blind grandmother's laments.

Doña Eulogia spoke of her grandson in the third-person singular as someone who was (or had started to be) absent. She repeatedly said, "I should have died with such a suffering, not this son of mine, this young son of mine."

This repeated lament contains a commentary about the precariousness of life and the injustice of death among these Quechua-speaking villagers. Should elders not die first?, Doña Eulogia seems to be asking when she asserts that she should have died, not her young grandson. She contrasts the strength, health, and youth of her grandson with her own weakness, sickness, and old age. An emergent vitality (*animu*) that has just started its way to plenitude is opposed to a declining vitality that is making its way toward death. There is something unnatural in the fact that she, a grandmother, is mourning her grandson's death, and not the other way around. After all, her lament suggests, she has already completed her life in this world and is ready to depart. Hers is a declining duration, while his was a dawning one. Is life not something that needs to be affirmed and completed in all its vitality and potentiality— which is to say, in all its *animu*?

Doña Eulogia uttered her laments in a soft, pained voice addressed to nobody in particular, and yet every person in the wake room felt she had spoken to them. She also made an indirect reference to her grandson's form of death, which she found unnatural on account of the physical suffering it entailed and not necessarily because of its source. "I cannot imagine his suffering [*ima sufrimientowancha wañuram*]," she said. The fact that he took his own life was not relevant. No accusation or search for intention, as we found in the work of the law, inhabits her laments. Only grief. If there is any reproach of his action, it refers not to the action itself but to the consequences of that action, that is, that he has left her (them) and that with his departure a number of other relationships in (and with) the world have been severed. But even if uttering her lament in the form of reproach against her grandson's irrevocable decision, Doña Eulogia did not speak *to* him directly: "He was supposed to bring me some fruit. . . . He was supposed to nurture me. . . . What was he thinking? Did he do that for not nurturing me? . . . Ah my beloved son, my young and healthy son. He had to nurture me; he had to bring me some fruit. Now, who is going to do that for me?"

By speaking of her grandson in the third person, the blind grandmother speaks as if he were away but still able to hear. This opens a window into the rhetorical operations by means of which language registers the shift in the victim's subject position in the world. It is the shift from the subject position of someone who is ready to offer care and affection to his or her elders, to the subject position of someone who is gone and will not be able to respond to these expectations. As elsewhere, human relations in these

Quechua-speaking Andean villages are imagined within a deep temporality that not only connects generations, but also crosses the frontier between life and death. In the moral economy of vitality (*animu*), new generations are supposed to nurture the older ones, even beyond death, as the latter nurtured the former. In life, the younger take care of the material needs of their elders; in death, of their memory. One of the ways in which this care is manifested is through the sensuous materiality of food, the ultimate source of vitality. The image of fruit in Doña Eulogia's lament is a charged symbol because fruit is scarce, and thus highly appreciated, in Accomarca. As gifts, fruits show the donor's consideration and affection but also evoke the idea of life as vital substance. Thus, when Doña Eulogia speaks of the fruits that her grandson was supposed to bring her as an expression of his care for her, of his love for her, and of his nurturing of her, she refers to a complex interlocking between the material and the moral worlds as if there were no possibility of speaking of one without speaking of the other.

With the sudden loss of her grandson, this promise of care in life and death embedded in the moral economy of vitality is lost. A world is lost with his departure. But more than that, this sudden loss is also perceived as a loss of relations with oneself. At a certain point in her litany, Doña Eulogia connected the deep grief her grandson's death brought to her life with her condition of being blind: "What is this life? Always walking in darkness. [Imam kay viday, tutapuriyllay]." Here, there is a mutual absorption between the moral and the material. She grieves that her grandson decided to abruptly sever his relationships with the world and others in this world. Her blindness works here as metonymic displacement for this loss of relations, but also for the uncertainty of relations in human sociality. Her despair at not being able to see the world speaks for her despair at not being able to be certain of the world and others in the world—to be certain, for instance, of what was in Lucho's mind when he made such a radical decision ("what was he thinking?"). And her lament here emerges as an acknowledgment that walking in darkness is perhaps all that life is about; one is condemned, as it were, to not knowing when, how, and why people do what they do. Relatives will never know why this young man took his life, and at the end they do not need to know. They only know that he is not with them anymore and that they will have to continue walking in life in the darkness that his loss brought to their lives.

In his well-known work on death, women, and power, Maurice Bloch (1982, 226) argues that women's engagement with pollution, emotions, grief, and mourning represents everything that needs to be symbolically vanquished to reconstitute the (male) social order in the aftermath of death. Seremetakis (1990, 1991) has offered a critique to this synchronic view, arguing that it is through the genres of lament and grief that women write the biographies of the deceased and the stories of the events leading to death. She suggests that insofar as these stories are told in the passage between life and death, it is women who have the last word about how social relationships have been lived and what their future implications are for the bereaved. In the ethnographic scene above, we have seen how women in the Andes also weave the biography of the deceased along with their own biographies. In response to the state, which claims certainty about motivation, behavior, and intent in order to distribute legal and moral responsibilities, the female relatives of the deceased emphasize the uncertainty of relations. The beloved young man was not mad, nor was he a criminal or an irrational person. Nor do the families need to be blamed for bad shepherding. His loss is to be attributed to the contingency of life and the inexplicability of the world. By means of enduring pain and laboring through grief, to make a home for the dead, women in the Andes have the last word, too.

Unnamable Death

No part of this complex assemblage of practices, objects, and representations through which Andean people govern tragic death was mobilized to cope with the massacre of 1985. The massacre was an event of an entirely different kind for which there was no language and whose resolution lay beyond the reach of the usual forms through which these villagers dealt with *malamuerte*. Thus, the mass graves where survivors hurriedly buried the remains of their slaughtered relatives stood, for several years, as a material reminder of the punishment anyone suspected of terrorism would ineluctably receive at the hands of the state. The villagers never attempted to transport these remains to the village cemetery and offer them burial because the event required a different kind of reckoning. For them, this was a political problem, not a ritual one—although they did ritually visit the site every year on the anniversary of the massacre and on the Day of the Dead.

To explore how this political reckoning started to take shape, let us return to the evening in Mama Benita's kitchen when she and Basilia and I talked about the young suicide's *alma*. The mere mention of this *alma* provoked conversation about other *almas* and *animus*. Mama Benita and Basilia told stories of frightening encounters between humans and specters, narrating the accounts of other people and also their own personal experiences. Mama Benita, for instance, told of a recent experience she had one night when she was sleeping alone in her hut in Llocllapampa—the ravine where the 1985 massacre occurred. The mass graves where the victims lay buried are very close to her dwelling. She told us that at a certain moment in the night she woke up suddenly with a sense of something very heavy and sinister sitting on her body, almost to the point of choking her. Terrified, she could barely move; after reciting several prayers silently, she began to slowly recover her breath. She concluded her story saying, "Tullus kausam [It is said that bones are alive]," which for me, in that moment, meant that she was associating her frightening experience with the proximity of the human remains buried in the mass graves.

I was struck by this implicit association between the *alma* of the suicide and the *animus* of the villagers slaughtered several years ago that, as the notion of *tullus kausam* denotes, would continue to reside in their hurriedly buried bones. It was clear that the *alma* of the suicide, rejected by God as a sinner, would wander dangerously for a time until the living assumed the collective responsibility of enabling its passage to the afterlife by means of special rites. However, the case of victims of the massacre was entirely different. They had been killed more than two decades before, and they were not sinners in any sense. Nor could their agency be assimilated to that of the ancient ancestors whose bones are thought to lie, unburied, in inaccessible caves.[29] Why, then, did the *animus* of the victims continue to roam and frighten the survivors? Why did Mama Benita speak of them, twenty years after those deaths, in the same framework as the *alma* of the suicide?

At the time of our conversation I did not understand that with their seemingly random going back and forth between the notions of *animu* and *alma*, my interlocutors were actually making a subtle allusion to the idea of two deaths—namely, the material reality of death as biological event (to which *animu* in its sense of vital force refers) and the reality of death as social event (to which *alma* in its sense of moral person refers). While intimately related, both are distinct entities. Both inhabit the liminal zone between two deaths that emerges when someone ceases to exist and lasts until such a loss is assimilated, reabsorbed, and incorporated by the community after a prolonged period of mourning. This liminal zone is dangerous, and such a danger becomes more prominent when the death in question is "unnatural" or transgressive. Mama Benita's notions of *kutichimunsi*, referring to the suicide's *alma*, and *tullus kausam*, referring to the *animus* of the victims of the massacre, alluded to this sense of heightened danger. It is as if death remained incomplete until the community finds suitable means to cope with the transgression and reincorporate the dead into the moral order by reinventing their moral persons.

Yet, while both the *alma* of the suicide and the *animus* of the villagers roamed in the same liminal space between two deaths, they concerned different problems and placed different kinds of demands on the living. In the case of Lucho's suicide, it was a moral transgression, and completing his death, so to speak, required a special treatment from the community—which, as I show above, involved accommodating legal and cultural norms prescribed for this kind of case in order to abate the pain that the unexpected death brought upon the community at large.[30] In the case of the victims of the massacre, as said before, moral transgression was not involved, nor were prescriptions available to the community to help them cope with such an unprecedented kind of death. In this case, what kinds of demands were the victims' *animus* placing on the living?

It might be possible to say that with the words *tullus kausam*—it is said that bones are alive—Mama Benita was referring to another kind of problem within the broad category of *malamuerte*: the postmortem harms inflicted upon the dead body such as autopsies, desecration, or the absence of funerary treatment. When this happens, it is believed in the Andes that the specters of the dead roam around their untreated remains until those remains are offered proper funerary rights.[31] If we take this view, villagers would have assimilated the massacre as a kind of *malamuerte* and would have believed that the *animus* of the slaughtered victims were wandering until ritual treatment was offered to their desecrated remains. However, such a culturalist reading would obscure the extent to which, for these villagers, the massacres defy categorization and the slaughtering of those sixty-nine villagers cannot be assimilated as *malamuerte*. What then?

Mama Benita's implicit association of the suicide and the victims of the massacre reveals also a crucial political register. In colonial Peru, suicide was considered a crime, in addition to being a mortal sin against the sovereignty of God. It was thus prosecuted and harshly punished by the state, with such penalties as confiscation of the suicide's property, burial in unconsecrated ground, denial of burial rites, and even postmortem desecration of the body.[32] In contemporary Peru, these legal penalties of the desecration of the bodies of suicides are no longer imposed, but they have left their traces in social memory in the form of fragments of myth. The anthropological archive of the Andes is full of tales about how the mortal sinners' moral exile should be inscribed upon their dead bodies.[33] However, ethnographic evidence of this kind of burial is scant, to say the least, and as far as I can tell, no present-day anthropologist has attended them. Stories about disposals of the *condenados* circulate in the register of rumor, transmitted orally in forms of speech such as "I was told," "it is said," or "I heard this story is true."

While modern Peru no longer permits the desecration of the bodies of suicides and mortal sinners, sanctions to punish de facto other mortal crimes against the terrestrial sovereignty of the state, such as rebellion, are very much alive. Offenses against the state are treated as "sacrilege" and hence are to be violently repressed.[34] During the counterinsurgency in Peru, the punishment for "sacrilegious" sin against the state was inscribed upon the bodies of "sinners" by means of publicly desecrating them and/ or preventing their proper burial, as in Accomarca. Kernaghan (2009, 114) rightly observes that killing during Peru's internal war was not only concerned with eliminating one's direct enemies but also aimed at communicating a most basic point about a (new) legal order and thereby defining the terms of political belonging. The figure of the mutilated corpse played a pivotal role in this task of defining political allegiances. In other words, as with the mortal sinners of yesteryear, the political mortal sinners of today were given a *malamuerte* in order to define the terms of political belonging and obedience.[35]

But the victims of the massacre in Accomarca were children, women, and elders, not the direct transgressors whose bodies were meant to bear the signs of sovereign violence. Not only did the state kill villagers who could in no way be suspected of being "dangerous terrorists," but it also made use of technologies of killing, with the purpose of desecrating the victims' bodies beyond recognition, that were utterly unknown to the villagers. This was an unprecedented kind of death for which the community had no name and for which the defenses that traditionally would have been available to them were simply nonexistent. In fact, I may go so far as to say that the massacre was such an unthinkable and unnamable event that it did not leave behind any *almas* in the way a transgressive form of death, such as a suicide, would leave behind. During my fieldwork, I heard several stories of ghosts, but none concerned the victims of the massacre, with the sole exception of the allusion Mama Benita made the night we were speaking of the suicide's *alma* in her kitchen.[36]

Here is where her allusion to the *animus* of the victims of the massacre reveals how their demand was political and not merely ritual. I note that the conversation in her kitchen happened just a few months after the forensic excavation of the mass graves in Llocllapampa had begun, in which the bodies of the first three identifiable victims (among them Mama Benita's mother) had been recovered at that point. If her scary experience was "recent," as she told us, then I can safely conclude that the ghosts Mama Benita encountered in Llocllapampa belonged to the victims of the massacre who had started to emerge following the legal and forensic intervention in the case, removing their bones. These were, then, not moral specters but *political* ghosts.[37]

Survivors left the shattered and desecrated remains of their loved ones in the places where they had been killed until the state returned to legally and politically confront its own atrocity. Reckoning with the massacre needed first and foremost a political story that would start by naming the event for what it was. As there was no term for it in their language and tradition, the Quechua survivors adopted a modern one: genocide. The legal and forensic exhumation had opened the public space for them to politically prosecute the massacre as a form of reckoning: it was genocide (see Chapter 1). Yet the modern state was unwilling to accept the term because in the "official story," the massacre was an instance of individual "excess." Nonetheless, it is in the midst of this political struggle over authoring the story of the massacre that the *animus* of the victims of the massacre could reappear in their way of becoming *almas* and then ancestors.

Concluding Comments

In this chapter, I have shown why political massacres in the Peruvian rural Andes cannot be assimilated under the general category of "tragic death," as the CVR attempted to do. Quechua villagers are familiar with various kinds of "unnatural" and violent death, such as suicide or murder, which they include within a broad category they call *malamuerte* (bad death); and they have available a complex assemblage of ritual practices, objects, and representations they mobilize to cope with those forms of violent and tragic death. By contrast, mass killings such as the massacre of

Accomarca are events of an entirely different kind. There is no language for these unthinkable events, the resolution of which lies beyond the reach of the usual juridico-medical-cultural assemblage through which Andean villagers govern violent and tragic death in everyday life. As elsewhere in the Andes, villagers in Accomarca never attempted to transport the remains of the victims of massacre to the village cemetery and offer them proper burial. For them, reckoning with state atrocity was first and foremost a political problem, not a ritual one.

This conclusion is central for the overall argument of this book because one of the presuppositions of the Peruvian version of the necro-governmentality of postconflict, as seen in Chapter 1, is that Quechua relatives and survivors are primarily interested in offering proper burial to their fallen loved ones. In this view, Andean mourners are portrayed as a kind of cultural automatons, preoccupied with following cultural rules rather than concerned with modern problems such as, say, whether in the defense of the body politic the modern state can go beyond the thresholds of life and death within which these Andean villagers test what a human form of life is. I have shown how, by contrast, for these villagers any ritual reckoning with atrocity has as a condition of possibility a political reckoning as well.

In Accomarca, such a political reckoning begins to happen in the context of the forensic exhumation of the mass graves where the victims of the massacre were hurriedly buried when survivors adopt a modern term to name the atrocity for what it was and is: genocide. The issue of publicly naming the event thus becomes an issue of political contention, but the fact that survivors seize the moment and enter into this disputation shows how they are able to escape the state's necro-governmentality of postconflict and, in this move, to reclaim for themselves the subject position of the people that challenges the spurious nature of the sovereign's power to arbitrarily kill with impunity and beyond any limit within which a human form of life is imagined in these Andean communities. In the next chapter, by looking at the forensic exhumations at the military base of Los Cabitos, in Ayacucho city, I begin an ethnographic exploration of how this political prosecution occurs when the body of the victim of state terror is not available.

3

Excavating State Atrocity

Since everything lies open to view there is nothing to explain. For what is hidden, for example, is of no interest to us.
—Ludwig Wittgenstein, *Philosophical Investigations*

ON A HOT August afternoon in 2006, Santiago, the forensic archaeology legal expert of the Legal Medicine Institute (IML) in Ayacucho, takes a break from his arduous work to brief the Quechua-speaking mothers of the disappeared about the progress of the forensic excavation. We are in La Hoyada, a dusty and stony narrow depression adjacent to the main barracks of the fortress of Los Cabitos that the military used as a site for shooting and training (Map 2).[1] Taking the attendants on a tour around the area, Santiago offers a detailed explanation of the team's findings and an account of the various phases of the forensic investigation since it began. The mothers listen attentively to the legal expert and, from time to time, interrupt his exposition to fill gaps in the evidence by telling their own stories. In many respects the forensic investigation is simply proving what they have long asserted about the atrocities committed in Los Cabitos. Perhaps the time for justice has finally arrived, after more than two decades of denial. In response, Santiago repeatedly emphasizes his team's commitment to find the truth, the objectivity and impartiality of which are guaranteed by their scientifically informed work. "Nothing is done in secret here," he concludes. "Our work here is strictly technical."

This assurance by the forensic archaeology legal expert of fairness, transparency, and objectivity in search of the truth is a manifestation of the Peruvian legal institutions' political commitment to establishing a clear contrast between their postconflict practices of justice-making and their wartime practices of denial, impunity, and complicity with state terror. Science and technology appear in this assurance as both rational foundation and path to truth and justice ("our work is strictly technical here"). Here, the expert alludes to the recent incorporation of archaeology as a forensic discipline into the work of the law dealing with the problem of clandestine mass graves scattered in former war-torn areas. Never before in the history of violence in Peru had this discipline been given such a prominent role in the criminal investigation of wartime atrocities, and its inclusion created enthusiastic expectations of truth and ensuing justice. The relatives of the disappeared in particular were hopeful that they would finally be able to locate their missing loved ones and recover their remains. The emergence of the figure of the forensic archaeology expert in postconflict Peru had brought to the search for justice a new optimism, which was associated with the truth-making capabilities of anthropology in the investigation of contemporary mass atrocity. It indexed the Peruvian reception of what I am conceptualizing as the necro-governmentality of postconflict.

This optimism partakes of a global optimism about the contribution anthropology can make to human rights, peace, and democracy in the aftermath of mass violence. In this view, forensic anthropological practices—particularly at the gravesite, through archaeological techniques—contribute decisively to efforts to lay the legal, cultural, and political foundations for a new postconflict democratic order, because they perform a crucial and essential function: a controlled recovery of the past. As I show below, this "technological optimism" about the truth-making capabilities of archaeological practices builds on the modern idea that the world is knowable under certain conditions of the pursuit of logic and procedure. It draws on what Valverde (2003) has defined as the "epistemology of the clue"—the idea that as a trained and detached observer, the knower is able to read clues and traces left by the past and thus gain access to otherwise inaccessible truths. It also presupposes that the past, as an object of knowledge, is stable and fixed.[2] The forensic archaeology legal expert thus personifies, in a single figure, the power and rationality of both the law and science working together to unmake the irrationality, violence, and arbitrariness of the past and to enable a controlled recovery of that past in a way that prevents its poisonous elements from seeping into the present and future.

This chapter interrogates this notion of the "controlled recovery of the past" that the legal-scientific complex of forensic anthropology is believed to produce through its investigation of state atrocity. I tell the story of the forensic excavation of clandestine mass graves in search of the disappeared conducted between 2001 and 2009 at the military fortress of Los Cabitos in the city of Ayacucho. Los Cabitos was the regional headquarters of the counterinsurgency campaign during the 1980s and 1990s. The CVR concluded that the fortress was a major center of detention, torture, and disappearance of suspects of "terrorism" during the 1980s. Subsequently, the forensic archaeological investigation revealed the presence of dozens of mass graves on the premises, containing hundreds of bodies of unidentified people who were executed at close range. It also uncovered heaps of ashes and burned fragments of human bones, alongside the ruins of industrial-style ovens where bodies were presumably incinerated in order to dispose of them without a trace and thus erase evidence of practices of state terror.

If a single truth emerges from the forensic excavation at Los Cabitos, it is that the event of truth-making proclaimed in terms of the "controlled recovery of the past" cannot entirely capture the excess of the event of atrocity. This impossibility is manifest in three interrelated aspects, as I show in this chapter. First, as mentioned above, most of the human remains recovered at Los Cabitos were ashes and fragments of bones that could not be individualized and identified. This excess of violence against the victims' bodies makes impossible the promise of bringing the disappeared back into society as legal, moral, and cultural subjects within the institutionalized structures of legal and disciplinary power. Second, a forensic investigation that set out with the aim of recovering bodies of the disappeared ended up revealing practices of state terror that resembled what Hannah Arendt called the "fabrication of corpses," referring to the factory-like production of mass death and the destruction of bodies in concentration camps (Arendt 1968). This practice cannot be captured in the highly formalized vocabularies and grammars of the law and forensic science. Third, the truth of state atrocity comes into being not as an ineluctable result of the technologies and practices of the law and forensic sciences, but as a result of agencies that are, in fact, always already excluded from their framework.

I argue that this "failure" of forensic anthropology in its project of "controlled recovery of the past" raises questions regarding the kind of

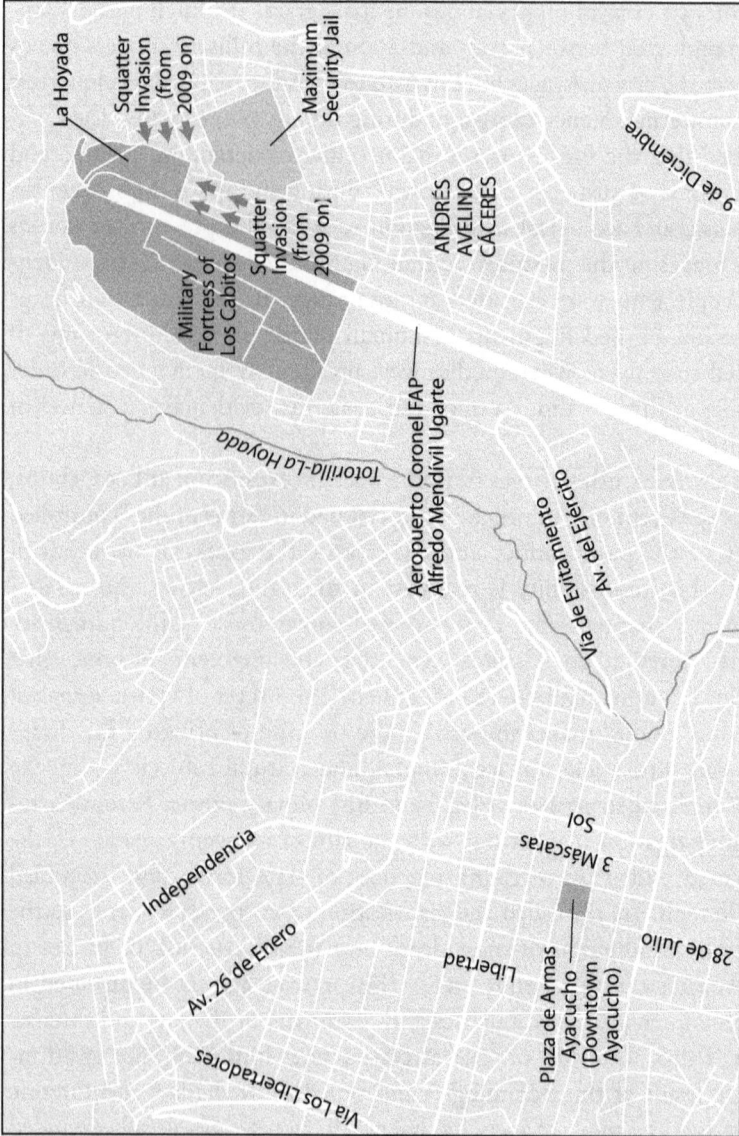

MAP 2. Map of Ayacucho city, showing the fortress of Los Cabitos and La Hoyada, 2016.

object "state terror" is, and whether this "object" can be entirely captured within the rational strictures of the law and science. I approach my analysis of the disjuncture between the "controlled recovery of the past" and the event of state atrocity at Los Cabitos with three questions. First, how do survivors of state atrocity relate to the investigation at Los Cabitos to make the legal and forensic truth happen without themselves becoming "legal subjects"? Second, how do legal and forensic experts relate to their "object" and the kinds of witnessing they embody at the site of atrocity? And third, what does translating the event of atrocity into the formal languages of the law and science of the "controlled recovery of the past" entail?

Unearthing State Atrocity

The military base of Los Cabitos is located on the northeastern out-skirts of Ayacucho city, in a desertlike natural fortress formed by ravines and steep hillsides that flow into the canyon opened by the Huatatas River in the east (see Map 2). In October 1981, the Lima-based national government declared a state of emergency in three rural provinces of the department of Ayacucho to combat the emergence of Shining Path guerrillas in the area. In December 1982, the government extended the state of emergency to the neighboring departments of Huancavelica and Apurimac and transferred all political powers to the military through the establishment of a *comando politico militar* (political military command) that was charged with the task of squashing the armed revolt and restoring the state's absolute control over the region. As the most important military base in the area, Los Cabitos became the all-powerful and inaccessible regional headquarters of the counterinsurgency campaign in the central southern Andes.

Soon, as human rights organizations reported at the time and the CVR documented later, Los Cabitos grew into a major center for the detention, torture, and disappearance of suspects of terrorism. The relatives of detained people spent hour upon hour in front of the checkpoint that controlled access to the barracks, waiting impotently for any news about their loved ones (Figure 3.1). At the time, everybody in Ayacucho knew that the fate of every detainee at Los Cabitos was already sealed, but this knowledge circulated only as rumor. No one dared to speak out: even the legal authorities chose not to interfere with the counterinsurgency operations despite allegations of atrocities carried out by the military in their

FIGURE 3.1. The military base of Los Cabitos, Ayacucho, October 2006.

barracks. Throughout the internal war, a proper legal and forensic investigation was never conducted. Immune to any legal inquiry, Los Cabitos stood for years as an unshakable symbol of the Peruvian state's sovereign power to kill with impunity.[3]

This situation changed with the advent of the democratic transition in late 2000 (see Chapter 1). Criminal investigations into gross human rights violations were reopened when the IACourtHR repealed Peru's 1995 amnesty law and the prosecutor's office intervened in Los Cabitos in late 2001 for the first time in two decades. Led by a special prosecutor, a forensic team from the IML in Ayacucho, with no training in archaeology, started to explore the premises and surroundings of the military base in search of mass graves. In September 2001 they found nine clandestine tombs that had been sacked and collected scattered fragments of human bones as well as cartridge cases and shreds of clothing. In December 2002, in a second intervention, the team found the remains of a furnace built of bricks and adobe that had been demolished. In two further interventions in January and September 2003, the team found five more clandestine tombs that had also been sacked. For the prosecutors these initial findings, despite their importance, constituted only circumstantial evidence that did not conclusively prove two major allegations: first, that Los Cabitos was a major site for the extrajudicial execution of terrorism suspects; and second, that the military had built a blast furnace on the premises to incinerate the bodies of their victims as a means of disposing of them without a trace. The crucial evidence that was missing was the victims' bodies.

The prosecutors felt hindered in their work by the lack of forensic personnel trained in archaeological theories, methodologies, and techniques. In response, in early 2004 the IML appointed a specialized forensic archaeology team with an archaeologist, a sociocultural anthropologist, and a dentist and charged it with the responsibility of conducting forensic exhumations in the region of Ayacucho.[4] The arrival of these experts, particularly of a *perito arqueólogo* (archaeology legal expert), renewed the prosecutors' optimism in the investigation. This forensic archaeology team launched a more specialized search, reexamining the initial findings of the previous explorations; however, they found nothing different. They also found only scattered fragments of human bones and circumstantial evidence such as cartridge cases and shreds of clothing. They found no clandestine mass graves containing human remains.

By late 2004 the search for hidden mass graves seemed to have stalled. Then, a leading Peruvian investigative journalist published a book based on the testimony of a former leading member of the army's secret death squads about previously unknown crimes committed by the Peruvian military during the counterinsurgency campaign (Uceda 2004).[5] One chapter, "La Ladrillera," confirmed the existence of mass graves and blast furnaces to burn the bodies of those killed in La Hoyada and provided details about the machinery and operations of "terrorist" extermination. The book claims that between 1983 and 1984, at least five hundred suspects were summarily executed and buried in mass graves in this area and that in 1985, in an attempt to eliminate the evidence of these crimes, the military sacked these clandestine tombs and burned the bodies of at least three hundred victims.

This new evidence reanimated the forensic investigation, and this time the team focused squarely on La Hoyada. Until then, their work had been guided by survivors' testimonies and recollections of former army privates, both collected through proper legal channels, following the formal procedures of the law.[6] If the voice of the survivor framed in the grammar of the law had thus far been an unsuccessful guide to truth, perhaps the perpetrator's voice articulated in a journalistic text would be more effective. Adopting the book as a central reference—but only after making it a legal text in the form of textual evidence—the forensic investigation resumed in January 2005. The guiding hypothesis was that at least two hundred bodies remained buried somewhere in La Hoyada, and following the lead of the book, the archaeologists opened dozens of exploratory trenches in the area. After two weeks of intense work, however, the investigation had made no significant progress. Like previous interventions, all they managed to collect as evidence were dispersed fragments of burned human bones, shreds of clothing, and fragments of burned bricks and some debris.[7] At the end of the excavation season, the forensic team seemed to be trapped in the snares of uncertainty and frustration and, in the face of this new disappointment, began to consider abandoning the investigation altogether.[8]

This somber scenario of disappointment and failure turned into one of expectation with an unexpected intrusion that entirely altered the fate of the investigation.[9] On the afternoon of the last day of the season of early 2005, the disheartened forensic team was packing up to leave the site with no clear idea of how or whether to continue its work. A drunken man showed up and, speaking in Quechua, began to make fun of them. The intruder, who was entirely unrelated to the ANFASEP mothers, said that the investigators were working in the wrong place and that they should excavate in another area. Out of curiosity one of the forensic experts followed him to the area he was speaking of. Santiago remembers that moment as follows:

We were *desanimados* [disheartened]. We were about to give up and leave the site. The exploration had ended. Then this *borrachito* [drunken guy] showed up at the excavation. Apparently he had his *chacra* [plot of land] down there, near to the river. He began to make fun of us in Quechua. I do not understand Quechua, but both Juvenal and Manuel do. "You are working in vain here," he said. "You should work there," and pointed to another place. He led us there and it was an area full of trash and shrubs of maguey. I did not want to take this drunken man seriously for two reasons: first, because he was drunk; and, second, because, according to our professional criteria, there was no indication of the existence of any site of burial in the place he pointed to. So, there was no point for me in believing a guy who was drunk.

Santiago acknowledges that it was the female prosecutor (*doctora*) who insisted, despite his skepticism, on investigating the area pointed out by the intruder. "I thought it was a waste of time," he said, "but the *doctora* insisted. We started reluctantly that same afternoon only because the *doctora* ordered us to do so. We opened an exploratory trench and, then, right before dusk, *by luck* we found human remains. It was a clandestine tomb in which we later found two individuals, one man and one woman" (emphasis added). Santiago remembers vividly how stones covered the human remains in the tomb; the bodies had been blindfolded, and cartridge cases were found associated with them. To the expert, this evidence indicated that the victims had been executed on the spot and that they probably had been forced to dig their own graves.

After more than three years of inconclusive investigation, this was the first in a series of crucial findings that demonstrated categorically, for the first time in Peruvian history, the practices of state terror at Los Cabitos. The prosecutor extended the timeline of the excavation season by two weeks, and the forensic team recovered four more bodies, among them the remains of a teenager dressed in a school uniform. In June 2005 the forensic team recovered eight more bodies from the same area. All of the victims had been shot at close range; all of them had been blindfolded; all of the tombs had been filled with stones to cover victims' bodies; all of them showed traces of quicklime, presumably used to accelerate the decomposition of the bodies; and circumstantial evidence such as cartridge cases, coins, and clothing associated with the bodies was recovered from all of the tombs. In short, not only did the forensic anthropology team recover fourteen complete bodies, they also uncovered hard evidence of how Los Cabitos operated as a killing field during Peru's "war on terrorism" (Figure 3.2)

The forensic legal expert's association of this major discovery with the notion of luck, even in passing, does not seem casual. Had the *borrachito* not intruded, they probably would not have found human remains in hidden graves. The drunk man, whose name they don't even remember, accompanied them for a few more days—always intoxicated. They came to learn that when he was a child he had by chance witnessed executions and burials in the area. His family lived in the vicinity of Los Cabitos, and he was responsible for grazing their cattle. At times, he reached La Hoyada inadvertently, and on one of these occasions, he observed the military's activities. But he was spotted, and the military detained him for snooping around. When the child was about to be executed as an undesirable witness, a captain acquainted with his family saved him from certain death. This captain used to visit the child's house frequently to rest and get some

FIGURE 3.2. In 2005, the forensic team recovered the first fourteen complete bodies at Los Cabitos.

free food. The military then released the child, but not before threatening him and his family with death if he said a word about what he had seen and the experience he had endured. With the word "luck," then, the archaeologist seems to refer to a chain of chance events that happened to facilitate their expert work, eventually allowing them to uncover and conclusively document patterns of state atrocity in Peru.

The Legal Expert's Double Authority

Some archaeologists have emphasized their discipline's rigorous and science-based truth-making capabilities, which, they argue, can contribute to forensic investigations of mass atrocity through a controlled recovery of the past. Saunders (2002), for instance, says that forensic archaeology can counter denial, provide evidence of human rights abuses, confirm survivors' accounts of atrocity, uncover the circumstances of victims' deaths, identify victims, inform victims' relatives so they can achieve some closure, and deter future human rights violations by demonstrating that the actions of the past are always recoverable. Blau and Skinner (2005) note how both traditional and forensic archaeology are interested in the controlled recovery of the past. The goal for both is to investigate material remains, whether they are objects, corpses, or residues, in terms of reconstructing activities of the past. Both are concerned with the understanding, recognition, control, and interpretation of space, site history, site formation, and the context and attributes of buried features and evidence (artifacts) within a defined area.

This picture of how archaeology can contribute to the forensic investigation of mass atrocity draws on the "epistemology of the clue" (Valverde 2003, 67). It presupposes that both archaeology and the forensic sciences share the venerable belief that real truths, even truths about morality and politics, leave interpretable physical traces in the world; they therefore share the modernist postulate that the world and others in the world are knowable under certain conditions of logic and procedure. Both disciplines operate on the epistemological assumptions that Ginzburg (1989) defines as the "evidential paradigm," the idea that seemingly insignificant, but visible, clues and traces provide access to inner and invisible truths. Thus, the authority of forensic experts and of archaeologists emerges from their ability to read these clues and produce narratives about otherwise unobservable phenomena. Since, according to this line of reasoning, both archaeology and the forensic sciences dwell in the same epistemological region, archaeologists may perfectly become forensic experts, as they possess the ability to produce knowledge and truth about inaccessible pasts that is necessary for the work of the law.

Yet another crucial presupposition frames the work of archaeology in postatrocity settings. The legitimacy of postconflict states is predicated on their ability to break with the violence and atrocity of times of war. The central problem they face is how to retrieve those facts of terror from the past without letting their toxic effects spill over into the present and poison the pursuit of justice that aims to end suffering and prevent future conflict. Informed by discourses of liberal rule, the mainstream view states that only a controlled recovery of those facts of terror, through the rational means of law and science, guarantees a productive access to a toxic past by regenerating the present and opening up possibilities for the future. The implicit corollary is normative: "state terror" must be treated as a stable object always already situated in the past, since the facts of terror are located in the past.

Trials or forms of restorative justice such as truth commissions have customarily been seen as the best mechanisms for such a controlled recovery of the past. For instance, Minow (1998) argues that any intervention into the past needs to make sure that it breaks the cycles of violence and revenge, and that truth commissions are the most appropriate means to that end. Taking a different approach, Ost (2005) highlights the role of trials in dealing with atrocity and says that by re-presenting crime in the ritualized and highly controlled forms and languages of the law, the trial does not limit itself to repeating the past. Rather, in stabilizing a linear succession of clear-cut distinctions between past, present, and future, the law performs a controlled repetition of conflict to bring it to a close and thus open up a negentropic and creative time in which a fractured past is healed to make a return to social peace possible. Postconflict state interventions, whether in the form of truth commissions, trials, or some other state-sponsored mechanism, operate on the crucial presupposition that clear-cut distinctions can be made between past, present, and future because time flows in a linear direction (see, among others, Rojas-Perez 2008, Wilson 2003, and Grandin 2005).

Because of this normative element with regard to time, archaeology's association with the law in forensic investigations of mass state atrocity leads to a series of transfigurations in how archaeology approaches its object and constitutes its authority. The law has its own forms of knowing and reasoning, both individualizing and forensic (see, among others, Valverde 2003 and Bourdieu 1987). In determining what counts as *a* legal fact, which in turn will ground *a* legal judgment with universal implications, the work of the law circumscribes particular events and thereby requires the constitution of particular legal subjects and objects in the form of *a* victim, *a* perpetrator, *a* crime, *a* witness, which can relate to preexisting universal rules. Within the legal universe, the site of excavation becomes *a* crime scene—a space defined (almost literally) by what is inside and what is outside the law, where only those legally authorized can participate in the game of establishing the legal truth. And the archaeologist becomes an expert witness—a legal subject endowed with the symbolic capital necessary to assist the law in gaining certainty. To perform this role accurately, Tuller (2015) and others argue, the archaeologist is required to submit to strict regulations with respect to the production and circulation of legal evidence.

More importantly for our purposes here, the law establishes a particular relation with the lay voice. As Bourdieu (1987) argues, the abstract
claims of the equality and universality of the law hide the fact that, by
definition, one of the first operations of the legal field is to either exclude
the ordinary voice or subordinate it to that of the expert. The law is a semi-
autonomous social field in which questions of who speaks, who is listened
to, and how to speak are mediated by forms of symbolic power that determine both the competence to speak and the authority to be heard. Thus, if
a controlled recovery of the past implies, by definition, the political need
for a circumscribed social field in which experts endowed with symbolic
capital participate in the games of truth out of which knowledge is produced, the law imposes additional power determinations. In the postconflict legal and political assemblage dealing with past atrocity, the ordinary
voice is always already *doubly* excluded or subordinated to the voice of the
legal expert.

Archaeologists appointed as legal experts thus embody two determinations of power: that which comes from their being experts in their discipline, and that which comes from their being the legal authorities at the
excavation site. In this condition, bearing the double authority of one who
knows how to know and one authorized by the law to produce a particular
knowledge about the past, the voice of the forensic expert cannot relate to
the lay voice except by either excluding or subordinating that voice. In this
sense, the irruption of the *borrachito* at the excavation site could only be
explained as a stroke of luck and good fortune accompanying the legal and
technological undertaking. At any rate, it is the presence of contingency
disguised as luck.

Objecting Voices

If the past is the "object" of the law and the forensic sciences, then we
could say, following Latour (2000), that through the irruption of the *borrachito*, the past objects to how it is being produced and spoken of within
the strictures of those disciplines. This objection is voiced from outside the
legal universe, not only because the "drunken guy" is not a (formal) part
of the legal investigation, but also because he voices an experience that has
been excluded from the particularizing work of the law. Moreover, he enters a scene that is highly charged with symbolic power and challenges the

forensic gaze that has been trained to read traces and clues and gain access to the invisible past. The Quechua-speaking intruder *objects* to the authority of the Spanish-speaking expert witness on the basis of the authority of his own experience as a survivor. The *borrachito* may be external to the legal universe, but he is internal to the event of violence and state terror that lingers in the present and of which Los Cabitos is a gruesome trace.

How is it that the voice of the survivor emerges to animate the event of truth in the context of an investigation of state atrocity? Put otherwise, when and how do survivors speak of the known but unsaid—that is, when others opt to remain silent? As the region most heavily affected by the internal war, Ayacucho is a "place of stories" in which everyone has a story to tell. The worst has come to be known here and for that reason one's pain, small or large, "need not go unsaid and unaccompanied" (Cavell 1994, 12). Whether directly in one's own experience, such as that of the unknown drunken man, or through that of a relative, a neighbor, a friend, or even an acquaintance, each person living here has witnessed how terror and violence devastate individuals, families, and communities and how, because of their mechanical repetition, violence and terror became ordinary affairs. Personal biography and place are thus intimately linked in the experience of pain and suffering resulting from violence. However, these stories of pain, small or large, can be said or accompanied or authored only under conditions that make possible such speech, its acknowledgment, and, crucially, the arrogation of voice.

Sanford (2003) rightly observes that large-scale political and legal processes in the aftermath of violence and terror, such as democratic transitions and peace processes, have effects at the local level and allow for the recuperation of voice. Broader shifts in power relations bring about shifts in language and thereby create possibilities for breaking the silence that is the quintessential manifestation of state terror that prolongs itself beyond physical violence (see also Green 1999 and Burnet 2012). Sanford's emphasis on power relations helps us to see the process of breaking this silence not as a straightforward instauration of the will to narrate trauma, as if everyone has been waiting for the moment in which they can speak truth to power, but as something to be attained through the work of desire. In a similar vein, Coxshall (2005) argues that most discussions of the effects of state violence based on the psychoanalytic model of trauma take for granted this impulse to narrativize.[10] This perspective obscures rather than explains how it is that people can or cannot tell their stories in the aftermath of terror and devastating violence. In contrast, Coxshall asserts that while broader processes of truth-telling call for narration, power relations at the local level continue to mediate who speaks what and to whom. Silence can, in fact, be one mode of truth-telling.

How, then, is the survivor's arrogation of voice to speak truth to power possible? The unknown drunk's arrogation of voice in the context of the criminal investigation into practices of state atrocity at Los Cabitos does not appear to be tied to questions of rights or the rule of law—in the sense that he feels morally compelled to tell the truth or to appeal to the law in search of justice. Since he is external to the legal universe of the criminal investigation (and precisely because of this very externality), he could have remained silent, out of indifference, complicity, fear, or simply denial. In fact, one of the most striking features of criminal investigations into state atrocity in the south-central Peruvian Andes was that Quechua-speaking survivors did not want to speak to the law. The prosecutor spoke to me of her difficulties in collecting testimonial evidence. "In most of the cases," she said, "we have to work with hearsay evidence. We have reliable information in just a few cases. People do not want to talk; even some relatives say it is useless to say anything."[11] By contrast, the "drunken guy" speaks truth to the law even when he has not been interpellated as a witness by the law.[12] More precisely, he speaks this truth as a kind of phantasmal apparition that disrupts the legal and forensic proceedings.

Penelope Harvey (1991) argues that drinking behavior in the Andes, as elsewhere, reveals complex social practices and cannot be reduced to either individual pathology or collective escapism. Despite the cultural salience of drinking, she continues, little attention has been paid to the verbal aspects of drunken interaction. Harvey shows how "drunken speech" is particularly revealing about the role of power and personal authority in linguistic interaction and builds on Bourdieu's notion of "practical competence," according to which people tend to remain silent when they lack the symbolic capital to endow their speech with authority and thus to be heard. By contrast, she argues, interlocutors who are drunk tend to speak rather than remain silent and are far less sensitive to the constraints of symbolic capital and relative authority. The most salient feature of "drunken speech" is the way in which the norms of sober linguistic interaction are flouted: "When drunk, speakers are less constrained in their linguistic choices by considerations of individual linguistic competence and of differential status between speaker and addressee. Cultural norms of heightened potency and diminished responsibility allow drunken speakers to extend their linguistic repertoires and to challenge established social relations" (ibid., 2).[13] Harvey further argues that while drunken behavior appears cross-culturally similar, drunken speech reveals a particular set of meanings embedded in specific historical experiences. In other words, drunken speech reveals particular historical and cultural configurations of power relations and structures.

Quechua-speaking people in the Andes are well aware of how the highly hierarchical structure of power in Peru is distributed along lines of race, class, gender, age, ethnicity, and linguistic competence. They are also well aware of how the arbitrariness of the Spanish-speaking law, a manifestation of the symbolic violence of the state, has historically played a crucial role in maintaining and reproducing such a power structure. They know that in their search for legal justice, the Spanish-speaking law may suddenly (and regularly) turn against them.[14] This awareness among Quechua-speaking rural peasants of how power relations have been historically negotiated in the Peruvian Andes is central to understanding why the sober survivor tends to remain silent before the law—as the difficulties faced by the prosecutor in collecting testimonial evidence show—and why the drunken survivor arrogates voice to himself *only* in the state of diminished responsibility and heightened potency of intoxication. It is as if, in the Andes, you have to be drunk to speak truth to the law—all the more so if what is to be spoken reveals the violence of the state itself. The Quechua-speaking survivor, in his drunken state, is "irresponsible" enough and feels encouraged enough to speak truth to power—to speak what usually goes unsaid in the sober state. In doing so, he disrupts the hierarchy of established social relations and challenges the (symbolic) violence of the Spanish-speaking state.

His being drunk also allows the work of the law to enter into the realm of excuses. J. L. Austin (1957, 7) famously argued that if ordinary language is to be our guide, "it is to evade responsibility, or full responsibility, that we most often make excuses." The sense here is that ethical or legal norms of responsibility cannot fully operate without the complement of a realm of excuses. In the case of the *borrachito*, he can excuse himself, or be excused, for his intrusion on the basis that it was not him who was speaking or behaving in a disruptive way, but another agency operating in him that cannot be accounted for—say, the agency of alcohol. By the same token, the law can excuse itself from constituting him as a legal subject—a person with a name who can be morally and legally accountable for his words. As far as I can tell, the legal authorities never attempted to locate and summon the drunken man as an eyewitness. Perhaps they reasoned that his testimony would not count in a court of law anyway, since he was a drunk, that is, a person who is unreliable because he is not sufficiently responsible for his words, and even more so because he was a *vicioso* (alcoholic).[15] Thus, with his legal agency always already evacuated, because of his being (always) drunk, the unknown drunken man was never considered a proper legal subject. In the highly formalistic realm of the law, for all practical purposes he was considered a non-person.

I did not happen to meet the *borrachito* during my fieldwork the following year, nor did I attempt to find him later to talk with him and learn about his motives. What could be added to the event of truth he animated if one were to learn from him, perhaps in his sober state, that he had done what he did because of this or that motive, when the whole efficacy of his apparition derives precisely from its phantomlike character? I wanted to register his presence in the way it was made known to me, that is, in the traces he left in the recollections of the experts as well as the relatives of the disappeared who were present on the day of his sudden appearance. The unknown drunk has become a kind of ghost in the history of the excavation;[16] this association is culturally resonant because in the Andes parallels are drawn between drunks on one hand and the dead and mountain spirits on the other. As Harvey (1991) argues, this connection is sometimes made explicit, for instance when people say that the dead are drunks, though most of the time it is made by association—when people group together drunks, the dead, and the mountain spirits in terms of their unreliability and disruptiveness. Their strong potential for good, Harvey says, is always qualified by the trouble they cause. "In some senses, they could be seen as operating in the same social space. It is usually drunks who see Awkis [mountain spirits]" (ibid., 13).[17]

Truth in Los Cabitos, then, arrives from the outside. It is an event resulting not from the legal and disciplinary technologies of truth-finding that aim at a controlled recovery of the past, but from the disruption caused by an impersonal witness. Truth in Los Cabitos occurs as a result of the unknown survivor's objection that forces its way through the controlled process by means of which the experts produce the past. He occupies a "zone of irresponsibility" from which he arrogates voice to himself, to speak truth to power and to introduce a context that the law and forensic sciences will never be able to capture fully in their formalism and rationality: that is, the event of terror itself that in its excess lingers in the present. It is from this zone that the (drunken) survivor speaks for each and every person in his community who has pain, small or large, that needs "not to go unsaid and unaccompanied" (Cavell 1994, 12). It is a singular voice; and because it is singular, it is universal. The *borrachito* shows that the past lingers all over this place of stories, perhaps awaiting the disruptive moment in which somebody arrogates voice to himself or herself and speaks for everyone while speaking of his or her own biography—singular but universal.

Desánimo, or the Legal Expert's Soul

I joined the forensic excavation at Los Cabitos in August 2006. The semirural area had a pleasant atmosphere of bucolic ordinariness that, given the story of atrocity associated with La Hoyada, felt uncanny. During that first visit I observed police and military personnel pleasantly strolling about when not in training as well as peasants of the neighboring *chacras*

FIGURE 3.3. Now-unused oil tank at La Hoyada, Ayacucho, August 2006.

collecting firewood, prickly pear fruits, and *molle*;[18] grazing their cattle; or simply walking to their homes in the surroundings. Except for a disused cement oil tank and the fading remains of recent archaeological excavation trenches, nothing indicated that during the 1980s La Hoyada had been a site of mass killing of disappeared suspects of terrorism (Figure 3.3). At the time of my arrival, rumor had it that urban squatters led by former *jefes ronderos* (peasant patrol bosses) were planning incursions to take over the area to build houses (*invasiones*). This looming de facto expropriation presented a threat to the forensic work, and I could sense an urgency among the legal and forensic personnel to continue making progress in their investigation.[19]

In this excavation season the small team of three forensic anthropologists began to dig in an area the military had used as a garbage dump in the past, on a steep slope in the northeastern part of La Hoyada (Map 3). They had what seemed to be a solid lead, and the expert in charge was very optimistic about finding more bodies, in addition to the fourteen recovered in the successful season of 2005 as a result of the drunken survivor's information. The public prosecutor had received the classified testimony of a former army private who had served at Los Cabitos during the early 1980s, in which he claimed that approximately thirty bodies had been buried in the area of the garbage dump. The forensic team had opened exploratory trenches to corroborate the testimony and found artifacts indicating the presence of clandestine graves. Their optimism prevailed despite their scarce resources and the scale of preparations required before they could start digging. The area was full of debris, trash, stones, and undergrowth, and they could count on the help of only two unskilled workers hired by ANFASEP.[20]

However, after three weeks of intense work, the forensic team had not found any more complete bodies, and feelings of disappointment returned. Throughout my fieldwork I repeatedly heard the archaeologists uttering the Spanish word *desánimo* to express their disappointment with the outcomes of their work. *Desánimo* as a noun can be translated as disheartenment, discouragement, sadness, or disappointment. It is the opposite of *ánimo* (enlivening, encouraging). It seemed to me that, in strictly forensic terms, there were no reasons for such disappointment; their work was making slow but steady progress in collecting evidence to prove that a killing field had indeed functioned in these former regional headquarters of the counterinsurgency campaign. In the excavation season of

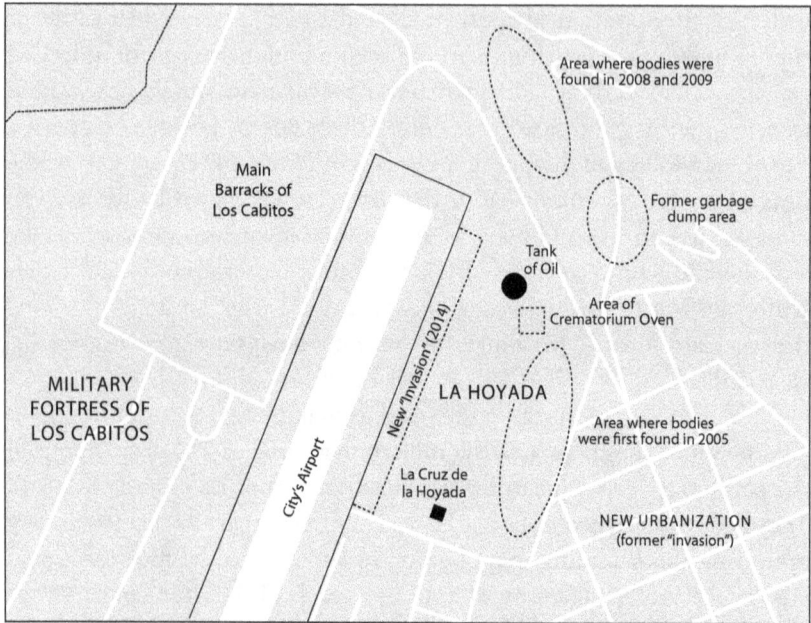

MAP 3. Map of La Hoyada, 2016.

August 2006, for instance, although the archaeologists were unable to find more complete bodies, they nonetheless uncovered crucial evidence indicating that the perpetrators had used the former garbage dump as a site to dispose burned human remains. They found agglomerations of ashes and fragments of human bones as well as circumstantial evidence dispersed uniformly throughout the excavation site. This pattern indicated that the burned human remains had presumably been transported in wheelbarrows from elsewhere and buried in the garbage dump. The team also uncovered evidence of what they called *arrastre* (dragging) of burned bricks and debris from a demolished structure, presumably a furnace. This evidence indicated that the former garbage dump had been not so much a burial site as a site for the disposal of burned human remains and even of demolished furnaces.

In the excavation season of October 2006 the team continued to dig in the area of the former garbage dump and also started to excavate in the vicinity of the disused oil tank (see Map 3 and Figure 3.3). Here, the archaeologists uncovered the foundations of what had presumably been a large furnace. As part of these foundations, they found combustible pipes

FIGURE 3.4. Foundations of an industrial-style oven, around which ashes and charred fragments of human bones were found in March 2007.

connected to the oil tank and three-phase electrical wiring that ran to the main barracks of the fortress. An electrical system of this kind is usually installed for industrial purposes. The experts therefore adopted the hypothesis that an industrial furnace had functioned here. During the excavation season of March 2007, the team made another crucial discovery: they uncovered ashes and charred fragments of human bones associated with the furnace's foundations (Figure 3.4). For the first time in the investigation they exposed evidence that linked the mass graves, the furnace, and the former garbage dump. In the seasons of June and July 2007, the team expanded the excavation and uncovered evidence of other ransacked graves, which indicated that the contents had been disinterred, presumably to be burned in the furnace. They thus established another crucial forensic link.

By the end of the excavation season of July 2007, when I concluded my fieldwork at the site, the forensic findings had objectively established that La Hoyada had been used as a site for the mass killing of disappeared terrorism suspects and for the industrial-style disposal of their bodies. Most of the complete bodies recovered from clandestine mass graves showed signs of people having been tortured and blindfolded, with their hands tied behind their backs, before being killed. Circumstantial evidence indicated that the victims had probably been forced to dig their own graves. In these graves were found stones that covered the bodies and traces of lime that had probably been used to accelerate their decomposition. Most of the tombs had been sacked, the bodies disinterred and then burned in blast furnaces. The ashes and remains of the burned bodies were subsequently disposed of in a garbage dump in the surrounding area. Finally, the perpetrators demolished the furnaces and dumped the debris in the same garbage dump. All of this was conclusively established as a result of the evidence collected by the team from 2005 to 2007. The highly professional, methodical, detailed, and painstaking application of disciplinary logic and procedure had indeed allowed the archaeologists to make a controlled recovery of the past and to establish the truth of what happened at the military base. Los Cabitos was shown to have been a site of the mass "fabrication of corpses."

If their work was making a decisive contribution to the criminal investigation of one of the major cases of state atrocity in modern Peruvian history, why is it that these experts were still *desánimados?* I contend that this disappointment arose from the fact that in almost two years of work they had not been able to find a single complete body, aside from those found in 2005. All they could recover during this time were heaps of ashes and an immeasurable quantity of fragments of charred human bones. Not being able to find more complete bodies was a source of *desánimo* for them, and this strikes me as a paradox because, in purely legal terms, they already had "bodies of evidence" for prosecution.[21]

We may argue that this anxiety about finding complete bodies is related to the fact that the "humanitarian aspect" of the excavation—the expectation that the archaeological work should facilitate the return of individual bodies to their relatives for proper burial—was missing.[22] In the project of the necro-governmentality of postconflict the recovered missing body has a crucial role because, in addition to providing evidence for the work of the law, it serves as a site for completing a story of suffering and redemption through which relatives can attain closure and return home (Wagner 2008; Rojas-Perez 2010, 2013). However, I suggest that *desánimo* comes not only from the humanitarian domain, but also from the fact that the archaeologists at Los Cabitos are themselves witnesses of the violence and suffering that now, in their role as experts, they study as an "object."

In search of certainty, both the law and the forensic sciences demand that archaeologists objectify and distance themselves not only from the investigated object, but also from their own personal experience of it. However, the forensic archaeologists at Los Cabitos were engaged in what Buchli and Lucas (2001, 10) define as the "archaeology of the contemporary past"—namely, an archaeology that deals not with the "recent past," but with the present and, as such, with contexts that are textually and discursively rich. For these authors, "recent past" implies closeness in time, whereas "contemporary past" refers to now. The difference is between proximity and identity. In the former, the "object of study" remains at some distance; there is still some gap, no matter how small, between the archaeologist and what is studied. In the latter, any gap is constantly contested and collapses because the archaeologist is implicated more immediately than in any other kind of archaeology.

The most immediate way in which their "object" implicated the archaeologists at Los Cabitos was that the contemporary past they were delving into was a central part of their own biographies. They were Peruvian archaeologists and, like myself, belonged to a generation directly affected by the internal war. The three of them came from working-class families with rural, indigenous origins who lived in regions of the Andes and Amazonian basin particularly affected by the violence of the Shining Path and the state; they had been first-generation college students who studied in public universities that likewise were infiltrated by the forces of war; they made vital decisions in a context of violence, mass death, and political instability; they knew stories of some peers who joined the forces of war, while others decided to either emigrate or retreat into their private lives, and still others joined citizen movements for peace and human rights.

In other words, like most Peruvians and Ayacuchanos of their age, they were familiar with the experience of violence and massive suffering, the material remains of which they now found themselves studying as forensic scientists. The internal war in Peru marked their biographies and, just like the *borrachito*, they inhabit a "place of stories." The archaeologists also know, only too well, numerous personal stories of suffering and devastation pertaining to a friend, a colleague, a classmate, an acquaintance, a relative, or even themselves. In this sense, the contemporary past they are investigating is, in several respects, an ongoing past—it is their "now." We may therefore ask to what extent and in what ways such experiences of suffering came back to them at the excavation site, particularly when they recovered ashes or fragments of human bones. We may ask what it means for them to return to the site of devastation as "experts."

Joyce (2015) compellingly argues that human remains are not simply inanimate matter. They are more than just evidence (see also Crossland 2009). During my fieldwork I observed how, while scrupulously adhering to archaeology's disciplinary rules and assumptions, at certain moments the forensic experts turned the procedure into a kind of ritual in which they treated the shattered human remains as anything but mere objects or artifacts. They handled these remains with a certain reverence and referred to them as belonging to a person who was present. "It is *his* knee," "it is *his* femur," "it is *his* rib," they said whenever they found fragments of bones and recovered them for site analysis. This use of language reveals a tension between two modes of relating to the remains: the body as evidence and the body as person (see Crossland 2000, 2002, 2009; and Joyce 2015). As persons, the dead have agency, and one specific way in which this agency is expressed is providing the information they possess (see Fredy Peccerelly in Carrescia 2008).

But to speak of the body as a person is also to speak of the body as a set of relations. At the site of excavation, the native archaeologists move between two deaths—between the brutal termination of biological life and death as human experience—in an attempt to bring the remnants of atrocity back into familiar webs of meaning and relations by means of attaching those remains to a name. In doing so, they also attempt to come to terms with their own contemporary past. The inability to recover these bodies at Los Cabitos thus gets translated not only into the inability to remake one's relation to them—say, in terms of offering them proper burial—but also the inability to remake one's relation to oneself—say, in terms of becoming a mourner. Something very personal thus continues to be missing with the missing body or is ultimately lost when one realizes that those human remains found at the site are beyond recovery, and *desánimo* speaks of that loss of one's relation to others and of being lost to oneself in this site of devastation.

Becoming Text

Das and Poole (2004, 6) show how operations of inclusion/exclusion of certain aspects of human life, and segments of human community for that matter, are necessarily constitutive of the state itself: "The forms of il-legibility, partial belonging, and disorder that seem to inhabit the margins of the state constitute its necessary condition as a theoretical and political object." Nowhere is this operation of inclusion/exclusion inherent in the work of the state illustrated more clearly than in the documentation of the investigation's outcomes and the eventual destiny of the recovered remains. By January 2009, when the forensic archaeology investigation came to a close, the forensic team had exhumed eighty-two more complete bodies, including a number of children. They also recovered parts of bodies of about forty more individuals as well as an unquantifiable amount of ash and charred fragments of human bones. It was impossible to determine how many more individuals were included among these remains. Most of the complete bodies recovered had their hands tied behind their backs, and their skulls showed that they had been shot in the head at close range with light automatic rifles. When I was in the field I observed how these remains, after they were registered by the public prosecutor (Figure 3.5),

FIGURE 3.5. The public prosecutor registering the findings of the excavation season of October 2006.

were carefully removed from the site of excavation and placed in bags labeled with the number of the unit and sector excavated, denoting the precise location where they had been found. These bags were then packed into cardboard boxes and sent to the IML headquarters for laboratory analysis to individualize the remains, identify the victims, and determine their cause of death.

All these findings were carefully documented by the lead prosecutor and the forensic archaeologists, in corresponding legal and expert texts that would later substantiate prosecution of the case in a court of law. Since these texts acquire a life of their own in subsequent legal proceedings, the materiality of the event of state atrocity became a background or, simply, was left behind. On one hand, the site disappeared as a material site of mass killing to become (legal and forensic) text. It is well known that in contrast to a typical archaeological excavation, forensic excavation, as well as the removal of human remains and other relevant evidence, necessarily entails destruction of the site. On the other hand, the recovered human remains ended up inside labeled cardboard boxes that were piled up in storage rooms at the IML in Ayacucho, as evidence that could not be used in the criminal prosecution of perpetrators because these remains could not be identified.[23] In the work of the law, with the end of the forensic investigation in the field, the event of state atrocity came to acquire a fundamentally textual life. Not only had the event been translated into the strict grammar and controlled vocabulary of the law and the forensic sciences in order to acquire legal efficacy; for that same reason—namely, to have legal efficacy—all the affects that accompanied, and to a certain extent constituted, the work of the state at the excavation site were necessarily excluded from the (legal and forensic) text thus produced. This is what a controlled recovery of the past entails.

Concluding Comments

In this chapter I have shown how the intervention of forensic anthropology is decisive in providing hard evidence to constitute a legally authorized truth about state atrocity and, hence, in establishing conditions of possibility for justice. Yet, I have also shown the tense and complex relationship that emerges between the field of expertise within which the forensic truth must be produced and its legally constituted outside—as epitomized in this case by the sudden intrusion of a drunken survivor who, despite not being part of the legal procedures, made possible crucial forensic findings at the site. Not only are the boundaries between both at times blurred, disrupted, and contested, but also there is a necessary and intricate flow of power and affect between the two. Without the outside, conditions of possibility for truth and justice could not be established, and all the more so given the nature and scale of atrocity that far exceeded anything that was previously known and possible in the country's recent history.

What I emphasize here for the argument of this book is that while the law, on the one hand, opens up the space for the forensic truth of atrocity to be established, on the other hand it folds such a truth into the highly regimented assemblage of rules, procedures, and languages of the trial. It is a double movement through which the law claims the forensic truth for the purposes of adjudicating violations to the law. Not only does it necessarily exclude certain aspects of the outside, but it institutionally appropriates and adapts the truth of suffering to the needs of the legitimacy of postconflict state institutions—that is, to a project of postconflict state-making. And yet, both the possibility of justice and the impulse to remake a world in the aftermath of state atrocity, while grounded in the work of the law, cannot be confined to the narrow and controlled realm of the law or, more precisely, of the trial. Although they are related, state-making and justice-making are not the same project. An irreducible dimension of justice in the face of state atrocity, its substance as it were, needs to be found, and founded, elsewhere.

We have seen how for Andean survivors and relatives of victims, any possibility of justice entailed first and foremost a political reckoning and not a ritual reckoning. In this chapter we have gained a sense of how such a reckoning stands in a relation of inside/outside vis-à-vis the work of the law and forensic sciences. In the next chapter, I begin an exploration of how the illiterate Quechua mothers of the disappeared inhabit the space of truth opened by the law at Los Cabitos and how they appropriate the forensic truth for their own struggle for justice and political reckoning with state atrocity in a gesture that at once stands inside and outside the law. Specifically, I look at how they reclaim the history of state atrocity by means of ordinary languages that are always already excluded from the work of the law.

4

The Cry
Memories of the Present

ONE MORNING IN March 2007, as soon as we arrived at the excavation site, a group of mothers of the disappeared approached the edge of the "crime scene" to greet the archaeologists and hear their initial briefing. While waiting for the experts to approach and talk to them, Juana, a middle-aged woman in search of two missing brothers, spontaneously volunteered to brief the mothers who were visiting the site for the first time on the progress of the forensic excavation. As an active member of ANFASEP, she had been closely following the investigation and was well informed of its developments. Speaking in Quechua, Juana described in detail the work the *doctores* had been doing and emphasized that all they had been able to find in the previous three seasons of excavation were charred fragments and ashes of human bones, as well as debris from a furnace where those bodies had presumably been incinerated. At this point in Juana's exposition, Mama Anki, a first-time visitor who now lived on the coast, suddenly burst into tears, crying out the name of her missing son. "Dario, where are you, sweet little man, boy, where are you, sweet little man? Please, tell me 'I am here,' I beg you [Dario, dónde estás? . . . papá lindito, niño, ¿dónde estás, papacito? 'Aquí estoy' ñiykamuway]," she uttered, in a cry that was both supplication and command.[1]

Heard all over the site, Mama Anki's painful cry opened up a moment of sorrowful silence among those at the excavation that morning, including the legal and forensic personnel. Mama Esperanza and Mama Natividad also broke down and began to weep softly. Everybody at the site was clearly moved by these mothers' display of pain, and some tried to console them. Juana herself told Mama Anki to stop crying, affectionately saying that if she continued to grieve like that, the earth might take over her soul: "The earth [*pacha*] may seize you [Pachapas qapirusunkinman]," she said in Quechua.[2] Amalia and Elena, nurses from La Red,[3] hastened to give these mothers emotional support. "Stop crying *mamita*, it may be more hurtful for you," Amalia told Mama Anki in Quechua. Embracing her kindly, Elena spoke additional words of consolation. "We are with you," she said in Spanish. I also mumbled some words of comfort. But Mama Anki was inconsolable and did not respond immediately to her companions' efforts to help her contain her grief. "Dario, please, tell me 'I am here,' I beg you," she cried once again. Amalia then whispered to me quietly in Spanish, "Está traumada esta señora [This lady is traumatized]."

We handed Mama Anki some water, and she slowly began to calm down. Then, still in tears, she addressed Mama Natividad, with whom she used to walk in search of their missing children during the worst moments of the counterinsurgency campaign in the early 1980s:

> Mama Anki: We did not come to this site, Mama Nati.
> Mama Natividad: They [the military] did not allow us to enter here; that is why.
> Mama Anki: They did not; they did not at all.
> Mama Teodora: [*Jumping into the conversation*] We could never gain access to this site; it was impossible.
> Juana: This place was under tight surveillance, ma'am. They used to send us away, saying, "They are not here."
> Mama Anki: Dear God, if I just could find my little son. If I just could . . . my God . . .

Mama Anki uttered this last phrase with less distress, and after drinking some more water, she started to tell us the story of the last time she had seen her missing son. He had been in a military barracks, and she could not rescue him. Eerily, at the moment she began her retelling, we heard shots from a machine gun ringing out somewhere not far from the site.

During my fieldwork, I witnessed other similar moments of despondency among these Quechua-speaking mothers when they were confronted for the first time in several years with the truth the forensic investigation was uncovering before their eyes: human bodies destroyed and incinerated beyond recognition. I saw a mother start to convulse at the sight of ashes and charred fragments of bones lying within the excavation pits. Another mother, seeing the shattered human remains for the first time, could articulate her pain only by bursting out into a mournful *harawi* song.[4] Thus, in several respects, Mama Anki's cry at the site speaks for them all, giving expression to that region of experience in which these mothers have been living since the disappearance of their children: "¿Dónde estás? . . . 'Aquí estoy' ñiykamuway [Where are you? . . . (tell me) 'I am here,' I beg you]."

Voiced at the site of excavation, the mother's cry is an agonizing gesture of both interpellation and instruction that attempts to reverse the work of state terror and relocate the son in relation to a certain place and a certain duration, in the present. It is interpellation in that the mother hopes to constitute both a subject who is called to identify himself with his name and a subjectivity that conforms to this naming by responding to it.[5] Yet, as the missing son does not—cannot—respond to the call of his name, the cry of the mother moves toward a gesture of instruction in a futile attempt to teach him how to respond to her call. After uttering his name, the mother's appeal enters into an intimate register ("papa lindito, niño, ¿dónde estás, papacito?" [sweet little man, boy, where are you, sweet little man?]). She addresses him as any mother would address her son in an everyday interaction in which she wished to reconvene with him, express her love, or simply teach him the forms of sociality and culture that everybody must learn to have a life together with others. Then, the mother speaks as if the return from the state of not-being in which the forces of terror have walled up her son would necessarily entail the need to reacquire language: she teaches her missing son how to pronounce the words that would respond to her call ("'Aquí estoy,' ñiykamuway").

This scene shows at once how the event of state terror is as much about the disappeared person's disappearance from language as it is about the disappearance of the body. The disappeared have suddenly stopped responding to their names: they have become names without bodies and (shattered) bodies without names. If, as Althusser (1971) says, the state constitutes its subjects through interpellation, then the cry of the mother unmasks how the work of terror in the form of forced disappearance consists, first of all, in the obliteration of the possibility of constituting both subjects and subjectivity through the usual "ideological state apparatuses," such as naming. State terror shatters the intimate relationship between a body and a name.[6] For the disappeared to reappear, this intimate relationship between body and name needs to be restored and ascertained in both life and death—that is, if alive, individuals must respond to their names;

if dead, their remains must be reattached to their names. The cry of the mother at the excavation site bears witness to the current impossibility of this reappearance. It bears witness to the presentness of the event of state terror and the ongoing nature of the disappearance.

The cry "¿dónde estás? [where are you?]," then, defines a region of language and action that both the state and the mothers share in their search for the disappeared. But for the state, reattaching names to bodies has to do primarily with the task of regaining control over its population and territory by means of certifying individuals' identity, their legal status, their state of being, and their residence. By contrast, for their mothers these individuals are unique, irreplaceable people with singular biographies. Their names are more than just legal identities that are stored in bureaucratic records, as they actually express how these singular people are embedded in a dense set of social relations. This fundamental disjuncture of what the disappeared are for the state and what they are for their mothers opens up a field of political struggle to ascribe meaning to the contemporary search for the disappeared in terms of how the event of state terror should be accounted for and how one should to respond to its longstanding legacy.

In this chapter I look specifically at how the mothers of the disappeared resituate the event of disappearance as an ongoing event in the new context opened up by the legal and forensic investigation. As we saw in Chapter 3, one of the central presuppositions of the necro-governmentality of postconflict is that the event of atrocity is situated in the past, from which it must be recovered in a "controlled" manner for the purposes of justice and mourning in the present. By contrast, as the event of disappearance has not ended, for these mothers state atrocity is an ongoing past. Yet the regime of truth in which the event unfolds has shifted from wartime denial and silencing to postconflict acknowledgment and an official search for truth. This shift allows these mothers to occupy the site of mass killing and compose a collective story of how the event of state terror has come to be embedded into their everyday lives. This "minor" story speaks not of individual "trauma," but of an ongoing (political) wound in the social body.

I start with an analysis of how the event of forced disappearance cannot be reduced to the framework of trauma. Then I analyze the double temporality in which the forced disappearance of alleged terrorism suspects unfolds as an ongoing event. I go on to analyze the daily routines and practices of authority through which the disappearance has been actualized, as they emerge from the memories of terror and suffering the mothers retell at the excavation site. Finally, I elaborate on how these stories are not memories of the past but of the present.

The Event's Present Tense

It might be tempting to contain the mother's cry within the clinical discourse of trauma. In fact, the mental health practitioner's straightforward characterization of the mother's gesture as a traumatic reenactment of her injury ("está traumada esta señora") is an invitation to participate in such a discourse. This comes as no surprise since in Peru, as elsewhere, the popularization of languages of trauma has made a particular set of ideas and tropes from the world of mental health sciences readily available for understanding and speaking of human suffering. It responds to the emergence of what LaCapra (1999, 712) calls the "culture of trauma" or "wound culture." As Fassin and Rechtman (2009) show, this "culture of trauma" corresponds not to the successful dissemination of a concept elaborated in the scientific world of psychiatrists and then exported into the "social space of afflictions," but to the emergence of a new moral economy. The fact that trauma has become so pervasive in our contemporary world is rather "the product of a new relationship to time and memory, to mourning and obligations, to misfortune and the misfortunate" (ibid., 276).

Nowhere else has this new moral economy articulated around the notion of trauma so patently manifested than in postcatastrophe scenarios. In Peru, as elsewhere, the official declaration of victory against the Shining Path in late 1992 brought about a particular kind of postconflict humanitarian intervention that has the notions of trauma and victimhood as central grammars of intelligibility. In association with the discursive practices of the human rights legal regime, this humanitarian intervention purported to provide "innocent" victims of political violence some form of therapeutic healing of the trauma that had visited them and devastated their lives during the protracted internal war. This humanitarian intervention acquired full legitimacy with the advent of the democratic transition in 2001 and in the context of the transitional justice project, particularly the work of the CVR. Notions of trauma and victimhood have since gained such salience that, as we saw in Chapter 1, even legal investigations of human rights violations are informed by a particular concern for humanitarian restoration to heal trauma, in addition to the typical concerns for prosecution and deterrence. These are internal to the apparatus of postconflict governance that combining notions of rights and unjust suffering aim at constituting victims of violence as both citizens and trauma patients.[7]

It is this moral economy's new relationship to time and memory that particularly concerns me here. Trauma theories concur on the idea that a traumatic event overwhelms ordinary human adaptations to life. The pain and distress it brings about to the life of the victim are so devastating that the event cannot be fully assimilated as experience by the traumatized individual. The victim's response to the traumatic event happens, in the words of trauma theorist Cathy Caruth (1991, 181), "in the often delayed, and uncontrolled repetitive occurrence of hallucinations and other intrusive phenomena." This destructive repetition, or acting out, governs a person's life, and the victim is unable to give expression to his or her wound. Thus, in Caruth's (1996, 4) interpretation, trauma is much more than a pathology or the simple illness of a wounded psyche; rather, "it is always the story of a wound that cries out, that addresses us in an attempt to tell us of a reality or truth that is not otherwise available." This rendering of trauma suggests that the traumatic event is in the past and that its devastating present-day manifestations are due to the fact that it is an "unclaimed experience," unrepresentable and unknowable to the sufferer. Healing requires the traumatized person to externalize the event by articulating and transferring the event to another self (the listener) outside the suffering self and then returning to a self that is now able to claim the event as experience.

Seen from this perspective, it might be possible to argue that the cry of the mother at the excavation site is a manifestation of the trauma visited upon her by the violence of the state ever since the forced disappearance of her son. Unable to distinguish between "then" and "now," the mother would not only be claiming experience in the present by compulsively repeating the past, or acting out, but also manifesting her inability to recognize the present and its promises as a consequence of her trauma.[8] Her cry would be bridging two distinct moments—namely, a past marked by an unbridled arbitrary violence and a present governed by the rationality of the law and promises of justice—and in its very reenactment or acting out, it would allow for the possibility of therapeutic recovery. Because she is unable to recognize the signs of possibility in the present, working through her trauma would require some form of expert mediation to facilitate a reflective claim of her experience. In other words, the temporality of trauma would allow us to clearly situate the event of state terror in the past. The disappearance, implicitly equated with the moment the missing person was last seen, would belong to the past, and it would return to the present only as a reverberation through the mother's acting out of her trauma that in turn requires expert mediation to facilitate recovery.

What renders this view inadequate in understanding the temporality in which the mother cries out is that the disappearance of her son is a matter of not just the past, but also the present. It is an ongoing event.[9] Déotte (2004) argues that what makes a disappearance a disappearance is that it lasts forever—and what lasts forever is the fact that we cannot say anymore that a person who responds to a name is either present or absent. In his words: "The disappearance is midway between the ascertained presence and the absence, for we need to insist in this regard: the disappeared is not an absentee. Absence is a mode of being in relation to a certain place. Conversely, the disappeared 'is not here, nor is there.' He 'is' in between the 'nor' . . . the 'neither'" (ibid., 324). The only certain thing we can say about the disappeared, Déotte goes on, is the last time and the last place he or she was seen alive. The disappearance suspends the possibility of connecting a name with a place and so of establishing a destiny. Because the disappearance suspends any ontological thesis about the being in the world of the disappeared, it is a problem not of representation or of memory, but of designation. "The [event] of disappearance," Déotte says, "is always already an ontological failure of designation rather than a 'perturbation of representation' or a hole in memory. It is not that representation is forbidden . . . but designation, for a name is not an image. The problem is, thus, not of the inability to represent—i.e., of the unspeakable [unutterable], of the sublime, etc.—but of the inability to name [*lo innombrable*], but not in an ethical sense (this is not a question of value)" (ibid., 327).

Déotte's insight helps us situate the ongoing character of the event—its present tense, as it were. But because it invites us to focus exclusively on the moment of the "last seen," it may also blind us from seeing how the relatives engage with the event. The cry of the mother at the excavation site certainly erases the distance between the past and the present. It is one of those instances in which the whole past is contracted into one moment in response to the appeal of the present (Deleuze 1988). It summons at once all the feelings associated with the experience of the forced disappearance of people whom the state considers terrorists. Yet it presents that region of the past that most overtly displays the violence and devastation visited upon the social body by the event of violence and seems to announce that the work of state terror has been completed.

Such a conclusion—that the work of state terror has been completed—would transpire if we remained locked in *just* listening to the cry of the mother, with our gaze fixed on the mother as she hopelessly tries to animate a response from her missing son as a means of bringing him back into being, unable to do anything but ask where is he and teach him how to respond—a gesture that has had no response since he was taken from home and most probably will never respond. If we remain fixed on this image, we stay suspended in the moment of the "last seen," when the body disappeared and the subject ceased to respond to his name, and we are mired in contemplating how it is that the state can suspend its work of interpellation at will, as a full manifestation of its sovereignty over life and death. Further, we are led to consider the cry of the mother as an act of witnessing *in* terror, similar to what trauma theory does by mobilizing the notion of acting out, and conclude with Déotte (2004, 327) that "the disappearance does not permit discourse to go on. Or alternatively, it permits it to go on only through the question 'where is she/he?'"

From the Cry to the Search

There is another way we can listen to the mother's cry at the site, however: we can extend our listening to what accompanies the cry, to what dwells in its surroundings. If we shift our listening to the dialogue between the mothers that follows the cry, we begin to see that the work of state terror is actually not complete, that witnessing *in* terror is not the only available form of testimony these mothers have to express their pain and that discourse goes on not only through the question "Where is she/he?" Let us consider the exchange again:

Mama Anki: We did not come to this site, Mama Nati.

Mama Natividad: They [the military] did not allow us to enter here; that is why.

Mama Anki: They did not; they did not at all.

Mama Teodora: [*Jumping into the conversation*] We could never gain access to this site; it was impossible.

Juana: This place was under tight surveillance, ma'am. They used to disperse us away, saying "They are not here."

Mama Anki: Dear God, if I just could find my little son. If I just could . . . my God . . .

This exchange introduces a subtle shift from the cry to the search— or, more precisely, to the history of the search. It brings back at once the whole experience of the mothers' search—the experience of how, despite the fact that their missing relatives were last seen at Los Cabitos, they could never access the military base in their search for them: "We could never gain access to this site; it was impossible [Kaymanqa manam yaykuran-chikchu karqa miki]." The exchange brings back how at the beginning, when they still hoped to find the disappeared alive, the mothers wandered around police stations, military garrisons, hospitals, and clandestine detention centers where security forces might have their loved ones detained. Then, as they were unable to find their missing relatives among the living, the mothers started to search for them among the dead, wandering around *botaderos*,[10] bushes, ravines, rivers, hills, or caves where the Peruvian military had disposed of their victims' bodies during the early years of their campaign of terror. The relatives hoped to find at least their loved ones' remains to offer them burial. But they never reappeared, alive or dead. Los Cabitos remained the only inaccessible site, concealing a truth that could only be imagined and circulated in rumor, since the state both prohibited access to the site and denied the event.

It was the mothers' search that allowed them to eventually gain access to the formerly forbidden site and the truth of the atrocity it concealed. Had it not been for their search, the law would not have eventually intervened at the site. The fact that the mother reenacts her cry at the excavation site, from a "here" to which they had never previously had access, and the fact that together these mothers articulate their memories of the impossibility of entering this "here" in search of their missing relatives show that the ongoing event of the disappearance no longer occurs in the context of denial and silencing. Rather, it occurs in a context in which the law promises to bring the disappeared back into legal, moral, and cultural being. The attempt to recover, individualize, and identify unknown human remains found at the site attests to the fact that state power has swung from the power to kill to the power that cares. However, as we saw Chapter 3, these attempts at producing the missing bodies as individuals with names can fail. Thus, since the law and forensic sciences intervened at Los Cabitos, the event has taken on a double status that encompasses both the disappearance itself—that is, the fact that the disappeared are still missing—and the truth of atrocity—that is, the possibility that the disappeared might be among those charred fragments of human bones.

I contend that the forensic excavation at Los Cabitos opens up for the mothers of the disappeared, for the first time in more than twenty years of vain searching, the possibility of a "where" in which the bodies of their missing relatives *might be* dwelling. As the scenes of devastation uncovered by the excavation unfold before their weeping eyes, these mothers realize that those charred fragments and ashes of human bones *might be* their missing relatives' remains. However, because it is impossible to identify those remains, uncertainty is not entirely dispelled. Nevertheless, a crack is introduced in the temporality of disappearance. The possibility of assigning their missing relatives' remains a "whereness,"[11] an ubiety, or at least an imperfect locality, affects the indefinitely prolonged uncertainty that has long engulfed these mothers' lives. It punctuates the duration of the disappearance.

The subtle shift in the mother's cry from the reenactment of interpellation to the enactment of desire also registers this shift of context. Just after these mothers articulate their memories of failing to gain access to Los Cabitos, Mama Anki says, "Dear God, if I just could find my little son. If I just could . . . my God." This utterance still expresses the ongoingness of the event of disappearance; however, it no longer directly appeals to the missing son, demanding that he respond as a means of calling him back into being. The cry of the mother has shifted to the register of desire and moves in an ambiguous region between invocation, imploration, and lament. Her cry of "wawachallaytay tariykuyman [if I just could find my little son]" indexes the fact that, since the process of legal and forensic inquiry into the fate of the disappeared in Los Cabitos began, the mother has been uttering her cry from a different region of the event. This region is a new zone of indiscernibility that emerges in between the ongoing event of the disappearance and the event of truth-making concerning the disappearance.

A zone of indiscernibility is where desire is reconfigured in a new form of becoming. The mothers have finally gained access to the only site they were not previously able to access, and this means that their encounter with the state is now happening in a different modality from the murderous one they encountered during the state of emergency. And yet, the truth the law reveals to the mothers is that they will probably not be able to find the missing bodies this time, either. *Wawachallayta tariykuyman* indexes their desire for something else to happen again, beyond the limits of the present. It is as if, after all these years of suffering since their children were last seen, these mothers have learned that all they have left is a chronic search for that small move, that small difference, that small crack in the duration of the disappearance that will transfigure their pain yet again.

This chronic search for possibilities in the face of the indeterminacy of reality is what Good (1994, 153) has referred to as "subjunctivizing reality."[12] In the remainder of this book, I show how these mothers inhabit this new zone of indiscernibility and collectively compose a new becoming.

Wasinchis (Our Home)

"Akuykusunchis, doctor, tiyaykuy wasinchispi [Let's chew coca together, doctor; make yourself at home in our house]." With this sentence, Mama Natividad used to invite me to join the mothers' conversations in the improvised tent we had erected at the excavation site to protect ourselves from the morning sun. It was an invitation to listen to their stories of suffering associated with the disappearance of their missing children. As in ordinary contexts, these conversations started with a generous sharing of coca leaves and an opening moment of divination and reading of what "Mama Coca" announced today for both the chewer's personal life and the eventual fate of the excavation. Are the *doctores* headed in the right direction with their work? Will they find bodies today? Will bodies ever be found? While most of the mothers were familiar with the arts of deciphering the omens of Mama Coca, they preferred the reading of their elder peers. In most of these readings, Mama Coca announced upcoming difficulties in the work of the forensic investigation that nonetheless would eventually be overcome. Mama Coca always asked for patience.[13] And patience, translated into the mood of waiting, became the main modality in which the mothers engaged the work of excavation once the dramatic moment of the first encounter with the site of atrocity receded. In the grammar of patient waiting, the mother's cry became retelling.

For these mothers, a typical day during a season of excavation started early in the morning in the front doorway of the two-story house of ANFASEP, located on the opposite side of the city from Los Cabitos. The relatives attending the exhumation gathered around 8:00 a.m., often arriving on foot and rarely by bus or *mototaxi*.[14] In the meantime, people accompanying them to the site—nurse practitioners from La Red, interns from human rights organizations, or anthropologists such as myself— bought snacks and drinking water in the neighboring *mercado* (street market) for what would be a long day of work. Each trip to the excavation site looked like a small expedition. Depending on the number of travelers, we usually packed ourselves into two or three taxis for the half-hour ride that crossed the narrow streets of downtown Ayacucho and the dusty dirt roads of the shantytowns that surround the military base and the city's airport.

In strictly formal terms, any person visiting the excavation site had to enter through the military checkpoint and be subjected to the usual rituals of control, inspection, and verification of identity—such as surrendering personal identification cards and using provisional ones while on the military premises—through which the state performs its sovereignty. However, the mothers preferred to access the site by an alternate route that, despite being longer, allowed them to avoid the military checkpoint, a much-feared locus of arbitrary power associated with their worst memories of terror. Every time we entered the site through the checkpoint, the mothers remembered having to spend hours waiting there for any fragment of information about their missing relatives and the many times they had been frightened away by death threats from military personnel.

Once at the site, at the beginning of my fieldwork we protected ourselves from the sun under the shadow of the unused oil tank that was part of the crematory oven at Los Cabitos. As the excavation progressed toward this area, we had to move to a different zone and find shelter under the shadows of shrubs of maguey and hawthorn abundant in the area. This was not comfortable, and one early morning I found myself buying plastic cloth and twine fiber in one of the *mercados* of Ayacucho to set up a makeshift tent at the excavation site that would protect us more from the heat of the morning. The mothers liked the idea and helped me extend and fix the plastic cloth over the shrubs and clean up the sitting area to get rid of *locachas* (venomous spiders). Then we arranged stones as seats that the mothers covered with their *mantillas* for further comfort. These arrangements became a matter of daily routine, and on several occasions, the mothers jokingly commented, "Wasichakuchq'anchis [We are building ourselves a home]." Thus arranged, the makeshift tent was comfortable enough for us to spend hours at the site while awaiting the daily briefing from the *doctores*. At a certain point, the mothers christened the makeshift tent *wasinchis* (our home) (Figure 4.1).

The word *wasinchis* conveys both the notion of shelter (as in house) and sense of belonging, domesticity, and intimacy (as in home). In using this word, then, the mothers were referring not only to the material fact of having a provisional roof over their heads for protection from the sun, but also to their gesture of making themselves at home in the site. This gesture indexes these mothers' powerful move, in the context of the excavation,

FIGURE 4.1. Mothers of the disappeared sit under the makeshift tent they called *wasinchis* (our home), at the excavation site, March 2007.

toward domesticating state terror and reinhabiting the site of devastation in a gesture of mourning. In the following chapters, I explain how this move occurs. For now, I emphasize the sense of *wasinchis* that conveys the mothers' desire to establish an atmosphere of intimacy and confidence in which they could share their experiences of suffering as if they were indeed at home and with people who would listen to them. The generous sharing of food and coca leaves contributed to this atmosphere of intimacy and domesticity, as if certain forms of materiality and consumption were conditions of possibility for some conversations to occur. In fact, as we saw in Chapter 2, consumption and conversation are central components of the grammar of mourning in everyday life. In this sense, by inviting me to share coca leaves and food with them and to make myself at home in their *wasi*, these mothers were inviting me to be part of their conversations not only as a listener or empathetic audience, but also as a companion in their move toward mourning. It was not I who invited them to my tent, but they who invited me to their *wasi*.[15]

As the idea of being invited to their *wasi* suggests, mine was not a clinical encounter between the expert who knows and those who lend themselves to be known. In fact, from the beginning I had the sense that these mothers were addressing their stories not to me in particular, but to one another, *again*, since in all these years of walking together in search of their missing relatives, they ended up knowing one another's stories of suffering very well. Moreover, throughout the years since their relatives had disappeared, they have been telling these stories to any audience willing to listen—including legal authorities, human rights activists, journalists, researchers, and members of the CVR, among others.[16] These stories reemerged at the excavation site as stilled and yet vivid scenes of suffering and devastation. Since they were not addressed to an external agent for the purposes of, say, denunciation, as part of a human rights report, or clinical healing in a psychotherapeutic transference, I wondered why these mothers were telling these stories to one another again. Soon I realized that the reemergence of these somehow stilled scenes in these mothers' retelling paralleled the material reemergence of the fragments of human remains in the forensic excavation. It seemed as if the mothers wanted to give these unknown fragments some form of lived context, to wrap them in words and thus situate them within a history of terror whose driving force was its own denial of itself. It seemed as if they were trying to stitch together the emergent fragments of human bones with the fragments of the history of violence and terror of which these remains were the material evidence.

Below I offer fragments of these stories, in no way pretending to give a full account of them nor to convey the full intensity of their performative force. If, as I said before, these stories gesture toward opening up the possibility of memory as a means of mourning, it is important to pay attention to the distinction between the narrated *I* and the narrating *I* (Desjarlais 2003). The narrating *I* sits with her peers in the *wasi* at the excavation site speaking of the encounters the narrated *I* had with the state in her search for her missing son during the campaign of state terror (Figure 4.2). Two temporalities are intertwined in the mothers' retelling: they spoke of the doubleness of the event, and they conveyed a sense of how the event had come to be embedded in their everyday lives and how, in engaging the event, they had come to constitute themselves as a collective subject. An anthropological listening to this retelling helps us understand how, in their

FIGURE 4.2. Mothers of the disappeared observing the forensic excavation at Los Cabidos, October 2006.

iterability, these stories both open up the possibility of a different mode of composition of the history of violence and terror in Peru and show the extent to which this is not a history of the past but of the present.[17]

Performances of the Exception

All the relatives attending the forensic exhumation recall the abduction of their loved ones as the foundational moment of their stories of terror. Most of the disappeared were (are) young men, and the stories of their kidnapping are similar to one another, as if they were from the same script. The military has taken over political control of the region and has established a stringent curfew; police and military patrols exert tight surveillance in the city, and nobody else walks in the streets. That is when it happens. Late at night, when everybody is sleeping, a military squad breaks into the house of the person who is soon to disappear. Taken by surprise, the relatives are first paralyzed by terror but then react and vainly try to resist. The heavily armed squad overpowers their resistance and subdues them with the threat of death. In a hopeless last attempt to rescue their loved one, the relatives run behind the vehicle in which the kidnappers are taking him away, but the attackers fire their guns at them. When the curfew is lifted the next morning, the relatives rush to every military and police post, only to hear the same response: nobody knows or has heard or seen anything. Their kidnapped relative has simply vanished.[18]

The story is well known and has been thoroughly documented by both official and unofficial institutions. The massive disappearance of terrorism suspects in Peru's central southern Andes started in 1983, when the military took over political control of the region in the context of the state of emergency. A political military command was established in Huamanga, the provincial capital of Ayacucho, and the military fortress of Los Cabitos became the regional headquarters of the counterinsurgency (see Chapters 1 and 3). The number of disappearances skyrocketed in this region between 1983 and 1984. As the internal war spread throughout the country, so did the practice of forced disappearance. Between 1983 and 1992, Peru became one of the countries with the most disappearances worldwide. Historically, with 3,004 cases, it is among the five countries in the world with the most disappearances documented by the UN Working Group on Disappearances.[19]

The official and unofficial documentation of these abuses has been crucial in demonstrating that the forced disappearance of alleged terrorism suspects was a central component of the counterinsurgency campaign in Peru and, consequently, that it was not a sporadic occurrence but a systematic and widespread practice.[20] However, this reporting defines the event of disappearance in terms of human rights violations. In this framework, instances of forced disappearance are crimes, and it is the state itself that is required to address these legal transgressions by means of the law. Written in legalistic and positivistic genres, as it is primarily focused on documenting transgressions of the law, this way of reporting captures and freezes the stories of the relatives of the disappeared in the moment of the "last seen." The event of disappearance is thus congealed in time in the criminal moment when a person went missing.

By contrast, a focus on the search allows us to go beyond the moment of the "last seen" and consider the extent to which the practice of forced disappearance is not so much a crime as it is a form of state rule. To understand this, we need to return to the excavation site and listen to the mothers' stories in an attempt to "restore to accounts of political violence both the surrounding social relations and an associated range of subjective meanings" (Wilson 1997, 135). In these stories, the military operation to kidnap the mothers' relatives from home was never silent. Typically, the kidnappers tried to placate the families' resistance by presenting their attack as an ordinary arrest, shouting over and over, "Mañana vienen al cuartel; mañana lo devolvemos [Come tomorrow to the fortress; tomorrow we will release him]." Since the state of emergency suspends fundamental rights, such as a warrant being required for detention, the perpetrators cited the law to produce their arrest and promised to return the arrested person when their investigation was over. But in the context of the state of emergency, this "mañana vienes" becomes a "never again," because the arrested person simply vanishes.

Consider the case of Mama Anki. Dario, her nineteen-year-old son, was kidnapped from the family home. After several days of wandering around police stations, Los Cabitos, and other detention centers, Mama Anki somehow received a message saying that Dario was being held at the military barracks of Quicapata and urgently needed medication. She immediately asked for help from a Catholic priest who was a friend of the family and then ran to the barracks with her scared children in tow. Perhaps because of the presence of the priest and the children, the military officer in command of the barracks allowed Mama Anki to see Dario. As she recalled events at the excavation site, the scene was both painful and terrifying. Her son was badly beaten but still able to walk. They ran toward one another. She held onto him tightly and, rebuking the military personnel for having beaten him so badly, demanded his immediate release. The military personnel separated them by force and pushed her away. At that moment, she suffered a panic attack. When she recovered, she resumed her struggle, simultaneously begging for and demanding the release of her son. Here is how she recalled the scene:

[*In Quechua*] Then the officer made me swallow a pill saying, "Drink"; then he asked me, "What do you want?" I got down on my knees, I prostrated myself as before God, saying, "Release my son, please, return him to me; my son works, my son is a student; he's lost five days of classes so far." I told him, "My son gets the best grades; he is lagging in his work, please," I kneeled down before him, crying. [*Shifting to Spanish*] "Do not kneel down. We are not God. Stand up!" he says to me; then he pulls me up. I stood up. "What do you want with your son? Your son is *terruco* [terrorist]," he says to me. "How can you say that he is *terruco* sir?" I said. "What have you found in my house? What incriminating evidence [*prueba*] have you found? You have searched my house over and over again for three nights, and what have you found in his room? What piece of evidence? Any document? What have you found, sir? He is innocent."

It was at this moment that Mama Anki heard one of the signature phrases of state terror, "mañana vienes":

> Anki: Then he said [*shifting to Spanish*], "Ma'am, do not worry, we will release him; you will get him back. Now, you give him the medicine you brought, and then go home with your children." Then he says, "Tomorrow bring him a blanket; also bring him shoes, a sweater, his ID; bring him whatever you have for him."
>
> Eudosia: [*In Quechua*] Ahh, so he even told you that . . .
>
> Anki: [*In Quechua*] Yes, he told me that: "You will bring everything early in the morning, at 6:00 a.m." But at 6:00 a.m. the curfew is still in effect; people do not walk in the streets at that time, and I said to him [*shifting to Spanish*], "Sir, how am I going to bring this at 6:00 a.m. if the curfew is in effect until 7:00 a.m.?" He said, "You just bring it, early in the morning, tomorrow—his ID."

Mama Anki returned to the barracks early the next day, but she did not see her son then or ever again. "Ay mamacha, noqaka confiaranim [Dear God, I foolishly trusted them]," she concluded her retelling, lamenting in retrospect having trusted the words of the military officers.

From time to time, when Mama Anki retold this story, the mothers at the excavation site interrupted their attentive and compassionate listening to confirm that things had happened in the way that Mama Anki was narrating them. Her story closely mirrors their own. They also had these kind of face-to-face encounters with the state in their search for their missing relatives; they also confronted military and police officials when attempting to rescue their loved ones from the places where they were presumably confined; they also heard variations of the unalterable "mañana vienes" and "su documento traes" as these officers' response to their demands for the immediate release of their relatives; they also had no choice but to trust these words; they also lament having trusted these words, because they have not seen their loved ones ever since; they can also tell that, along with the disappearance of the body, something essential is disappearing in language: trust in words and conventions ("Ay mamacha, noqaka confiaranim"); they also came to know that people can disappear from the face of the earth in such a casual, matter-of-fact manner, at the snap of the state's fingers whenever the state sees itself threatened.

What is striking in the scene Mama Anki describes is the altercation between the mother and the military official in their encounter in the "space of death" (Taussig 1984). Both mobilize ordinary idioms and pictures of the bureaucratic work of the state, either to protect life or to complete an act of state violence that, according to the state's own normative order, is criminal. At the time this scene occurs, it is already well known throughout the region that the forced disappearance of alleged suspects of terrorism is usually followed by the reappearance of the victims' bodies, badly mutilated and dumped in *botaderos*. *Botaderos* such as Purakuti and Infiernillo allow everybody to see how dogs, pigs, and other scavengers complete the destruction of those human remains among swarms of *chiririnkas* (flies of death). Ayacuchano people know that the intervention of the Peruvian military has created a very efficient machine of state terror and mass killing with full impunity in the context of the state of emergency.[21]

It is not surprising, then, that the anguished mother of a young man detained and tortured in a military barrack kneels down before the commanding officer, simultaneously demanding and begging for the immediate release of her son, in a desperate gesture to rescue him from imminent death. She knows that, because of the state of emergency, the decision over the life or death of her son has become a prerogative of that officer. In the space of death that the state of emergency has opened up in the region, he has come to embody the state's sovereign power over life and death. In her anguished imploring for the life of her son, the mother goes as far as to touch that political idiom which, from colonial times, has historically connected political sovereignty with religious sovereignty to make legible and legitimize the absolute power of the state over the life and death of its subjects: "I got down on my knees, I prostrated myself as before God, saying, 'Release my son, please; return him to me' [Qunqurakuykuni diosta qina nispa: 'wawayta señor soltaykuwaychik, quykapuwaychik']."[22]

The military officer orders the mother to stand up, saying, in a typical modern gesture of authority, "Do not kneel down. We are not God. Stand up! [No estamos Dios para que rodillas; levántate!]." This gesture asserts the rational basis of the secular liberal state and evokes the widely accepted notion that there is a clear distinction between the irrational and arbitrary forms of power typical of premodern times and those based on procedure and legal rationality that are, in theory, typical of the modern liberal state. After all, the counterinsurgency war was being waged in the name of the defense of liberal values and democratic institutions. In this new fold of the altercation, the mother shifts to the state's idiom of the good citizen. Her young son is a responsible and accomplished student who is lagging in his studies as a result of his fateful encounter with the state. He is responding positively to the investment the state has made in educating him as a good citizen. The officer then retorts by charging her son with terrorism—"Your son is *terruco*"—by definition the worst crime in the eyes of the state, since it endangers its very life.

In response to the military officer's dangerous indictment, Mama Anki shifts register again and mobilizes the legal language of evidence (*prueba*) to confront the state with its own claims about the rationality governing the administration of its violence. Drawing from common understandings of what constitutes criminal evidence in Peruvian legal culture, she asserts that the military has found no incriminatory evidence in the extensive searches they conducted in her house and, consequently, that her son cannot be arbitrarily charged with terrorism. Such a serious accusation needs hard evidence, but where are these *pruebas*? Have they found any evidence that incriminates her son? The scene suggests that Mama Anki seems to accept the idea that in the state of emergency a military officer can take over the roles of both prosecutor and judge to expeditiously determine the guilt or innocence of people charged with the crime of attacking the life of the state. She even seems to accept the idea that in such a case, the state can take the life of the transgressor. But for that to happen, guilt has to be unmistakably demonstrated with *pruebas*. The state may be a godlike entity with sovereign power over life and death, but it cannot capriciously take the life of its subjects. The state of emergency may have invested the military with such sovereign power, but it cannot kill at random. It is the mother who now mobilizes the idea that a modern state has rules, procedures, and institutions to establish people's guilt or innocence and that these are especially crucial when the life of the accused is at stake.

It is at this point that the military officer resorts to the languages and images of ordinary bureaucratic paperwork ("mañana vienes"; "su documento traes") to force the mother to leave, evoking the idea that documents and rational procedures provide access to guarantees and rights. Utterances such as "mañana vienes" and "su documento traes" populate the legal, regulatory, and performative landscapes of state bureaucracy in the Peruvian Andes. Quechua-speaking peasants have become all too familiar with these bureaucratic practices and utterances; they have invested their desire for justice in the state in response to its promise that proper documentation, procedure, and rationality secure access to justice. Poole (2004) has shown how this desire for justice is usually betrayed: the documents the state demands from peasants tend to drift endlessly from office to office without being completed. For Quechua peasants, justice appears not as something that occurs as a necessary result of bureaucratic procedure, but rather as the unpredictable "slippages between threat and guarantee" that happen in those ephemeral moments when they come into contact with "the languages, institutions, spaces, and people who represent justice and the law" (ibid., 37). The utterance "mañana vienes" perhaps most clearly gives expression to the temporality that governs the life of documents drifting endlessly within the corridors of the bureaucratic machinery, but it also has become perhaps the most visible (or audible) index of the arbitrary nature of state power, moving between threat and guarantee in everyday life.

In the context of the state of emergency, the state's ordinary practices, idioms, and performances slip swiftly into death-dealing machines. The real objects trafficked within the Kafkaesque bureaucratic apparatus are not documents but human bodies—bodies that are supposedly protected by the fundamental rights and guarantees of the liberal order and whose probable final destiny is implicitly announced by the way they were taken away from home and the arbitrary charges leveled against them. In ordinary contexts, the fact that it is paperwork that is subjected to an endless drifting from jurisdiction to jurisdiction makes the experience of the "mañana vienes" bearable, often mockable, always contestable, and more crucially, deferrable in the expectation that perhaps *mañana*, in yet another encounter with the bureaucratic apparatus of the state, something distinct might actually occur. But in the context of the state of emergency, the "mañana vienes" governing the clandestine circulation of bodies does not admit deferment. There is no possible *mañana* when the lives of people detained by the military are at stake.

One can only imagine the mother's terror in facing the decision of whether to leave the barracks, leaving her son and trusting the military officer's "mañana vienes" and "su documento traes." In possession of the public knowledge of what happens to people the military kidnaps on charges of terrorism, she refuses to leave the place, knowing that at this point her presence is perhaps the only guarantee of her son's life. And yet, perhaps because of the need to protect the safety of her other children, who have come with her to the barracks, or perhaps because of the advice of the Catholic priest who has accompanied her, or perhaps because her experience with the arbitrariness of state power tells her that "mañana vienes" and "su documento traes" may perchance work in protecting the life of her son—that the state might abide by its own rules, procedures, and rationality in the administration of its justice or that the state officials might abide by their words—she reluctantly leaves the place.

Mama Anki returns to the garrison the next day, early in the morning, only to find at the checkpoint that nobody there knows anything about any detained person, that nobody has seen or heard anything, that nobody remembers anything about her visit the day before, that she perhaps had imagined or dreamed it. Thus the mother finds at the checkpoint not only that her son has disappeared, but that her desperate attempts to rescue him the day before have also vanished from reality. For the state, that encounter never happened; it could have happened only in the mother's imagination. This time, there is not even a message of "mañana vienes" and "su documento traes." This time, the mother finds plain denial—that is, the creation by means of words of a nightmarish world in which reality itself has come to be suspended.

Many years later, when retelling her experience to her peers at the excavation site, she ends this part of her story with words of lament and regret for having trusted the military officer's words. She conveys in retrospect her sense that, for her, state terror acquired a material presence by means of words. The disappearance of her son was secured not only by the state's global betrayal of its promise that documents, rules, and procedures provide access to justice, but also by the state authorities' withdrawal of responsibility for their words. Moreover, with the subsequent denial of the forced disappearance of her son, she found out that the denial was more than just deception and betrayal. She came to learn that perhaps more than the *formal* suspension of fundamental civil and political rights, the state of emergency brings about a de facto radical suspension of the usual senses and meanings of words embedded in ordinary language. In ordinary interactions, mistrust in the authorities' words is always present, since one is never certain what their will is and where it will go. But in the context of the state of emergency, their ultimate will seems to suspend reality itself by unmooring words from their usual referents in the world. In the state of emergency, language becomes simultaneously both victim and weapon of state terror.

The Disappearance of the Disappearance

Like Mama Anki, the relatives retelling their stories at the excavation site recalled that the official denial of the disappearance was for them the most intolerable and damaging aspect of the campaign of state terror. They knew from the beginning that, after being shuttled from one military or police post to another, their kidnapped loved ones would eventually be clandestinely transported to Los Cabitos. And the relatives knew that in following their loved ones' tracks, they, too, would end up gathering at the checkpoint of the military base to inquire about them and demand their release. The military would never let them past the checkpoint, and the relatives would then spend hour upon hour, day upon day, and week upon week in the area, waiting for news. It was at the checkpoint that, in response to their demands for information about the whereabouts of the captives, the distraught relatives would hear again and again that there were no detainees in the military base; that no one had seen or heard anything; that the military had nothing to do with the task of detaining suspects; that detaining people was the job of the police; that if their relatives really had been detained, then they were certainly being held in police posts; that their relatives surely had joined the terrorist ranks; and that, in fact, they had probably eloped with their lovers. Here is how Mama Isabel recalled these performances of denial:

We came to this barracks almost every day. "There is nobody here; there are no detainees [*preso*] here," the military told us. At that time, they were surely burning those detainees here, but they denied having them here: "There is nobody; there are no prisoners here; their fellow terrorists [*terrorista masin*] surely have taken them with them; surely they are terrorists and they joined the terrorist ranks." Nothing. Outright denial. We came here [Los Cabitos] with several other women. We waited and waited here, but nothing. Surely, at that time those prisoners were already here in this very site [*pampa*]; surely some of them were already killed, and the rest were burned. Oh dear God [*Ay dios mio*] . . .

Mama Isabel's final "Ay dios mio" emerges here not as a rhetorical expression of sorrow and incredulity, but rather as a testament to how words seem to fail these mothers when they attempt to describe the practices of state terror. In possession of the evidence provided by the forensic excavation, what the mother finds difficult to articulate in ordinary words during her retelling is the boundlessness of denial. It is the corroboration of the fact that at the very moment when the military was denying having captives in its barracks, they were actually torturing the detainees, extrajudicially killing them, disposing of their bodies in clandestine mass graves, and eventually burning their bodies to erase the evidence of the atrocities committed there.

The mothers never accepted the speech of denial that blamed their missing loved ones for their disappearance, and they kept insisting that the military authorities release the detainees. Because of this, they themselves were targeted by the military's war of words. This is how Mama Isabel recalled that part of the story:

They [the military] brought them here, but they denied it: "There is nobody here, there is nobody here." Total denial. We insisted: "But you have brought them here." And then they said: "You must have gone insane; you must be drunk; you are lying; you should have raised your son well so he would not become a terrorist; you yourself must be a terrorist."

The world of fantasy created by the operation of the state's denial not only suspends reality but also recasts people who uphold such realities as insane, liars, drunks, and, ultimately, terrorists. Denial reverses reality and fantasy and creates dreamlike worlds in which the state—the same state that is waging a brutal campaign of terror against perceived dissidents—appears outside any unlawful exercise of force and is portrayed as the ultimate source of order, rationality, and rights. In the fantastic world that the state's war of words creates, not only the victims are responsible for what has befallen them, but also their relatives, particularly their mothers, who have failed to properly educate them to become virtuous citizens of the state.

Unlike the language of rumor, the language of suspicion, insinuation, and culpability through which the disappeared and their families are blamed for their suffering has a signature: the signature of the state. But like rumor, this speech has been conceived to enter into and spread through the social body by infecting ordinary language with terror's talk. It has been conceived not only to govern social understandings and responses to state terror, but also, and fundamentally, to reassert the idea that state terror (if acknowledged at all) is not arbitrary or irrational. It has been conceived to paralyze the response of the victims' relatives to state terror by casting suspicion upon them only because they are relatives of suspected "terrorists." And if, as in the case of the mothers, someone contests the state's terror talk, this speech is designed to silence such contestation by presenting it as an act of madness. In the words of the state, the mothers who started to walk in the streets, calling for the release of the victims and their return home, were "irresponsible," were not able to properly educate their children, and can only be liars, madwomen, drunks, or, ultimately, terrorists themselves.[23]

The state's performative operation of mobilizing language as a weapon of state terror comes full circle with the work of the legal institutions in the context of the state of emergency. During the long hours we spent at the excavation site every day, a recurrent topic of conversation among the mothers was their ill-fated encounters with the state institutions whose discursive raison d'être is to protect the rights of citizens and enforce the rule of law. Let us listen to a fragment of the exchange that followed Mama Anki's retelling of her failed attempt to rescue her missing son from the garrison of Quicapata. Here the mothers ask Mama Anki whether she immediately went to the Fiscalía to announce that her son was being held by the military.

> Juana: Didn't you go to the Fiscalía right away?
> Anki: I went, of course!
> Eudosia: [*In Spanish*] But of course, they would not pay attention to her claims! [Qué le van a hacer caso!]
> Juana: [*In Spanish*] That's true; they would not pay attention to our claims, right?
> Eudosia: [*In Quechua*] Sure, they just would not want to do anything.
> Anki: No, they did not. They [the legal authorities] told me, "There must be some reason [por algo será]. We do not want to meddle with it [this problem] anymore; since we have been meddling too much for those *terrucos*, we've got problems and conflicts with them [the military]. We have arguments with them [the military] because of the *terrucos*, they told me.

The mothers' skepticism regarding the legal institutions' response to their plight ["qué le van a hacer caso"] is informed by their familiarity with the kinds of relations that have bound the Spanish-speaking state and indigenous Quechua-speaking rural people since colonial times. Peruvian legal culture belongs to the genealogy of the civil law tradition. It is built on the idea that the law is a hierarchical system of codes that are written to be read and that these written rules and codes equally bind and protect everybody in the political community. The promise of justice derives from the ability to read the law. In this act of reading, the authorized reader, in search of the truth, picks out some rules and norms according to certain conventions and procedures and applies them to facts to establish judgment and a decision. However, the ordinary experience of illiterate Quechua-speaking peasants with the law and the judicial system has been shaped by unwritten forms of power, such as the traditional impunity of local and national elites and the disciplinary practices through which the law is read and forensic, clinical, and legal evidence is collected (Poole 1987, 1994, 2004). Customarily, the Spanish-speaking legal authorities in Peru do not pay attention ("hacer caso") to the plight of Quechua-speaking peasants despite the written rules.

This state of affairs deteriorates further in the context of the state of emergency. At the excavation site, the mothers recall how, in their desperation to rescue their missing children, they appealed to the legal authorities, going to their offices and filing formal complaints in the hope that the legal apparatus would somehow serve to locate their missing relatives and protect them from torture and imminent death. Without such paperwork, they were told, the legal institutions would not act. Moreover, the legal authorities would ask the mothers to bring more paperwork to document the disappearance ("su documento traes"). Many years later, at the site, these mothers recall that as illiterate people, they did not know how to deal with all these written procedures and had to try to learn on the spot how to do so (Muñoz 1998, 453). They also recall that they had to walk the corridors of the Spanish-speaking legal institutions, back and forth from office to office, waiting hours for any sign or response, following the endless drift of paperwork from office to office and never finding any positive answer to their requests.

It has been thoroughly documented that the legal institutions complied with the campaign of forced disappearances by means of either negligence or plain abdication of their role in protecting citizens' fundamental rights.[24] Less documented has been the legal authorities' active involvement in the circulation of "terror's talk" (Taussig 1989) by means of ordinary language. As these mothers recall many years later, "por algo será" (there must be some reason) was the usual response they received from the legal authorities to their requests for intervention in their cases. The authorities insinuated that the disappearance could not be a random event; that if the victim was missing, it certainly was because he or she was involved in terrorism—the presupposition being, of course, that only terrorists ended up being disappeared at the hands of the state. In the relatives' memories, the legal authorities appeared to be taking for granted that the disappeared were terrorists and therefore deserved what was happening to them.

While the formal pronouncement of the law concerning the events is suspended or delayed until greater certainty can be attained—which in most cases demands more paperwork—the law makes a spurious judgment outside of any rational and legal procedure, casting blame upon the victims of the state. In a context in which the mothers were attempting to mobilize the legal institutions in the urgent task of protecting life, the perlocutionary force of "por algo será" uttered by the legal authorities acquired the force of something resembling a pronouncement of the law. When spoken by legal authorities, "por algo será" sanctions the idea that, for the law, it is not the state that must be suspected in its practices of violence and terror, but the victims themselves, who no doubt deserve their fate.

Moreover, in the picture that emerges from the mothers' retelling, the legal authorities appear to be considering issues concerning *terrucos* to be outside their jurisdiction. To inquire about the fate of the disappeared is to "meddle" with the business of the military—a view that implicitly exempts the military from the purview of the law. The mediating plane between these two jurisdictions—the jurisdiction of the law and the (unstated) jurisdiction outside the law—is the political category of terrorism. Labeling someone a terrorist, or simply casting suspicion upon that person, always already situates the victim outside the purported protection of the law. The condition of possibility for gaining the law's protection in the view of the legal authorities, as portrayed in the mothers' memories, is to be innocent of the charge of terrorism. But the determination of such innocence, in the face of the evacuation of any legal procedure that in theory guarantees the rationality of law, belongs to the domain that is outside the purview of the law and therefore depends on the arbitrariness of sovereign power.

In this sense, uttered by the legal authorities, "por algo será" acquires a perlocutionary force that completes two different, but related, tasks to consummate the disappearance: first, it recasts the arbitrary violence of the state as rational violence, and second, it redirects blame against victims and situates them in that zone of indistinction outside the purview of the law. If the law demands the exposition of the self as a condition of possibility of political action, then what we see here is an abject retreat of the law, which, rather than demanding the exposition of victims, blames them in absentia for their atrocious fate at the hands of the state.[25]

Memories of the Present

Taussig (1989) argues that terror's talk is above all a "war of silencing" that is quite different from the mere production of silence, and that the point of the silencing and the fear behind silencing is not at all to erase memory. Rather, the point is "to drive the memory deep within the fastness of the individual so as to create more fear and uncertainty in which dream and reality commingle" (ibid., 15). That the Quechua mothers of the disappeared bring vivid memories of their experiences of terror and suffering to the excavation site seems to speak to this idea: in its work of reestablishing its rule upon the social body, the state has managed to inscribe memories of terror in the fastness of the individual. And yet these memories are also full of gestures of resistance and escape from the determinations of state terror. Like others in Latin America and elsewhere, the Quechua mothers of the disappeared have struggled to resituate the "social location" of the facts of terror from the private sphere, where the state seeks to locate them, to the public sphere, where the mothers seek to place them.

The retelling of these memories at the excavation site at Los Cabitos belongs to this genealogy. As this chapter shows, in this new iteration, these memories are put to work not to imagine or reconstruct the whole of the mothers' past experience, but to emphasize those dimensions of their experience that the official denial of the disappearance of their loved ones has most devastated. And they are put into circulation once again to articulate the fact that denial, which is a conspicuous manifestation of terror's talk, has not ended with the formal end of the campaign of state terror, the transition to a postconflict democracy, and the opening of criminal investigations of past atrocities at Los Cabitos. Despite these broader political and legal changes in the country, denial continues to circulate in everyday life, infecting ordinary language to blame the disappeared and their families for their fates. In this sense, the circulation of these memories in this new iteration acquires a forensic dimension if we consider "forensic" in terms of its Latin root, *forensis*; namely, what belongs to the *forum* or the public. At the excavation, the forensic experts put material fragments in relation to one another to produce an imagination of the whole; similarly, in their storytelling, the mothers put fragments of life in relation to one another to produce an imagination of the specific conditions (social, political, and cultural) that underwrite denial of the disappearance from its beginnings until the present.

We can now see why the experience of forced disappearance cannot be reduced to the framework of trauma. The repetitive character of the mothers' stories does not speak of an unclaimed experience that finds expression only through the mechanical and compulsive repetition of the traumatic situation. Rather, it speaks of their forensic, that is, public, character. Through repetition, these stories have been working ever since the moment of the "last seen" to resituate the social location of the facts of terror from the private sphere, where the state seeks to locate them, to the public sphere, where they belong. The forensic evidence found at Los Cabitos backs these mothers' claims of truth and opens up a new space from which they can continue their political reckoning with state terror as a means of establishing conditions of possibility for justice. In the next chapter, I explore another political dimension of their experience, namely, how in their struggle against state terror they have become a collective subject.

5

Caprichakuspa
Witnessing Before Terror

Warmilla caprichakuspa purimuyku [It was women who walked, stubbornly disobedient].
　　—Mama Isabel

ONE DAY AT noon in late October 2006, Mama Isabel and I approached the edge of the excavation site to observe the progress the archaeologists had made during the morning. The experts were taking a short lunch break and had left the carefully dug *cuadrillas* (trenches) open to plain sight. From the edge, we could see the parts of human skeletons, fragments of burned human bones, heaps of ashes, and other human remains they had exposed in almost two weeks of work. Another season of excavation was coming to an end, and while the experts had made enormous progress in uncovering hard evidence concerning the blast furnace in which human remains presumably had been incinerated, they had not been able to find any new complete bodies beyond those they had found in earlier seasons. All they had managed to expose this time were more human remains scorched to ashes.

Contemplating this scene of devastation, Mama Isabel began to retell stories of similar scenes she had observed during the early years of the counterinsurgency campaign in the 1980s, perhaps one of the darkest moments in the recent history of the region and the country. In those days, the military regularly dumped piles of cadavers in what the people in Ayacucho came to know as *botaderos*—the spaces at the outskirts of the city where the military disposed of the mutilated bodies of those who dared to challenge sovereign power—and the mothers searched for their missing children in these places. Mama Isabel recalled the first time she had gone to one called Infiernillo,¹ where she saw a scene that still haunts her: seven bodies with visible traces of torture and shots to the skull; dogs and pigs had been eating these bodies in the midst of swarms of *chiririnkas* (flies of death). Despite their damaged state, Mama Isabel could see that five of the bodies were male and the other two were female. That is all she would ever know about them. There was exhaustion in her words as she talked about those unknown shattered bodies, as if the words that came into contact with the material remnants of atrocity also ended up burned and numb.

Mama Angélica joined us at the edge of the excavation (Figure 5.1); she, too, associated the scenes of devastation before us with those they had seen in the *botaderos*. She, too, started to retell stories about those early experiences, but unlike Mama Isabel she preferred to speak in her Quechua-inflected Spanish, as if to ensure that I did not miss any of her words. In retelling these scenes, her words nonetheless sounded similarly exhausted. At one point, however, after alluding to the violence those bodies and the

FIGURE 5.1. Mothers of the disappeared at the edge of the forensic excavation at Los Cabidos, October 2006.

ones before us must have endured—badly tortured, executed, and ultimately ground to dust—Mama Angélica's voice gathered force from some deep recess of life to say: "This is not small to just forget it. Not considering they [the victims] were people, human people . . . Okay, one can punish . . . one can make them suffer; but, doctor, to kill them in such a way . . . that is what *capricha* me strongly [Eso no es poco para olvidar. A pesar gente, gente humano . . . Bueno, puede castigar; allí puede sufrir, pero matar esa forma, doctor . . . Eso me capricha fuertemente]."

The word *capricha* expresses a gendered form of agency that emerges against the intolerable, the passage of time, and the weaknesses of memory (Marks 2003). It has no direct translation into English because it is one of those words that bridge two languages, Spanish and Quechua. The word has Spanish roots, and Mama Angélica uses it as a verb, which in the infinitive form would be *caprichar*. And yet, the verb *caprichar* does not exist in Spanish. The closest would be the pronominal verb *encapricharse*, which in English is translated as either "to develop a crush on; to take a fancy to" or "to persist in; to insist on." In this second connotation, the verb *encapricharse* evokes ideas of being stubborn, which is the primary sense in which Mama Angélica uses the word. A second word similar to *caprichar* is the Spanish noun *capricho*, which in English is translated as "whim," "(passing) fancy," or "caprice." *Capricho* evokes senses of desire, which are also present in Mama Angélica's use of the word *caprichar*.

The ethnographic record sheds more light on how Quechua-speaking people in Peru's rural Andes use the term. In her work in the Southern Andes, Robin (2008) found the notion of *capricho* attached to the distinction Quechua peasants make between the sexes. In this view, women have seven souls whereas men have only three, and having more souls makes women more "capricious" and/or "stubborn" than men—a difference that alludes to an ontological distinction. As Robin (2008, 51) says, "a narrow-minded or unruly character would be determined by the number of souls a person has,"[2] echoing the Andean idea that the concentration of soul—vital force—influences the general condition and force of an individual's character. Robin shows that the idea of women having more souls than men is a male representation—which does not necessarily mean that women do not participate in it. It manifests a male anxiety about establishing gender difference by attributing to women characteristics that men would not possess, say, unreasonableness, unruliness, narrow-mindedness, stubbornness, and volatility.

In the context of the state of exception, *capricharse* acquires political salience to index the gendered dimensions of the internal war. Because the term connotes senses of stubbornness, unruliness, and unreasonableness, it is mobilized to reenact the long-standing distinction between the "political" and the "prepolitical." On one hand, it is put in circulation to berate, confine, diminish, and ultimately govern particular forms of (female) political action. On the other hand, the Quechua-speaking mothers of the disappeared occupy the subject positions the term entails to contest the practices of state terror during the counterinsurgency campaign. *Capricharse* is the only way these mothers have to forcefully question and challenge the sense that, in the name of defending the body politic, the sovereign can go beyond any limit and subsume everything, including the rights of the dead. *Capricharse* is their response to state atrocity, previously during the internal war and now during forensic excavation of the truth of state atrocity.[3]

In this chapter I explore the gendered dimensions of the response to state violence and terror. In particular, I interrogate the long-standing wisdom that women engage politics in contexts of violence motivated only by their desire to protect the sacred rights of their families as opposed to the rights of the sovereign. As is well known, Hegel (1999) most eloquently articulated this polar opposition in his reading of the Greek myth of Antigone. In his view, the state is the intrinsic source of rationality and preoccupation with the entire body politic, while its subjects, particularly women, possessed by irrational love for their families, are able to act only in terms of their lineage and descent.[4] Hegel thus confines Antigone's agency to the realm of the prepolitical sphere of the family as opposed to the political sphere of the community.

In Peru, the action of the Quechua-speaking mothers of the disappeared has also been portrayed as motivated by their passionate love for their family and has thus been situated in the realm of the prepolitical. The CVR, for instance, recognized the "persistence" of these mothers and concluded: "Even in the worst moments, with tenacity and bravery these women kept alive the flame of hope for the recovery of their loved ones, and that justice would be applied to those responsible for the disappearances" (Comisión de la Verdad y Reconciliación 2004, conclusions 147 and 148). The prepolitical character of these mothers' actions is further confirmed by the fact that, in the racialized and gendered hierarchy of Peru's political culture, they are seen as "more Indian" and, as such, as unable to enter the game of modern politics.[5] The CVR, again, offers an example of this view by asserting that the victims' organizations were "relatively weak" because most were composed of "poor peasants with little consciousness of their rights, for whom access to justice was difficult, and who had weak social networks with few urban contacts." The CVR concluded that this weakness "worked to the advantage of impunity for the perpetrators of human rights violations and crimes" (Comisión de la Verdad y Reconciliación 2004, conclusion 147).

By contrast, in this chapter I show how these mothers started and persisted in their search for their missing loved ones out of their love for them; but in this search they ended up engaging the crucial question concerning the possibility of political community in the face of forms of state violence that have gone beyond the thresholds of life and death within which Andean people test what a human form of life is. The decisive experience here is their becoming a collective subject by means of which they engage the sovereign in terms of movement and escape, as opposed to the sovereign's search for stasis as a crucial means of political control. There is thus a double witnessing: how to relate, in terms of escape and movement, to the sovereign's mercurial power to kill in the state of exception; and how, in this gesture of disobedience as a form of political action, these mothers' mobilization in the context of the state of exception evokes the figure of the people walking away from the sovereign's binding and shepherding powers.

I start with the question of what the intolerable is for these mothers in the state's practices of killing. Then I offer an account of the ways these mothers render their collective mobilization against state terror as a gesture of disobedience. I go on to show how they encounter and confront sovereign power in the space of death and how, in their gesture of walking away from the sovereign, they evoke the figure of the people. I further show how the sovereign's effort to send them back home has a male counterpart in the domestic sphere; and I conclude by showing how, because of their resilient collective mobilization, these mothers are eventually able to politically and historically indict the sovereign's practices of the "fabrication of corpses" from the very site of atrocity.

The Intolerable

To delineate the contours of the intolerable against which *capricharse* emerges as a gendered response to state terror, let us return to the scene at the edge of the excavation site. Mama Isabel and Mama Angélica were recalling their earlier experience confronting unprecedented forms of state violence. Of course, violence and death came from both the Shining Path and the state. In a horrific pedagogy of terror, mutilated bodies thrown in public sites to rot before everybody's gaze became the main visual language the contending forces used to communicate their political projects. On one hand, the Shining Path typically killed opponents in theatrical displays of power that encompassed maiming their bodies and prohibiting their burial, while also carrying on punitive strikes against villages that fought back. On the other hand, the Peruvian military massacred Andean villagers whom it considered supporters of the Shining Path, disappeared terrorism suspects, and established the infamous *botaderos*.

Anthropologists have documented the brutal impact this visual politics of dead bodies had on the population. Theidon (2006, 438), for instance, aptly argues that the war in rural Ayacucho was experienced as a "cultural revolution," that is, as "an attack against cultural practices and the very meaning of what it is to live as human beings in these villages." She emphasizes how people were forced to leave their dead loved ones wherever they had fallen, returning, if they could, only to "bury them hurriedly like animals" (ibid.).[6] At the excavation site, the relatives of the disappeared recalled those moments of violence, terror, and death. For instance, here is how Mariela, whose brother was disappeared in the early 1980s, retold her story:

Almost every single day there were dead people. That was not news anymore. When we went to the school early in the morning, we used to run into killed people thrown in the streets early. Sometimes those bodies were hanging on electrical posts showing signs of knife cuts. Sometimes when my mother asked me to go to the grocery store, I also encountered dead bodies. It was horrible. At the beginning we were terrified, but then, after a while, the kids got used to it. Conversely, we used to run where killed bodies were found to find out who had been killed that day. It was as if it were a game . . . We were traumatized, but then not that much.

At the time, Mariela was a little girl. Her retelling at the excavation site conveys how the world as she had known it had been turned upside down—not only because of the sudden irruption of terror at home, materialized in the forced disappearance of her brother, but also because the gory scenes of mutilated unknown bodies in the streets had gradually become part of the landscape of her everyday life. At some point, she and other children started to be at once "traumatized" and "not traumatized" by these scenes of terror, taking their encounters with atrocious death as a matter of play—a scene that captures the blurring of limits between the ordinary and extraordinary that came with the eruption of violence in urban Ayacucho. Reflecting upon these scenes, the relatives at the site conveyed the sense that the true horror for them was not so much (or not only) having witnessed indiscriminate killing, as having started to get used to it. Horror, for them, lies in the gradual conversion of unspeakable mutilation into something usual, as if such mutilation had to be accepted as part and parcel of everyday life and as if numbness and paralysis were the only way to survive the material presence of terror. Horror lies in the realization that basic fabrics of meaningful social relations in everyday life were being shattered before their eyes and they not only could do nothing about it, but had started to get used to it.

In his study of violence and memory in the Upper Huallaga valley, Kernaghan (2009) says that violence was aimed at the whole population as a method of "making a people." The boundary-marking use of violence that he calls "the political" aimed at "forging a new collective and shaping the individual subjectivities that will fall within through the designation, discovery, and the elimination of public enemies that fall outside" (ibid., 123). The political requires violence, Kernaghan argues, but not all violence involves the political. The violence of the political was channeled through the display of human corpses that proclaimed a new law in the making.[7] Those images circulate along two temporal strata—wartime and postwar times—and do different kinds of sense-making work corresponding to different political conditions. But as Kernaghan suggests, senses of the intolerable are associated with violence both as experience and as memory. From the perspective of townspeople—that is, from the perspective of the population—living through the violence and later remembering it, what is (was) intolerable is (was) not violence per se, "but violence with no clear course" (ibid., 208).

During my work as a human rights activist in the late 1980s and 1990s, I frequently heard these kind of comments concerning senseless violence encapsulated in rhetorical formulas such as "matar por matar" (killing for no purpose). Ordinary people living under the state of exception, but not directly affected by violence, soon learned to navigate danger by learning to read the signs of this violence. In a context of existential threat, they rapidly crafted a sense of orientation that allowed them to anticipate atrocious death. But whenever such violence appeared or became utterly random, this sense of orientation disappeared, and terror engulfed their everyday lives. Kernaghan is right in saying that the townspeople find (found) this senseless violence intolerable. In the balance of terror, the violence of the state not only was the most feared, but also eventually appeared as having sense. Rhetorical formulas such as "por algo será" (there must be a reason) served to connect the rationality of the state and its atrocious violence.

From the perspective of the mothers of the disappeared, the picture of the intolerable is of a different nature. Mama Angélica's comment, "Okay, one can punish . . . one can make them suffer; but, doctor, to kill them in such a way?" conveys a sense of what these mothers consider intolerable in the practices of state violence. The sense of these words is that the state can legitimately inflict pain and suffering upon the transgressor's body, and these words even seem to suggest that, in extreme situations, when its life is at stake, the state can kill the transgressor. However, in punishing transgression to its rule, the state cannot go beyond the agreed-upon human forms of life that it is supposed to protect and, ultimately, embody. At sites such as the *botaderos*, these mothers saw human bodies desecrated and destroyed beyond recognition. At Los Cabitos, they see more human bodies pulverized and desecrated beyond any recognizable human form (Figure 5.2). These are the bodies of the disappeared. It is these violations of the human body that the mothers see as, echoing Veena Das (2007, 90), "being 'against nature,' as defining the limits of life itself."

Transgressing and defying the rule of the state entails risking reprisal that may involve death, but in the view of these mothers nothing justifies the disappearance or utter destruction of the body. This idea came up over and over in our conversations at the excavation site. Mama Natividad, for instance, once said: "Even if it were true that our sons were involved [with the guerrillas], they [the army] should have killed them and thrown their bodies at the front door of our houses. We would have just buried them, crying and pained, but with our hearts in peace knowing where our relatives were." There is a sense of boundary here. The intolerable for these mothers is not whether violence makes sense, or has lost its clear course, but whether, in the task of (re)constituting a population subject to sovereign power, violence can go beyond some thresholds within which Andean peoples test what a human form of life is. The intolerable for the mothers is not that the state can kill, but that in punishing transgression against its rule, the sovereign assumes the right to vanish the bodies of

FIGURE 5.2. Charred fragments and ashes of human bones at Los Cabitos, October 2006.

suspected transgressors in the ways that occurred at Los Cabitos, to the point that these victims were put beyond the reach of any agreed-upon form of human action that might somehow redeem their memory. As we have seen these ideas echo Arendt's (1968) notion of the "fabrication of corpses." At Los Cabitos, the intolerable is that not only were individuals' lives anonymously taken away, but their deaths and the memory of their deaths were also eliminated. The victims were subjected to forms of asocial death—death without mourning, rituals of remembrance, and even grief; death robbed of its meaning as the end of a fulfilled life.

Caprichakuspa Purimuyku

These mothers awoke to this problem—that is, the problem pertaining to the question of whether the violence of "the political" can subsume everything, including the funerary rites of the dead, thus endangering the possibility of being together with others in society—only when they found that their suffering was also the suffering of other mothers and started a collective search for their disappeared. This collective dimension animates their *capricharse* against what they see as intolerable in the practices of state violence. This awakening resembled a kind of brutal "initiation" through which these mothers transfigured themselves from being townspeople (a population learning to navigate violence to avoid lethal encounters with it) to people (subjects who, defending life, openly contest violence and atrocity.)

The mothers' brutal initiation with state terror typically started when the military stormed their houses to take away a family member for "interrogation" (see Chapter 4). The prospect of never seeing that family member again prompted these mothers to start a frantic search for their missing relatives. The manner in which victims were taken away announced a brutal destiny for them. Inevitably they would be tortured and most probably killed. Their mutilated bodies would then be thrown in the *botaderos* to rot before everybody's gaze. The mothers (as townspeople) knew that such was the typical fate of the disappeared. This terrifying prospect brought the mothers to the street. This is how Mama Isabel recalls those moments:

At the very beginning, the mothers of those who were taken away from their homes first stayed in that *parque* [small town square] without knowing what to do . . . We were there just crying. Then we started to talk to each other: "What happened to you?"; "My son is missing"; "My son is missing too," we told each other, crying. "What are we going to do now?" we asked ourselves. "We will file a complaint," we said. Always crying. Then we said we would return the next day to do it. "Yes, *mamay*, we will return tomorrow, but how are we going to do it? They [the Intelligence Service] are persecuting us." They did not want us to gather and talk. "We will stand silently, and we will talk in passing, two people at a time," we planned. After that, we started to meet daily.

In this scene, the mother, out of grief, suddenly moves from the private sphere of home to the public sphere of the street. Her sense is of having been suddenly uprooted from home and thrown onto a landscape of devastation, lost in pain and tears, not knowing what to do, where to go, whom to ask, or how to start the search for her loved one. She began to wander aimlessly. In the street she finds other women who have also been suddenly exiled from home, and they start to share their agony, even in a mode of confession, recognizing each other in the street by their tears and the visible signs that pain had started to inscribe on their bodies.

The face-to-face encounter of mothers in the street and their mutual acknowledgment of their common suffering were the beginnings of their collective mobilization. Harassed and persecuted by the secret services, they started to meet surreptitiously, inventing forms of meeting that would help them escape the military surveillance that sought to prevent their gathering and coordination.[8] Such meetings were always in the street—sometimes in squares and other times in markets, at front doors of public institutions, in churches, or simply at any crossroads. They were always quick encounters just to exchange information about their incursions to the *botaderos* or to coordinate legal demands, and it was always women who participated in this mobilization. Mama Isabel recalls this gendered collective mobilization: "It was women who walked [*puriy*]. Men did not walk. Men should not walk in those dangerous times. It was only women who walked *caprichakuspa* [stubbornly disobedient] [*warmilla caprichakuspa purimuyku*]. Then, other women began to show up more and more [Warmilla masta puriniku, mana karika purinchu, mana karika peligrowan purinmanchu, warmilla caprichakuspa purimuyku. Chaymanta mastaña, astaña rikuriyku]." Many years later, reflecting on their earlier experiences, the Quechua-speaking mothers of the disappeared articulate their mobilization in search for their missing relatives as an act of willful, gendered disobedience (*caprichakuspa*) in response to the practices of terror of the patriarchal state. Let us consider the senses encapsulated in the expression *warmilla caprichakuspa purimuyku*.

In its basic form, the Quechua verb *puriy* denotes movement.[9] It can be translated as "to walk," "to go," or "to wander," among other related senses. As a noun, *puriy* denotes senses such as "conduct [behavior]," "current [flow]," or "functioning." In ordinary contexts, *puriy* appears in a dense variety of uses that fall into the realms of the moral, the technical, and the political. For instance, accompanied by an adjective of value such as *allin* (good), *puriy* becomes a verb denoting moral behavior, as in *allin puriy* (to behave rightly) or *mana allin puriy* (to behave badly). It also refers to the idea of functioning, as in *purich'qanmi* (it is functioning) or to the notion of current as in *mayu puriy* (river's flow). We also find *maypapas puriy*, which denotes wandering or roaming. In the context of the internal war, this is the sense Quechua peasants use to denote the guerrillas. Throughout rural Ayacucho, villagers referred to the Shining Path as *tuta puriq* (those who roam at night) or, simply, *puriqkuna* (those who roam).

In her analysis of these terms, Theidon (2006, 443; 2001, 548) privileges the perspective of a house-centered morality present in some uses of the notion in northern rural Ayacucho. In her view, villagers used both *tuta puriq* and *puriqkuna* to index the "inhumanity" of the members of the Shining Path, or, more precisely, their having fallen "out of humanity." In the first case, *tuta puriq* equates Shining Path members with the *condenados* (the damned souls)—those asocial, monstrous, and sinful ghosts that wander in the *puna* haunting living human beings. In the second case, *puriqkuna* refers to those who are always walking, those who never remain in one place—"transgressive people who are out of place, not belonging anywhere." Theidon sees these transgressive wandering figures as acting in opposition to what, in her interpretation, is the index of humanity for Andean peoples; that is, to have a home and family. Humans have ties with both people and places.[10] Thus, she associates *puriy* with moral transgression—with having gone astray or deviated from a moral course. Those who wander (*puriy*) and are out of place have fallen out of the human moral community.

The experience of the illiterate Quechua mothers of the disappeared offers an entirely different picture. We may say that in their case, *puriy* (walking) does not index deviation from a moral course and that, on the contrary, it is because of a moral imperative and their bonds with their children that these women leave their "proper" place at home and wander in search of their missing loved ones. As we have seen in Hegel's discussion of Antigone, we may say that they were possessed by their ethical responsibility toward their family members.[11] But their *puriy* is more than just a moral action. It is true that these mothers leave home and go to the streets out of their individual grief and suffering, but in the streets they find that their collective *puriy* is the only possible way for them to attempt to rescue their children. Since this collective *puriy* directly confronts the state, it becomes a political and not merely a moral movement, and these mothers begin to walk (*puriy*), stubbornly disobedient (*caprichakuspa*), on political tracks that are customarily reserved for men.

Puriy as a form of engagement with the state is a familiar image in Quechua-speaking Andean communities. As Sharma and Gupta (2006, 17) say, people's encounters with the state shape their imagination of what the state is and how it is demarcated "but also enable people to devise strategies of resistance to this imagined state." People learn to use the same bureaucratic techniques that alienate them from official justice to gain institutional access, subvert official scrutiny, and further legal procedure, or simply to establish authority over others. Poole (2004) shows that in Peru's Andes, the "drifting" of paperwork from one state office to another for years without being finalized indexes the kind of relationship that binds peasants to a state whose promise of justice takes the form of endless procedures and inconclusive filing of written documents. Yet despite the law's self-referentiality, peasants continue to assert claims on the state and its promise of justice by learning to navigate the Kafkaesque paroxysm of procedure.[12] *Puriy* belongs to this repertoire. If paperwork "drifts" from one state office to another, peasants wander (*puriy*) behind this paperwork in a stubborn attempt to gain some form of justice from the state. *Puriy* is the flip side of "drifting."

As most Andean ethnographers know, local authorities are not usually in town because they are doing business in the district or provincial capital. Villagers refer to these out-of-town political activities with the Spanish verb *gestionar* or the Quechua verb *puriy*.[13] And when *gestionar* does not work, *puriy* also serves to denote social protest. In this political sense, *puriy* has the positive connotation of assuming public responsibility and putting oneself in motion to obtain something from the central authorities in the context of Peru's highly hierarchical and ritualized forms of power and the state's "rule by abandon" (Heilman 2010, 9). An effective *puriy* is valued in these communities, and whoever shows it usually holds a position of authority. It usually involves gift exchange and other networking mechanisms, and it particularly demands the ability to speak and write in Spanish, as well as familiarity with the state bureaucracy's procedures, tropes, and performances of authority. Thus, an effective *puriy* demands particular forms of symbolic, cultural, and social capital that enable Quechua-speaking people to deal with the Spanish-speaking state's proceduralism and reliance on literacy and written documents.

Since this proceduralism and reliance on literacy and written documents shape, encode, and reinforce class, ethnic, and gender privileges in the Andes, *puriy* is gendered. As mentioned above, most indigenous Quechua-speaking women are monolingual and illiterate and come from peasant backgrounds and are therefore seen as "more Indian" in the racialized and gendered hierarchy of Peru's dominant political culture (de la Cadena 1995, 2000). It is taken for granted that state officials do not pay attention to women's petitions, so men are usually in charge of the community's affairs. Quechua-speaking men customarily have some level of literacy, are bilingual, and have experience with state institutions such as the army. Thus, typically, men walk in the public sphere conducting political business while women stay at home taking care of the household.

These everyday practices of the Spanish-speaking state always already determine this sexual division of labor in political affairs and are legitimized and reenacted by discourses associating ethnic, class, and gender identity with place. As de la Cadena (2000) shows, Peruvian intellectuals have imagined the indigenous Quechua-speaking woman's place in the nation-state in a variety of ways. The *indigenista* variant of the early twentieth century imagined that the proper place of the Indian woman is the rural community where she can preserve the purity of the race. The *neoindianista* variant of the 1930s imagined the mestizo woman (the *chola*) as the prototype of Peruvian racial formation. The populist imagination of the mid-twentieth century, purporting to eliminate racial thinking by privileging class analysis, subsumed the figure of the Andean woman within the broad class category of "peasant." Despite their differences, these hegemonic discourses all postulate that the Indian woman's proper place is at home under the control of the right kind of man.[14] Here I emphasize two images that run through these discourses: first, the image of a woman out of her "proper" place as a source of transgression and social disorder; and second, the image of women's collective action as irrational, emotional, and premodern (because it entails being out of their "proper" place), as opposed to men's, which is rational, enlightened, and modern. In short, by establishing a distinction between prepolitical and political action, these hegemonic discourses always already situate Indian women's collective action at the margins of the modern political community, and more so if they are illiterate and monolingual.

The relentless, extensive, and systematic attack of state terror against the family and kinship makes unsustainable any house-centered morality and, paradoxically, releases female political agency from its cultural, moral, and ideological containers. When the campaign of state terror sent scores of women to the streets in search of sons, brothers, fathers, or husbands, the military authorities found themselves with the problem of what to do with these unruly women who were now populating public space despite efforts to send them back home (*caprichakuspa*). Their counterinsurgency strategy sought to break social solidarity and paralyze society by terror, localizing people at fixed places and stilling their movements. But the result was the opposite: hundreds of women surreptitiously started gathering in the streets, overcoming their fear, to support each other, exchange information, coordinate action, file paperwork, visit the offices of the legal authorities to demand their intervention, wait at checkpoints for long hours to demand a response from the police and military authorities, visit hospitals and prisons, run to places where new corpses were being found, and infiltrate the *botaderos* to find out whether their relatives' bodies had been thrown there. In short, as they started to walk in search of their missing relatives, the Quechua-speaking mothers of the disappeared started to develop forms of sociality and political practice that the military authorities then sought to break and paralyze by terror. This is what the phrase "*warmilla caprichakuspa purimuyku*" encapsulates.

Ingold and Vergunst (2008, 1) contend that walking is a profoundly social activity, that in their timings, rhythms, and inflections, the feet respond as much as the voice does to the presence and activity of others: "Social relations, we maintain, are not enacted *in situ* but are paced out along the ground." In their walking (*puriy*), the Quechua mothers of the disappeared are responding to the voices, presence, and activity of others and are receiving responses from these others; they are enacting social relations that come to constitute a collective response to the individualizing and paralyzing practices of terror. They are not just responding to the state's attack as members of kinship networks—their response is not simply a response from a collection of individual families; rather, it is a response from a new collective entity that (à la Durkheim) emerges from the social interactions they have while walking.

This moving collective entity has the form of not an organism, but a band—at least during the early years of the counterinsurgency campaign, when the number of disappearances peaked in the region. Recalling Deleuze and Guattari's (1987, 358) description of a band, we can say that the mothers' collective response was more a machine of "immanent relations" than an organism with stable powers. Their walking (*puriy*) was of the rhizome type rather than of the arborescent type. The mothers became an organization only after some time had passed and they had begun to encounter modern human rights institutions. Under the influence of these institutions' modern languages and practices, the mothers transfigured their walking (*puriy*) to make it more suitable for formal interaction with modern state institutions.[15]

This image of a band of unruly women disobeying the sovereign (*warmilla caprichakuspa purimuyku*) evokes the idea of walking away from the social contract that, in modern theories of the state, binds a political community's subjects to sovereign power. John Dewey's (2012) concept of "the public" will help us here. As Bennett (2010) puts it, the public for Dewey consists of a "confederation of bodies" that are drawn near to one another not so much by choice as by a shared experience of harm that, over time, coalesces into a "problem." The public is not a social organization, nor do the members of the public belong already to the same community. What they share is that they are all affected by the same problem. In that sense, a public does not preexist its particular problem but emerges in response to it and lasts as long as such a problem persists. Problems emerge as a result of conjoint action.[16] Thus, not only is a public a temporary association but also there are different publics coexisting around different kinds of problems.

With their collective walking, the Quechua mothers constitute a public in the sense Dewey gives to the notion—that is, a public systematically cares for the consequences of a conjoint action that has become a problem. But it is the problem around which they walk that makes the public that the mothers constitute not just different from others but assume the figure of the people as opposed to that of the population. The problem is whether in the name of defending the body politic, the state can go as far as destroying fundamental agreements in forms of life upon which such a body politic claims to be erected. While the population joins the action of the state by means of justifying and finding rationality in the consequences of the campaign of state terror ("por algo será"), the mothers bring to the fore of the public arena the central question of the limits of sovereignty in constituting a body politic. While the population does not care for the lethal consequences of conjoint action, the mothers walk away from the formula of sovereignty encapsulated in the campaign of state terror. Let us explore further the image of the Quechua-speaking mother walking away from the rule of the (male, Spanish-speaking) sovereign.

Viejas Locas (Mad Old Women)

As in the myth of Antigone, the sovereign cannot bear to see a woman commanding rule.[17] The Peruvian state responded to the mothers' *puriy* by mobilizing images of female irrationality and immorality—images that drew on long-established male fears and anxieties that equate a woman out of her "proper" place with transgression and social disorder.

These anxieties were heightened by the fact that the women who were out of their proper places in this case were Indian women walking in overt challenge to the sovereign's rule. Thus state authorities went beyond simply not paying attention to these women's claims (*no hacer caso*) and blaming them for not having properly raised their children; they also mobilized a gendered and racialized war of words. This war of words presented the mothers as the "irrational and immoral other" that needed to be sent back home to reconstitute the order that the insurgency had altered.

Furthermore, in these attempts to send them back home, the military authorities used, or threaten to use, force against these women. This was particularly the case when these mothers entered the stages (the *botaderos*) where the sovereign exhibited the shattered bodies of the enemy that could be seen but not approached. The mothers were the only ones who dared to go to the *botaderos*. Walking in search of their missing relatives had become dangerous, and the mothers were well aware of these dangers. In our conversations at the excavation site, they recalled the various strategies they had used to avoid military surveillance. The expression *paca pacalla purimuyku* (we walked to those places behind their backs) encapsulates the sense behind their strategies. But sometimes, they could not avoid confrontations with the sovereign. Here is how Mama Angélica recalls one of those moments:

> Angélica: (*In Spanish*) I went to Purakuti [a *botadero*], *mamá*. I arrived and searched everywhere in the *huayco* [hollow]. I found a hole there, a very deep hole. I saw swarms of flies [*chiririnkas*] hovering around it. Then, I bent into the hole and cried the name of my son, "Arquimedes," in tears, thinking that maybe he was there *deshauciando*[18] . . . Then, "*paq, paq*," bullets burst around me. When I looked at—*mamá*, at that time, there were no houses at all in Purakuti; it was a wasteland that was full of cadavers dumped all around. Nowadays, Purakuti is full of houses—
>
> Isabel: (*Interrupting in Quechua*) Yes, at that time there were just maguey shrubs all around. There were no houses at all.
>
> Angélica: (*In Spanish*) Then they yelled at me, "Get out from there, fucking old lady, or we will kill you right there." "Kill me," I responded meanly. "Kill me, you fucking shit. Where is my son?" At that time, *mamá*, I am not afraid of being killed, truly. I am not afraid of dying. Then, after too much pressure and threats from them, I got out. Then, in the Purakuti flat ground, all these soldiers surrounded me [*murallado*]. "You crazy old lady. We will shoot

you [*fusilar*]." I replied, "Yes, I am crazy; I became crazy because of my son. Where is my son?" I retorted. "I have five *soles* in my pocket"—at that time five *soles* was some money—"I have five *soles* in my pocket. You might say 'I want to shoot that old lady, but I will waste my bullets on her'; but I am going to pay you for your bullets to shoot me. But, first, show me my son. Only then will I die in peace." I told them so. Then, one of the privates dared to say, "Do not do that to that poor lady; we all are born from a mother." He had not finished saying that yet, when his fellow soldiers started to beat him. Then all of them surrounded me, threatening, "Do not waste time; let's shoot the crazy old woman." A captain then arrived and said, "Okay, leave that lady alone; send her home in a car." I refused: "I do not want it, sir; I do not need it. I have feet; I have eyes to walk by myself. Thanks, but what I need is my son. You give me back my son." I escaped in this way, *mamacita*. They wanted to kill me.

To descend into the *botaderos* was to assume that missing loved ones were dead. However, as Mama Angélica's retelling shows, these women entered those spaces of death with the agonizing hope of somehow finding a remaining shred of life. In the scene she recalls, Mama Angélica cries out the name of her missing son, hoping that he is still able to respond. As the word *desahuciando* conveys, this was a hope against hope.[19] Mama Angélica's use of *desahuciando* carries two senses simultaneously. In one sense, the word conveys the idea that her missing son's body may have been evicted, or thrown into this space of death. In another sense, *desahuciando* conveys the idea that while he may have been irremediably condemned to death, he is not dead *yet* (as someone who is terminally ill is not dead yet). In a space of death where exposed, mutilated corpses proclaim the brutal violation inflicted upon them, the mother hopes against hope for just one word or a slight movement indicating that life somehow still exists here. But the only response that greets her is silence and swarms of excessive numbers of flies that index the material reality of excessive death.[20]

The warning shots the sentinels fired toward Mama Angélica announce that she has not only descended into the space of death, but also entered the stage of the sovereign; they announce that she is not only transgressing the sovereign's law, but also disrupting the staging of his power. In this space of death, her life is at the mercy of the sovereign; she can be killed without legal consequences or disappeared without a trace and without a witness (Agamben 1998). Yet in this scene, Mama Angélica's transgression does not immediately condemn her to death. The sentinels threaten her with death in an effort to force her out of the sovereign's stage, where shattered unknown bodies were intended to be seen but not approached or retrieved for burial. It is not only an ominous visual statement of the fate that awaits those who dare to challenge the sovereign power, but also an assertion that getting close to the dead means risking getting killed too: "Get out from there, fucking old lady, or we will kill you right there [sal carajo vieja, o ahí nomás vamos a matar]."[21]

The confrontation that follows evokes the myth of Antigone in terms of the emergence of a gendered voice on the stage of the sovereign and at the moment of transgression. The illiterate Quechua-speaking mother not only challenges the Spanish-speaking male sovereign to make good on his threat, but also questions him—face to face, in his own language, and in the same space of death where he has staged the plenitude of his power—about the whereabouts of her missing son: "Kill me, you fucking shit. Where is my son? [Mátame, mierda. ¿Dónde está mi hijo?]." In search of her missing son, Mama Angélica not only defies the sovereign's prohibition by entering that zone where the distinction between life and death is entirely up to his will, but also questions him about the limits of his power ("¿Dónde está mi hijo?"). It is an act of stubborn challenge (*caprichakuspa*) to the sovereign's power over life and death.

The sovereign sees the mother's gesture of defiance to his power as an act of madness. The sentinels surround her, announcing that they will end this act of madness by shooting the madwoman on the spot: "You crazy old lady. We will shoot you [Vieja loca. Vamos a fusilar]." In response to this interpellation to her as a madwoman, the mother assumes the new subject position, but only to reverse the sovereign's claims and confront him again with his own crime: "Yes, I am crazy; I became crazy because of my son [Si, loca por mi hijo]."[22] She reasserts the strength of the maternal bond, which society widely demands and otherwise celebrates. If she has become a madwoman, it is because the sovereign has vanished her son from the face of the earth without a trace, and she is demanding that the sovereign account for her son's whereabouts. A human body cannot simply vanish from the face of the earth without a trace, in the name of protecting the political community from a vital threat. Her madness denounces the criminality underlying the state's order.[23]

In a further gesture of defiance, the mother offers to pay the sentinels for the material costs of her execution, since they presumably believe that killing her is inconsequential. Here the mother touches on the cultural grammars of gender, class, race, ethnicity, and age that always already situate Indian women in a position of political insignificance within the Spanish-speaking political community. Defining the contours of the political community and establishing the social contract are issues for men—more precisely, for white, urban, educated Spanish-speaking men. An old, illiterate, Quechua-speaking peasant Indian woman—who, in addition, has gone mad—cannot represent any serious threat to the power of the sovereign. And yet, the mother challenges the sovereign to take her life if he pleases—but only if he can first bring her missing son back from wherever he has placed him: "I am going to pay you for your bullets to shoot me. But, first, show me my son [Voy a pagar . . . su bala; pero primeramente a mi hijo enséñame]."

What we see in this confrontation up to this point amounts to the Hegelian idea of conflict between two principles of law—the law of the state and the law of the family. The gesture of defiance of the old Quechua-speaking woman only confirms in the eye of the sovereign her madness. She has gone insane because of her love for her missing son. As long as we are mired in this exchange, the scene seems to have no other meaning. But I would call attention to the scene that follows. Killing this woman is obviously inconsequential for the sovereign, so he decides to send her home instead. Home is a proper place for her. At home, under the authority of her husband or some other "proper" male figure, this woman will return from madness to normality. At home, the mother will not be *vieja loca* any longer: "Okay, leave that lady alone; send her home in a car [Déjenlo a esa señora; lleven en carro para que vaya a su casa]." At home, she becomes a *señora* (lady).

In this picture, the sovereign power swiftly becomes a form of pastoral power able to conduct the mother's conduct. The sovereign oscillates between the power to kill and the power that shepherds. This stage where the sovereign exhibits the rotten bodies of those who dare to challenge his power is not a place for her to stay; she should not endanger her life but instead should go back home to take care of her other children. The sovereign will take her safely home, talking with her on the way and perhaps giving her advice about how to safely conduct herself and her children in those dangerous times. The implicit assumption is that she should forget about her son, who is probably dead, and care for the living.

At work here is a powerful cultural theme. Like other countries with a Catholic colonial history, in Peru the figure of the Virgin Mary, the sorrowful mother of Jesus, has been a dominant patriarchal frame of reference for shaping gender relations and subject positions within the family and the cultural imagination at large. We can say for Peru what Aretxaga (1997, 62) says for Ireland: "As cultural ideal the Catholic mother represents the emotional foundation of the family. She is the source of unconditional love, expected to protect and forgive her children and to mediate on their behalf when trouble befalls them." During the campaign of state terror, as in the scene narrated here, the mothers of the disappeared came to occupy an ambiguous position. On one hand, as "mothers of terrorists" they were always already suspects and, hence, vulnerable to state violence. On the other hand, as "proper mothers" they were just doing what any other "proper mother" would do for her children. The mothers embraced and mobilized the "proper mother" aspect of the equation, and sometimes the sovereign appeared disconcerted as to how to react toward her: "we are all born from a mother." Shepherding her back home is the answer.

Yet in a further act of stubborn defiance, the mother refuses to be returned home by the sovereign, who has suddenly transformed into a kind of political shepherd that cares for life. "I do not want it, sir; I do not need it. I have feet; I have eyes to walk by myself [No quiero señor, no necesito, tengo pie, tengo ojo para ir]," says the mother. She refuses the sovereign's offer to guide her back to her proper place, because, for her, the only way back home is to find her missing son.

I want to highlight three themes here that are central for my argument in this chapter. The first is the oscillation of sovereign power between the poles of the power that kills and the power that cares and shepherds. This image of two poles of sovereignty, akin to Dumézil's (1988) idea that sovereignty has two heads, questions those understandings that see sovereignty primarily as an omnipotent power to kill and/or to let die.[24] Second, in the scene above, the missing body of the son short-circuits the sovereign's oscillation between the power to kill and the power to administer life, and the mother's demand for the son's return exposes this short-circuit. The power that cares is unable to unmake the effects of the power to kill to effectively shepherd the mother back home. Third, the image of the mother walking away from the sovereign because she cannot have her son returned evokes the figure of the people walking away from the binding and shepherding powers of sovereign. If the population (evoked in this chapter by the notion of the townspeople) submits to the sovereign's power to kill and administer life, the people conduct themselves as if they are not part of the population—as if they are putting themselves outside of it. "I have feet; I have eyes to walk by myself," the mother powerfully says. The image evoked here is akin to the Foucauldian notion of counter-conduct (Foucault 2007). "The people" here is this kind of public that, in the face of practices of terror that have gone beyond the thresholds within which a human form of life can be tested, now walk by themselves on their own feet, guided by their own eyes, refusing to submit to the formula of sovereignty encapsulated in those practices of terror.

Terror at Home

The walking (*puriy*) of these mothers in search of their missing loved ones met with suspicion at home, particularly from their husbands. During our conversations at the excavation site, the mothers recalled feeling betrayed by their male next-of-kin on several occasions in the midst of the campaign of state terror. Their accounts make it clear that state violence hits home not only by physically disappearing family members, but also by poisoning family relations and devastating the family world as the family members knew it. Mutual accusations and self-recriminations ravaged families, as if the responsibility for what was happening to them could be found in the deep recesses of the family structure rather than in the practices of the state. These accusations and self-recriminations came hand in hand with the problem of not knowing how to respond to this unprecedented violence and protect their families from further suffering. These mothers' sense of betrayal bears witness to this corrosive effect of state terror. This, for instance, is how Mama Anki recalls her experience with her husband:

Because I got back home late, even my husband beat me. He did not want me to walk [*puriy*] late. He beat me, *mamá*. He said to me, "Surely they will release your son soon. Where have you been until so late? Your other children have not had their meals yet. You must have a lover; this is why you are out so late." But, *mamá*, I was walking in search of my son. What else could I be doing?

I did not meet Mama Anki's husband during my fieldwork; the family moved to the coast long ago, and she is the only family member who returns to Ayacucho from time to time to follow up on the criminal investigation into her missing son's disappearance. But a glimpse of his side of the story comes from the memories of Ernesto, a human rights lawyer from APRODEH who came to know the family well after becoming their attorney when the criminal investigation of the case was reopened in 2003. Ernesto recalled that on one occasion, when the couple visited his office, he asked Mama Anki's husband why he had beaten her when he knew she had been late because she was searching for their missing son. According to Ernesto, he replied: "I went crazy, doctor, I went crazy. I was afraid. I worked hard during the day, and then, when I got home, she was not there. There was no dinner; my children had not eaten during the day; they were totally neglected. I went crazy." More than two decades after the events, a husband who walks with his wife running legal errands for their missing son's case sees the violent husband as someone who has gone crazy.

The husband does not use insanity here as an explanation for the general problem of wife beating. Indeed, domestic violence against women is quite frequent in the Peruvian Andes, but this "ordinary violence" can be dealt with, negotiated, contested, and even forgotten.[25] What years later comes to be seen as a burst of (male) insanity is the fact that the "ordinary" violence of the husband against the wife happens simultaneously with the "extraordinary" violence of the state against the mother. Blinded by his own fear and male skepticism, the husband thought that the only way to protect his family from further violence and suffering was to bring the wife and mother back home to her proper place by disciplining her through violence. For the mother and wife recalling these moments many years later, it is difficult to disconnect the violence of the husband and the violence of the sovereign. Both sought to bring the woman back to her proper place—that is, back home under the authority of a male figure.

The blurring of the distinction between these two forms of male violence bears witness to the loss, in the context of the campaign of state terror, of criteria as to what it is to be a father or husband and a mother or wife and what it means to protect the family from state violence. Coming from the same cultural roots, both kinds of male violence presuppose that a woman outside of her proper place—at home, under the authority of her male kin and taking care of her children—is already a suspect of betrayal against both her husband and the state. In the context of the state of emergency, the Quechua-speaking mother of the disappeared walking (*puriy*) in search of her missing son is always already suspected of adultery and of being an accomplice of terrorists for not having properly educated her children to become worthy citizens of the state. Furthermore, when she confronts the sovereign to demand her son's return, she is always already convicted of madness. Terror's talk portrays these mothers in search of their missing children as madwomen (*viejas locas*), Indian whores (*indias putas*), and terrorists (*viejas terrucas*).

In the stories the mothers recalled at the excavation site, their resentment at their husbands' betrayal is not primarily about having been suspected of disloyalty as wives and even beaten out of jealousy. They can live with that. What seems much more difficult for them is their sense that their husbands betrayed their children.[26] In other words, these mothers attribute their male kin's betrayal not to their failure as husbands, but to their failure as fathers. For instance, Mama Isabel recalled with disappointment how, out of terror, her husband did not help her at all in her struggle to protect their son from being kidnapped from home. A military squad stormed their house at night to take away her son. She wrestled with the attackers, but her husband lay petrified in bed and did nothing. In a last attempt to rescue her son, Mama Isabel ran behind the military vehicle that was carrying her son away. When she returned home, she confronted her husband. This is how she recalls the moment:

> Mama Isabel: You might have thought that he would get out of bed . . .
> Mama Elena: He did not get up?
> Mama Isabel: No, *mamá*, not at all. He did not get up. No, no. He didn't even care; he didn't even go to the police. I had to do everything by myself. I did not get any help from him.
> Isaías: He did not help you at all?
> Mama Isabel: No, doctor, no [*with disappointment*]. I filed the complaint by myself; I walked, doing this all alone. He did not walk with me anywhere, not even when I was searching for our son among the dead, as in Purakuti. I walked over there all by myself. [*Silence*] Even the day I was wrestling to protect my son, do you think he got up? No, he did not get up. He wrapped himself in his blankets face down. He did not get up. This is why, when I returned home, I confronted him: "You rogue, why didn't you get up when they were kidnapping our son?" He said, "No, I could not. They also beat me. They also knocked me down to the floor and kicked me badly." This is how he tried to justify himself. No, he never helped me.
> Isaías: Surely he was terrified.

Mama Isabel: Terrified, yes. I walked by myself then, even when I went in
search of my son among the dead, turning over corpses. I was not afraid
of them anymore. [*Deep sigh*] I used to be afraid, but then I was not afraid
anymore.

Here, Mama Isabel seems to be implicitly asking what kind of father
this is who has lost his ability to acknowledge his son's existence. How is
it that while the mother fiercely defends their son, the father surrenders to
fear and listens, paralyzed, to his son's kidnapping? How is it that while the
mother starts an anguished search for their son, the father seems simply
not to care about it at all, as her words "ni preocupacunchu" (he didn't
even care) suggest? In this scene, it is not the wife who is disappointed
with the husband, but the mother who is disappointed with the father.
The husband may betray the wife in several ways—say, by beating her or
committing other kinds of abuses against her in the construction of his
masculinity—and be forgiven. But there is a responsibility that the husband must not fail to honor: his role as a father when the life of his son is
in danger. The mother's disappointment with her husband in his position
as father suggests that, in the view of the mother, criteria as to what makes
a father are ultimately tested at the moment when the life of the son is in
danger. And yet, simultaneously these mothers asked their male kin not to
join them in their mobilization because it was dangerous for men to do so
("Men should not walk in those dangerous times"). This ambiguity shows
the fragility of context in the state of emergency and how these women
had to find ways to navigate the irruption of unprecedented devastation
into their lives.

At the excavation site, I heard other stories that conveyed a sense that
fathers had betrayed their sons by not responding as expected when the
lives of those sons were at stake. In these stories, fathers appear either wrap-
ping themselves in fear—in a sort of triage in which they opt to maintain
the safety of their own lives over their children's—or performing hyperbolic forms of virility and machismo that, in an uncanny impersonation
of state terror, end up blaming their sons and their mothers for their own
suffering. Mama Teodora recalled one such instance. Her husband had
refused to walk with her in search of their missing son, and whenever she
confronted him for his neglect and abandonment, he would respond with
the same condemnatory statement: "Fuck him; if he wanted to mess with
stupid things, fuck him; he should be a man [and assume the consequences

of his actions] [Que se joda, carajo, si se ha metido en cojudezas, que se joda, para eso es hombre]."

The stories retold in our *wasinchis* at the excavation site reveal how state terror, by seeping deep into the recesses of the world of the family and kinship, destroys primary social relationships.[27] Forms of skepticism and betrayal that shadow human relationships in ordinary life are exacerbated in the context of unprecedented state terror and unrestrained violence, to the point that people become different people. Terror turns the familiar into the lethally strange. But these stories also reveal how the experience of violence and state terror is inhabited and contested differently according to gender. The father's moral discourse articulates the idea that a "proper man" faces the consequences of his actions and decisions, establishing a link between morality, gender, and masculinity. It does not matter whether such consequences entail the possibility of being disappeared. Thus, as someone who is supposed to teach and embody masculinity, the father simply allows the son to risk and face annihilation. In his view, virility is more important than fatherhood.[28] By contrast, in the mothers' moral discourse, it is clear that transgression against the rule of the sovereign is to be punished. Physical punishment is tolerable. What is intolerable is when, in punishing transgression, the sovereign goes beyond any limit and grinds the body of the transgressor to dust. Punishment cannot entail the destruction of the transgressor's body to the point where any social relation with him becomes impossible.

The Indictment

"Now, they cannot say that we are madwomen; they cannot say that we are drunks; they cannot say that we are liars; they cannot say we are 'terrorists.'" Mama Angélica stands at the edge of the excavation site, looking at the shattered remains uncovered by the forensic experts: parts of skeletons, ashes, and charred fragments of human bones carefully exposed in the excavation pits. She speaks calmly, but her voice is deep and moving. Other mothers stand by her side, looking with tearful eyes upon the scene of devastation. In more than two decades of searching, they were never able to find their missing loved ones, and now they are standing in front of shattered human remains that most likely belong to those loved ones. For all these years, because they never submitted to the rule of the sovereign and stubbornly contested denial, these mothers have been persecuted, harassed, and confined to a ghetto of suspicion, labeled as mothers of terrorists, liars, drunks, or madwomen. Now the work of the law was exposing the state's lies. Words played a crucial role in these operations of terror, and now, before the human remains that bear witness to atrocity, the mother raises her indictment against the state: "Now, they should watch their 'masterpiece' [*obra maestra*]; now they should come here and, in front of all this evidence of what they have done, they should dare to deny it: 'No we did not do this.'"

There is rage in Mama Angélica's words. She reclaims the past not only in terms of truth and knowledge, but also in terms of affect: fear gives way to rage. But her words also indicate that something new has been found at Los Cabitos, as the derisive expression *su obra maestra* suggests. Terror and repression are not new in this region as state violence has historically been essential to state formation in the Peruvian Andes, as elsewhere. And, as we saw above, during the counterinsurgency campaign, these relatives witnessed unprecedented forms of violation of the human body. But the forensic excavation at Los Cabitos reveals a different kind of ethical and political problem. The mother registers this new problem in her reaction to this revelation: "Okay, one can punish . . . one can make them suffer; but, doctor, to kill them in such a way? [Bueno, puede castigar . . . allí puede sufrir, pero ¿matar esa forma, doctor?]."

The state's *obra maestra* that the forensic excavation reveals as a new problem is that, in the name of defending the body politic, the state set up an industrial-style machinery of killing in which hundreds, if not thousands, of perceived enemies of the state were tortured, summarily executed, buried in clandestine mass graves, and then exhumed to be incinerated in ovens and disposed of without a trace. The forensic evidence proves that some practices of state terror in the central southern Peruvian Andes in the 1980s resulted in an Andean version of Arendt's "fabrication of corpses."

But *obra maestra* refers not only to the actual physical extermination of human lives, but also to the set of ideas; the political, legal, institutional, and moral practices; and the practices of denial, silencing, and the war of words that made such an event possible. The mother of the disappeared indicts the whole assemblage of practices, ideas, and languages that enabled, allowed, and even justified the occurrence of something like the "fabrication of corpses" in the name of defending the body politic from a vital threat. And she utters her political and historical indictment from the very site where these atrocities were carried out. Denial of atrocity is not the last word. The last word is the mother's indictment, but for that to happen she appropriates the work of the law and forensic sciences for her claims of truth.[29] The mother's indictment emerges and inhabits the space of truth that the law has opened after years of denial, complicity, and collusion with the sovereign's power to kill.

A specific picture of the relationship between the witness and the law emerges here. To delineate its contours, let us bring Agamben (1999) into the conversation. In his comment on the Kantian differentiation between the *quaestio juris* and the *quaestio facti* in relation to the problem of witnessing and the Holocaust, Agamben renders this difference as a dichotomy to assert that truth cannot be confined to juridical language: "The decisive point is simply that the two things not be blurred, that law not presume to exhaust the question. A non-juridical element of truth exists such that the *quaestio facti* can never be reduced to the *quaestio juris*." He goes on to say that this nonjuridical element of truth—that is, the *quaestio facti*—is precisely what concerns the survivor: the survivor is concerned with "everything that places a human action beyond the law, radically withdrawing it from the trial." For Agamben, law is not directed toward the establishment of justice, "nor is it directed toward the verification of truth. Law is solely directed toward judgment, independent of truth and justice" (ibid., 17–18).

We saw in the previous two chapters that the mothers of the disappeared are also primarily concerned with the *quaestio facti*. However, in contrast to Agamben's view, in the case of Los Cabitos there is a juridical element of truth that does matter to them, because the problem at stake is secrecy and denial, that is, the establishment of the *quaestio facti* in itself. Agamben's abstract and totalizing view reduces the question of the law to the problem of the trial and does not allow us to see how crucial the work of the law has been in opening a space to establish the (forensic) truth of atrocity. At Los Cabitos, the facts themselves needed to be established and brought into public view. The establishment of the *quaestio facti* required a forensic move, and a *quaestio juris* allowed this move to happen.

A view of the law focused on the trial would also prevent us from seeing both how the mothers' collective mobilization made possible the intervention of the law at Los Cabitos, after many years of denial and secrecy, and how these mothers appropriate the forensic truth to bring into being particular ways of reinhabiting the world in the face of devastating violence. This forensic truth allows the illiterate Quechua-speaking mothers of the disappeared to speak truth to power and reclaim the past for their own project of justice and reckoning with state atrocity. It allows them to utter their political and historical indictments from the very site where those atrocities were carried out in a gesture that certainly goes beyond the trial, and stands outside it, but has been made possible by the law.

Concluding Comments

In this chapter I have shown how in the individual search for their missing loved ones, the mothers of the disappeared ended up becoming a collective subject and engaging crucial questions concerning the possibility of political community in the face of practices of state terror that they saw as lying beyond the thresholds of life and death within which Andean peoples test what a human form of life is. In their struggle, the mothers learned to relate to sovereign power in terms of escape and movement, as opposed to the paralysis the sovereign seeks to produce as a means of political control, in a gesture that evokes the figure of the people walking away from the sovereign's binding and shepherding powers to conduct themselves as political subjects in their own right.

This enduring collective mobilization (*puriy*) allowed these mothers to eventually indict—politically and historically—the assemblage of practices, ideas, and languages that enabled, allowed, and even justified the occurrence of something like the "fabrication of corpses" in the name of defending the body politic. The oscillation of the pendulum of sovereign power from the pole of necropower to the pole of necro-governmentality opens up a space of forensic truth that the mothers inhabit in their own terms. In the last two chapters we saw how they retell their stories to collectively compose and author a minor history of state atrocity in the region, one that is within and outside of the official versions of this history. In doing so, they reclaim the past for their own projects of reckoning with state violence and terror as a means of establishing conditions of possibility for justice and mourning.

One of the central claims of this book is that in cases of political mass violence, a political reckoning is necessary for any ritual reckoning to take place. We are now ready to see how, in addition to political and historical reckoning, the forensic truth of atrocity enables relatives to start a move toward inhabiting the former site of the "fabrication of corpses" in a gesture of mourning and reclaiming death as human experience, even in the absence of an individual body. This ritual reckoning that comes after, or along with, the political and historical reckoning has a political salience of its own. The following chapters are devoted to understanding how this move occurs.

6

Talking Soul
Reclaiming Death as Human Experience

Why do I think that if there are human souls the human body is the
only fitting locale for them?
        —Stanley Cavell, *The Claim of Reason* (1982)

ONE MORNING IN early March 2007, soon after we had arrived
at the site for another day of observing the development of the forensic
excavation, Mama Natividad began to talk about the *chiririnka*—the dark
blue fly that Quechua-speaking people associate with death.[1] At this point,
the archaeologists had already uncovered crucial evidence demonstrating
that La Hoyada had been a site for killing disappeared terrorism suspects
and that industrial-style disposal ovens had been used to dispose of their
bodies without a trace. They had found the foundations of a blast furnace
and exposed combustible pipes that connected an oil tank with the blast
furnace, as well as electrical wiring that connected the blast furnace with
the military base's main barracks. They had also uncovered traces of human
remains associated with the furnace's foundations—a crucial finding since
it provided hard evidence to show that the furnace had in fact been used
to burn human bodies. Yet they had not found any other complete bodies
since 2005. All they had been able to recover were more heaps of ashes and
fragments of charred human bones.

At first, nobody responded to Mama Natividad's comments about
the *chiririnka*. But she repeated her comment despite this initial silence,
and eventually Margarita, who was standing beside her, felt compelled to
respond. This is how the dialogue unfolded:

Mama Natividad: Even the *chiririnka* is hovering around.

(*Silence*)

Mama Natividad: (*More loudly*) Even the *chiririnka* is hovering around very nicely.

Margarita: Is it hovering around you, *mamaya*?

Mama Natividad: Mmm. Don't you hear it, *mamita*?

Margarita: No, I don't [*Manam.*]

Mama Natividad: It is buzzing nicely.

The initial *manam* of Margarita did not discourage Mama Natividad. A couple of minutes later, she brought up the topic again, seeking to involve others in the conversation. Margarita said she did hear the fly this time, and other relatives said so too. The discussion continued:

Mama Natividad: The little *chiririnka*, the little *chiririnka* . . . see?

Margarita: Oh yes, the little *chiririnka*; who knows which of our relatives it is.

Mama Natividad: See, see. It is me that it is hovering around. It has been hovering around me since the other day.

Sonia: It is a soul, isn't it?

Victoria: Surely, it must be a soul.

Margarita: There it is; it is coming back again.

Animated by Mama Natividad's insistence, other mothers eventually acknowledged the presence of the *chiririnka* at the excavation site that morning. They listened to its cadenced buzzing, but nobody actually saw it. Mama Natividad's use of the Spanish verb *ve* (to see) did not refer to the actual *seeing* of it, but to the *hearing* of it, of sensing it being there. She wanted to confirm that her interlocutors could hear the buzzing of the *chiririnka* as she could.

Mama Natividad went on to tell the story of how, several years earlier, a *chiririnka* had announced the death of her older brother. She recalled that one afternoon, a *komer siquicha chiririnka* (dark green fly) had alighted on her wrist, then on her forehead and cheeks, and then again on her arms and hands. Her heart filled with a premonition, because she knew that the hovering of this fly around one's head is an announcement that death will strike home. Hours later she received a message from her siblings in Lima saying that their older brother had died earlier that day. "I can tell that what is said about the *chiririnka* is indeed true [Qamuqmi kachsqa],"[2] Mama Natividad concluded, presenting her experience as evidence for a larger claim establishing the *chiririnka* as a harbinger of death and an intercessor between life and death. Margarita confirmed what Mama Natividad said about the fly:

> Margarita: It is said that it announces it [death], *mama*, that green one.
>
> Mama Natividad: Yes, it announces it [death]—that green one, *mama*, the green one.
>
> Margarita: There it is; it is coming back.
>
> Mama Natividad: Yes, it is coming back.

The association of flies with death and the dead is a long-standing cultural motif in the Peruvian Andes.[3] Thus, for the mothers that morning at the excavation site there was no question that the *chiririnka* was a bearer of a human soul. Rather, the question for them was to which of their families that soul belonged, which of the disappeared was being expressed by that *chiririnka*. It was a question of belonging, and hence of identity. Mama Natividad asserted that the fly was hovering around her, suggesting thus that it was her missing son's soul. But the silence that met her claim, along with the fact that the *chiririnka* hovered around without alighting anywhere, left the question of identity open. It wasn't clear to whose missing loved one that soul belonged. It must have crossed the other mothers' minds that the wandering soul could be that of their own sons.

Anthropologists have widely reported the presence of the fly of death in Andean contemporary funerary rituals.[4] Typically, it shows up in two distinctive temporalities. First, as in Mama Natividad's story about her older brother, it appears as a harbinger of imminent death. In this perimortem apparition, hours before death occurs, the fly senses those who are about to die and hovers around them and/or their close relatives.[5] Second, the fly appears in ritual contexts, including those dealing with funerary rites to dispose of the dead, and on All Saints' Day and the Day of the Dead, when Andean people commemorate their ancestors.[6] In these postmortem apparitions, the *chiririnka* carries a human soul that is either about to depart for the afterlife—following death—or an ancestor who is returning temporarily to renew relationships with the living.

The internal war in Peru brutally brought about a third kind of presence. At the excavation site these mothers repeatedly returned to the image of the *botaderos* during the early years of the counterinsurgency campaign, where, in search for their missing relatives, they encountered swarms of *chiririnkas* hovering above the mutilated bodies of unknown people that had been thrown there. This image of swarm after swarm of *chiririnkas* indexed the new brutal reality that had emerged in the region—the reality with no immediate precedents of atrocious and anonymous mass death (see Chapter 5).

That morning of the apparition of the fly at the excavation site, the mothers did not talk about it in the ordinary senses—as a harbinger of death, a departing soul in a funerary context, or a returning soul in a ritual context. Nor did they talk about it in terms of their brutal experience in the *botaderos*. So, if the *chiririnka* did not appear in the culturally sanctioned temporality of premonition or repetition, or in the frozen temporality of atrocious mass death, in what temporality did it hover above the site that morning? What were these mothers to make of the solitary presence of the fly of death at the former site of the "fabrication of corpses"?

In this chapter I begin to explore how the Quechua-speaking mothers of the disappeared reclaim death as human experience in a powerful response to the sovereign's "fabrication of corpses." Concerning what happened at Los Cabitos we can echo what Arendt (1968, 452) says about what happened in the concentration camps: "The concentration camps, by making death itself anonymous (making it impossible to find out whether a prisoner is dead or alive) robbed death of its meaning as the end of a fulfilled life. In a sense they [the killers] took away the individual's own death, proving that henceforth nothing belonged to him and that he belonged to no one. His death merely set a seal on the fact that he had never really existed." All that is left of those who were last seen at Los Cabitos are some unrecognizable and shattered human remains that bear witness to the utter destruction that was visited upon them. The mothers want to restore the victims to their human condition by means of bringing their unspeakable deaths back into some kind of human form and grieving lives and deaths that the state deemed ungrievable and, hence, unmournable.[7]

I suggest that the flight of the solitary fly of death at the excavation site signals that such a work of grieving and mourning has begun among the mothers of the disappeared at the level of kinship. It is an index of both a mother's subjunctive acknowledgment of the truth that her missing son's remains might be among those the forensic exhumation is piling before her eyes and her desire to make a home in death for him, thus restoring some kind of relationship with him. For this purpose, the mother brings to the site of mass killing ordinary languages, practices, and technologies through which Andean people cope with loss in everyday life. She thus can constitute a performative body to be mourned, recognize signs of the various temporalities of death, and imagine some form of witnessing to the death of her son as opposed to the death without witnessing that state terror sought to impose upon him. It is a gesture that envisions the figure of the mother moving between two deaths—death as biological termination of life and death as human experience—attempting to bring the disappeared back into some form of social being. This gesture is in itself a powerful indictment of the practice of the "fabrication of corpses."

I begin by briefly looking at how anthropologists have approached the presence of the fly of death in contemporary Andean funerary rituals. I then offer an ethnographic example from the village of Accomarca to explore the relation between genealogical kinship and death in ordinary contexts, of which the fly of death is an index. I go on to examine how this relation is altered when devastating violence hits home. Finally, I return to the excavation site at Los Cabitos to explore the ways the mothers of the disappeared mobilize everyday practices and technologies to produce an imperfect form of grieving and mourning that I conceptualize as "subjunctive mourning."

Scientific Flights

The fly of death is an object of archaeological, ethnohistorical, and ethnographic study. In archaeology, corresponding to recent developments in Andean studies in the archaeology of death,[8] a specific approach known as archaeoentomology is devoted to the study of these insects in the contexts of graves and their associated remains. The fundamental theoretical presupposition is that knowledge of the biology and habits of entomofauna relevant to the grave can cast light on the funerary practices of ancient societies. Huchet and Greenberg (2010, 2846) argue that although it is impossible to estimate the postmortem interval in an archaeological context, "the faunal combinations associated with a burial, and the biology of the recovered species, might provide valuable information on the 'history' of the cadaver." Applying this insight to the study of the pre-Columbian Moche civilization on the north coast of Peru, Huchet and Greenberg offer new insights into this society's burial practices and fine-tune contemporary understandings about life and death among the

Moche.[9] Archaeoentomology thus contributes to the epistemological and methodological reorientation in archeology that aims to study death, in ancient societies, in terms of its relational aspects or, in the words of Shimada and Fitzsimmons (2015), in terms of "the living-dead relationship."

The fly of death has also left its imprint in iconographic and textual representations of pre-Columbian Andean societies. The Moche iconography, for instance, depicts an intimate relationship between flies and the dead in ritual contexts of sacrifice and burial (Hocquenghem 1981; Huchet and Greenberg 2010). The same relationship is described in the seventeenth-century Quechua text known as the Huarochirí manuscript—a compilation of myths and rites from the Huarochirí region in Peru's western central Andean slopes that is considered a testament of ancient and precolonial Andean religion (Urioste and Salomon 1991). According to this text, on the fifth day after death, the soul (*anima*) escapes the body of the deceased in the form of a fly. It further states that the fly of death returns temporarily during the funerary rituals before departing for the land of the dead (Taylor 1987, 411–23). Drawing upon this ethnohistorical material, Salomon (1995, 329) suggests that these representations encapsulate distinctive Andean conceptions of life and death: "The simplest generalization about the theory of life and death compatible with consistent motifs in the [colonial] documents is that a human being consisted of perishable soft parts (softer in younger people); a durable skeleton and hide, which became the lasting person or mummy; and a volatile personal shade or spirit (called *anyma*), sometimes visualized as a flying insect, which departed from both soft and hard parts to return to the place of origin (*pacarina*) whence the person came."[10]

These pre-Columbian origins have led some anthropologists to interpret the presence of the fly of death in contemporary Andean funerary rituals as evidence of cultural continuity. For instance, Valderrama and Escalante (1980, 241) argue that colonial Catholic evangelization was never totally accepted in Andean rural communities and that the longevity of such representations and practices are evidence of a fundamental continuity of pre-Hispanic cultural traditions and the vitality of ancient categories of thought. Robin (2008, 13) has rightly criticized this kind of approach for reifying these Andean communities' representations within a reality that appears arrested in time, "as if they were utterly situated in the margins of the national society, impermeable to historical changes following the Spanish conquest."[11]

Another interpretation links Andean ritual practices and representations of death (including the *chiririnka*) to agriculture. In this view, practices associated with death in any specific society are part of an overarching social organization and are a stage for other social dramas—and in Andean rural societies the central social drama is the regeneration of life, in that life is a limited good. Thus the commemoration of the dead in November is but a moment of reciprocal exchange between the living and the dead inscribed within a broader scheme of labor recruitment and the (re)organization of social relations before the beginning of the annual cycle of agrarian production. November is an occasion for the living to feed the dead in exchange for the rain the dead provide.[12] More generally, in this view, as Ferraro (2008, 263) puts it, "human burial is considered a kind of sowing or a ritual of passage from the dry to the rainy season, and prayers on the graves are seen as structural equivalents to the sowing of seeds."

None of these interpretations helps us understand the work of the *chiririnka* at Los Cabitos. We thus need to go beyond problems of cultural continuity or synchronic analysis of Andean death rituals and avoid the "flattening effect," as Joyce (2015) calls it, of treating "objects" of study in terms of abstractions instead of addressing the concrete circumstances in which people mobilize those objects and the purposes for which they do it. I thus take the view that the living-dead interactions are experiential and context specific to explore the presence of the *chiririnka* as an index of the relation between death and genealogical kinship in ordinary, everyday contexts. A view from the ordinary, I suggest, reveals the ways death is seen as part of the fabric of life, mediating continuity and separation within a deep relationality that connects not only humans with humans, but also humans with nonhumans.

This deep relationality is usually expressed in terms of kinship and alludes to what Sahlins (2013) conceptualizes as the "mutuality of being." In the Peruvian rural Andes, as elsewhere, notions of kinship encompass a broad field of relationships, including both genealogical kinship and performative kinship (Isbell 1977; Leinaweaver 2008). In its immediate manifestation, death and the cultural representations and ritual practices associated with it gravitate toward the pole of genealogical kinship, but death can only be reckoned with within the broader economy of the "mutuality of being." An ethnographic example from the Andean village of Accomarca illustrates this relation between death, biological kinship, and the mutuality of being.

Ordinary Flights

When I arrived in Accomarca in the early afternoon of October 31, 2006, people were already in a mood of celebration for All Saints' Day and the Day of the Dead. Some villagers were in the village's main grocery store, having drinks and discussing the latest happenings. As usual, I first visited César and Benita, the elderly survivors of the 1985 army massacre with whom I had developed a close relationship since the beginning of my fieldwork. I found them busy preparing for the celebrations. They were sorting dry maize and leaving it ready to prepare *mondongo* and tamales, the customary dishes for the occasion.[13]

Given our mutual affection, I was not surprised when they invited me to spend All Saints' Day with them and share the traditional lunch at their home.[14] What did surprise me was that César and Benita observed All Saints' Day at all—at least certain aspects of it—as she had converted to Protestantism long before and he was considering doing so as well. Protestantism combats celebrations inspired by Catholicism and demands that adherents refuse to participate in them. But participants often decide themselves what to refuse and what to honor, and César and Benita decided to hold the typical All Saints' Day lunch. They also invited Basilia, a relative of Benita's and fellow churchgoer who lived by herself and frequently visited the house. However, in compliance with Benita's church's views, they did suspend the *mesada* (offering) commonly given to returning souls, which is a central feature of the commemoration.[15]

The next morning, while Mama Benita and Basilia spent time together in the kitchen cooking and gossiping, I helped César rinse the maize for the *mondongo* one last time before handing it to Benita. Then we went to work in their small garden, and César started to instruct me on the plants, teaching me their names, their medicinal and alimentary uses, and the care they required. He also taught me how to prepare firewood with different types of axes. As we worked, he spoke—for the first time without any prompting—of the 1985 massacre and the history of violence in the village. Later, as we were taking our seats in the small kitchen to have lunch, César called me *karichuri* (son), declaring, "You are now like our *karichuri* [Kamka, karichurinchis q'ina kamki miki]."[16] Benita confirmed her husband's declaration with a smile on her face: "Yes, indeed, he is now like our *karichuri* [Au, payq'a karichurinchis q'ina miki]."[17] Since that day, I have sat at their table as *karichuri*.

That as an ethnographer I was incorporated affectively into César and Benita's kinship is hardly exceptional. What needs to be highlighted here is that my adoption as *karichuri* happened at that moment of the year when social relations among the living and the dead are ritually renovated. I had arrived in their lives as a stranger who asked questions about violence and death. Soon, a friendship developed as my visits became more frequent. On each trip I ran errands for them in the city and brought gifts for them upon my return, and during my stays in the village, they invariably invited me for breakfast, lunch, or dinner, which almost always turned into long conversations in their small kitchen. I would listen for several hours to their stories of life in the community. I saw them cry but also laugh, and I answered their endless questions about my life and work in the United States, and my family. We became friends, and our relationship could certainly have continued in the register of friendship.

The desire to shift our relationship from the realm of friendship to that of kinship is an example of how kinship as a "mutuality of being" operates in everyday life in these rural Andean villages. The Quechua term that alludes to this mutuality of being is *kuyaqkuna* (those who care for us and whom we care about). It is an elastic term that encompass both genealogical kinship and ritual kinship, but it is irreducible to any of these categories. In the Pampas River valley there are three categories of relatedness: *ayllu* (near relatives), *karu ayllu* (distant relatives), and spiritual relatives such as *compadres* and *ahijados* (godfathers and godchildren). While the first two refer to a grid of social relationships constituted by blood ties and marriage ties, or genealogical kinship, the third denotes one of the typical forms of adoptive, or ritual, kinship in the Andes.[18]

Kuyaqkuna is "legitimized" and spoken of through kinship terminology, but it is distinct, and as mutuality of being, it goes beyond genealogical and ritual kinship. Ideally, care, love, and esteem should circulate within these established networks of kinship, but this is not necessarily the case. Relationships within genealogical kinship (*ayllu* and *karu ayllu*) are fraught and often complicated by grudges and feelings of hatred and envy associated with questions of inheritance, law, and property, and ritual kinship is always haunted by the possibility of betrayal. People thus tend to *also* find their *kuyaqkuna* outside the realms of the *ayllu*, *karu ayllu*, and spiritual relatives through various kinds of alliances that include but are not limited to forms of performative kinship. Simply put, in the Andes you do not necessarily have to be blood relative, affinal relative, or spiritual relative to be *kuyaq*.

In this sense, the question of mutual care, love, and esteem—that is, the mutual participation in each other's lives—is independent of whether the relationship is legal, spiritual, or biological. It does not depend upon the certitudes of the law, religion, or biology. But that fact does not make the mutuality of being denoted by the notion of *kuyaqkuna* less real or fictive. The mutual care, love, esteem, and the shared substance that circulates within the grid of *kuyaqkuna* are real and crucial for life in these villages. But for the very reason that they are not built upon certainties, relationships within *kuyaqkuna* are not given once and for all, and who your *kuyaq* are is always an open question. In the Andes, as elsewhere, the presence of others in our lives, as well as our presence in the lives of those others, is not taken for granted and needs constant renewal.

Kuyaqkuna as mutuality of being also extends to entities such as ancestors, earth-beings, and the dead. It is the participation of these "third parties" (Sahlins 2013) in the life of the Andean rural villagers that is celebrated and renewed during the commemorations of All Saints' Day and the Day of the Dead. The central moment of this renewal is the *mesada*—an offering for the dead that typically is arranged by noon of November 1 and remains for at least twenty-four hours. The *almas* (souls) arrive anytime during this period to accept and consume the offering of food and drink. The sign that announces the arrival of the *almas* is the appearance of a *chiririnka*, which hovers for a while and eventually alights on the offering. When this happens, it is a sign that the *almas* have accepted the offering. Only then will the relatives proceed to serve their own lunch without touching the food and drink of the *mesada*. Once the *almas* have eaten or accepted the offering, the contents become tasteless. The *almas* take the *alma* of the food left for them.

How villagers in Accomarca continue to set up the *mesada* became evident to me when I visited Emilia, another survivor of the 1985 massacre, in the afternoon on November 1 after my lunch with Benita and César.[19] When I arrived in her house, she had already finished setting up the *mesada* for her returning souls. Florencio, her husband, had gone to their plot of land to complete some unfinished work, and Falco, their eleven-year-old son, was playing on the patio. "So, you guys have already had your *mondogo*, huh?" I teased her.

"Yes, doctor," she replied.

"Oh, so the *chiririnka* has already been here," I asked her in a tone of complicity.

". . . Yes, doctor . . ." she replied hesitantly, as if wondering how I knew about the *chiririnka* or how she was going to explain it to me if I asked more questions, perhaps trying to "make sense" of it. I did not ask more questions. I knew that the *chiririnka* had already been there.

Emilia had arranged the *mesada* in the main room of their little two-room adobe house, which indicates the solemnity with which the visit of the *almas* is awaited, as the main room is where all interactions relating to formal matters take place. The offering was situated across the main entrance of the house and arranged with a great deal of care in its details and expressions of abundance. It was on Emilia's only table, which she had covered with a brown poncho made of sheep's wool, which is usually an expensive possession for villagers. Over the poncho, Emilia had put the best tablecloth she owned: a white cloth decorated with multicolored flowers and birds embroidered in the corners. Presiding over the offering was a bunch of *amancaes*[20] in a white cup labeled with the emblem of the European Union. Behind the flowers, a small basket covered with a white cloth containing two *t'anta wawas* (bread babies) was the *mesada*'s centerpiece.[21] The lavishness of the arrangement contrasted with the modesty of the room.

As the offering has to include the dishes and drinks the *almas* liked the most when they were alive, it required Emilia's best effort. On both sides of the *amancaes* were a pair of tamales. Behind them and on the right were two pieces of sweet bread and a green *tuna* (prickly pear). On the left side were two apples and a mango. Five generously served dishes distributed around the central arrangement completed the *mesada*. They were prepared with local agricultural products. On the right side of the table, Emilia had placed both a soup made of wheat and a *segundo* (second dish) consisting of boiled rice and pumpkin stew. At the back of the central arrangement was a plate with *mondongo*, the customary dish for this commemoration. Finally, on the left, Emilia had put two more dishes: a soup of oats and a *segundo* made of a combination of potato and pumpkin. In stark contrast to the frugality of their ordinary meals, the *mesada* was a luxurious banquet (Figure 6.1). It could not be otherwise: they were expecting the yearly visit of their *almas*—an event that needs to be celebrated with respect, devotion, and joy.

As mentioned above, a synchronic analysis of the ritual explains the lavish *mesada* in the Peruvian Andes as an effort to ensure the arrival of rains for the upcoming growing season. Yet as Ferraro (2008) suggests, this perspective obscures questions of conviviality, intimacy, and everyday

FIGURE 6.1. The *mesada* (offering for the dead) in Accomarca, November 2006.

practices. From this perspective, I came to see the ritual of the *mesada* as a central moment of instruction and initiation into the body and life of kinship. For instance, as soon as he heard people talking in the main room, Emilia's young son Falco returned from the patio and began to frolic around us. At this point, her husband had also returned from their plot of land, and while his parents and I were talking about happenings in the village, Falco began to tease his mother, pretending that he was going to eat the delicious food she had arranged in the *mesada*. In turn, Emilia was trying to stop her son from doing so, pretending that she was getting mad. It was a familial scene full of life and joy—an ordinary scene in which a child moves among his elders to steal language, as it were.

This is the atmosphere of intimacy in which children are usually introduced to and become acquainted with their ancestors. Except when death strikes home in entirely unforeseen ways (such as Lucho's suicide in Chapter 2, for instance), the first thing children learn about death is not the painful experience of loss, but this privileged moment of the year when the souls of their ancestors return home momentarily to show that they continue to care for the living. These returning souls do not constitute an undifferentiated group of anonymous entities that are (just) bringing rain with them; rather, they are a set of individuals with names and personhood. In the intimacy of home, children come to learn that they belong to a wider social body and soul that extend in time. The child learns to experience singular, named ancestors whom he or she did not know personally as presences constituting the temporal depth of his or her own personhood. In other words, the child comes to sense that his or her personhood has a "relational and distributed" form spanning the living and the dead (Gillespie 2001).

Perhaps more importantly, the child is initiated into a particular cultural grammar in which this "relational and distributed" form of his or her personhood encompasses networks of human and nonhuman relations. The child thus comes to know that the human is constituted in relationships with both other humans and nonhumans, some of which are present in our present, and some of which are present in our past. Further, the child learns that these relations to the world and to humans and nonhumans in the world are to be lived by the terms of a dynamic of continuity and separation, caring and mourning. Referring to our relationship to the past, Ariss (2004, 31) writes: "to remember is never solely to recount the past, but to put forward one's relation to it," as "a validation of continuity (or caring) and discontinuity (mourning) that each person experiences in relations with others."

The successful yearly visit of the *almas* to their living relatives is conditional upon the dead having been properly dispatched and their bodies being localized in a socially sanctioned place where the living can reciprocate their ritual visit. This happens on November 2, when villagers spend the whole day in the cemetery. They take water, candles, and white flowers for their *almas*, and food, cane alcohol, and *chicha* (maize beer) for their extended kin, neighbors, and the community at large. As elsewhere in Peru's rural Andes, in Accomarca there are two main categories of tombs: niches for the wealthier villagers and plain graves for the poor. Whether they are visiting a niche or a plain grave, the villagers behave as if they are fixing up their *almas'* houses. They weed the tombs, fix and repaint the crosses that preside over them, hang wreaths on the crosses, and arrange bottles of water and candles on the tombs. Once these tasks are complete, the relatives pray in a contrite way. Finally, when they have given this material and spiritual attention to their *almas*, they visit the *almas* of members of their extended families and neighbors.

The mutuality of these visits is an occasion for reunion with both close and extended relatives as well as *kuyaqkuna*. At these reunions, food, coca, *chicha*, and cane alcohol circulate profusely. Some families bring music and play their recorders; others bring musical instruments to play *pumpim*, which is a musical genre typical of the region of Pampas (Ritter 2002). After a while, some people begin to dance. As on no other day in the year, the cemetery is taken over by a festive, multicolored, and vociferous multitude. *Rezadores* (prayer-givers) circulate from tomb to tomb offering prayers for the dead and receiving, in return, portions of the food and drink the relatives have brought to the celebration. After spending the whole day in the cemetery, families return to their homes at dusk, usually stopping by their affine relatives' houses to continue the celebration for a little while longer. Clearly, the *almas* have propitiated reencounters in the extended network of kinship and have reconstituted the community. In renewing relationships with their dead, the living renew relationships among themselves.

There does not seem to be room for the *chiririnka* in this context. In any case, its flight at the cemetery does not have the symbolic force that it has at home. Perhaps this is why, writing on the neighboring region of Huaquirca, Gose (1994) opposes the *chiririnka* as a sign of mourning to the *paqpako* as a sign of the victory of life over death. The *paqpako*, Gose says, is an owl (sometimes called a *paqo-paqo)* whose cry announces an imminent human death. The night after All Saints' Day, a human representation of the owl does the rounds of all the houses where vigils are taking place. During the commemoration of the Day of the Dead, this same human representation mocks mourners by dancing on the tombs of their dead loved ones. For Gose, the idea that a fly expresses the human soul is evidence of the transformation the dead are said to undergo in the afterlife, and their return during the Day of the Dead expresses nostalgia for life and reattachment. He says further, "They [the souls] never completely lose their affinity for physical and social incorporation that characterized their life, any more than they are completely forgotten by their kin. It is this state of affairs that leads both living and dead back to the mutual attachment of the mourning period, and undoes the separation previously achieved in funerary rites" (ibid., 14). By opposing the *chiririnka* to the *paqpako*, Gose argues that death and its collectivization are causes for celebration, not mourning. The *paqpako's* message is clear: "there can be no consolation, let alone renewal, by means of grief" (ibid.). The regeneration of life comes on the basis of the triumph of the social over the death of individual members of society. The work of the *paqpako* is nothing but the work of the social disguised as a nonhuman form of agency that unmakes the individual. Thus, within the ethnographic tradition in which Gose writes, grief and individualization appear as problems for the collective regeneration of life. Associated with the home and the figure of the woman at home, grief, emotions, individual loss, and mourning embody everything that needs to be negated and vanquished if the social order and the life of the community are to be symbolically reestablished following individual death (Bloch 1982; Bloch and Parry 1982).[22]

An emphasis on kinship and relationality, as outlined above, offers us a different understanding of the apparition of the fly of death in ritual contexts of both mourning and commemoration. It is a culturally specific index of the double temporality in which humans situate themselves in response to the presence of death in their lives: separation (the irreversibility of death) and continuity (the memory of the dead). Levi-Strauss tells us that one of the functions of rituals is to integrate and overcome the opposition between reversible and irreversible time. While present and past are theoretically distinct, rites of mourning carry the present into the past by placing the dead irrevocably in a separate time-space as ancestors. By contrast, rites of commemoration bring the past into the present by recreating the "sacred and beneficial atmosphere or mythical times in which the living can mirror their ancestors and their deeds" (Levi-Strauss 1966, 236–37). The two processes, Levi-Strauss clarifies, are not equivalent: "mythical heroes can truly be said to return, for their only reality lies in their personification; but human beings die for good" (ibid.). The *chiririnka* flies in these two temporalities, which, although distinct, are intimately connected and reckoned with primarily in the realm of genealogical kinship.

Suspended Flights

In contrast to the excitement that surrounds the yearly ritual visit to the dead in the village cemetery, the visit to those killed by the Peruvian Army in 1985 was frugal and circumspect. The survivors had buried the shattered remains of these victims in a mass grave at the site where the massacre occurred and never attempted to move them to consecrated land (see Chapter 2). Until the exhumations of 2006 and 2007, the relatives typically visited the mass grave two times during the year: on August 14, the anniversary of the massacre, and on November 2, the Day of the Dead. On both occasions, as I had the chance to observe, they brought candles, flowers, and water for their slaughtered loved ones; weeded the burial site; rearranged the low fence of stones that surrounded it; prayed; and stayed at the site for a while. Coca leaves, cigarettes, and some cane alcohol circulated among the attendants. The conversation invariably centered on retelling the massacre, showing how relatives continued to grieve the loss more than two decades after the slaughter (Figure 6.2).

On the occasions when I had the chance to accompany these relatives on their visit to the mass grave site, I did not observe or hear about the presence of the *chiririnka*. Nor did I hear of any ritual return of the souls of these victims to renew relations with their surviving relatives. It was as if the ways in which these victims were massacred and hastily buried in a mass grave had determined that their souls should wander around, trapped in the murky passage between life and death, until justice was served. The suspended ritual flight of the *chiririnka* indicated that the ritual circulation between the past and the present was still blocked. But the presence of the

FIGURE 6.2. Survivors in Accomarca visiting the mass grave where their slaughtered relatives were hastily buried in 1985, August 2006.

shattered remains, imperfectly buried, as well as having a story to tell about these remains, had allowed the relatives to develop some form of imperfect mourning and imperfect commemoration. Both temporalities remained somehow suspended, waiting for the moment when the event of atrocity could be politically and historically prosecuted, something that started to happen following the exhumation of the first three victims (see Chapter 2). Only then, the ritual circulation between the past and the present could be unblocked, and perhaps only then the fly of death would ritually reappear in the context of commemoration.

Following the forensic exhumations of 2006 and 2007, the surviving relatives stopped their ritual visit to the former clandestine mass graves. Without human remains, those burial sites lost ritual significance for them. This became clear to me the day I asked Emilia whether she was going to visit her parents' former site of burial for the commemoration of the Day of the Dead. "No, doctor," she replied. "My *almas* are not there anymore. They have been sent to Ayacucho [Manam, doctor. Almaymi mana chaypichu. Aparunkum Ayacuchuman]." Emilia was referring to the fact that, after the forensic procedure, her parents' remains had been transported to Ayacucho for laboratory work, leaving their former site of burial empty. There was no reason to ritually visit an empty tomb. Memory and the soul travel with the human remains. The dead body thus anchors in time and space the set of interactions between continuity (care) and separation (mourning) that bind together the living and the dead in their mutuality of being.

This is why there is particular anxiety about the location of the dead body in the Andes. For instance, in Accomarca, the relatives of the victims whose remains were sent to Ayacucho after the exhumation became deeply concerned about the return of these remains. Whenever I arrived in the village, the first thing villagers asked me was whether I knew when the legal authorities would send these bodies back home.[23] Telling in this respect is Mama Benita's anxiety about the return of her mother's remains. As a converted Protestant, she did not set the *mesada* and did not go to the cemetery to pay a visit to her *almas*, but she remained attentive to the fate of human remains. Her anxiety to recover the body of her loved one led her to develop *pensamiento* (deep anxiety).[24] Because of her new religious allegiances, she might no longer perform Catholic-inspired rituals, but she continues to believe that human remains need proper burial and a resting place.

By contrast, the absence of the body gives way to an experience of hyperbolic uncertainty in which even the idea of death is suspended. No funerary rites can be performed, no ritual return of the dead can take place, and there can be no commemoration of any kind. The missing body means that something is missing in the social fabric itself. Ezequiel, another survivor of the 1985 massacre in Accomarca, articulated this suspended state of being in which even death is in abeyance:

> We have not been able to bury our [missing] parents. Many people ask me, "Why have you not worn *luto* [mourning clothes]?" How should I? I do not know whether they are dead or alive. I do not know where they are. I do not know. People ask me, "Why haven't you offered a mass for your parents?" "Why haven't you gone to Huamanga to offer a *misa de difunto* [mass for the dead]?" they say. I respond, "Maybe they are alive . . . maybe they are alive." We have been living with this anxiety for many years. Until now, we have not worn *luto*.

Ezequiel's parents were kidnapped by the army and disappeared without a trace following the massacre. Since then, Ezequiel and his siblings have been searching for them, and like many other Quechua-speaking villagers in the Peruvian Andes, they have never been able to find them, either dead or alive. This is why, despite the many years that have elapsed since the disappearance, Ezequiel and his siblings hold on to an agonizing hope against hope that the lack of remains might indicate that their parents are somehow still alive. But even if they were to assume, finally, that they are dead, the absence of the bodies prevents these relatives from engaging the work of mourning, even an imperfect one. Nor are they able to resituate their loss in the web of life, and, by redefining their relations with the dead, redefine themselves—or, otherwise put, to have the possibility of reconstituting their mutuality of being. Their parents cannot return home in the context of the commemoration and renewal of relations with the dead.

Mourning the Unmournable

Now we can understand the work of the solitary *chiririnka* at Los Cabitos. The flight of the fly of death signifying the presence of a human soul at the excavation site indexes a shift of context from one centered on the grammar of disappearance to one centered on the grammar of death. It thus signals that a time of mourning has come, a time for mourning those who the practices of state terror deemed unmournable. Two developments

allowed for the configuration of this new situation: first, the forensic intervention at the former secret site of mass killing opening up a possibility of
some form of justice and indictment of atrocity, as seen in Chapter 5; and
second, the establishment of what in Chapter 4 I call the "whereness" of
the missing body. Since their disappeared were last seen at Los Cabitos, the
mothers at a certain point began to acknowledge the possibility that the
shattered remains found at the forensic excavation *might* be those of their
missing relatives. This whereness, or the possibility of assigning their disappeared a place, an ubiety, or, at least, an imperfect locality, punctuated the
indefinitely prolonged uncertainty that had engulfed the mothers' lives all
the years since their relatives' disappearance.

The flight of the *chiririnka* at the excavation site thus signals the
emergence of a form of mourning I call "subjunctive mourning." Situating
herself in this temporality of subjunctive mourning, the mother moves in
the zone between two deaths, the physical termination of life and the symbolic absorption of it, to make a home in (symbolic) death for her missing
son through a series of performative gestures that are meant to bear witness
to his death and symbolically constitute a body to be mourned. Consider
the following scene: the morning after the appearance of the *chiririnka*, we
were as usual in our makeshift tent, talking about some recent happenings
in the excavation, when Mama Natividad changed the subject to tell us
about a relatively recent art contest to which she had submitted two songs
of her own creation. The contest was part of a broader therapeutic project
administered by a local NGO with funds from international donors. The
aim of the project was to help relatives of the disappeared to cope with
trauma, and the NGO considered that therapeutic labor and the narrativi-
zation of experiences of suffering were useful ways to proceed. The NGO
decided that a song and poetry contest would help materialize some of the
organization's goals and offered small prizes for the winners to encourage
participation.

Mama Natividad told us that the two songs she presented were adaptations of the melodies of some popular *huaynos*—the most popular musical genre of everyday song in the Peruvian Andes[25]—set to lyrics she
composed about the disappearance of her son, a high school senior taken
away from home in 1984. Sonia and Rocío, my research assistant, asked her
to sing her compositions for us. At first, Mama Natividad refused, gently
saying that if she sang, she would surely cry: "Waqaruymam [I may cry]."
But then, on second thought, she decided to sing both songs. This was her
first song:

84, 85 Purakutipi purillarqani	I wandered in Purakuti in 1984, 1985.
Purakutita riqsillarqani	I then came to know Purakuti.
Chiririnkam war, waryachkasqa	Only *chiririnkas* fluttered all over the place.
Chiririnkam muyullachkasqa	Only *chiririnkas* hovered all over around.
"Kaypichum kachkan wawallay" nini	"Is my beloved son here?" I asked myself.
"Tarirusaqchu wawayta" nini	"Am I going to find him here?" I asked myself.
Manama nunca tarillanichu	But I could never find him again.
Manama nunca rikullanichu	But I could never see him again.
Uyachallanta muchaykunaypaq	To give him one more kiss on his sweet face,
Makichallaypas qaywaykunanpaq	To hold our hands together one more time.
Puñuykullanim, puñuykullanim	Exhausted, I fell asleep, I fell asleep,
Rikcharillanim, maskaykullanim	And when I woke up, I searched for him again.
Chayaramunchu wawallay nispa	Asking, "Has my beloved son returned home?"
Kutiramuchu tesoruy nispa	Asking, "Is my treasure back home?"
Wawallaytaqa uywakurqani	I was bringing up my beloved son.
Wawallaytaqa qispichirqani	I was raising my beloved son,
"Qori qollqillam wawallay," nispa	Saying, "My son is my gold and silver."
"Tesorochallam wawallay," nispa	Saying, "My son is my treasure."

Chayta nillaspa uywakullaptiy	When I was bringing him up with that hope,
Chayta nillaspa qispichillaptiy	When I was raising him with that hope,
Brazollaymantam kitaykullawan	They took him away from my very arms.
Makillaymantam qichuykullawan	They wrenched him away from my very hands.

Remarkably, Mama Natividad sang this song in the mood of a *harahui*—although she never explicitly referred to her compositions as *harahuis*. In contrast to the popular *huayno*, as Arguedas (1978) explains, *harahui* is a type of mournful ceremonial song that is sung only on special occasions such as weddings, the beginning of the sowing season, the end of the harvest, the farewell or welcoming of loved ones, and funerary ceremonies. By the time Mama Natividad sang her songs at the excavation site, the atmosphere was already infused with sentiments of mourning. This was not only because of the flight of the wandering soul the day before (the *chiririnka*), but also because Mama Natividad had said, on various occasions during the excavation season, that they, the relatives and their companions, were attending the excavation as if it were a wake. Her songs made explicit the mood of mourning. By changing the lyrics, Mama Natividad had transfigured popular *huaynos* into mournful *harahuis*. These were not songs of protest or denunciation. Their work was to tell a story—the story of how state terror entered into the fabric of her life.

In the first five stanzas, this first song presents the familiar picture of the mother descending to the space of death in search of her missing son. In this picture, the swarm of hovering *chiririnkas* indexes the experience of death in excess in the context of the state of exception—that is, death beyond what these Andean peoples until then knew how to harness within the ordinary boundaries of sociality and culture. If the fly of death is the carrier of the human soul, then its disproportionate numbers in this space of death speak of bodies of suspected enemies dumped in the open for all to see, yet that nobody could claim, as visible manifestations of sovereign power. The swarm of hovering *chiririnkas* at this site of death was an index of asocial death, death uncontainable, in sheer excess. Clinging to her last

hope, the mother searches for her missing son among these unknown bodies to find him and kiss him goodbye or hold his hands for the last time
(see Chapter 5). But she cannot find him here either. There is a confession
of failure and exhaustion in the verses of the song, as if to say that beyond
this space of death there are no more places to go. It is a confession of failure at the limit of the possible.

In the sixth and seventh stanzas, the song presents another familiar cultural motif in the Andes: finding the dead loved one in dreams. In
dreams the soul leaves the body and encounters other souls, particularly
the souls of the dead. In dreams one can converse with these souls and
learn about their pains and desires (see Chapter 7). In her mournful song,
unable to continue her search, the mother eventually falls asleep. Perhaps
her missing son will appear in her dreams. But her dreams are blind in that
respect. The song subtly suggests that the missing son does not appear even
in that region inhabited by the souls to which dreams offer access. If he is
not there, then he is still alive. The mother wakes up with the hope that
her missing son is back home, among the living, since he is not in the land
of the dead ("Has my beloved son returned home?"). But he is not back
home, so, trapped in hopeless repetition, she starts her search all over again.

In the last four stanzas the song presents a picture of how an ordinary
life can be brutally assaulted by state terror. Like any other parent in the
Andes, Mama Natividad had put all her hopes in her missing son, bringing him up according to the unstated rules dictated by the promise of a
better life, of social mobility. Her son was a smart and diligent high school
student who stood out among his peers. The mother had high expectations for him and hoped that he would care for her and the entire family
after he succeeded. There is nothing extraordinary in her thinking of her
son as her project. She speaks not only from those regions of patriarchal
desire where male offspring are more valuable than female offspring, but
also from those regions of modern discourse where education is a path to
success. The song shows the fatal injury caused to this ordinary project,
nurtured by the state, when the violence of those not named in the song
but whose signature is readable in the terror they wage against the social
and physical body entered into her everyday life.

The song's affective work in the context of the forensic excavation is
noteworthy. Sung at the site where shattered remains of the disappeared
are being uncovered, the song introduces a contrast between the times of
terror and suffering of which it speaks and the times in which it can be

sung. Perhaps the clearest sign of this temporal, affective differentiation is the contrast between the picture of the swarm of *chiririnkas* the song talks about and the scene of the solitary, wandering *chiririnka* the day before. This is also the contrast between death in excess, beyond any conceivable human form, and the attempt to somehow domesticate such an excess within by means of ordinary cultural grammars of mourning. In Chapter 2 we saw how mourners facing devastating loss in ordinary contexts need to tell the story of those who are leaving them and how their mutuality of being has been brutally torn by the loved one's sudden departure. In her song at Los Cabitos, Mama Natividad similarly tells the story of her son's life and how his sudden disappearance brutally devastated her life as she knew it.

In her second song, Mama Natividad gives voice to her missing son, producing an antiphony of pain in which the disappeared young man bears witness to his mother's suffering and tries to bring her back from the zone of inexhaustible pain where she has been exiled since his disappearance:

Mayuchum apan qori wawayta	Is it that a river has swept along my precious son?
Qaqachum ñitin kuyay wawayta	Is it that a landslide has carried away my beloved son?
Manaña nunca tarillanaypaq	So I could not find him anymore.
Manaña nunca rikullanaypaq	So I could not see him anymore.
Ama mamallay waqallayñachu	[*The son*] Oh, my beloved mom, stop weeping.
Ama mamallay sufrellayñachu	Oh, my beloved mom, stop suffering.
Cariñollayta yuyarispayki	When you remember my love,
Retratollayta qawaykuspayki	When you look at my portrait,
Parata qinam waqallaptikim	When you weep and your tears flow down like rain,
Yakuta qinam waqallaptikim	When you weep and your tears flow down like water,
Ñawillaykita tutayarini	Your eyes become blind (because of me) . . .
Ñawillaykita. . . antayarun.	Your eyes fade away (because of me).

At this point, Mama Natividad broke down in tears and could not finish her song. But in her words, we could all hear the voice of her missing son asking the mother to stop suffering for him, to accept the separation. It is not only the mother who suffers for her missing son; the missing son also suffers as he witnesses his mother's pain. This song tells in two voices the story of pain and suffering linked to state terror. It calls for consolation and witnessing—or, better said, it calls for consolation *as* witnessing.

In the first stanza, the song portrays the forced disappearance of a person as an event so absolute that it seems to have been caused not by human action, but by forces of nature. In search of her missing son, the mother has exhausted every possible site where she might find him. Where else can she go if there are no more places to go? Or has a mighty river or landslide swept him away? It seems that only a catastrophic irruption of nature could explain the disappearance of her son without a trace. The only thing she knows for sure is that she can no longer find or see him: "Manaña nunca tarillanaypaq / Manaña nunca rikullanaypaq." The son inhabits a zone to be found nowhere.

In the second stanza, the missing son speaks from this zone of no-where, asking his mother to stop weeping and suffering for him. He asks her to stop recalling his love and looking at his portrait, as if some forms of memory are toxic and lead only to darkness, paralysis, and more death. At work here is the idea that excessive, irresolvable grief is an all-consuming, debilitating, and paralyzing force. It inscribes itself upon the body and manifests itself through the body. Thus, in the iconography of the body depicted in the song, the mother weeps and suffers in excess, to the point that her tears resemble the rain or a river. Such weeping and suffering can only consume a person and lead to blindness. The missing son's voice warns his mother that if she continues weeping for him so inexhaustibly, she will subject her eyes to irremediable darkness; she will go blind because of him. The eye that weeps in excess blinds the eye that sees.[26] And an eye that has gone blind cannot bear witness; a voice that falls silent, overwhelmed by pain, cannot retell the story. Consolation and separation are needed, the missing son's voice suggests, for the task of bearing witness to the pain and suffering brought about by state terror.

There is a political subtext to this song: excessive grief, leading to blindness, means the survivor's extinction; thus it must be avoided. This formula equates seeing with power and agency. Mourning and consolation have to begin at some point to keep the survivors from going "blind" so they can bear witness to the atrocities committed against the social body. But the idea of "going blind" because of suffering formulates the body itself as a potential witness. In fact, the idea of "going blind" present in her second song incited Mama Natividad to expound, this time in the register of testimony, on how the (female) relative's body bears witness to the disappearance of a loved one without a trace. Addressing Mama Victoria for validation of her claims, Mama Natividad said: "But *mami*, when you have to walk like that, it is true that your eyes go blind; it is true that they go into darkness; they cannot see any more, oh dear. That is true."

Going blind is not a metaphor but a material sign of how grief can consume a mother's body. Mama Natividad presented her own experience as evidence of her claims, but she generalized her reflection to speak for all the mothers of the disappeared who, like her, had walked in search of their missing loved ones during the worst moments of the counterinsurgency campaign. In Mama Natividad's account, going blind speaks of how, at one point, these mothers started to wander aimlessly and with such grief that their sense of judgment abandoned them and they were no longer able to engage in basic bodily activities such as eating or sleeping:

... at that time we lost even our sense of judgment [*pensamiento*]; we just lost it, oh dear ... At that time I used to walk dazed as if I were drunk. Even my mouth got dark, because I could chew only coca leaves. Because I cried that much, my eyes even became sick. I could not even remember my name, oh dear. Perhaps one might think that at that time, around 1984, that we were able to enjoy our food in peace, that we were able to sleep sweetly ... [Not at all]. We had to walk with just some water to drink and some coca leaves to chew ... We had to walk like that.

Here, Mama Natividad recalls how her grief transformed her into a different person. She walked dazed, as if she were drunk. She was not even able to remember her name. Speaking for other mothers and relatives who, like her, were in search of their missing loved ones, Mama Natividad says that they lost their taste for life; they could not enjoy their food or sleep comfortably. The only thing that kept them alive was the search. They survived the search just drinking water and chewing coca, which eventually left marks on their bodies. Mama Natividad also recalls becoming another person physically. Her body was not hers anymore:

Even my waist got very thin; I became so thin that, to my shame, even my underwear got tangled between my legs, oh dear god [*mamallay mama*]. Do you think I would have lunch? Do you think I would have dinner? Coca leaves were my only food; water was my only drink; or was it otherwise [*asking Mama Victoria*]? Our waists were so thin that even our belts did not fit us anymore. They were so thin . . . If you eat, at least your waist will be normal. But if you do not eat, your waist gets so thin that you cannot believe it.

Many years later, reflecting at the excavation site, Mama Natividad tells us how the bodies of the mothers bore witness to the disappearance of their loved ones. They walked dazed like the blind; they were disheveled and gradually got thinner because they were so consumed by their pain that they could not eat or sleep. They became different people; they did not fit in their clothes anymore; they did not recognize themselves anymore. With the loss of their children, they lost themselves. In some respects, the forced disappearance of their loved ones made them disappear themselves. Walking in the streets or the *botaderos*, they became ghosts, their bodies denouncing the injury that state terror had inflicted upon the bodies of their missing loved ones. Their bodies announced what had happened to the body of their families and kinship. Both the bodies of the disappeared and the bodies of their surviving relatives are on a continuum of pain and suffering. This is what mutuality of being is about. It is an illustration of how kin "live each other's lives and die each other's deaths" (Sahlins 2013, 28). The wound has been commonly inflicted on this mutuality of being.

Impersonal Body

But the mother survived to bear witness to the wound state terror inflicted upon the body of kinship and, by extension, to the social body at large. As seen in chapters 4 and 5, this witnessing takes the form of a collective retelling through which the mothers not only indict the brutal and unspeakable assault that devastated their lives, but also resituate the facts of terror to where they belong: the public sphere. Here, this witnessing assumes a gesture of (subjunctive) mourning through which the mothers bring the disappeared back into some form of being, even if this is their being in death. Mama Natividad pictured the death of her son thus: "With his tears flowing from his eyes like rain, with his tears flowing from his eyes like water, my beloved son must have suffered so much pain when they burned him. My son must have died in so much pain. He must have cursed the day when I gave birth to him. He must have cursed my breast that nursed him." In light of the evidence the forensic exhumation had uncovered, these mothers seemed to have no other way to imagine how their loved ones were presumably tortured and killed. It was an atrocious death that, in a mother's imagination, must have led her missing son to even curse the day of his birth and the very breast that nursed him. This mother's imagination reverses the economy of pain that makes life possible. A mother endures pain to give life and goes through moments of pain to nurture this life and make it blossom. This is the natural course of things. But the pain that state terror inflicts upon the victim's body is of such a nature that the victim wishes not to have been born or nurtured. In this scene of retelling, the mother seems to be wishing not to have given birth and nurtured a body that would eventually be destroyed in such a way. In imagining the atrocious death of her son many years later, she seems to be lamenting the day she brought him into life.

It seems, then, that the work of state terror has attained completion, that the state has been successful in "eliminating" "terrorists" and deeming their lives and deaths ungrievable and unmournable. It seems that the sovereign has the last word as it reveals the fate that awaits those who dare to challenge its power: their bodies will be destroyed beyond recognition and exiled beyond any human action that could redeem them, and their relatives will live with the eternal disgrace of having had "terrorists" in the family and the guilt of having failed to raise them as virtuous citizens.

However, the work of mourning breaks through the paralyzing effects of state terror to restore the movement of life. In contradistinction to, or alongside with, the endless presentness of the disappearance, another temporality emerges in which some form of distinction between a "before" and an "after" can be acknowledged and reckoned with. It is the temporality of death which sanctions an ontological distinction between past and present. The ritual traffic between the past and the present that Levi-Strauss considered to be central to the social fabric of society can thus be restored. The gesture of mourning carries the present into the past by placing the disappeared/dead son irrevocably in a separate time space, and the gesture of memory (retelling) brings the whole past into the present to bear witness to his disappearance/death in a gesture that stands in opposition term by term to the kind of death without witnessing that state terror attempted to inflict to these people. Thus, in the absence of an identified individual body that can be mourned and redeemed, the mothers' gesture of subjunctive mourning composes an impersonal body to be mourned and honored. First, they imagine the site of mass killing to be the ultimate container for the human remains found there. Despite the careful and painstaking work of the forensic experts, who recovered what they could, it is impossible to recover those human remains that have been shattered to dust and burned to ashes. These irrecoverable remains will remain mixed with the soil of the site of mass killing. The materiality of the site and the materiality of those human remains that remain have become indistinguishable. Second, the mothers imagine a form of impersonal witnessing to the form of death without witnessing that the sovereign inflicted on the disappeared. Consider the following exchange:

> Mama Natividad: Who could possibly listen to his screams in this site? Only these rocks echoed them; perhaps only the doves that fly high heard them; this soil must be the only witness to them. [*She begins to weep.*]
> Mama Victoria: There was nobody to witness it. They must have tortured them. Who knows what else they did to them? They must have ordered them to dig their own graves, but who was there to bear witness to it?
> Elvira: Nobody, nobody indeed! [*They begin to speak at the same time, visibly agitated.*]

On several occasions, I heard these mothers refer to the site of killing with the Quechua notion of *chunniq*, which describes a very isolated and remote place where human presence is rare. At the time of the killings, this site was *chunniq* not primarily because of its remoteness, but because access was restricted by the military's tight control of the area. Because the site was *chunniq*, it was impossible for any human to witness the torture and death inflicted upon the people executed here. Implicit in this recounting is the fact that perpetrators cannot be witnesses. The "fabrication of corpses" they executed was meant to sanction a form of death without witnessing, an asocial death, a form of death that prevented anyone from listening to the victims' pain and bearing witness to their deaths.

But the perpetrators were wrong. There were witnesses, nonhuman witnesses that heard, saw, and contained all the suffering that happened at this site. These witnesses include the soil, the surrounding hills that echoed the victims' screams, the sky, the air, the dust, the rocks, the doves that flew over the site and saw everything. This *chunniq* site is thus impregnated not only with the blood of those who were executed here, but also with their pain and suffering because it bore witness to their unspeakable deaths. It is impregnated with the event of atrocity whose material remnants linger there despite the passage of time. It is, then, an impersonal witness that tells the story of those whose lives and deaths state terror deemed to be ungrievable and unmournable. We can now understand the work of the solitary, wandering *chiririnka* with whose flight we began this chapter. It indicates the presence at the site of the impersonal bodies of the disappeared and gives expression to souls that are now moving between the temporalities of mourning and remembrance.

Concluding Comments

In this chapter we have seen how, following the forensic revelation of the truth of atrocity at Los Cabitos, the mothers of the disappeared initiate a move toward mourning their still missing loved ones. It is a gesture that indexes the *imperfect* shift from the grammar of disappearance to the grammar of death that the forensic intervention, unable to identify the remains, brings about. The mothers engage this imperfect shift and, entering into a mood of subjunctive mourning, bring to the site of mass killing ordinary languages, practices, and forms of relationality through which Andean people cope with loss in everyday life. They thus can constitute an impersonal body to be mourned, recognize signs of the different temporalities of death, and imagine some form of witnessing to the death of their missing relatives as opposed to the death without witnessing that state terror sought to impose upon them. While coming along with the gesture of indicting state atrocity, politically and historically, the mothers' gesture of subjunctive mourning is in itself a powerful indictment of state practices of the "fabrication of corpses."

The way these mothers imagine, in their subjunctive mourning, the connections between the bodies of the victims, the soil of the site of mass killing that contains their shattered remains, and the landscape as witness to their unspeakable suffering and death brings into our discussion the question of space. The legal and forensic intervention engages the former site of mass killing as a plain and neutral container of evidence, but the mothers engage it as a haptic space, that is, as a space of affects, intensities, and events. In the next chapter I discuss these different understandings of space and their implications for the task of reckoning with state atrocity and mourning victims of practices of the "fabrication of corpses." An account of how these mothers move from the intimate scenes of mourning their missing children to scenes where they begin to mourn all the victims of atrocity as a collective subject will help us in that task.

7

The Magic of Justice
How to Ensoul the Work of Law

Where our language suggests a body and there is none: there, we
should like to say, is a spirit.
— Ludwig Wittgenstein, *Philosophical Investigations*

AFTER HAVING SPENT some time exploring the rocky terrain of La
Hoyada, Mama Lidia and Mama Isabel eventually found an appropriate
place to perform the *pagapu* (payment to the earth) in the environs of the
site.[1] It was an early morning in August 2006, and a new season of excavation had just begun. The team of archaeologists had decided to excavate a
different area from the one where they found the first fourteen complete
bodies in 2005. They had a lead from a former army private who had suggested that more than thirty bodies had been buried on a steep slope in
the northeastern part of the site, which the military had formerly used as a
garbage dump (see Map 3). Because of this lead and the successful findings
of the previous year, the experts were cautiously optimistic about the possibility of finding more bodies. But there was also some uneasiness in the
air, because former president Alan García had recently been reelected to a
second term. He had been unsuccessfully accused of human rights crimes
carried out during his first term, and he decidedly opposed this kind of
legal investigation. The future of the forensic investigation at Los Cabitos
had thus become somewhat uncertain.[2]

I had just returned from fieldwork in the village of Accomarca to
participate in the new season of excavation at Los Cabitos. I was not able
to determine where the idea of performing a *pagapu* at the site came from,

or how it originated, but what was abundantly clear was a particular excitement among those attending its realization. It was customary that leaders of ANFASEP participated at the beginning of a new excavation season, and so Mama Angélica, Mama Feli, Mama Lidia, and Mama Isabel were at the site that morning. As usual, they were accompanied by their lawyers and practitioners from a mental health support network for victims of violence. Cecilia and Pamela, a lawyer and psychologist, respectively, both based in Lima, were the most enthusiastic. They said that Cristina, the public prosecutor, was also very interested in participating in the ritual. Cecilia even implied that it was she who had suggested performing a *pagapu* at the site. However, much to her frustration, Cristina had to unexpectedly return to her office and could not attend the ritual.

I was excited too, perhaps even more than the other professionals there. I had the sense that their excitement was related not just to a modern fascination with the exotic, but to a genuine belief that the intervention of forces we do not control, such as fortune or providence, could perhaps help in the discovery of more bodies during this new excavation season. I certainly shared those sentiments, but as an anthropologist I was more intrigued by the performance of this ritual outside its usual context. A *pagapu* is neither a mortuary nor a commemorative ritual, of the kind Durkheim describes as piacular rite. Rather, it is a propitiatory ritual whose object is life, fertility, and abundance. Customarily, peasant families propitiate beings of the earth such as the Pacha Mama (Mother Earth) or the *Wamanis* (mountain earth-beings) in February, May, and August, to seek help or avoid their wrath and ensure the fertility of crops and livestock and the well-being of humans. These months are central in the agricultural calendar, and several important events take place, including the start of the sowing season, the harvest, and the branding of animals. It is said that at these times of year, the Pacha Mama and the *Wamanis* are particularly receptive to offerings.[3]

Moreover, it is customary that only men perform *pagapus*. Women are typically forbidden from participation because they are assumed to be too weak to deal with the powerful masculine forces of the *Wamanis*. *Pagapus* usually also require the intervention of ritual specialists who mediate between the sponsor and the earth-beings. No less important is the fact that *pagapus* are usually performed in secret, at night, at remote sites that families consider sacred and that therefore need to remain either inaccessible or hidden from animals and other people. Finally, customarily individual households perform the ritual, not collectives.[4] We are therefore led to ask what kind of work is being done when a rite whose object is life, fertility, and abundance is performed at a site of mass killing where a forensic investigation of atrocity is taking place.

The *pagapu* belongs to the assemblage of everyday practices of truth-making and ordinary technologies of the self that the mothers bring to the site of mass killing to animate the work of justice in response to state atrocity. These are practices, languages, and technologies that modern politics tends to see as premodern relics and vestiges of "magical" practices. I show how the work of these "magical" practices enters into a relationship of adjacency with the work of the law and forensic science to together confront, in their own distinct terms, the long-standing legacies of state terror and atrocity. While these "magical" practices depend for their efficacy on the work of the law and forensic sciences, they go beyond the rational limits and foundations of the latter to create affective conditions of possibility for truth and justice in the face of practices of state terror that have gone beyond the thresholds within which Andean peoples test what a human form of life is.

Specifically, the work of these "magical" practices at the excavation site is to produce a particular kind of space where forms of other-than-human agency can be seen doing *also* their own work for justice in response to state atrocity. While the law and forensic sciences engage the former site of mass killing as a plain and neutral container of evidence, the mothers' practices invest the site with realms and meanings beyond the rational discourse of law and science and unfold a space of affects, intensities, and events, more than properties, akin to what Deleuze and Guattari (1987) conceptualize as haptic space. Through these practices the mothers show that the problem of justice at Los Cabitos concerns not only questions of rights, recognition, and rule of law, but also reweaving the web of life that the state's "fabrication of corpses" has torn apart.

In this chapter, I first discuss how the *Wamani* is enlisted in the work of justice against state atrocity. Then I situate the *pagapu* in its historical context to see how it draws on a long-standing political grammar through which Andean people have historically coped with various forms of state power. I then analyze some specific ways in which the work of these ordinary practices and technologies of self and truth go beyond the work of the law and forensic science. I go on to show the ways these practices bring the disappeared back into being through dreams and ghostly apparitions. I conclude by showing how this reemergence, in turn, asks for a new sacred landscape, a landscape in which mourning can begin to take place.

Mast'ay (Spreading)

The mothers decide to perform the ritual at the foot of a rock surrounded by maguey, which is located in the vicinity of the former garbage dump where the archaeologists are digging new exploratory trenches. The rock is at the head of a steep slope of a canyon that goes down about five hundred meters to the banks of the Huatatas River. The mothers have chosen this site after a careful search of the area for the most suitable location for the small shrine that will house the offering, with a view to minimizing potential human or animal disturbance of the shrine in the future. With the exception of Augusto, the mothers' Ayacuchano lawyer, those in attendance respectfully move back to allow the mothers to prepare the ritual. Mama Lidia, Mama Isabel, and Augusto collect *tabla-rumichas* (small flat stones) from the surroundings to put together a stone box that will serve as the shrine for the *pagapu*. But before they proceed, the mothers and their lawyer engage in an exchange regarding the name of the *Wamani* to whom the ritual will be addressed. Usually, a nearby mountain is believed to embody the earth-being specific to a given location. The mothers know that the official name of the neighborhood in which La Hoyada is located is Yanamilla, but they are not sure whether the local mountain to which the *pagapu* will be offered has the same name. The following exchange occurs:

> Mama Lidia: I wonder what the name of this *orqo* [mountain] is?
> Augusto: No idea what its name is.
> Mama Lidia: What name would that be?
> Mama Angélica: We will name it Yanamilla, then, I guess.
> Augusto: Yanamilla.
> Mama Angélica: Yes.
> Augusto: Lord of Yanamilla.
> Mama Lidia: We will name it "Lord of Yanamilla," I guess; what else could we name it?

In this exchange, a new earth-being is recognized as the governing *orqo* (mountain) of the site where those individuals who were interned at Los

Cabitos during the counterinsurgency campaign were, as the mothers have come to know, tortured, killed, and their bodies burned to ashes. The mothers immediately invest the *orqo* with the notion of "lord" to proclaim his hierarchy, nobility, and the profound respect he commands as the sovereign of this locality. "Señor de Yanamilla" is therefore the name of the *Wamani* to whom these mothers address the *pagapu*.[5]

Once the name of the *Wamani* is established, Mama Lidia distributes coca leaves among the participants while Mama Isabel and Augusto assemble the small shrine with *tabla-rumichas*. Mama Lidia arranges a *kintu* for herself, and others do the same.[6] She places three coca leaves on top of one another, with two leaves pointing away from her body and the third crossing them to form the shape of a cross. Then, after whispering "coca-chataya akuykusaq [I will chew some sweet coca]," she carefully folds the leaves and puts them in her mouth. Coca is a key ingredient of the ritual. It is a shared substance that both constitutes a community among the participants and prepares their bodies and souls for the rite. The liminal moment when humans enter into contact with the *Wamani* is invariably one of danger, as the earthly forces that the ritual unleashes attempt to seize the bodies of those who take part. This seizure happens by means of a *mal aire* (bad air or bad wind) whose symptoms are usually an acute stomachache, a sudden drop in blood pressure leading to fainting, or even a chronic weakness that can lead to death.[7] Coca shields the ritual participants from the *mal aire*.

While participants must protect themselves from the *Wamani*'s powerful forces, it is just as important to speak to him. He not only sees but also listens, and Mama Lidia reminds Mama Isabel of the need to talk to him: "Rimachakuspayki [speak persuasively to the mountain]," she tells her. Mama Isabel, who has now taken charge of arranging both the shrine and the offering by herself, proceeds as advised. While chewing her *kintu*, she addresses the *orqo* in a whisper and invokes his presence: "Ay wamani, ay wamani." Words are as important as substances, gestures, and symbols in the ritual, and they are uttered according to particular performative conventions. The mothers address the *orqo* in a tone of persuasion rather than of interpellation or begging. When Mama Isabel completes the preparation of the small shrine, she tips her hat to indicate the beginning of the invocation. The other mothers who are attentively following these preparations from behind tip their hats as well. They whisper prayers in a gesture that resembles a Catholic prayer, but from what I hear they address their invocation to the *Wamani*. The rest of us follow suit and join the mothers in their appeal to the *orqo*.

The moment of invocation gives way to the *mast'ay* (spreading), which is the key moment of the ritual. Mama Isabel asks for someone to hand her some pieces of paper on which she can spread the *ofrenda* (offering), which consists of natural crops such as fruits, flowers, and coca, as well as transformed products such as cookies, candies, cane liqueur, cigarettes, and candles. She then asks that someone hand her the fruit, but both Mama Feli and Mama Lidia remind her that coca leaves must be spread first. The *mast'ay* has to be done properly; otherwise, the offering may be rejected and the ritual end up in failure. Mama Isabel proceeds to first spread the coca leaves, forming a bed upon which she will later present the rest of the offering. She also places a bunch of flowers that Augusto has tied together in the form of a cross. Then she asks that a cigarette be lit for her (*cigarrucha*) and blows smoke over the bed of coca leaves. The other mothers follow suit and likewise blow their cigarette smoke over the *mast'ay*, as if they were aromatizing or warming it. The rest of us are respectfully silent, listening to their whisperings intermingled with the soft hiss of the morning breeze (Figure 7.1).

After spreading some more coca leaves, Mama Isabel and Mama Lidia together look at how these leaves have fallen to find out whether the *orqo* is receiving the *mast'ay*. Mama Lidia then whispers softly, as if she were talking to herself: "Kayqa sumaqllaña mastakuykun [There it is; coca has spread beautifully]." Mama Isabel replies, also softly: "Kusiska [The orqo is pleased]." She spreads more coca leaves to confirm the omen, after which she softly announces: "Kusiska kachkam; kichaska kachkam [The orqo is pleased; it is opened (receptive)]." Mama Lidia confirms her reading: "Kusiska chaskikuchkam [The orqo is accepting the offering and is very pleased]." The *Wamani* lets them know, through the coca leaves, that he is very pleased to receive the offering. Mama Isabel asks for more cigarettes to blow more smoke over the bed of coca leaves, and Mama Lidia asks her to also blow smoke under the cross of flowers: "Cruzlla pachampi cigarrochatapas fumaykuy [Blow some cigarette smoke underneath the cross]." The mothers then proceed to place the candies, cookies, and fruit within the shrine.

In the final moment of the ritual, the mothers light four candles in a gesture that seems to allude to their missing relatives. One by one, they place their candles within the shrine, while whispering prayers. Finally,

FIGURE 7.1. The mothers of the disappeared offer a *pagapu* to the earth-being governing La Hoyada, August 2006.

Mama Isabel carefully places a bottle of cane alcohol, which is the last offering, and starts to cover the small shrine with more *tabla-rumichas* with the help of Mama Lidia and Augusto. At that moment, Mama Feli, who has been following the ritual from behind, reads the ashes of her cigarette and proclaims, "Tarisunchis [We will find]," and adds in Spanish, with a tone of hope, "Vamos a encontrar, papa [We will find, o dear]." Mama Lidia confirms this proclamation by noting that the way the coca leaves fell in the *mast'ay* constitutes an excellent omen. "Sayanpakunraq [The coca leaves even appeared upright]," she says. We are all thrilled with the announcement and return to the excavation site with a sense of optimism, after the task of covering the small shrine with more *tabla-rumichas* has been completed. The *Wamani* has spoken. *Tarisunchis* (we will find) is the generic form in which the Quechua mothers translate his announcement.

As we start back to the excavation site, Augusto speaks to Manuel, the only member of the forensic team who speaks Quechua and who has observed the ritual from a distance, to tell him the outcome:

Augusto: Manuel, Manuel, the spirit of the mountain says that we will find. The coca says that it is going to be a little bit slow, but we will eventually find.

Manuel: We will have *ánimo* [enlivenment] then!

Mama Lidia: Yes, *ánimo*!

Santiago, the lead expert, also uses the expression *ánimo* when Augusto announces the news to him at the excavation site. With obvious enthusiasm, Augusto says that the coca leaves in the ritual declared "we will find." "But it is not going to happen soon," he clarifies. Santiago receives Augusto's announcement positively, even though he did not participate in the ritual. "I hope so," he says, "because, damn, when one does not find [bodies] . . . one starts to lose *ánimo*." I note here that while the mothers use the generic formula *vamos a encontrar*, the experts interpret the omen as announcing that they will find more missing bodies. I discuss this difference below.

Geographies of Power

The mothers addressed the *Wamani* as a being in itself, a separate all-powerful being with its own will. As anthropologists have long documented, this is how Quechua peasants address the *Wamani* throughout Peru's central southern Andes. Take, for instance, the case of Peruvian writer and anthropologist José María Arguedas. In his ethnographic study of cultural change in southern Ayacucho, conducted in the early 1950s, he asked some Quechua elders from Puquio about the *Wamani*, and he received the following answer: "Pin kaqmi wamani . . . que" (in Spanish, "El wamani es el que es" [the *Wamani* is he who is]). That is, the *Wamani* is not about meaning or representation, but about being. It is about an other-than-human being, on which humans depend for their subsistence. As the same elder told Arguedas (1964, 235): "It is he who nurtures us, he who gives us our food [Uywakuninchik, mikuchiqninchik]." It is, in short, about the being of the earth, about its agency as universal, life-giving energy. (See also, de la Cadena, 2015).

The *Wamanis* are personifications of this being. Each has his own name and locality. They preside over a mountainous landscape populated by both humans and nonhuman entities (spirits of the dead, ghost ancestors, evil beings, and spirits of animals, among others) that constitute and inhabit a constellation of relations through which life circulates, materially and spiritually. The *Wamanis* own all the plants, animals, raw materials, and elements essential for life, such as water, that are found in their domains, and in dealing with these elements for their own subsistence, humans are required to ask the *Wamanis'* permission and duly pay them back for the use of their possessions. Failure to do so provokes their wrath. As one of the elders Arguedas interviewed said: "Terminuntan pagayku. Piñachakumanmi mana chayta pagaptiykuqa [We have to pay him (the *Wamani*) back his share. If we don't do that, he gets very angry]."[8] If angered, a *Wamani* can devour human hearts and cause miscarriages, infant deaths, malformations, and illnesses among humans and their animals. He can also bring about drought, frost, hail, or other natural disasters that lead to the loss of crops (Isbell 1978, Ansion 1987, Arguedas 1964).

   Wamanis, then, hold the power of life and death over the people and all other forms of life that fall within their jurisdiction. Quechua peasants speak of this power as *munayniyoq*, a notion that can be translated as "he whose will is command."[9] The *Wamanis* are *munayniyoq* as they have the dual capacity to bring life and fertility, but also misfortune and death. Put otherwise, the earth has a creative force that in its potent circulation can be either beneficial or destructive for human beings. In its beneficial aspect, the earth provides everything all living creatures under its care need to live and flourish. But to benefit from it, humans need to collectively domesticate the destructive aspects of this force by exchanging work, energy, food, and wealth with the beings who personify and express the earth's other-than-human power. Humans thus establish internal relations with this force and are obliged to properly attend to them. Any rupture in these relations due to oblivion, bad faith, greed, or deceit provokes the fury of the earth, resulting in death and calamity.

   De la Cadena (2015) has rightly criticized the tendency in anthropology to reduce the relational regime of earth-beings, people (*runakuna*), and the interactions between them to the frames of religion and/or cultural belief. Such an approach, she says, builds on the foundational distinction between nature and humanity that is consubstantial to modernity, which is both consequence and maintainer of the colonial condition that still lies beneath the ongoing destruction of highland Quechua peasant worlds. Instead, she offers the concept of "being-in-*ayllu*" to think of these worlds in their ontological complexity:

The entities (runakuna, tirakuna [earth-beings], plants and animals) that compose it [the world] are like the threads of the weaving; they are part of it as much as the weaving is part of them. In this conceptualization, in-ayllu humans and other-than-humans are inherently connected and compose the ayllu—a relation of which they are part and that is part of them. Accordingly, being-in-ayllu is not an institution that presupposes humans on the one hand, and a territory on the other. Neither is external to the ayllu . . . "being-in-ayllu" means that runakuna and tirakuna emerge within ayllu as relationship, and from this condition they, literally, take-place. (ibid., 101–2)

I am sympathetic to this project of decolonizing modern forms of knowledge and power by short-circuiting the foundational distinction between nature and humanity. However, for my purposes in this chapter—which is to understand the work of the *Wamani* and the *pagapu* at the site of state atrocity—I focus on how this being-in-place that de la Cadena powerfully envisions as "weaving" has been affected by both colonial and postcolonial state power. I thus draw attention to a paradox: while earth-beings are essentially *ayllu* insiders, in their human appearance they resemble quintessential foreigners or outsiders. Andean people usually portray the *Wamanis* as wealthy white males with blond beards who reside in palaces sumptuously furnished in gold and silver and ride on beautiful white horses—images that evoke the figure of the white colonial ruler or the modern *hacendado* (landowner).[10] Also, many Quechua terms about the cult of the mountains—such as *pagapu, terminu, derecho, armada*—have Spanish etymological roots.

Gose (2008) argues that the appearance of mountain spirits as white rulers corresponds not to essentialized notions of racial identity but to entirely different dynamics. He sees the contemporary regime of mountain worship as a recent historical innovation rather than a remnant of pre-Hispanic religion. In his view, it emerged as a combined result of large historical processes such as the spatial restructuring of sacred places during colonial forced resettlement, struggles over whether Andean ancestors should rest in Catholic churches, and the links between an ancestor cult and colonial political authority. Gose argues that the decisive shift from a cult of ancestors to a cult of mountains occurs as a result of the final decomposition of *curaca* authority [Indian native authority], which followed the failed Túpac Amaru rebellion in 1781 and the advent of the modern state in 1821. Until then, the *curacas'* mummified lineages were the axis of social and political organization. The regime of mountain worship emerged without lineages, and hence without the hierarchical effects of genealogical descent, and more attuned to the nascent republican form.[11]

According to Gose, this evolution responds to a political strategy that Andean peoples have historically deployed to accommodate and assimilate the brutal colonial enterprise: incorporating invaders as ancestors. They do not simply submit passively to colonial power; rather, as Gose (2008, 299) says, "Andean people invoke the image of these white political authorities only to subject them to their own forms of sociality, and thereby ideally remake them into a power that is no longer alien, one that they can live with." In doing this, Andean people extend into the colonial situation a long-standing political script whose traces are inscribed in pre-Hispanic mytho-history. Gose builds on the well-known fact that most myths through which Andean societies explain their own formation have as a central storyline the assimilation of powerful beings that come from outside the narrators' realms. Once taken within, these powerful external beings become ancestors. Society, in these legends, is thus genealogically built on the inside-outside dyad. This dyad in turn becomes the conceptual mechanism for incorporating external gods into indigenous pantheons.

For my argument here, I draw three implications from this notion of the dyadic inside-outside construction of society. The first alludes to the two geographies of power within which Andean peasants live their everyday lives. On one hand, their "being-in-*ayllu*" in a dense weave of internal relations between humans and other-than-human beings, who inhabit the space both materially and affectively in certain ways, is ideally meant to make life blossom and flourish. Local *Wamanis* are very much involved in peoples' everyday lives as ordinary affairs are usually dealt with at the domestic level, and it is only when a plight is beyond the reach of their power that other *Wamanis* intervene. The plight travels in an inside-out direction toward more abstract and uncertain levels of power.[12] On the other hand, the geography of state power has a center that is elsewhere, but its material presence is experienced as a force that comes from the outside to colonize everyday life, and Andean peasants are always coping with it. For them, life unfolds at the material intersection of these two geographies of power.

Second, the material intersection of these two geographies of power produces entangled notions of sovereignty. Both the *Wamanis* and the state are *munayniyoq*, since both hold the power of life and death over the common people, and as Earls (1969) observes, there is a flow of power between both. At the local level, he explains, "it is not at all easy to disentangle the sheerly physical and economic aspects of political domination from those firmly embedded in the religious system of the Quechua Indians" (ibid., 71). Political domination has historically been in the hands of local bosses (*curacas*, *hacendados*, *mistis* [small town mestizos]) who draw their power from being the local manifestation of the state, and this power has historically materialized as an oscillation between the power to kill with impunity and the power to make live, or between sovereignty and government, or, in more familiar terms, between the sword and the cross. As Earls and Gose explain, Andean peasants have historically subjected state power to their own forms of sociality in an attempt to domesticate its destructive aspects and to accommodate its aspects of governance to their needs. Ritualization expresses this domestication in symbolic form.

Third, the historical interaction of these material geographies of power and the entangled forms of sovereignty and government that emerge from it are inscribed on the landscape in the shape of particular modes of sacralization—that is, certain modes of folding and unfolding spaces of life as well as spaces of death, redemption, and transgression; the kinds of other-than-human entities that populate these spaces; the modes of acknowledging these entities; and the sets of norms and practices for addressing and relating to these entities and spaces, among other elements, are all intimately connected to specific regimes of power. As much anthropological work shows, the cast of characters on the stage of the sacred, their moral condition, the forms of their manifestation, and the scripts for relating to them have historically changed alongside political transformation. The forms that the sacred takes in the Andes is a contested and moving realm (Gose, 2008; Allen, 1988; Isbell, 1978; de la Cadena, 2015).

I therefore propose that the work of the *pagapu* at Los Cabitos can be situated within this long political genealogy of domesticating and accommodating state power to configure the framework for life together in society at the local level. The *pagapu* engages the nondestructive and enabling aspects of state power, embodied in this case in the work of the law and forensic sciences, to confront the destructive and dangerous aspects of state power. Its work seeks to resacralize the political space in two intimately related respects: reestablishing the thresholds of life and death within which a life together in society can happen *again*, after atrocity; and opening up the political space where those whose lives and deaths were banished from society by state terror can be brought back into *political* being. The disappeared can then populate, as newcomers, a reconfigured sacred space where some kind of social relationship can be reestablished with them. Let us see now how this work occurs.

Time for Justice

With the expression *kichaska kachkam*, the mothers announced that the *Wamani* was pleased and hence receptive to their *pagapu*. The Quechua word *kichaska* has two parts: the verbal root *kichay* or *kichariy*, which translates as "open," and the suffix *aska*, which indicates the state of being of the verb's object. *Kichaska* therefore means "it is open." The word *kachkam* introduces a temporal qualification in this general statement, specifying that such a state of being is transitory. It is open for now, in the present moment, and it is uncertain how long this opening will last. In addition, it is an opening that brings possibility, but it also brings danger and vulnerability for those involved. Its outcome does not necessarily depend just on closely following the rule.

This is the usual sense in which the *pagapu* is performed in ordinary contexts. Possibility and renewal do not arrive simply as mechanical consequences of following the rules. The sponsor may duly comply with the cultural prescriptions of the ritual—say, performing it during particular months of the year or on a particular day of the week or hour of the day, offering the right kinds of goods, or having ritual specialists mediate between the sponsors and earth-beings. Moreover, these prescriptions may be fulfilled in good faith and sincerity. But a desired outcome does not necessarily follow, and the ritual may end in failure. No one can predict whether the *Wamani* will be *kichaska* or, even when that is the case, whether he will deliver what has been asked for and in the form asked for. After all, to be *kichaska* is the *Wamani*'s prerogative, as is the kind of response he offers. He is, let us remember, *munayniyoq*.

The mothers' *pagapu* at Los Cabitos evokes these senses of possibility and renewal, and also of danger, uncertainty, and vulnerability. In performing the rite, they followed the cultural prescriptions for its realization and fulfilled them in good faith and sincerity, pleasing the *Wamani* with their offering, who then made himself available to respond to their query. But the mothers knew, before the rite began, that his answer would not necessarily conform to their hopes and expectations. He could have responded that it was over, that there was nothing left for them to do in their search for justice, that it was time to go home. Instead, however, he indicated that the path to justice was still open, although he did not specify what kind of justice it would be. The mothers translated his response into words with the generic and unspecified expression *tarisunchis* (we will find).

Things are not very different with the work of the law. The forensic investigation has opened a time of possibility but also of danger, uncertainty, and vulnerability for the mothers' plight. Like the *pagapu*, the legal and forensic rules have been closely followed, the practices have been performed in good faith and sincerity, and the law has made itself available to hear the mothers' demands for justice. But the mothers' historical experience with law and violence tells them that this moment is precarious and cannot last indefinitely, as the sovereign may cancel it at any time, without warning. And even if the law is still available and inclined to hear their plight, they are aware that the form that justice will take and whether it will conform to their hopes and expectations cannot be known in advance.

This unspecified promise of justice is one of the ways in which the work of the *pagapu* and the work of the law and forensic sciences enter into a relation of adjacency. Both events of inquiry in search of justice share a condition of possibility in the shift of state power that has opened up a time for justice, and both work on their own terms to unmake the long-term effects of state terror and atrocity. There is also a circulation of affect between the two, in the task of creating the conditions of possibility for justice, in the form of the advent of a new situation. While the *Wamani* can speak at the site only because the law has made the forensic investigation possible, the law takes affective force (*ánimo*) from his omen, as seen above. We can picture this adjacency, as the work of the law and the work of the ordinary coming together on their own terms to bring about justice, as an ongoing singularization of a new situation whose specific contours are not known in advance.

However, in the case of the law this unspecified promise of justice has a particular ontological and epistemological horizon—the discovery of missing bodies that can be individualized, identified, examined, and returned to their families for proper burial. In fact, most of the modern practitioners at the excavation site on the morning that the *pagapu* was performed—including the forensic archaeology experts themselves—interpreted the *Wamani*'s omen ("vamos a encontrar") as a straightforward announcement that they would be able to find more complete bodies, which in turn would enliven (*animar*) the work of the law in bringing about justice. In this view, not finding bodies brings about only *desánimo* (despondency), as experts Santiago and Manuel put it (see Chapter 3). We may not know in advance the specific form justice will take, but without bodies, the search for justice is weakened as the work of the law gets mired in its inability to recover the missing body.

Here we find the first of three regions of reality in which the work of the ordinary, as embodied in the *pagapu*, goes beyond the rational work of the law and forensic sciences, while presupposing it. In a modernist understanding, the possibility of justice is anchored in the recovery of the missing body. In terms of retribution, the individual body is a site of forensic evidence; in terms of restoration, it is the object of mourning; in terms of historical truth, its presence serves to dismantle official denial and silencing. In more general terms, recovering the missing body is vital for the legal work of constituting particulars—a victim, a perpetrator, a crime, a witness, etc.—that can then operate as instances of the law's general transcendence. To pronounce judgment and restore the social order, the law needs these particulars to dramatize the infraction of the general rule, prove the perpetrator's responsibility beyond reasonable doubt, and ensure compensation for the victim's harm. Individualization is the central grammar the law uses to constitute particulars as actuals, or ordinary points, from which a new situation can emerge as a result of legal judgment.

The work of the ordinary is, of course, also concerned with the problem of the missing body. After all, the mothers initiate the ritual to enlist the *Wamani's* support in finding out whether there are still bodies to be discovered at the site. But the movement toward justice that the *pagapu* embodies does not stop when these bodies cannot be found, or cannot be identified when found, as is the case with the work of the law whose initial promise comes to a halt. The *Wamani* concerns himself with the well-being of individuals, but above all he concerns himself with the weave of life in which these individuals happen to have their ontological dwelling. As mentioned above, the world in which he dwells encompasses not only living human beings, but also the dead, their spirits, and other-than-human beings such as animals, plants, and the earth itself. The question of justice, then, is how to reweave this weave of life that the practices of state terror and atrocity have torn apart. In this sense, the *Wamani's* unspecified promise of justice is precisely this reweaving of life, which presupposes the work of the law but cannot be completed by the rational means of the law alone.

A second region where the work of the ordinary goes beyond the rational work of the law and forensic sciences concerns the problem of the social location in which the facts of terror are to be placed. Taussig (1989) rightly argues that the point about silencing state terror, and the fear behind silencing it, is not to erase memory but to drive it deep within the fastness of the individual so as to create more fear, uncertainty, and paralysis. He goes on to say that this is what makes arresting the simplest of public-space talk, such as the mothers of the disappeared speaking the names of their disappeared in public spaces, together with displaying their photographs, because such a ritual-like act resituates the facts of terror where they belong. In Chapter 5 I showed how the Quechua mothers developed this kind of response to state terror. Here I show how the *pagapu* also works to affectively resituate the facts of terror where they belong. A brief excursion into what the ritual does in everyday contexts will illustrate the point.

In their work on rituals of payment to the earth in Peru's southern Andes, Bolton and Bolton (1976) identify two distinctive types. The first is preventive: individual households perform the ritual *before* misfortune strikes as a payment to the earth in exchange for good fortune, health, fertility, happiness, or conjugal compatibility. The second is restorative: individual households perform the ritual *after* misfortune has struck and as a response to an existing problem, such as theft, illness, or witchcraft. Bolton and Bolton argue that the two types of rituals should not be confused, even though both can be performed after harm has been done, to prevent additional damage. While the first involves an act of generalized positive reciprocity in which good is exchanged for good, the second involves an act of negative reciprocity in which evil is returned for evil. The first is nonspecific and offered on a calendric basis to address any random, impending, or possible misfortune by appeasing the earth-beings' anger and potential retaliation. In contrast, as response to specific *daños* (harms), the second is performed on particular occasions.

For my purposes here, I draw attention to the ways the two types of ritual address social relationships and make sense of the circulation of death and misfortune. On one hand, in their cyclic repetition, the preventive type serves to remind individual households that the spiritual and material circulation of life is bound to the care they pay to their relationships with both human beings and other-than-human beings. Failure to do so causes harm. On the other hand, in restorative rituals sponsors inspect their close relationships to identify the source of misfortune and interrogate their position within those networks as a way of obtaining a remedy. Thus, both types of ritual speak of the fragility and precariousness of social relationships. While preventive rituals are reminders that these relationships are always haunted by the possibility of betrayal or obliviousness, restorative rituals address relationships that are lost to households. Yet, while both rituals require that sponsors be aware of the fraught nature of their close relations, they also allow for the possibility that the capriciousness of earth-beings may be identified as the source of their actual or potential suffering. Sponsors can then free themselves from being responsible for their misfortune and can go on with the task of living.

Unlike ordinary contexts in which individuals can assign responsibility for harm and misfortune to earth-beings' capriciousness, thus deflecting personal responsibility for their own suffering, state terror shuts off such a possibility by squarely blaming its victims for their suffering and forcing them to accept responsibility for it. It blocks and paralyzes the movement of life. This blocking and paralyzing power cannot be undone *just* by means of sanctioning perpetrators of atrocity. A collective action is *also* needed, to symbolically and affectively purge practices of terror and atrocity from human sociality—this is the work done by the *pagapu* at Los Cabitos. Here, the liminal time that the ritual opens does not serve as the moment when the sponsors' close relationships, their wakefulness to them, and the earth-beings' capriciousness are reviewed and assessed as sources of misfortune and harm in order to produce a new situation.[13] Instead, it works as a propitious moment to expel what blocks and paralyzes life, and to restore life's vital flux.[14]

A third region where the work of the ordinary goes beyond the rational work of the law and forensic sciences concerns the kinds of space for justice that both open. In Chapter 8 I offer a more systematic analysis of the different kinds of spaces that are entangled at the excavation site at Los Cabitos. For now, I point out that while the law and forensic sciences engage the former site of mass killing as a plain and neutral container of evidence, the *pagapu* shows the ways the mothers engage this site as a haptic space, that is, as a space of affects, intensities, and events, more than one of properties (Deleuze and Guattari 1987). As we will see in what follows, this is the kind of space in which the ghosts of the disappeared and unknown dead reemerge to reestablish some connection with their surviving relatives and make their own claims for justice.

Ghosts of Atrocity

In her ethnographic work on dreams in Ayacucho, Arianna Cecconi (2011) found that in the aftermath of the internal war, *Wamanis* started to appear as soldiers in addition to the figure of the *hacendado*, particularly in areas where the violence of the military was worse. In the dreams she collected, these *Wamani* soldiers threaten villagers with violence and death, or attempt to seduce women, in the same ways that the military did during wartime. Villagers interpret these dreams as premonitions of pain and sickness sent by the *Wamanis* to which they must attend if they do not want to fall sick. Cecconi suggests that although *Wamanis* also appeared as soldiers before the war because of their close connection with *hacendados*, "it can be assumed that the recent armed conflict has had an impact on the frequency of dreams and visions during which the divinity appears as a soldier" (ibid., 420, n. 11).

That *Wamanis* appear more frequently as soldiers as a result of the war is an index of how mass violence affected the Andean night and its terrors. In some cases, the "traditional" cast of nocturnal beings that typically terrified the living simply vanished, as Theidon (2012) shows. Andean villagers became terrified not of *condenados* (damned spirits), but of their living neighbors. In other cases, new kinds of haunting beings emerged as people were killed in ways unknown to these rural villages, or were left unburied, or were simply disappeared without a trace. During my fieldwork, I heard several stories of disappeared brothers, husbands, sons, and fathers returning home in dreams, much to the joy of their distressed relatives, only to vanish again when the survivors awoke.[15] These traces that historical events leave on people's lives, manifesting themselves in dream-visions, ghost apparitions, and haunting images of mountain spirits and the dead, among other manifestations, can be taken as forms of historical seismographs.[16]

It is not surprising, then, that when a regime of violence and terror shifts to a regime of law and regulation, or, when necropower shifts to necro-governmentality (see the Introduction), this shift is registered in the sensitive world of dreams, spirits, and ghosts. This is the case at Los Cabitos. Before the forensic excavation began, stories about ghosts at the military base had become a kind of urban legend in Ayacucho. In one of the most well-known stories, ghosts were said to haunt military privates who happened to be on sentry duty in a particular watchtower that faces an area of the fort where, it was known, military intelligence squads tortured and executed suspects. Privates did not want to go there at night because ghosts appeared to them as dark lamenting figures, wildcats, or in some other menacing human form that would attack them as soon as they dozed off. These stories widely circulated as rumor to affectively signal what was known but unsaid about Los Cabitos. These accounts lacked signature. Nobody knew who these ghosts were, or who had seen them, or where and when they had specifically appeared, or how the stories originated; but everybody spoke of them as real.

When the excavation started at Los Cabitos, a new set of stories emerged, as if the ghosts of atrocity had eventually found a place and a time from which to address the living. One morning in March 2007, Mama Victoria told me of her personal encounter with one of these ghosts around the time the excavation began. She is in search of her disappeared brother. A very likable person, she was one of the most devoted relatives and attended the procedures almost every day. If she did not come, it was because something urgent had kept her away. She lived in a nearby neighborhood, which facilitated her almost daily presence. Like everybody else in the vicinity, she went around La Hoyada on her way to the slopes that face the Huatatas River, in search of firewood. One evening she was returning home after a long day working on the riverbanks. As she reached the environs of La Hoyada, she heard a sorrowful cry from somewhere nearby:

They [the ghosts] also made me hear their grieving laments: "Way, way," as if a woman were sobbing. Then I went back to see where the cry was coming from. I searched. I did not want to leave it. I was thinking, "Maybe the military are hurting somebody." "Señora, señora," I called softly. "Maybe they have hurt a goatherd child," I thought. I searched here and there but did not find anything. There was nothing. Then I headed home looking, frequently checking behind me. But I was not tranquil anymore. I was agitated. At that time, this area was clear. It was flat. All around was flat. There were no mounds of dirt around like nowadays. Before leaving the area, I sat somewhere nearby. Then somebody whistled. "Or are they military?" I looked around, but there was nothing. I went home and said to my grandson, "Pitacha, let's go back down there to the river." And we went down there to the river. There I picked up some more firewood. Then, on our way back, at a distance I saw a woman who was crying up there. I became very agitated. I saw her. But when we reached that point, there was nothing. I told my grandson to go home. Then I searched everywhere. "But how is it that somebody laments and there is nobody?" I searched everywhere but found nothing. "Perhaps here, perhaps there." Nothing. I didn't find anything.

In Chapter 2 we saw how, in the Andes, ghosts and spirits roam where there are unburied human bones. Human bones are not just inanimate things. They signal presence.[17] The work of the law is to produce the victim's body, and as the legal and forensic experts started to recover and move the human bones clandestinely buried at La Hoyada, a parallel movement of the ghosts and spirits associated with those bones began to occur. Stories of apparitions became even more frequent as the excavation exposed human remains to plain view.

What is distinctive about the ghosts at Los Cabitos is that they are strangers to the more familiar ghosts and wandering spirits that populate the Andean night. Notable among these familiar beings are *umas, qarqachas,* and *condenados,* who have distinctly evil characters as a result of their moral transgressions of the rules of reciprocity that shape the circulation of life in the Andean world.[18] As anthropologists have long documented, practices of exchange and reciprocity between humans and other-than-human beings are cornerstones of the human community's vitality in the Andes, and refusing to participate in them is simply to put oneself out of the moral community. Ansion (1987) lists some of these moral transgressions, which in turn produce specific forms of evil being: incest breaks cultural norms governing exogamous marriage; avarice breaks the exchange of goods and labor; promiscuity is disorderly and dangerously selfish. The evil beings emerging from these transgressions prey primarily on their kin to expiate their sins.

Condenados are particularly terrifying beings. They are living dead that wander the mountain peaks because they have been rejected from the world of the dead as a result of their moral transgressions and so have not been able to complete their transition to the afterlife (*quq vida*). They are usually portrayed as spectral beings dragging chains or surrounded by fire; sometimes they wear cassocks or black blankets. Usually they hide their faces, which have become skulls. The *condenado* seeks to take over a human being's soul and eat the brain; the victim is usually a close family member. The most common reason for becoming a *condenado* is incest or avarice, which fundamentally affect the realm of kinship. Eating close relatives is analogous to the idea of incest, which is seen in the Andes as the worst moral transgression (Allen 1982, 187).

The ghosts at Los Cabitos may share some features with ordinary evil beings, but their genealogy and condition are entirely different because they are not moral transgressors. For instance, they may wander like the *condenados,* but they do not terrorize ordinary people or prey on their kin because they have not broken any relations of reciprocity within their kinship networks. Nor are they the familiar *animus* (souls) that roam for a while after biological death as they try to find their way to the afterlife. The ghosts of Los Cabitos are in fact newcomers in the Andean night whose demands for redemption have a decidedly political character. Moreover, they contribute to the global search for justice in the face of atrocity. On occasion, they help to establish the identities of the disappeared and thus help relatives come to terms with their loss.[19]

Take the story Mama Lidia retold, of a ghost that appeared in 2005 when the archaeologists exhumed the first fourteen bodies. Back then, the police used to watch over the excavation site at night to prevent intruders from entering the crime scene and disturbing the evidence. One night, three policemen were sitting in their truck when they saw, at a distance, a human figure standing in the middle of the site. It was a young man wearing a soccer outfit, with a ball in his hands. The policemen thought that he was a neighbor who had lost his way, and one of them took a flashlight, climbed out of the truck, and walked toward the intruder, shouting, "Hey, fella, what are you doing here? It is not okay for you to be here now. It's forbidden." The stranger remained mute, standing immobile in the middle of the site. Since the stranger seemed not to notice him, the policeman looked back toward his colleagues to ask for help in case an intervention was needed. When he turned around again, the intruder had vanished. The policemen searched all over the site, but the stranger had disappeared without a trace. The next day they spoke with the forensic personnel to check whether any of them had returned to the site without warning the previous night. They had not. Laughing nervously, the policemen said that they had then encountered a ghost.

The mothers told me that the first time they heard the story they immediately thought that the young ghost was Mama Juliana's missing son, who was kidnapped and disappeared while playing soccer in his neighborhood in Ayacucho and was last seen at Los Cabitos. "It must have been his soul, wandering in pain [Almachan waqakuchkancha miki]," they told me. Of note in this story is not so much that the mothers seemed unsurprised that ghosts could appear at the former site of mass killing that still contained victims' remains, but the almost forensic character they collectively assigned to the apparition. Given the circumstances surrounding the disappearance of Mama Juliana's son, there seemed to be no alternative but to conclude that the ghost was his. For the mothers, the apparition simply confirmed what they already knew.

At work here are everyday practices of truth-making in the Andes. Apparitions have a revelatory character. Like dream-visions, they come from the outside.[20] A brief detour into Andean theories of dreaming will help us here. Quechua people make loose distinctions between different types of dreams. The first is between ordinary dreams, which villagers dismiss as unimportant, and dreams that they consider significant because they relate to people's deep concerns. Significant dreams are in turn classified into "dreams from inside" and "dreams from outside." As Cecconi (2011) explains, while dreams that come from inside are defined as dreams *con pensamiento*—that is, dreams born in deep concerns, sorrow, and inner thoughts—dreams that come from outside occur without *pensamiento* or connection to inner states of being.[21] Only dreams that come from outside have revelatory powers because they occur for one of two reasons: either the dreamer's *animu* (vital principle) temporarily leaves the dreamer's body to go forth and encounter other *animus*, or the sleeping person receives the visit of external beings such as *Wamanis*, ghosts, or the dead. In either case, the dreamer cannot leave the dream unattended without risking harm.

Dreams and apparitions are the typical means by which the dead place demands—sometimes heavy ones—on the living. Ordinary spirits usually make such demands in terms of respect, expenses, and attention and may be a capricious crowd, "an awfully envious lot" (Taussig 2001, 309), even more so if they were violently killed. It is different with the disappeared. Besides revealing where they were killed or where their bodies were buried, I heard stories of dreams in which they visited their surviving relatives to console them.[22] Take the story of Mama Juliana's son, whose ghost the policemen saw at Los Cabitos. The other mothers told me that he had visited his mother in her dreams. He had been an excellent soccer player. In her dreams, he and Mama Juliana were at the airport because he was about to take a trip to play a tournament in Lima. She was very worried about his trip, but he told her that she should not be, that he was just taking a short trip to do something he enjoyed. He would return soon, he said, to be with her always.

I cannot confirm whether she had this dream before or after the excavation began, because I did not meet Mama Juliana. But the manner in which the mothers told the story to me conveyed the sense that, like the apparition of his ghost at the site, this consoling visit in her dreams occurred after the excavation began. The sense was that with the opening of forensic procedures at the former site of mass killing, after relatives had searched in vain for several years, some kind of partial and imperfect reconnection began to occur between the disappeared and those grieving relatives. In this case, the intimate and individual dream visit of the missing son with his mother has the purpose of consoling her in her grief and facilitating her work of mourning. It is a vision-dream that asks surviving relatives to awaken to their own lives and acknowledge a limit in their responsibility toward the disappeared. It is a vision-dream which teaches that "the problem of the other is not that of (or only that of) establishing connections but also [of] suffering separation" (Das 2010, 33).

Haunting the Political Community

If the ghosts of atrocity do not haunt their relatives, who do they haunt? They haunt the political community in the name of which those atrocities were committed. The visits of consolation—in which the disappeared appear to teach their grieving relatives that moral questions are not just about following the rules but about being awake to life—have as their counterparts visits of revelation—in which they teach that the question of being awake to life has not only moral aspects but also political and historical ones. The excavation is an occasion at which the ghosts reveal themselves as a collective subject, that is, as a group of people defined by a certain common characteristic—being seen by the state as terrorism suspects. In contrast, "traditional" ghosts, souls, and dammed spirits appear as utterly solitary, lonely individuals. A dream that Mama Victoria had after one of her first visits to the excavation site illustrates this:

> Mama Victoria: After I came here, I started to dream. The first time I came, I had this dream. In the dream I saw many women and men here [at the excavation site]; they were naked; they were running here and there and there. Then, they just disappeared.
>
> Isaías: In your dreams, the first time you came here?
>
> Mama Victoria: Yes. [*Shifting to Spanish*] These people had their hands tied behind their backs; some of them do not even have hands; some others are covered in blood; they are running here, and there and there. . . . Then they just disappeared. [*She sighs.*] [*Shifting back to Quechua*] I woke up agitated. "Huh, huh, huh" [*breathing heavily*]. I could not even cry . . . I woke up. Then I got up and promptly prayed. "I had this dream," I told my husband, and he said, "That place must be full of all these people's spirits."

"Yes," I said. "Spirits are wandering there, suffering." "Surely that was how they were tortured; that is why you saw them in that way in your dream," he said.

Mama Victoria tells us how her body was affected by the dream, which is a usual motif in dream narration. When the spirits appear, the body registers their presence (*ñitiy* [To squish, to suffocate]). The ghosts in her dream-vision appear as a collective entity to reveal something that the relatives have not witnessed for themselves, namely, the unspeakable ways the victims' bodies were tortured and executed at this very site. They *ñitiy* her through her dreams.

As the conversation with her husband makes clear, the code of interpretation for Mama Victoria's dream is not symbolic, but *historical* ("'Sigoro chaynatacha castigarku; chaycha chiqui kawarunki' qinata nim"). Her dream-vision of tortured bodies running here and there at La Hoyada, only to suddenly disappear, alludes to the recent history of terror and atrocity in the region. It alludes to the peoples' lived experience and knowledge of the way sovereign power has historically been negotiated in the Andes. Paraphrasing Kwon (2008, 2), we can say that these ghosts are evidence of historical injustice. But they are not just symbols or ideas of history. They are first and foremost concrete historical identities whose existence, although belonging to a past moment, is believed to continue to the present time, not allegorically but empirically.

The historical and political character of the ghosts of atrocity at Los Cabitos also becomes evident in the kind of demand they place on the political community in the name of which those atrocities were carried out in the first place. They reveal themselves collectively not only to show that the unspeakable destruction inflicted upon their bodies needs to be seen as an injury to the social body itself, but also to collectively voice the forms of respect, attention, and acknowledgment of their suffering that this political community needs to offer if the path to justice and mourning is genuinely open. Another of Mama Victoria's dreams envisions the emergence of this collective voice. In this vision-dream, she encounters her missing brother and other unknown ghosts that are with him:

> Mama Victoria: The other night he told me in my dreams, "I am at the bottom of that hill near a corn plantation, exposed to the heat of the sun." He is exposed to the heat; he wants water; he asks for it, but there is none. "It's hot, it's cold; I cannot find any cover." This heat . . .

Isaías: He says that each time you dream with him?[23]

Mama Victoria: I always dream. . . . Now, he came accompanied by my
mother. They came together. Then my mother asked me, "Darling, have
you already found him? You haven't returned all his drink [aja] to him,
have you? He is thirsty; there are a lot of people here, people I know; people
I don't know; they are there, crying and suffering." Then my brother says,
"We are a lot of people here, all exposed to the heat, exposed to the cold."
"I cannot find anything to cover myself with," he said.

Isaías: Your brother?

Mama Victoria: Yes. "People are stomping on us; people are sitting on us [here
she refers to the fact that neighbors and animals walk freely at the site]. They
do not respect this site; nobody does; even animals are stomping on us."
He told me so. It is true; animals, people, just walked over this site. Then,
after that, he said, "People do not remember here. Nobody remembers us in
this place. They should encircle this area; they must isolate the area." When
I was about to ask him, "But who should do that?" I woke up because
somebody knocked on my door: "Tan, tan, tan." Then I prayed, and after
that I could not sleep anymore.

Three features of this remarkable dream stand out. The first is the
way the dream-vision connects cultural motifs and political commentary
against state practices of the "fabrication of corpses." This time, it is not
visions about shattered bodies but about the final fate of those who were
slaughtered. As mentioned before, in the Andes, spirits and souls roam
in the vicinity of human bones, and as much ethnographic work shows,
like the living the dead can be cold, hot, hungry, or thirsty or can suffer. I was told that when the dead appear in dreams expressing any of
these bodily symptoms, it generally means that they are not receiving from
the living the attention and respect they deserve. This is particularly the
case when their remains have not received proper burial. I heard of other
dreams in which the disappeared visit their relatives to complain that they
are hungry or thirsty or cold or hot, and the mothers typically read these
signs as a message from their missing loved ones that their bones are exposed to the elements in mountains or deserts and that they need to be
properly dispatched to a resting place.

But Mama Victoria's vision-dream goes beyond the plain enactment
of a cultural motif. It is not just about proper (private) burial. Her ghost

brother speaks of acknowledgment, respect, and memory from society, that is, of political problems. Being thirsty or cold or hot or not having anything to protect themselves from the elements refers, in this context, to the social and political denial of the kind of death they were subjected to at this site. Here, not only were individuals' lives taken away anonymously, but their deaths and the memory of their deaths were also eliminated. The victims were subjected to forms of asocial death—death without mourning, rituals of remembrance, and even grief; death robbed of its meaning as the end of a fulfilled life. Mama Victoria's ghost brother explicitly says that people do not want to acknowledge what has happened to them here, at this site of mass killing: "Manam yuyankuchu kaypi runakuna [People do not want to remember what happened here]." Such a lack of acknowledgment is experienced as social exile.

A second feature of the dream-vision I emphasize is its preoccupation with the collective. There are many ghosts in the same situation of despondency and suffering as Mama Victoria's ghost brother. There are people they know, people they do not know, people who are acquainted with the family, and people who are strangers to them. Her ghost brother speaks for all these people, familiars and strangers, to say that all share the same situation of having been exiled and condemned to social and political oblivion. He laments that their atrocious deaths have gone unnoticed and been forgotten—a notion conveyed by the image of people and animals carelessly walking above their remains that linger at the site ("Kawankunapi purikuchkanku"). During my fieldwork I did not hear of dreams before the exhumation in which the disappeared manifested themselves as a collective subject, which leads me to think that it was the initiation of forensic procedures that allowed these ghosts of atrocity to collectively present their pain and suffering.

A third feature is the instructional moment in which Mama Victoria's ghost brother speaks of the kind of remedy for their suffering that these ghosts of atrocity demand. The site where they were presumably tortured and killed and their bodies burned should be encircled and set apart to show the disappeared respect and attention and acknowledgment from society. "Rededorta qina ruwarumanku. Rededorta qina rurarkuchunku [They should encircle this area; they must isolate the area]," the ghost brother says. In other words, the site of mass killing where their remains linger should be transformed into a sacred site of social memory and mourning, as a means of offering the disappeared some form of justice. And when the sister is about to ask who should be in charge of doing that, the dream-vision ends, leaving hanging in the air the obvious answer that this is the task of the surviving relatives.[24]

These scenes of apparitions and dream-visions show how everyday practices of truth-making operate in those regions of life where the law and forensic sciences cannot enter because of the limits of their rational principles and procedures. It is clear that such truth-making practices would not stand a chance without the intervention of the law and forensic sciences, but is it also clear that they are just as important in creating affective conditions of possibility for justice and mourning in the aftermath of state atrocity. They open a space in which the unknown dead and disappeared, those who modernist epistemologies akin to the law and forensic sciences condemn to silence, can arrogate voice to themselves and voice the harm that has been inflicted upon the social body and teach about the kind of remedy such a harm calls for. But even if we are not prepared to concede that the dead can talk, in the telling of these stories by survivors and relatives there is a powerful political commentary against the state's practices of the "fabrication of corpses," as well as a demand to be awake to the ever-present possibility of the repetition of such atrocity.

This is the sense in which Koselleck (2005) considers dreams to be first-class historical sources, in his discussion of the distinction between *res fictae* and *res factae* in the work of history. He argues that while it is true that dreams belong to the sphere of human fictions, to the extent that they do not offer a real representation of reality, dreams nonetheless belong to life's reality. Dreams are real; and, for Koselleck, their salience for historical analysis derives from their ability to testify to a past reality in a manner that perhaps could not be surpassed by any other source. "Dreams," he says, "do occupy a place at the extremity of a conceivable scale of susceptibility to historical rationalization. Considered rigorously, however, dreams testify to an irresistible facticity of the fictive, and for this reason the historian should not do without them" (2005, 209). Subjected to a methodic analysis, dreams, or rather, dreamers' accounts of dreams, can render realities, such as mass violence and terror, that are not just dreamed but that are themselves components of those realities. "Terror is not simply dreamed; the dreams themselves are components of terror" (2005, 210).

Here I find a resonance with the Andean idea that dreams with revelatory power "come from outside" (see above). Yet, while the historian is constrained to infer this outside from the dreamers' textual accounts of dreams and their rhetorical aspects, the survivor reads (or dreams with) this outside in the material traces of the event—the site itself, the materiality of the bodies, the heaviness of memory, and the like. Dreaming, for her, is more than a revelation of a past long gone. It is rather a manifestation of a past that lingers in the present.

Concluding Comments

In this chapter I have shown how everyday practices of truth-making and ordinary technologies of the self, which modern politics would consider "magical," enter into a relationship of adjacency with the work of the law and forensic science, to together confront, in their distinct terms, the long-standing legacies of state terror. In particular, I have shown how the work of these everyday practices and technologies is to produce a particular kind of space for justice. While the law and forensic sciences engage the former site of mass killing as a plain and neutral container of evidence, the mothers' practices invest the site with realms and meanings beyond the rational discourse of law and science, in which forms of other-than-human agency can be seen doing their own work for justice in response to state atrocity. It is the kind of space that ensouls the work of the law and science at the site.

We have also seen that in unfolding a haptic space as a means of producing conditions of possibility for justice and mourning, the mothers constitute both the victims and themselves as collective subjects. In the next chapter I show how this haptic space that the mothers unfold at the excavation site is worded and translated into vehicular languages of the state so that society at large can hear and understand that the problem of justice at Los Cabitos concerns not only questions of rights, recognition, and rule of law, but also reweaving the web of life that the state's "fabrication of corpses" has torn apart.

8

"The Glory of the Disappeared"
Necropower, Necro-governmentality, and the People

ON THE SUNNY and hot early afternoon of July 16, 2011, as we wait for the inauguration ceremony of La Cruz de la Hoyada to begin, I sense in the atmosphere a certain mood of achievement, along with the prevailing mood of mourning. Some mothers wear photographs of their disappeared around their necks; others hold posters depicting enlarged identification photos of their missing relatives and the date they were last seen. A few of them wear black mourning clothes. A few others are dressed in the typical Ayacuchano *mestiza* garment for special occasions: white straw hats ornamented with black ribbons, white silk blouses, and blue mantillas and skirts. All of them hold flowers and candles and sit behind ANFASEP's blue banner (Figure 8.1).[1] Other attendants include representatives of local and national human rights NGOs as well as the mayor of Ayacucho city and the regional director of the Ombudsman Office, the only local authorities who participate in the ceremony. Tellingly, no national authority attends the event, and there is no national press coverage. But the mothers, familiar as they are with the national elites' practices of denial and silencing, are not surprised or bothered by this absence. For them what matters most is that, against all odds, they are finally going to inaugurate at least a modest memorial on behalf of those massacred at Los Cabitos.

The three-meter-high concrete Cruz de la Hoyada was hastily erected in early July 2011, just a few weeks after the trial on the human rights crimes at Los Cabitos began at a special court in Lima. The immediate purpose of installing the cross was to stop the imminent encroachment of the city into the site. Also, as we saw in the Introduction, the inaugural

FIGURE 8.1. Mothers of the disappeared waiting for the beginning of the inauguration ceremony of La Cruz de la Hoyada, July 2011.

ceremony of the cross coincided with the installation in Lima of the Cristo del Pacífico—the gigantic statue of Christ with which the coastal ruling elites wanted to bless the country's economic well-being and proclaim a brilliant future of prosperity for Peruvians. As we have seen, La Cruz de la Hoyada seemed to emerge out of nowhere to haunt the nation's celebration of its progress and to disrupt the dream of a society marching toward a prosperous future without facing up to its recent past of state atrocity.

I emphasize that erecting this small memorial on behalf of the disappeared and massacred at Los Cabitos would have been unthinkable a few years earlier. From the early 1980s, the military fortress remained a forbidden site for mothers searching for their missing loved ones and could not be investigated for allegations of human rights crimes. It was only in 2001, when the Fiscalía launched its large national project of the forensic exhumation of mass graves, that prosecutors could gain access to the site and initiate a criminal investigation into the atrocities carried out there during Peru's "war on terror." Only then could the mothers of the disappeared gain access to the site; in fact, as seen in Chapter 1, the legal authorities encouraged their participation in the forensic procedures as a means of helping them attain closure after being confronted with the truth of what happened to their missing loved ones. The investigation came to a provisional end in early 2009, and although the forensic experts thoroughly documented the ways in which egregious atrocities had been committed at the site, they were unable to recover and identify bodies of the disappeared in the ways it was initially expected. La Cruz de la Hoyada is the mothers' signature, inscribed on the site as a response to this unanticipated development.

In this chapter I explore the historical and political salience of La Cruz de la Hoyada and examine the ways it embodies a claim on political community in the aftermath of state atrocity. In doing so, I expand the exploration I initiated in previous chapters regarding the ways these mothers reclaim the former site of the "fabrication of corpses" as a space for justice and mourning. We have seen how they bring into the site an assemblage of everyday practices of truth-making and ordinary technologies of the self through which they invest the site with realms and meanings beyond the rational discourse of the law and science and unfold a space of affects, intensities, and events, more than properties, akin to what Deleuze and Guattari (1987) conceptualize as haptic space. I have shown how while coming into being along with politically explicit projects of historical reckoning, these ordinary everyday practices reclaiming the site articulate in themselves a powerful political commentary against state atrocity. La Cruz de la Hoyada brings these demands into the public sphere and thereby introduces another fold into the global project of historical and political reckoning with the state's "fabrication of corpses."

In contradistinction to the way the law and forensic sciences engage the site—that is, as a mere container of evidence and neutral space of inquiry—the way the mothers engage it conveys an understanding of space as a complex interlocking of senses that simultaneously encompasses physical space, a mode of inhabiting the space, and space as becoming. Following this insight I thus begin by showing how La Cruz de la Hoyada comes to constitute a physical border between the site of mass killing and the city. Then I examine the ways that the cross stands in its own right at the intersection of necropower and necro-governmentality to reclaim the site as a historical and political forum for reckoning with state atrocity. I go on to show how it is at this point that a collective voice emerges to indict the "fabrication of corpses" and make a claim on political community. I conclude by looking at the political embeddings in the space around the former site of mass killing to show how the mothers' response evokes the figure of the people emerging as a response to the event of state atrocity.

The Cross and the City

The origins of the idea of reclaiming the site of mass killing to honor the disappeared and massacred at Los Cabitos can be traced back to one morning of late October 2006. We were sitting as usual next to the excavation site and chatting about the upcoming celebration of All Souls' Day and the Day of the Dead a week later. Suddenly, Mama Natividad asked, with deep sadness, whether they would ever be able to find and recover the remains of their missing loved ones—a question that kept returning throughout the exhumation to haunt the mothers. Casting her eyes over some prickly pear cacti, she wondered whether bodies might be buried beneath them and whether it would ever be possible to answer that question in a space as large as La Hoyada. Other mothers joined her in these tormented musings, saying that surely there were more bodies buried there, and there, and there, gesturing toward one plant and then another, but that perhaps they would never be found. Then Mama Lucila asked, "This is why I ask, why it is that we do not claim this site for a 'campo santo'? [Chaytam ñuqa ninim, imanasqataq mana kay sitiuta reclamanchikchu campo santupaq]."[2]

Mama Lucila's question triggered a lively conversation. "Yes, for all of us [Aja, kay llapachanchik riki]," Mama Natividad said, stressing the collective dimension of the claim and potential appropriation. "Yes, we could then offer them [the disappeared] a mass here," Ana, a sister of a "disappeared," said. The mothers wondered to whom they should send a petition to convert the site into a campo santo. Mama Victoria then recalled that she had once posed that question to their attorney Augusto, and he had said this was a naive idea. The site had owners, and nobody (cualquiera) could just come and request its expropriation. Mama Lucila responded by saying that she was surprised that Augusto could say they were cualquiera. They were families of the disappeared, the people whose remains the authorities were trying to recover, and that very fact gave those families the right to request that the site be converted into a campo santo. Everybody agreed with Mama Lucila and decided to bring up the question for consideration during the next ANFASEP meeting at the end of the month. I attended the meeting and saw that with Mama Natividad's support, Mama Victoria brought the issue to the consideration of the assembly and received enthusiastic approval. From that point on, converting La Hoyada into a sacred site of memory and commemoration for the disappeared became part of ANFASEP's official agenda.

This scene shows how a sense of collective entitlement emerged among these mothers on the basis of their status as relatives of the disappeared whose remains still lie somewhere within the site and that the law is also in search of. At that point, it was becoming evident that perhaps the mothers would not be able to recover the remains of their missing loved ones. They thus wanted to convert the former site of mass killing into a sacred site where they could collectively mourn their disappeared. This symbolic inhabitation of the site would bring a partial and imperfect solution to two different though related problems derived from the law's inability to produce the missing bodies. First, the mothers would have a place to go to establish some kind of connection with their disappeared that the law and forensic sciences were unable to bring back home. In Chapter 6 we saw how, as the excavation progressed and revealed the truth of the atrocity, the mothers began to confront an agonizing ambiguity of knowing, but not being certain, that the unknown human remains *might* belong to their missing relatives. In response to this ambiguity, the mothers started to articulate a personal dimension of mourning in the mood of the "might be," an imperfect form of mourning I conceptualize as "subjunctive mourning."

Second, converting the site of mass killing into a sacred place would also respond to the problem of what to do with the unknown human remains recovered during the excavation—a concern that started to develop among the mothers as ashes and charred fragments of human bones began to accumulate without the possibility of identification. At one point Mama Lidia asked, "What are we going to do with these *huesitos sin dueño* [little bones without an owner]?[3] Where are we going to bury them?" It did not matter that these remains belonged to strangers. In the end, in the view of these mothers, nobody deserved the kind of death that the state inflicted upon these unknown people. Since these unknown dead could not be located within kinship networks, a sacred site where they had been annihilated would offer them a place to be buried, honored, and commemorated as human beings. This impersonal dimension of mourning is articulated in the mood of compassion and care for the stranger.

Claiming the site as sacred would also serve to stop the slow but steady periurban squatter invasion of the land around the site, which started at the same time as the investigation and had ever since threatened the integrity of forensic procedures (see the areas of "new urbanization" on Map 3). In 2005, for instance, the Fiscalía dealt with an invasion at the periphery of La Hoyada during which squatters allegedly threw away human remains that they found while building their houses. Of note here is that while *invasiones*, that is, informal urban settlements on the outskirts of Peruvian cities, typically have their origins in internal migrations and inorganic urban growth, in postwar Ayacucho they proliferated in the late 1990s and early 2000s under the leadership of former *jefes ronderos* (peasant patrol bosses). These leaders sought to legitimize such undertakings by arguing that they had successfully fought back the Shining Path, alongside the army, and that as such they had a right to have a place in the city.[4]

When I started my fieldwork in early 2006, the squatter invasion of the site was already a preoccupation for the mothers, their attorneys, and the legal and forensic authorities alike. At the time, the immediate area near La Hoyada was barely urbanized. The city jail constituted a kind of de facto final frontier between the site and the *invasiones* (see Map 2). But the mothers and the legal authorities feared that the situation could change at any time. In fact, rumor had it that squatter-led land traffickers had already developed plans to take over the site as soon as the opportunity arose. In the face of this threat, the mothers began petitioning various national authorities, both political and military, demanding guarantees for the protection of the site. But their petitions were ignored. Instead, they encountered the military's strenuous opposition to the idea of building a memorial at the site. This attitude only deepened the mothers' suspicion that the military was somehow behind the *invasiones*, as a means of erasing evidence and promoting forgetfulness of the atrocities committed there.

In 2009, when the forensic archaeological investigation came to a temporary end, the takeover of the land surrounding La Hoyada began in earnest. A new urban settlement emerged, with carefully designed streets, squares, and areas for public buildings. The settlers were mostly families of former and current low-ranking army officers. In mid-2011, when the squatters were about to take over La Hoyada itself, the legal authorities authorized the construction of La Cruz de la Hoyada as a means of stopping the settlement and protecting the integrity of the site of mass killing as a "crime scene." This is how the mothers were granted an opportunity to build the cross, as a first step in a broader project of erecting a Santuario por la Memoria (Sanctuary for Memory) at the site.

Indeed, the cross did effectively stop the encroachment of the city into the site of mass killing. At least for the time being, the mothers managed to reclaim the site as a *physical space* where they could erect a memorial for the massacred and disappeared at La Hoyada.[5] The sense of achievement that circulated during the inauguration ceremony was certainly warranted. In a subtle but intense battle for memory, the mothers had overcome the military's reluctance to allow memorials for "terrorists" in the surroundings of Los Cabitos. But perhaps more significantly, the cross had established a physical boundary between the city and the site of mass killing and thus made a political statement concerning the question of life together in the city. For most poor people in Peru, the only way to get a house in the city is by means of these *invasiones* on its outskirts. In postwar Ayacucho, this process seemed to be unfolding somehow oblivious to the recent past of violence. By stopping the encroachment of the city into the former site of mass killing, the La Cruz de la Hoyada arose to remind poor Ayacuchanos that as much as a place to live, they need a place in the city for their own memories.

Between Necropower and Necro-governmentality

Reclaiming the site of mass killing as a physical space to commemorate the massacred and disappeared at Los Cabitos also entails reclaiming it as a privileged public space, or forum, for reckoning with the state's practices of the "fabrication of corpses." This move is more clearly seen when the project of legal reckoning with state atrocity shifts from the site of excavation to the courtroom. After the forensic investigation at La Hoyada came to an end by early 2009, the trial on the case began at a special court in Lima on May 26, 2011. The Fiscalía charged seven former high-ranking officers with crimes against humanity for the torture and forced disappearance of fifty-four terrorism suspects in Ayacucho in 1983—the year the military seized control of the Peruvian south-central Andes. Yet because of a controversial administrative decree that turns over the adjudication of human rights cases to a special court in Lima (Sala Penal Nacional), the case was removed from the jurisdiction of Ayacucho—where the families live and the atrocities were committed—and was transferred to Lima—where the defendants live.[6]

La Cruz de la Hoyada was inaugurated on July 16, 2011—that is, just a few weeks after the beginning of the trial—and thus came into being at a moment when the transition from the excavation site to the courtroom occurred. As the courtroom becomes the primary forum for dealing with the event of atrocity, a new assemblage is put into motion in which people, things, objects, words, and relations are differently arranged in time and space than in the prior assemblage that focused on the excavation site. The event acquires a life largely embodied in legal and forensic texts, and all its material signs are moved into the background, as it were. The cross embodies the mothers' response to the series of changes that this transition introduces into the question of how to reckon with the state's "fabrication of corpses" and how to inhabit the event.

Consider some of these changes. To begin with, the site is left behind as merely a neutral container of evidence. The courtroom now is the forum, where experts initiated in the highly regimented language and grammar of the law and forensic sciences (lawyers, judges, expert witnesses, clerks) are the only players in the formal games of truth that seek to produce certainty, adjudicate responsibility, and offer recognition. The relation of adjacency between the law and forensic sciences, on one hand, and the everyday practices of truth and self that the mothers had brought into the site, on the other, and that had been instrumental in producing senses of justice and mourning at the site, as we saw in Chapter 7, is terminated and no longer valid in the courtroom.

Second, in these games of truth, the ontological status of the unidentified human remains shifts according to the legal categorization of atrocity. At the end of the forensic excavation, the experts had been able to recover about one hundred complete skeletons and an unspecified number of skeleton parts, as well as a large quantity of ashes and burned fragments of human bones. However, they were unable to identify these remains, nor were they able to determine with any certainty how many more individual bodies were included among the ashes and charred fragments.[7] The Fiscalía charged the alleged perpetrators with crimes of torture and forced disappearance. By definition, the legal category of "forced disappearance" presupposes that the victim's body is missing. In contrast, the category of "extrajudicial execution" presupposes that the victim has been identified. Because the exhumed unidentified remains did not fit any of the available legal categories, they were considered "contextual evidence"—that is, evidence that showed *what* happened, but not *to whom*. Therefore, these remains have ever since been kept in the storage rooms of the IML in Ayacucho.

Third, while the mothers could participate as a collective of plaintiffs during the forensic excavation, in the courtroom their participation was to be, by definition, on an individual basis. The Fiscalía defined Los Cabitos as a complex case of gross human rights violations carried out from at least 1983 through 1985. As a matter of expediency, the prosecutors split the case into two according to the year the crimes were committed—namely, Los Cabitos 1983 and Los Cabitos 1984—to be able to indict the specific officers in charge of the military base, who were rotated yearly.[8] As a result, only some of the mothers could participate as individual plaintiffs while others were excluded from the trial proceedings.

These shifts and changes brought about by the transition from the site of mass killing to the courtroom are, singly and cumulatively, significant. Perhaps the most significant development, however, occurs in the ways the event of state atrocity enters the mainstream national public sphere. The Los Cabitos case is possibly one of the most important in Peru's modern legal history and as such should have elicited widespread public attention in Lima. What was on trial was not, say, a massacre in a remote Andean village or killings by clandestine death squads, either of which could be justified as the result of individual "excesses" or as the actions of groups operating outside the control of the authorities. Rather, what was on trial was the transformation of the counterinsurgency's regional headquarters into a killing camp where the Peruvian military used Nazi-like technologies of body disposal. However, in striking contrast to the trial of former president Alberto Fujimori on charges of human rights violations (from December 2007 to April 2009), a wall of public silence encircled the Los Cabitos trial from the start.[9] The former proceedings were covered live on national television from beginning to end and provoked widespread national debate; the latter has received almost no press coverage and has not been a subject of public conversation. The hearings of the Fujimori trial were packed with people, including members of the political elite; few attended the Los Cabitos trial besides the defendants' relatives. In the former case, the relatives of the plaintiffs and defendant actively engaged the Spanish-speaking public to advance their case through newspapers and the media; in the latter, the Quechua-speaking plaintiffs could not even attend the hearings because they could not afford a twenty-hour round-trip bus journey from Ayacucho to Lima every week.[10]

We might attribute this silence *only* to the fact that who speaks and who is listened to in the public sphere is determined by conventions and structures of symbolic power distributed along ethnic, class, and gender-based hierarchies. Giving voice to an experience and inserting private memory into the public realm depends on one's ability to speak and be heard in this public domain, which in turn is determined by one's position in the socioeconomic hierarchy. However, what is *also* at stake here is the object "state terror" and the complex temporality of finished/unfinished pasts in which the postconflict state dwells. On one hand, the unfolding of a postwar time of recognition, rights, and democratic rule demands the folding into the past of wartime violence, atrocity, and arbitrary rule to separate and set it aside. The project of necro-governmentality aspires precisely to achieve that folding through the controlled languages of the law, forensic sciences, and humanitarian reason.

On the other hand, the actual killing may cease but the work of necropower does not stop. It cannot stop because, in the continuous re-founding of its order, the state constantly constitutes an "internal enemy" against which its violence and impunity can be legitimized and justified.[11] In Peru, discourses about the "ever-present" threat of terrorism remain alive despite the fact that the state defeated the guerrilla groups long ago.[12] The legal and institutional apparatus set up to wage the counterinsurgency (e.g., antiterrorist legislation) has been kept in place, and political technologies for controlling populations that proved to be "effective" during the "war on terror," such as the administration of fear, have been revamped for use during the postatrocity period. The past is unfinished in the sense that "terrorism," an object constituted during the internal war, continues to be an organizing principle of postconflict practices, as Theidon (2010) has rightly observed.[13] This temporality of the unfinished past indexes the work of necropower. It works to produce the network of affects necessary for controlling suspect populations, maintaining domains of immunity that rulers reclaim for themselves to face the "ever-present threat of terror," and shaping the collective memory of state atrocity through fear and silencing. This temporality of the unfinished past has the specific effect of perpetuating the ungrievability and unmournability of those whom the state massacred in the recent past as suspects of being the "internal enemy."

These are therefore two related forms of governing past state atrocity. On one hand, there is outright denial and silencing, which perpetuates the production of unmournable lives and deaths (imagined as the "internal enemy") as a manifestation of the work of necropower; on the other hand, there is the modulated speech that emerges from the joint work of the law, forensic science, and humanitarian reason, which by means of tested technologies of truth and self seeks to bring about a controlled recovery of the past in which the "internal enemy" can be brought back into the fold of the nation's citizenry as a moral, cultural, and/or legal subject, but not as a political subject. As Theidon (2010) suggests, the only way Quechua-speaking survivors and relatives have to "legitimately" enter the public arena dominated by the Spanish-speaking elites is by presenting themselves as victims and thus effacing their political agency.

La Cruz de la Hoyada stands at the crossroads of these two forms of postconflict governance and their related temporalities. It has a voice of its own and responds to both forms of addressing past state atrocity in the national public sphere. On one hand, it unfurls the public secret of the atrocities carried out at Los Cabitos that the work of necropower seeks to keep folded through denial and silencing and thus short-circuits the ongoing production of unmournable lives and deaths. On the other hand, it exposes the limits of the law and forensic sciences to address an event of violence that for these mothers has gone beyond anything conceived of as belonging to a human form of life. Reckoning with the state's "fabrication of corpses" cannot be effectuated through the rational means of the law and forensic sciences alone. Consider some of these responses:

First, the cross responds to the move toward individualization that the work of necro-governmentality initiates in the phase of the trial, by means of which only those victims whose remains have been duly identified are granted legal personhood and may aspire to some form of state justice and recognition. It speaks on behalf of both known and unknown victims of state atrocity, and in doing so it does not avoid a language of victimhood. An inscription on the horizontal arm of the cross makes an ecumenical claim: "In memory of the victims of La Violencia [en memoria de las victimas de La Violencia], 1980–2000." The cross thus claims to be a memorial for *all* the victims of the internal war. But on its vertical arm, this claim is qualified. Over a drawing of the iconic symbol of the disappeared in Peru—two hands cradling a photo ID of a disappeared person—is this inscription: "La Hoyada: Sanctuary for Memory. Between 1983 and 1985, hundreds of people were clandestinely killed, buried, and incinerated at this site [La Hoyada: Santuario por la Memoria. Entre 1983–1985 cientos de personas fueron asesinadas, enterradas e incineradas clandestinamente en este lugar]." Here, the cross refers explicitly to *all* the people the military disappeared and massacred at La Hoyada. It thus makes a global historical and political indictment of the practices of state terror and atrocity carried out at the site during the internal war.

Second, the cross goes beyond the law and forensic sciences in the task of dismantling the territoriality of state terror. Robben (2015) uses this notion in his work on disappearances in the Southern Cone of South America. He argues that the notion of necropower encompasses not only the power to kill, but also the power to decide how to dispose of the bodies of those annihilated on behalf of the body politic. He introduces the notion of "territoriality," or the absolute dominion over national territory, to refer to this manifestation of necropower. One of the two Latin etymological roots of the term "territory" means *terrére*, that is, to frighten and terrorize. Robben argues that disposing of the victims of state terror without a trace, by dumping them in clandestine mass graves or incinerating them or throwing them into rivers and bodies of water, manifests territoriality. Through the exercise of territoriality, necropower seeks to situate the victims outside society, even beyond death, to prevent their political memorialization and to paralyze dissidence. He contends that as long as these bodies are not recovered, state terror retains its "necropolitical hold" on society. He thus argues that exhumations dissolve the territoriality and necropolitics of state terror and contribute to the recovery of a democratic society. As shown in this book, the exhumations at Los Cabitos have indeed been central to dismantling years of denial and the state's necropolitical hold. Yet this dismantling also demands a political and historical resignification of the former site of mass killing, a task the law and forensic sciences could not undertake because by definition they treat the site as a mere container of evidence and neutral space of inquiry. Below I elaborate on the specific ways in which the mothers articulate in words this historical and political resignification.

Finally, let us also consider the kind of postconflict subject, who is concerned with the past and with the future of the political community, that the cross imagines. The inscriptions on the cross refer not only to the victims' fate, but also to the mourners' struggle. The back of the vertical arm on the cross features an image of a crying woman dressed in mourning black (*luto*). A veil covers her head, and she looks down at a burning candle in an allusion to the figure of the suffering mother, which in Catholicism is symbolized by the Virgin Mary. The image is accompanied by these words:

"The truth breaks through. We remember because we want to build a more just country [La verdad se abre paso. Recordamos porque queremos construir un país más justo]."[14] This statement connects the notions of truth, memory, and justice as cornerstones of a postatrocity political community. But more importantly, it shows that the mothers consider the realization of this project of a new political community to be their task. Here there is a subtle shift from a search focused primarily on their disappeared to a search focused on transforming the kind of political relations that enabled state atrocity.

Fragments of Soul: When Voice Emerges

To reclaim the former site of mass killing as a forum is also to reclaim voice and agency. In the courtroom, the survivor's voice is constrained and eventually drowned out by the expert language of the law and forensic sciences. Also, though in more subtle ways, some kinds of public discourse may end up drowning out the survivor's voice, as that discourse assumes to know and be certain of the survivor's pain and how to address it. In contrast, voice at Los Cabitos emerges in its own right to reclaim a history and a mode for reckoning and coping with that history. To see this, let us return to the inauguration ceremony of La Cruz de la Hoyada.

The ceremony consisted of three moments: an opening paraliturgy, the unveiling of the cross, and a series of speeches. The speakers were the mayor of Ayacucho city, the regional director of the Ombudsman Office, representatives of local and national human rights NGOs, and two ANFASEP leaders, among others. With the exception of the mothers, all the orators stressed ideas of recognition, forgiveness, and reconciliation, as well as the need to acknowledge both the suffering and courage of the mothers. They also variously referred to the disappeared as "victims," "people," and even "brothers and sisters," and all agreed that the site should be converted into a Santuario por la Memoria. Speakers agreed that the memory of what happened here should never die, not only because preserving that memory is a form of justice to the victims and their relatives, but also because it serves as a powerful preventive against the repetition of similar atrocities in the future.

These speeches reenacted the Peruvian version of the necro-governmentality of postconflict—using its vocabulary of recognition, preservation of memory, and learning from the past—but none of them attempted to educate the mothers on how they should understand the ceremony and its symbolism. A Catholic priest assumed that task during the paraliturgy, in an attempt to conduct the mothers' conduct toward conformity and consolation. He framed the ritual in the grammar of a typical mass for the dead. The obvious premise was that Los Cabitos was the last remaining place where the disappeared might be found, and the mothers had no other sites where they could continue their search once the forensic investigation at La Hoyada was over. Their missing loved ones would never be found, and common sense dictated that the mothers' search should come to an end, assuming that these mothers were interested only in their individual searches. He thus invited the mothers to think and speak of their disappeared as the dead people whose remains had been found at Los Cabitos so they would be able to offer them a symbolic burial. As part of the ritual, then, he asked the mothers to speak the names of their missing relatives as a means of evoking their presence in the ceremony.

In one of the most moving moments of the ceremony, the Quechua mothers rushed to respond to the priest's call. Initially, their voices merged into an unintelligible choir, but then, following his instructions, they began to pronounce their missing relatives' names one after another: "Teófilo Carrión," "Celestino Calderón," "Arquímedes Ascarza," "Américo Espinoza." Thus an invisible multitude of disappeared persons began to emerge, invoked by their grieving relatives. Then, the priest spoke of this invisible multitude of the disappeared as dead people:

We thank you, God, for the people we lost and whose deaths we are commemorating here. Their lives were important to us, and they were taken from this world. We thank you for the love they gave us, for their friendship, for the peace they spread around them. We thank you because their suffering teaches us to comply with the will of God, because in this way they have attained the true life and the love of us all.

In his final gesture, offering the dead a symbolic farewell, the priest asked the mothers to applaud in their memory and to light their candles as a final homage. "And in this very important moment for me," he said, "I would like each of you to light your candles and then give a round of applause for the departed." Following the priest's directions, the mothers lit their candles and applauded the dead (Figure 8.2).

Yet, while accepting the possibility that their missing relatives might be among those killed at the site whose remains are unrecoverable, the

FIGURE 8.2. Lit candles in memory of the disappeared, July 2011.

mothers do not conform to the Catholic ritual's call to accept loss, attain consolation, cancel their search, and return home. Below, we see how the mothers embark on a subtle struggle over words to impart their own sense to the inauguration ceremony as well as La Cruz de la Hoyada as a sign of the renewal of their search, rather than its termination. The cross is not just about commemoration, as implied in the priest's ritual. The remains found at La Hoyada *might be* those of their relatives, but as long as the identities of those remains are not determined, the uncertainty persists and their search is not over. The search, however, has been altered because it now incorporates questions arising from the truth of atrocity uncovered at Los Cabitos. The revelation of state practices of the "fabrication of corpses" must have implications and a response, so the mothers' search henceforth focuses not *only* on finding the individual missing bodies of their relatives, but *also* on transforming the conditions that made such atrocities possible. In this gesture responding to state atrocity, of maintaining their *puriy*, the mothers make a claim on political community.

To illustrate this, let us turn to the scene that followed the priest's ritual. Mama Angélica, the historic leader of ANFASEP, pronounced the inaugural words, half in Quechua and half in her broken Spanish, on behalf of the mothers (Figure 8.3):

[*In Quechua*] This cross is in the name of so many of our dead and disappeared. It is their presence, so we can respect them, so we can see them. It is the presence of the more than eight hundred people disappeared here. [*Shifting to Spanish*] It must be respected; we must be watchful about it, always; it cannot be left just like that, because we could never find our children. In this wasteland, many corpses, men and women, were thrown in [unmarked] pits . . . [*Here she speaks of a woman tortured and killed by the military.*] . . . a woman cried to death; they [the military] smashed her with stones, poor thing, and those military shot her. At that time, those military were savages; it is unnamable what those savages did. But this wasteland [witnessed] so much pain and sorrow, so many disappeared. This wasteland is their memory. It [the cross] must be respected; we must be watchful about it; we must not just leave it here and that's it, we do not come back anymore; that cannot do. We must always walk here; that is respect for the Holy Cross [*Señor Cruz*]. Of all the disappeared, of all those killed, this cross is the glory.

I take Mama Angélica's speech as one of those instances in which the whole of the past, all at once, appears actualized in a contracted form.[15] And yet, as she tries to articulate such a past in words, it can only emerge as fragments of scenes that come into being not to tell the whole story, but to define the affective qualities of the present moment.

Reflecting on her work on violence in India, Das (2007, 5) thinks of the notion of fragment not in terms of being a part or various parts that may be assembled together to make up a picture of a totality; "the *fragment,*" she writes, "marks the impossibility of such imagination." Das invites us to instead think of the fragment as alluding to "a particular way of inhabiting the world, say, in a gesture of mourning" (ibid.). In previous chapters, we have seen that similar notions of the fragment evoking the limits of representation are embedded in the ways Quechua mothers engage the truth of state atrocity revealed at the excavation site. Just as the ashes and charred fragments of human bones will never be brought back together to reconstitute a complete body, the fragments of stories of terror and suffering that the mothers retell in the context of the excavation cannot, nor are they meant to, reconstruct and represent the totality of the event. Rather, they bring these fragments back to define a particular way of inhabiting the present and occupying the former site of mass killing.

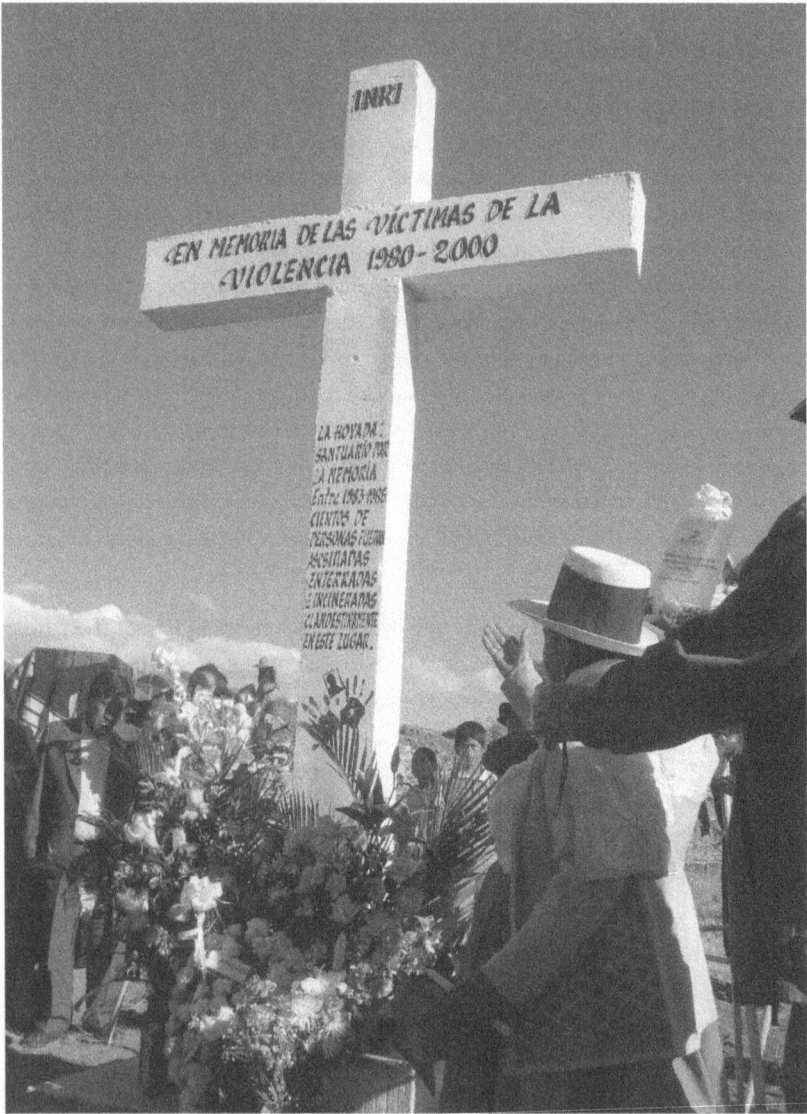

FIGURE 8.3. Mama Angélica pointing to La Cruz de la Hoyada during her speech at the cross's inauguration, July 2011.

Mama Angélica's speech translates into words these affective engagements with the truth of atrocity and the lingering effects of mass killing at the site. Through her words, the illiterate Quechua mothers of the disappeared arrogate voice to themselves and speak truth to power in what, echoing Deleuze and Guattari (1986), we may call a "minor language." These words embody the ordinary voice that, moving within and outside of two vehicular languages of the state, emerges to give expression to the mothers' experience of what it is to face state terror. The rational and evidentiary language of the law and forensic sciences serves to counter denial and anchor legal and historical accountability. The symbolic language of religion, which the Catholic, Spanish-speaking state has mobilized since colonial times to assert its "civilizing mission," serves to question whether in its self-assigned "civilizing mission" the state can go so far as to destroy the fundamental fabric of society within which a human form of life is agreed upon.

We thus attend here to a scene of the emergence of a collective voice. I emphasize that this time the mothers' voice speaks truth to power, not primarily to the sovereign that kills and allows the corpses of the enemy to rot before the public's eye as a sign of its necropower (see Chapter 5), but to the sovereign that recovers those bodies and counts, examines, identifies, and returns them to their relatives for proper burial. This collective voice emerges in the aftermath when the mothers' dilemma is not whether to obey or disobey the sovereign's law, as during times of war, but what to do with the shattered unknown human remains that the project of necro-governmentality has been unable to return home as legal, moral, and cultural subjects. In short, this collective voice emerges to articulate a response to the practices of the "fabrication of corpses," a response that builds on but goes beyond the controlled recovery of the past and in so doing reclaims the figure of the people reemerging in the aftermath as a political response to necropower and its ongoing production of ungrievability and unmournability.

To see how this response is articulated, let us follow Desjarlais (2003, 107), who tells us that if we want to grasp the dynamics of language, time, and political agency implied in ordinary words, we must listen to these words as would natives of the history these words speak of. For if we listen to these words as utterances alone, we miss the intonations in which they are wrapped, their implications, and how they relate to other words and situations in the speakers' lives. I hope that, by this point, readers are in some ways "native" to the history Mama Angélica's words speak of, in which case my task of conveying her words and the affects they articulate will be greatly facilitated. For this task, I transpose her spoken words into a series of textual fragments, which enables me to undertake a step-by-step exegesis that will situate these words in their historical, cultural, and affective contexts.[16]

First Fragment

[*In Quechua*] This cross is in the name of so many of our dead and disappeared. It is their presence, so we can respect them, so we can see them. It is the presence of the more than eight hundred people disappeared here. [*Shifting to Spanish*] It must be respected; we must be watchful about it, always; it cannot be left just like that, because we could never find our children.

> *Tanto wañunninchikpa, tanto chinkaqninchikpa, sutinpi kay cros; . . . paypa presencianmin; kay 800 y picos desapareciduspa presencianmin kay cros.* [Shifting to Spanish] *Hay que respetar, hay que mirar todo, todo tiempo, no hay que dejar así nomás, porque nunca encontramos nosotros nuestros hijos.*

In this fragment of speech, Mama Angelica establishes an internal relation between the cross on one hand and on the other the disappeared and unknown dead during Peru's "war on terror." At first sight, it seems that the mother thinks of the cross simply as a cenotaph for missing relatives who have presumably been executed at the site. This formula builds on two premises: the disappeared were last seen at Los Cabitos, and the forensic investigation demonstrated that most of their bodies were destroyed beyond recognition. It follows that the search is over and that, since there are no more places to look for their disappeared, it is time for the mothers to return home. The cross thus stands at the site as a symbol of remembrance and commemoration for the disappeared and unknown dead, as a substitute object for the mothers' loss. In this view, as articulated by the Catholic priest, La Cruz de la Hoyada means containment, symbolization, closure, and the eventual end of the searching.

But seeing things this way misses the unruly elements that the cross unfurls. Note the ways the mother's speech connects notions of indeterminacy and presence ("It is the presence of the more than eight hundred people disappeared here [kay 800 y picos desapareciduspa presencianmin kay cros]"). Let us recall that indeterminacy short-circuits the attempt of the state to bring the disappeared back into being through expert work. While proving that human beings were tortured, killed, and incinerated at La Hoyada, the technologies of truth of the law and forensic sciences cannot determine just how many people were slaughtered and who they were.

Indeterminacy thus impedes the state from unfolding a legal and moral space where, by means of counting and measuring, individual identities can be restituted, human bodies relocated, victim status distributed, and responsibility and recognition allotted.[17]

In contrast, in Mama Angélica's speech indeterminacy does not stop movement. Rather, it leads motion in a different direction as it works to restate the ontological status of the disappeared as an indeterminate multitude, a collective entity composed of an unknown number of unknown people disappeared and annihilated together by the state, whose shattered remains *may* have been found at the site but who themselves have not been found yet. Indeterminacy thus unfolds a space that the unknown dead and disappeared inhabit as ghosts, from which they return to haunt the dream that we can *again* have a political life together in society without grieving and mourning those who the practices of state terror deemed ungrievable and unmournable (see Chapter 7).

This contrast between the two kinds of space-time that indeterminacy effects resembles one of the distinctions Deleuze and Guattari (1987, 477) draw between a smooth and a striated space-time: "in a smooth space-time one occupies without counting, whereas in a striated space-time one counts in order to occupy." This insight helps us to see how, when Mama Angélica speaks of the cross as expressing the presence of an indeterminate number of disappeared, she does not speak of it as a plain cenotaph that represents the victims who have finally been found, recovered, counted, identified, and returned home. Rather, she speaks of it as a material sign of those who have simultaneously been found and not yet found, of those who inhabit a disruptive space-time that escapes the determinations of state power and that the disappeared occupy by right because they are not excluded by counting.

Second Fragment

[*In Spanish*] In this wasteland, many corpses, men and women, were thrown in [unmarked] pits . . . [*Here she speaks of a woman tortured and killed by the military.*] . . . a woman cried to death; they [the military] smashed her with stones, poor thing, and those military shot her. At that time, those military were savages; it is unnamable what those savages did.

En esa pampa muchos cadaveres [sic] enterrados, hombre y mujeres en huecos han puesto; . . . una mujer han gritado todavía, hasta esa fecha está machucando piedra, *entonces ahí han gritado pobrecita y han baleado todavía los militares; es un salvaje esa fecha esos militares, no tiene nombre esos salvajes.*

The shattered human remains emerging from clandestine mass graves bear witness to the time when the sovereign power to kill with impunity manifested itself to its fullest extent. In the mother's words, it was a time when members of the Peruvian military became "savages," a time when they carried out practices that cannot be articulated in language because they are *unnamable* ("no tiene nombre esos salvajes"). What is "savage" and unnamable is not so much that the state can kill, but that the forms of violence waged during the campaign of state terror went beyond the thresholds of life and death within which Andean peoples test the range of a human form of life. Mama Angélica's brief mention of an unknown woman smashed with stones and killed at the site recalls one sense of this beyond-ness, namely, the abject forms of violation of the human body through the act of killing. The other sense refers to the fact that the bodies of victims were made unavailable for some kind of resignification of their deaths as a form of human death. Both senses allude to a form of violence that is seen as "being 'against nature,' as defining the limits of life itself" (Das 2007, 90) because it is an assault against life itself and against those thresholds of life and death within which the possibility of a life together in society is imagined among Andean peoples.

The conceptual distinction between the notions of limit and threshold helps us to see what the stakes are for these mothers in the task of recovery from state atrocity. Deleuze and Guattari (1987, 438) say that "the limit designates the penultimate marking a necessary rebeginning, and the threshold the ultimate marking an inevitable change." In the mothers' formulation of the "unnamable" and "savage," the sense is that the atrocious forms of violation of the human body to the point that death as a human experience was made impossible for some people cannot be considered merely in terms of the limit. These practices are not just casual instances of excessive use of force that do not demand an interrogation of the nature of the social relations that made these practices possible—relations that make some Peruvians more killable than others and their deaths more negligible than others. They do not allow for a fresh beginning of the same kind of social relations that ultimately shaped those practices in the first place. Rather, with the state's "fabrication of corpses" at Los Cabitos, a threshold of life (and death) has been crossed, a transgression has occurred that marks the need for an inevitable change. La Cruz de la Hoyada marks the point at which our relationship to the political community, our sense of justice, and our sense of mourning can no longer be grounded on the same understandings and agreements that led to atrocity. It calls not for recognition—say, via rights and victimhood—but for renewed political relations within new assemblages. It calls for refounding.

Third Fragment

[*In Spanish*] But this wasteland [witnessed] so much pain and sorrow, so many disappeared. This wasteland is their memory.

Pero esa pampa tanto pensamiento, tanto desaparecido, su memoria esa pampa señores.

Here Mama Angélica's speech translates into words the material senses that the site of mass killing has for the Quechua mothers of the disappeared (see Chapters 6 and 7). The pain and suffering of the disappeared and unknown dead linger at the site, alongside their remains reduced to irrecoverable ashes and minute fragments of burnt human bones mixed with the soil of the site. The mothers' pain and sorrow for their missing relatives also lingers ("esa pampa tanto pensamiento, tanto desaparecido").

In her speech Mama Angélica connects this haptic space to the notion of memory ("su memoria esa pampa señores"). To say that the site is their memory is to initiate a move to offer the victims of state terror some form of acknowledgment. To be a human experience, death cannot go without witnessing. In ordinary contexts, as seen in Chapter 2, the witness is one who can tell the story of a life that comes to an end; he or she is one who mediates between the dead and the mourners to make them both understand that death is not the end of life, but a transfiguration into a new mode of existence. At Los Cabitos, the mother's words affirm that the only witness to the asocial death of the people killed at this site is the *site itself.* It is implicit that the perpetrators cannot be witnesses. In contrast, the site is a document of the atrocities carried out against defenseless people. It tells the story of death without witnessing at the time the site was *chunniq* (deserted, lonesome)—that is, when necropower composed a "death world" in the region.[18]

The site can be witness because it is impregnated with the blood of those killed and contains their bones reduced to ashes and unrecoverable fragments, despite the best efforts of the forensic experts to thoroughly collect such remains. At work here is the Andean notion that dead human bones have agency—a notion discussed in previous chapters.[19] In modern epistemologies, dead bodies are usually depicted as inert objects, and if they have any agency, even political agency, it can be attributed only to the meanings that the living assign to them.[20] In contrast, the idea that dead human bones have agency does not rely on the meanings dead bodies embody, but on their very materiality.[21] The disturbing, animating, constraining, and enabling power of human remains derives not simply from the ambiguity of dead bodies as uneasy subjects/objects or persons/things, but also from their being, as Stepputat (2014, 26) puts it, "flowing, transforming materials that are recognizably human, thus demanding stabilization into definable 'objects' and perhaps identifiable 'subjects.'" Human remains are thus more metonymic than metaphorical; they signal "presence" more readily than meaning.

This is the kind of presence evoked in the mother's speech. The human remains found at Los Cabitos have resiliently survived the attempts of necropower and territoriality to vanish them from the face of the earth. They have also escaped the attempts of necro-governmentality to both capture them within the power/knowledge grid of the law and forensic sciences and stabilize them into definable objects (individual bodies) and identifiable subjects (victims with proper names). Moreover, having been reduced to ashes and dust, many of these human remains are irremediably mixed with the earth, their substance becoming one with the substance of the earth, and thereby are beyond the reach of the rational procedures of forensic sciences and the law. But they are there, their presence remains at the site, and this is the sense of the utterance "su memoria esta pampa señores." It evokes the floating energies and affects around the unknown bodies found at La Hoyada, energies and affects that cannot be fixed or invested in techniques and signs but that have become forces that haunt the political community.[22]

Fourth Fragment

[*In Spanish*] It [the cross] must be respected; we must be watchful about it; we must not just leave it here and that's it, we do not come back anymore; that cannot do. We must always walk here; that is respect for the Holy Cross [*Señor Cruz*].

Hay que respetar, hay que ver todo, no hay que dejar así nomás ahora ponemos eso acá y ya, pero otra vez ya no venimos; no puede ser, siempre venimos, eso es respeto al señor cruz.

In this fragment Mama Angélica uses the Spanish verb *venir* (to come), which in this context I take to be a variation of the more general Quechua verb *puriy* (to walk). In Chapter 5 we saw how when their loved ones were taken away from home, these mothers were driven by their grief into the streets to search for them during the height of the counterinsurgency campaign. In the streets they discovered that their private grief was also the grief of other mothers, and in the streets they constituted a community of suffering that, mobilizing the patriarchal figure of the proper mother, emerged paradoxically as a collective response to the paralyzing practices of state terror. The Quechua mothers use the verb *puriy* to describe this experience of collective walking.

In Mama Angélica's speech, the subtle shift of language from "walking" (*puriy*) to "coming" (*venir* in Spanish) is an index of how La Cruz de la Hoyada stands at a point between two trajectories. The first is the trajectory of the mothers' experience of their collective search before the forensic investigation at Los Cabitos was begun. For several years, these mothers persisted in their search and did not give in to calls to forget about their missing loved ones, let them go, and return home. But in all these years of walking, they did not have a place to reconnect affectively, at least in the subjunctive mood (might be) with their disappeared (see Chapter 6). The findings at Los Cabitos at last allowed for the possibility of assigning their missing relatives a certain "whereness," an ubiety, or at least an imperfect locality, a physical space where they could rearticulate some kind of relationship with them (see Chapter 4). It therefore seemed that the time for these mothers to return home had finally arrived—that their search was over because the unknown remains found at Los Cabitos corresponded to their disappeared, as the priest suggested.

But here is where their search takes a different turn and embarks on another trajectory. Mama Angélica's call to always come to the cross is not an invitation to visit the site in the same way one regularly visits a cemetery to commemorate dead loved ones. Such a reading would miss the temporal and historical depth of her call. Her demand that the mothers always visit the cross is a call for a transfigured form of their collective walking, or *puriy*, in response to the practices of state terror. It is a call for movement as a means of giving life to what otherwise would be a lifeless symbol. It is as though these illiterate Quechua-speaking mothers know, from experience, that the only way to relate to the Spanish-speaking state, to force it to respond to their plight, to move it in the direction of justice, to escape the determinations of terror, is to continue their collective walking. The truth of atrocity does not cancel these mothers' *puriy*, as the project of necro-governmentality expects, but only transfigures it. Their continued movement will give life to what the cross stands for: the project of having a life together in society *again* in the aftermath of the state's "fabrication of corpses."

Fifth Fragment

[*Spanish*] Of all the disappeared, of all those killed, this cross is the glory.

   Todo desaparecidos, todo matanza, su gloria es ese cruz señores.

This fragment condenses the four previous ones. La Cruz de la Hoyada is the glory of the disappeared—all of them—and the glory of those unknown people the state killed—all of them. The Spanish term *gloria* (glory) derives from the Latin "gloria," and it is ordinarily used to express and refer to praise, reverence, worship, and wonderment. It circulates primarily in the religious sphere to speak of God's magnificence, supreme goodness, and unsurpassable honor.[23] It is also customarily used to express sympathy for the dead, as in the expression "que dios lo tenga en su gloria" (may he rest with God). Since the mother's use of the term dwells in this region of language, we might be tempted to take *gloria* in that sense of sympathy and farewell to the unknown dead and disappeared, somehow following the lead of the Catholic priest.

   But coming on the heels of the disclosure of the truth of state atrocity at Los Cabitos, Mama Angélica's *gloria* has a deep political and historical sense despite its religious wrappings. In her words, "glory" weaves materiality, biography, history, and nonhuman agency together to embody the presence of an undefeated component that the work of necropower is unable to reduce. It is the resilient element that survived the state's attempt to annihilate the "internal enemy," to erase that enemy from the face of the earth without a trace, in the name of defending the body politic against a vital threat. It is the resilient element that breaks through the postconflict denial and silencing of state atrocity and the ongoing production of ungrievable and unmournable lives and deaths. It is also the resilient element that escapes the state's attempts to bring these ungrievable and unmournable lives and deaths back into society as legal, moral, and cultural subjects through the individualizing technologies of truth employed by the law and forensic sciences, within a depoliticizing state-sponsored project of "controlled recovery of the past."

La Cruz de la Hoyada is the "glory of the disappeared" because it stands on its own political ground for the ungrievable and unmournable lives and deaths of those perceived enemies of the state annihilated at the site of atrocity. It is a political ground that unfolds its space in escaping the oscillation between necropower and necro-governmentality, a space that demands a certain mode of occupation and a certain kind of becoming. It is from this space that the Quechua mothers can proclaim that what is at stake in the postconflict response to state practices of the "fabrication of corpses" is more than just a problem of rights, the rule of law, and state recognition—at stake is the crucial question of the very possibility of political community. It is from this space, this political ground, that the mothers teach us that grieving and mourning the ungrievable and unmournable grounds such a possibility of political community, because the thresholds of life and death within which a life together in society can be imagined are thus reconstituted. It is also the space where a dissonant movement (*puriy*) unfolds as the only meaningful response to the ever-present threat of state terror and the creation of "death worlds." It is, in short, a space where the figure of the people emerges and becomes.

The Figure of the People

In chapter 5, I suggested that during the campaign of state terror the mothers' puriy constituted a public in the sense Dewey (2011) gives to the notion—that is, a public emerges not so much by choice as by necessity. A public comes together in response to a shared experience of harm, and cares systematically for the consequences of a conjoint action (the source of such a harm) that, over time, becomes a problem. I suggested that the problem around which the mothers walked made the public they constituted not just different from others but to assume the figure of the people as opposed to that of the population. At stake in this problem was the limits of sovereign power and the vital question of whether in the name of defending the body politic the state can go as far as destroying fundamental agreements in forms of life upon which such a body politic claims to be erected.

Many years later, the mother's words at the site of atrocity call for reconstituting a public. This time, however, the problem to be faced has a different form: what to do with the legacy of forms of violence that went beyond the thresholds of life and death within which Andean people test what a human form of life is. The project of a "controlled recovery of the past" is insufficient to reckon with this legacy and the mothers call for arranging things differently from how necro-governmentality arranges things to govern past atrocity. This gesture evokes, again, the figure of the people as opposed to that of the population. The people, Foucault (2007, 43–44) submits, are those who conduct themselves in relation to the management of the population, at the level of the population, as if they are not part of the population—that is, they conduct themselves as if they have put themselves outside of the population as a collective subject-object. The people, in short, are those who, refusing to be the population, escape governmentality and conduct their conduct in their own terms. I

FIGURE 8.4. La Hoyada after the end of the excavation, July 2011.

now to invite the reader to consider how this image of the people has been embodied in the territory around the former site of mass killing.

Visitors to La Hoyada in 2016 could still find the following spatial configuration of the site: in the northernmost area stands an old tank of oil that presumably supplied fuel to the furnace used to incinerate bodies. Facing the tank, and directly opposite it, stands La Cruz de la Hoyada. The cross now constitutes the precise border between the former site of mass killing and the city. These two signs stand at opposite ends of a terrain crisscrossed with fading exploratory trenches dug during the forensic archaeological investigation (Figure 8.4), which exposed the foundations of the crematory ovens and the clandestine mass graves where the victims were initially buried (see Map 3).

If these visitors were familiar with the history La Hoyada tells, they would recognize three political and historical trajectories embedded in this spatial configuration (Map 4). The first corresponds to the trajectory of necropower and territoriality in creating "death worlds" in the central southern Andes during Peru's "war on terror." The now unused tank of oil, the foundations and debris of the crematorium, and the fading traces

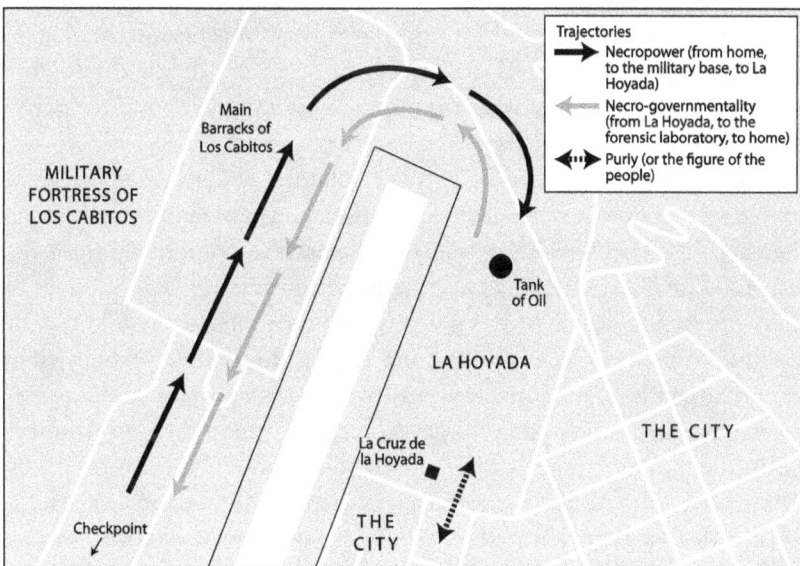

MAP 4. Trajectories of necropower, necro-governmentality, and *puriy*.

of former mass graves, among other signs, index this trajectory of state power in times of emergency. The second corresponds to the trajectory of necro-governmentality in attempting to shape postatrocity worlds. The fading trenches of the forensic excavation stand for this form of postconflict state power. The third corresponds to a form of political agency that evokes the figure of the people standing in their own right in response to the two aforesaid forms of state power. La Cruz de la Hoyada indexes this trajectory.

Our visitors would also recognize the complex set of relations of opposition and adjacency connecting these three trajectories. For instance, while the arc of necropower can be traced from victims being seized from their homes, interned in clandestine detention centers, tortured, and slaughtered and their bodies disposed of without a trace, the necro-governmentality of postconflict follows the same trajectory but in exactly the opposite direction: the bodies of victims are to be located and exhumed from their clandestine graves, taken away from the military premises, and interned in the forensic laboratory for individualization, identification, and forensic examination. Then, once the criminal evidence inscribed on these bodies has been collected, they are to be returned to their relatives for proper burial while the evidence is sent to the courts for the corresponding trial. Yet both trajectories involve state institutions, practices, technologies, experts, languages, forms of occupying the space and folding/unfolding time, and imaginations of what the object/subject of their power is (population, internal enemy, victim.)

By contrast, La Cruz de la Hoyada embodies a political and historical trajectory that does not need any institutional mediation but just walking together (*puriy*). Our visitors can now access the site directly from the city to be involved in the history it tells. In contrast, during the times of state emergency, access to the site was forbidden and one could not be involved without existential risks, and during the times of exhumation, the privileged way to be involved was by being a legal part of the procedures. Also, in contrast to necro-governmentality and necropower, whose embeddings appear now as fading ruins, the cross embodies a trajectory that is alive. The call of the mothers, as we have listened to it above, is to keep their walking alive. The cross proclaims that the only way to give life to the memory and presence of the massacred and disappeared at La Hoyada is through a renewed public mobilization. In fact, in response to this mobilization, following the inauguration of the cross, local authorities started to pay attention to the mothers' demands and took initiatives to expropriate the site for the purposes of building a Santuario por la Memoria.

But there is one more aspect that our visitors familiar with the history La Hoyada tells would not fail to recognize: the profound historical and political sense of the call for a permanent mobilization (*puriy*) around La Cruz de la Hoyada. The cross constitutes the physical and symbolic border between the city and the former site of the "fabrication of corpses," and when the mothers call for keeping their mobilization alive, it is not just to keep the memory of their disappeared alive but also to keep alive the symbolic border between the city and the site of atrocity. The historical and political statement the cross embodies becomes clear: the possibility of a life together in the city stands in polar opposition to the sovereign's capacity for the "fabrication of corpses." Otherwise put, the thresholds of life and death within which we imagine our life together in society cannot accept practices that in the name of defending the life of the city go beyond those thresholds. It is the task of the people to keep those thresholds alive.

Concluding Comments

In Chapter 7 I suggested that the historical coexistence of and interaction between different forms of power, say, sovereignty, discipline, and government, are inscribed on the landscape in the shape of particular modes of sacralization. Otherwise put, certain modes of folding and unfolding spaces of life as well as spaces of death, redemption, and transgression; the kinds of other-than-human entities that populate these spaces; the modes of acknowledging these entities; and the sets of norms and practices for addressing and relating to these entities and spaces, among other elements, are all intimately connected to specific configurations of power relations. In this chapter I have shown how the relationships of opposition and adjacency between three historical and political trajectories concerning state violence—that is, necropower, necro-governmentality, and the figure of the people—have been inscribed on the landscape around the former site of mass killing in the surroundings of Los Cabitos.

The distinction between the notions of necropower and necro-governmentality suggests a picture of sovereignty that is akin to Dumézil's (1988) idea that political sovereignty, or domination, has two heads: the magician-king and the jurist-priest, the despot and the legislator, the binder and the organizer, the fearsome and the regulated. As Deleuze and Guattari (1987) note, these poles stand in opposition, but they function as a pair, in alternation or, as I have shown, in oscillation. This picture of the two heads of sovereignty also has a family resemblance to Poole's (2004) formulation of how Quechua peasants in the Peruvian Andes see the work of state power as both threat and guarantee. In terms more familiar to the history of Andean Quechua peoples, we may say that it is also akin to the oscillation between the sword and the cross that has been a central grammar of power in Peru's political formation since colonial times.

The way this picture emerges in the Los Cabitos case allows me to make two claims. First, this picture of sovereignty differs from those other pictures, such as Mbembe's (2003), that put the emphasis on the omnipresence and omnipotence of sovereign power as the power to kill that is obsessed with the production of "death worlds." Instead, sovereignty, or political domination, also manifests itself in the task of governing a population. Second, this productive aspect of power is crucial to situate the question of the people as that of a possibility that both engages and escapes the oscillation between the two poles of sovereignty. It is a third element, working within and outside the determinations of state power.

In this chapter I have shown how, moving within and outside the state's vehicular languages—the languages of the law, forensic sciences, and religion—the mothers of the disappeared embody this third element, standing in its own right at the intersection of the two poles of sovereignty. First, they find voice to indict politically and historically the practices of the "fabrication of corpses" waged during the campaign of state terror, which made impossible even the possibility of death as human experience, as something that lies beyond the thresholds of life and death within which Andean Quechua-speaking people test what a human form of life is. Second, they also find voice to state that these practices of state atrocity sundered the fundamental fabric of society and put into question the very possibility of people living together in political community. Responding to this event of atrocity requires more than just the restoration of rights, the rule of law, and/or moral recognition. It requires a refounding of the political community, which in turn calls for the mothers' permanent mobilization (*puriy*). This gesture evokes the figure of the people reemerging from the remnants of atrocity to ground the possibility of life together in society again in the aftermath of devastating violence.

Afterword

ON JUNE 21, 2016, just as I was completing this book, the Peruvian government passed Law 30470 titled "Ley de Búsqueda de Personas Desaparecidas" (Law for the Search of Disappeared Persons) with the purpose of facilitating the search for people who were reported disappeared during the internal war in Peru between 1980 and 2000. The law is meant to expand, enhance, and accelerate current state-sponsored efforts to bring the disappeared back into the fold of the nation's citizenry, efforts that, as I have shown in this book, started in mid-2001 in the wake of the Fujimori regime's downfall. According to estimates by Peru's Ombudsman Office, one of the proponents of the law, approximately eighteen thousand Peruvians are still considered missing. Between 2002 and 2015, the government's special forensic team (Equipo Forense Especializado, EFE) exhumed 3,202 bodies from unmarked graves. The EFE has identified 1,833 of these. If these efforts continue at this slow pace, many more years will be needed to complete the official search for the disappeared. "With this law," said Eduardo Vega, head of the Ombudsman Office, "the process of search will be accelerated."[1]

The decisive and novel move the law introduces is to squarely situate this enhanced search for the disappeared within a humanitarian framework. In the law's own words, "to prioritize a humanitarian approach means that the search will seek that the process of recovery, identification, restitution, and proper burial of disappeared persons have a healing effect [*efecto reparador*] for bereaved families, and that such a search will neither encourage nor hinder the attribution of criminal responsibilities." In other words, the law unhinges the process of the search, exhumation, identification, and return of remains to families from its original moorings in the criminal investigation of human rights abuses and political crimes. Before the enactment of this law, the only way to initiate such a search process was by means of a criminal investigation on the cases of disappearance. According to the Ombudsman, this way of doing things was slow and trying and in the end prolonged the suffering of the families who have been searching for their missing loved ones for many years in order to offer them proper burial and attain closure.

With the new law, the government's executive branch takes charge of conducting this humanitarian search for the disappeared. For that purpose, the Ministry of Justice and Human Rights will "establish, execute, and supervise" a "national plan for the search of the disappeared." It also will manage a "national registry of missing persons and burial sites," which will be created through the same law. In addition, the ministry will promote and supervise psychosocial interventions focused on the "emotional and social recovery of bereaved relatives" throughout the process of the search. Likewise, the state institution will oversee that material assistance is provided to relatives throughout the process of recovery and identification. Last, and perhaps more important, the Ministry of Justice and Human Rights will be put in charge of planning and promoting the entire process of forensic investigation concerning the search for the disappeared. In short, the executive and not the judiciary branch of government will now be in charge of controlling the production and administration of forensic evidence in cases of human rights violations and political crimes.

The new law thus displays a variety of features that correspond to what I have called the necro-governmentality of postconflict. It retains and expands the central concept of the "right to truth" with which the project of the search and recovery of bodies was born in 2001. The law establishes that relatives "have the right to know the truth about the circumstances of the disappearance, the status of the missing person, including their whereabouts or, in case of death, the circumstances of their death and the place of their burial."[2] Yet in this new iteration, and in contrast to the CVR's project, the law is not meant to promote official ceremonies of reburial with the purpose of eliciting awareness and compassion among mainstream Peruvians toward their less fortunate compatriots directly affected by the war. Likewise, in contradistinction to post-CVR government actions, the new forensic interventions will not be aimed at prosecuting political crimes. Thus, the law assumes that rather than legal and/or political reckoning, survivors and relatives of the disappeared are primarily interested in achieving some form of ritual reckoning with the legacy of mass violence and atrocity. Based on the concept of the "right to truth" and on a humanitarian approach, the law posits survivors and relatives primarily as cultural rather than legal, political, or historical subjects.

The enactment of the 2016 law has been received with enthusiasm by associations of survivors and relatives of the disappeared in Peru as well as by the national and international human rights community, among them the members of the United Nations Working Group on Enforced or Involuntary Disappearances. It remains to be seen how the law will be implemented, what specific spaces of action it will open, and what technologies of truth and self it will deploy to govern the conduct of survivors and relatives and to govern the dead. One thing is for sure, however; as I have aimed to show in this book, Quechua-speaking survivors in particular and rural villagers in general will find ways to inhabit these new spaces and to articulate their own projects of justice and political and historical reckoning with atrocity and mass violence. Our future research must now turn its attention to these new engagements. In this book I have offered some insights that may help in such an exploration.

As Seery (1996) notes, death is not a usual topic for political theorization. Stepputat (2014) suggests that this neglect responds to two concurrent tendencies in Western epistemology: first, the modern move away from death that resulted in the marginalization, suppression, silencing, or even denial of death as an object of study (see also Aries 1974 and Lomnitz 2005); and second, a particular rendering of Foucault's elaboration on the shift from sovereignty to biopower. Rather than responding to changes in cultural representations of death and the dissolution of forms of social solidarity, the invisibilization of death expresses a fundamental shift in the regime of power that sanctions the emergence of Western modernity, as Foucault suggests. The apotheosis of power no longer manifests itself in the diagram of "to let live and to make die" but in "to make live and to let die." The power of the sword, and all the spectacle of death that accompanies it, gives way to a power that gives itself the function of administering life. As Foucault (1978, 138) writes,

In the passage from this world to the other, death was the manner in which a terrestrial sovereignty was relieved by another, singularly more powerful sovereignty; the pageantry that surrounded it was in the category of political ceremony. Now, it is over life, throughout its unfolding, that power establishes its dominion; death is power's limit, the moment that escapes it; death becomes the most secret aspect of existence, the most "private."

In this shift, death emerges as the limit of biopower because it is the end of life. "Death," Foucault claims, "is outside the power relationship" (2003, 248).

In this book I have interrogated this formulation of death as the limit of power or as the power relationship's outside edge. Much fine work in the burgeoning field of transitional justice echoes this notion that death is outside power relations. Scholars in this field have focused on the problem of how to prevent the repetition of mass violence and killing in the future rather than on the problem of how postconflict communities govern dead bodies as a means of legitimating the political transition of those communities from violence to nonviolence. They have rarely addressed questions about funerary rites and grammars of mourning, or, more generally, how to properly dispatch the dead, as if these questions do not pertain to problems of belonging, sovereignty, violence, and even senses of the sacred that are usually considered crucial for the (re)constitution of political communities in the aftermath of atrocity. I have suggested that this neglect is based on the assumption that death is considered as primarily a *biological* event and that any postmortem reckoning with it escapes rational debates and calculations of power in modern politics.

In contrast, following a long-standing anthropological tradition that sees death not just as a biological event but as a lengthy social process, I have offered ethnographic evidence to show how power relationships continue to occur beyond the limits of biological death. As suggested by Robert Hertz's (1960) theory of the double burial, I have followed the distinction between two deaths, that is, death as a biological event (the end of a life) and death as a symbolic event (the end of a story or a biography). Much anthropological work has long established ever since Hertz's pioneering work that, in most societies, the transition from life to death is usually highly regulated and ritualized in ways that are specific to political and cultural contexts. Various forms of political, religious, communal, or moral authority usually claim the right to govern dead bodies and the means of properly dispatching them. The modern state itself seeks to monopolize control of the transition from life to death by claiming the ultimate authority to define how the dead are to be mourned and disposed of within its jurisdiction. Because of this intense presence on the part of the state in the transition from life to death, the governance of dead bodies has often been a site of political contestation in ordinary contexts.

As historians and anthropologists have documented worldwide, political struggles over dead bodies are more intense when the bodies at stake belong to victims of political violence, war, and campaigns of state terror. The dead have thus been seen as having "political lives" (Verdery 1999) or populating political landscapes as "ghosts of war" (Kwon 2008) until survivors and postconflict authorities confront the fundamental questions concerning the localization of the bodies, the memories of the lives those dead lived, the acknowledgment of the atrocities committed against them, and the mourning of their loss, among others. The administration of the relation between the dead and the living following episodes of mass violence has thus been central for the constitution of modern states and political communities.[3]

While questions concerning the central place that the problem of governing dead bodies has in the constitution of political communities are not new in the history of the modern state, in this book I have given an account of some of the novel ways in which these struggles occur in our modern world. I have coined the notion of necro-governmentality to conceptualize a form of power that, as attested by the contemporary proliferation of projects of the forensic exhumation of mass graves in former war-torn areas, moves between two deaths attempting to shape postatrocity worlds. An assemblage of cutting-edge technologies including DNA testing and new forensic archaeological techniques has been mobilized to recover unknown victims of mass violence. In addition to an intense forensic scientific mediation, the novelty of these postconflict interventions is that they are articulated within the regimes of international human rights law and global humanitarianism as well as a new moral economy of suffering to which they give way.

This assemblage of science, human rights, and humanitarianism has come to provide the present-day grid of intelligibility to govern the postconflict traffic of dead bodies. The Peruvian case is just one illustrating how recovering, counting, individualizing, identifying, and disposing properly of dead bodies has become a central aspect in the reconstitution of postconflict political communities. I have shown how, in this context, survivors and relatives of victims trying to recover the remains of their missing loved ones in the aftermath of mass violence, such as the campaign of state terror in the Peruvian Andes, are now incited to stake their claims in terms of rights and humanitarian reason. Once largely left to the realm of "culture," the question of how people mourn and recover from mass death has been resituated within the biopolitical problem of "to make live" in terms of administering dead bodies, constituting certain kinds of subjects, sanctioning certain kinds of conduct, modulating languages of violence, and reorganizing time and space to secure the future of the body politic through material practices and rational technologies of truth and self.

I have suggested that this necro-governmentality of postconflict is the contemporary counterpart of the power to kill. While "massacres have become vital" (Foucault 1978, 137) and are no longer waged in the name of a sovereign who must be defended but on behalf of the existence of everyone in the political community, the administration of the legacy of those vital massacres is as crucial as their perpetration. However, differently from forms of negative power conceptualized as "necropolitics" or the "biopolitics of neglect," the necro-governmentality of postconflict is a positive form of power. It is a power of normalization, with simultaneous effects of individuation and homogenization. It has the form of governmentality because it aims to structure the field of possible action and speech of survivors, relatives of victims, and the population at large so as they are able to conduct their conduct as free subjects.

Looking at the work of the necro-governmentality of postconflict in the Peruvian context has allowed me to interrogate crucial questions of political community, authority, and belonging beyond the usual frameworks of rights and the law as well as the rationalist languages of modern politics that inform most transitional justice theories. To begin with, I have suggested that the presence of this form of power in postconflict settings asks for a reconceptualization of the notion of sovereignty beyond its usual characterization as the power to kill or let die. If I have persuaded you, the reader, that a form of power such as necro-governmentality exists, then perhaps we may agree in the idea that the question of sovereignty cannot be considered merely in terms of "necropower," or the power to create "death worlds," as suggested by theorists such as Mbembe and Agamben. The picture of sovereignty I have presented in this book resonates with Dumézil's (1988) characterization of sovereignty, or political domination, as a power that has two heads: the magician-king and the jurist-priest, the despot and the legislator, the binder and the organizer, the fearsome and the regulated (see also Deleuze and Guattari 1987). If the political requires violence to constitute a population (Kernaghan 2009), then we can say that the political, as suggested above, also requires the administration of the legacy of those killings committed in the task of capturing a population or protecting it from perceived vital threats.

This conceptualization of sovereignty as the oscillation between two heads of political domination is crucial to see the emergence of a third political entity that I have seen as evoking the figure of the people. I have documented how survivors and relatives of victims of state atrocity escape the normalizing and depoliticizing impulse of the official projects of reckoning with past atrocity. I have shown how this possibility can be best examined when technologies of truth and self through which the state seeks to govern past atrocity reach a material limit in their ability to individualize and identify the remains of victims of state terror whose bodies have been systematically destroyed beyond recognition—a practice that, following Hannah Arendt, I have called the "fabrication of corpses."

But to see the emergence of this third political entity, I have invited readers to go beyond the usual understandings of modern politics in terms of rights, the rule of law, and humanitarian reason and instead to pay attention to the ordinary practices and technologies of self and truth that survivors and relatives bring to sites of mass killing to cope with legacies of atrocity. In doing so, I have cast light upon the ways forms of agency that are not usually considered in rationalist studies of politics "object" (Latour 2000) official projects of reckoning with past atrocity. One such form concerns the agency of things—and particularly, the agency of human remains. The human remains that this book addresses have resiliently survived state attempts to make them vanish completely, and they simultaneously resist their capture within the modern power/knowledge grid of the law and forensic sciences as identified individuals. These ungovernable human remains remain as ghosts of atrocity haunting the political community, and survivors and relatives appropriate these haunting powers to reclaim the past on their own terms.

A second kind of objection pertains to the question of the reterritorialization of the political community. With the removal of bodies from their clandestine burial sites, the necro-governmentality of postconflict alters the wartime relationship between the geography of violence and the geography of memory as memory travels with the remains of the dead. By means of this traffic of dead bodies, the state seeks to reclaim sovereignty over a territory free from the material traces of the war and govern the memory of the war. Yet, as I have documented in this book, survivors and relatives contest this operation of depoliticization by means of ritually occupying former sites of killing. They thus inscribe upon the landscape their memory of violence—a memory the state seeks to individualize and privatize, thereby effacing its collective character.

A third kind of objection is the governance of the language used to speak about the violence of the past, and particularly of the atrocities of the state. I have shown how, as in other similar experiences, in Peru the necro-governmentality of postconflict entailed the establishment of an "official story" that frames a particular way of naming the events of the past that is highly selective, highlighting some aspects of the history of violence while obscuring others. By showing how survivors and relatives escape the attempts at governing the ways they should speak of the past, I have argued that the naming of violence does not reflect semantic struggles alone. I have documented the ways that ordinary language becomes for survivors and relatives the vehicle for bodying forth pain, sentiments, and stories of terror and suffering and how, in their naming and silences, they make a claim on political community.

These kinds of agency escape the normalizing and depoliticizing effects of the necro-governmentality of postconflict to assert that the question of how to reckon with state atrocity cannot be reduced to a problem of rights restoration, behavior modulation, and state recognition. I have shown how, in the two cases of state atrocity I discussed in this book, survivors and relatives seize the moment of the forensic exhumation to speak truth to power and denounce the practices of state terror that resulted in the "fabrication of corpses" such as occurred at Los Cabitos and the Accomarca massacre; but I have also shown how for these survivors and relatives the task of remaking a world in the aftermath of devastating violence demands to recompose fundamental fabrics of society torn by state terror as well as reconstitute fundamental agreements in forms of life that the state is supposed to protect and guarantee. The picture of politics that emerges here is thus one concerned with (re)composing a world rather than concerned merely with claiming rights, the rule of law, and state recognition.

In this sense of politics as (re)composition of a world, the Quechua-speaking survivors and relatives of victims of state atrocity in the Peruvian Andes repoliticize the problem of justice and mourning in the aftermath of devastating violence, in contrast to the depoliticizing and normalizing impulse that animates the project of the necro-governmentality of post-conflict. As suggested above, this gesture of escaping the project of govern-mentality echoes the distinction of "people" and "population" that Foucault (2007, 43–44) considered fundamental in the constitution of a political community of free subjects. By means of ordinary practices and technolo-gies of truth and self that escape the field of possible action and speech that governmentality structures to conduct the conduct of the Quechua survivors and relatives, those survivors and relatives mobilize a radical cri-tique against the practices of sovereignty that resulted in events such as the mass killing at Los Cabitos and the Accomarca massacre. Sovereign power has limits before a field of freedoms and rights whose nature the sovereign does not, and cannot, command. And the only way to protect those free-doms and rights is to become people—that is, to take back for the people the *constituent* power and reinstate the fact that sovereign power is always *constituted* power.

Notes

Introduction

1. "And when do the disappeared return? / Every time a thought summons them. / How do we speak to the disappeared? / With our emotions seizing us from inside." Unless otherwise indicated, all translations from Quechua, French, and Spanish in this book are the author's.

2. "Lima tendrá su propio Cristo del Corcovado." *El Comercio*, June 10, 2011. The statue is thirty-seven meters high, and according to Wrobel (2014, 78), is four meters taller than Rio de Janeiro's Christ the Redeemer.

3. Some in the opposition argued that García's Cristo del Pacífico, which they had re-named Cristo del Neoliberalismo, was an integral part of the broad efforts deployed by the ruling elites, since the runoff election period in the fall, to ensure that Ollanta Humala, the nationalist incoming president, keep the neoliberal economic model intact.

4. "Declaraciones del Cardenal Cipriani luego de bendecir 'Cristo del Pacífico,'" Arzobispado de Lima, http://www.arzobispadodelima.org/index.php?option=com_content &view=article&id=1133:declaraciones-del-cardenal-cipriani-luego-de-bendecir-qcristo-del -pacificoq&catid=169:junio-2011&Itemid=530 (accessed February 28, 2015).

5. Needless to say, it is Catholicism that claims for itself the de facto right to be an integral part of modern politics in Peru. This "right" has its roots in the Spanish colonial project, which materialized the brutal subjection of colonial subjects in the so-called New World by means of the joint work of both the colonial church and the colonial state. This has usually been illustrated as the joint work of the cross and the sword. As Nelson suggests in her work on postwar Guatemala, in several respects, this logic of power lives on in Latin America: the sword works through physical force, while the cross works more subtly on "hearts and minds" (2009, 34). For a critique of liberal understandings of the place of religion in modern secular societies, see Asad (2003).

6. Here, I follow the notion of "vehicular language" of Deleuze and Guattari (1986). They ask us to think of language not as a transparent means for exchange of information,

but as a hierarchic system structured by and structuring power relations. Following Henri Gobard, they speak of four kinds of language: a vernacular, maternal, or territorial language; a vehicular, urban, governmental, worldwide language (of business, commercial exchange, and bureaucratic transmission); a referential language (of sense and culture); and a mythic language (on the horizon of cultures). "The spatiotemporal categories of these languages differ sharply: vernacular language is *here*; vehicular language is *everywhere*; referential language is *over there*; mythic language is *beyond*" (Deleuze and Guattari 1986, 23).

7. A former director of the Instituto de Medicina Legal (IML, Legal Medical Institute) said that probably more than one thousand people had been disappeared at the site. Luis Bromley, "Cerca de mil personas fueron recluidas en Los Cabitos, y no salieron nunca." *La República*, April 27, 2008. The IML is the state institution that provides forensic science expertise and services to legal and other state institutions and agencies.

8. For the notion of "public secret," see Taussig (1999). See also Tate (2007) and Gonzales (2011).

9. In Chapter 8 I return to these words to elaborate on what is meant by the "glory" of the disappeared and how they condense a history of suffering and struggle into a single moment of instruction that, in reclaiming the past, makes a claim about the possibility of political community in the aftermath of state atrocity.

10. Translation modified by the author.

11. Translation modified by the author. The CVR's epidemiology of violence was based on seventeen thousand oral testimonies that the commission collected during its two-year mandate (June 2001–August 2003).

12. I use the notion here to refer to the logic of "letting die" as distinct from the logic of "taking life" that Foucault conceptualizes in his work on biopower (1978). The notion of the "biopolitics of neglect" also appears in de la Cadena (2015, xviii).

13. In his well-known analysis of the South African Truth and Reconciliation Commission (TRC), Richard Wilson (2001) offers the most systematic critique of the ways in which these commissions deploy a variety of metanarratives, such as "reconciliation," for reconstructing the nation-state and its hegemony in a top-down direction. The gap between national and local processes of reckoning with the legacy of the apartheid regime was notable, and the TRC did not attempt to bridge it.

14. History books in Peru are full of references to thousands of people killed in episodes of mass violence. But typically only the names of the major protagonists are known. For the most part, the dead in these episodes are anonymous people who enter history as statistics. For a sample of the most recent books about the history of political violence in Peru, see Walker (2014), Mendez (2005), Heilman (2010), and La Serna (2012).

15. The notion of "governing dead bodies" comes from Stepputat's notion of "governing the dead" (2014). See discussion below.

16. Translation modified by the author.

17. Rebecca K. Root (2012) offers more insights into the CVR's involvement with exhumations in her comprehensive case study of the Peruvian CVR. She conceptualizes such interventions as being part of "symbolic reparations." However, like Hayner, she does not mention the ceremonies of reburial that the CVR performed during its tenure. On the

CVR and transitional justice in Peru, see also Milton (2014), Saona (2014), Bueno-Hansen (2015), Boesten (2014), and del Pino and Yezer (2013).

18. From the time legal scholars such as Martha Minow (1998) and Ruti Teitel (2000) published their seminal books, transitional justice has become a field of inquiry. There are even specialized journals. In this vast literature the question of governing the dead is barely present. This is the case even in anthropological literature on transitional justice. For instance, in two otherwise excellent edited volumes on the topic, there is no allusion to questions of burial, funerary rites, or, more generally, how to properly dispatch the dead during violent conflict. See Hinton (2010) and Shaw and Waldorf (2010).

19. The CVR's final report (or sections of it) is also customarily offered as evidence in the project of accountability for past state atrocity. It figures prominently as evidence in most of the trials on human rights violations (Carlos Rivera, personal communication; Rivera is a well-known Peruvian human rights attorney representing the plaintiffs in several trials on human rights). Interestingly, every year groups of Peruvians in Lima and other regions gather on August 28 to celebrate one more anniversary of the release of the CVR's final report. Furthermore, every year, panels of academics in Peru and elsewhere are convened to evaluate the progress on justice, reparation, and institutional reform that the CVR recommended in its final report to prevent the repetition of violence in Peru.

20. Taussig (1984) argues that rational languages are insufficient to understand excessive violence and that we need to approach this through consideration of symbolic imaginary, mythic, and emotive aspects.

21. An example of this skepticism is philosopher Richard Rorty's (1991, 29) candid acknowledgment that the rational public debate entails the exclusion of what cannot be taken seriously: "We Western liberal intellectuals should accept the fact that we have to start from where we are, and that this means that there are lots of views, which we simply cannot take seriously." Cited in de la Cadena (2015, 91). For a fascinating account of what desecularizing modern politics entails in the Andean context, see de la Cadena (2015).

22. To emphasize how devastating the violence in this region was, the CVR projected the number of fatalities on a national scale in the following terms: "If the ratio of victims reported to the CVR with respect to Ayacucho were similar countrywide, the violence would have caused 1,200,000 deaths and disappearances. Of that number, 340,000 would have occurred in the city of Lima." Comisión de la Verdad y Reconciliación 2004, 433.

23. Citing official sources, Gloria Cano, executive director of the Asociación Pro Derechos Humanos (APRODEH), a prestigious and well-known human rights NGO in Peru, said that by mid-2015 around eighteen thousand Peruvians remain "disappeared." "Aprodeh: De Acuerdo a las cifras del Ministerio Público hay 18 mil desaparecidos en el Perú," ideele-RADIO, June 11, 2015, http://peruwp.zgeist.org/aprodeh-de-acuerdo-a-las -cifras-del-ministerio-publico-hay-18-mil-desaparecidos-en-el-peru/ (accessed July 11, 2016).

24. "Desaparecidos en Perú: "Encontraré a mi hermano aunque me tome toda la vida," BBC-Mundo, August 28, 2015, http://www.bbc.com/mundo/noticias/2015/08/150827_ peru_busqueda_familiares_ppb (accessed November 6, 2015).

25. Recounting her reaction when she first came to know about Auschwitz, Arendt (2000, 13–14) said: "It was really as if an abyss had opened. Because we had the idea that

266 Notes to Introduction

amends could somehow be made for everything else, as amends can be made just for about everything at some point in politics. But not for this. *This ought not to have happened.* And I do not mean just the number of victims. I mean the method, the fabrication of corpses and so on—I do not need to go into that. This should not have happened. Something happened there to which we cannot reconcile ourselves. None of us ever can" (emphasis in the original).

26. Arendt (1968, 452) writes: "The concentration camps, by making death itself anonymous (making it impossible to find out whether a prisoner is dead or alive) robbed death of its meaning as the end of a fulfilled life. In a sense they took away the individual's own death, proving that henceforth nothing belonged to him and that he belonged to no one. His death merely set a seal on the fact that he had never really existed."

27. On the notion of "forensic turn," see Anstett and Dreyfus (2015). For a synthetic history of the evolution of these new subdisciplines, see Rosenblatt (2015). He groups them under the label "human rights forensic investigation," which in his view is a distinct, networked field of global activism and scientific practice rather than a set of sporadic or idiosyncratic interventions (2015, 8). On the emergence of the forensic anthropological techniques in contexts of mass death, see also Wagner (2008), Renshaw (2011), and the collections edited by Crossland and Joyce (2015) and Ferrandiz and Robben (2015).

28. The anthropological archive, full of detailed descriptions of ideas about death and the afterlife as well as practices of mourning and disposal of the body among the natives, has registered the ghostly presence of the colonial state attempting to eliminate those native practices. See, for instance, Malinowski (1948), Rosaldo (1993), and Coklin (2001).

29. In the case of the Americas, for instance, by the midcolonial period, pre-Columbian sacred sites, ancestor worship, and cults of the dead were no longer at the center of the religious and political life of indigenous peoples; they had been replaced by colonial churches and the saintly world of the colonial Catholic imaginary. The notion of the "Christianization of death" comes from historian Gabriela Ramos (2010). For more on the "conversion" of the Andean Indians, see Estenssoro (2003). For an anthropological perspective on these historical processes in the Andean region, see Gose (2008) and Robin (2008). For Mexico and Central America, see Lomnitz (2005).

30. In this respect, see Sarah Wagner's (2008) remarkable study of the development of DNA technologies to recover and identify the Bosnian Muslim victims of the genocide in Srebrenica.

31. In his critique of Foucault's conception of power, Mbembe (2003) argues that the concept of biopower, as a form of power thoroughly invested in life in order to produce a healthy population, does not look at the ways a politics of death and killing continues to permeate its workings. This is particularly the case in colonial contexts and similar situations, such as apartheid in South Africa and the Israeli occupation of Palestine, where biopower ultimately manifests itself in the power to kill or to allow to live—that is, in terms of sovereign power.

32. In my use of the notion of "governmentality" here, I follow Fassin's (2011) observation that, contrary to what is often believed, governmentality is not about life but only about populations. He argues that Foucault invented the concept of biopolitics, but paradoxically

in his later work he avoided addressing the core of the issue—life itself. Instead, Foucault turned biopolitics into what is in essence a politics of populations, "a politics which measures and regulates, constructs and produces human collectivities" (ibid., 185) through a series of political technologies such as death rates and family planning programs, health regulations and migration controls. Governmentality is a form of normalizing power that seeks to produce human collectivities by means other than either violence and coercion or consensus as evoked in the figure of the social contract. As Foucault (2007) shows, at the center of this form of power is the problem of conduct or, more properly speaking, how to conduct the conduct of others—that is, the conduct of bodies, the self, families, children, populations, etc. Governmentality thus is about structuring and shaping the field of possible action and speech of subjects so they conduct themselves as free subjects (see Lemke 2011).

33. In Chapter 1 I describe how this form of governmentality came into being in the Peruvian case.

34. The anthropological literature on death, mourning, and burial is extensive. Some classic studies and collections are Hertz (1961), Malinowski (1948), Bloch and Parry (1982), Metcalf and Huntington (1991), Seremetakis (1991), Conklin (2001), Desjarlais (2003), Scheper-Hughes (1993), and Rosaldo (1993). For a relatively recent review of this literature, see Robben, ed. (2004).

35. The figure of the grieving woman inhabiting the space between two deaths is pervasive in anthropological literature. See particularly Bloch and Parry's (1982) analysis of the relationship between death, women, and power in different contexts. See also Seremetakis (1991) for a critique of the synchronic views of the role of women in the gendered division of labor in the work of mourning. See also Das (2007).

36. This fieldwork between October 2005 and August 2007 was part of my dissertation research and was funded by the National Science Foundation (project No. 0518950; title: "Law, Transitional Justice and National Reconciliation in Post-war Peru") and the United States Institute of Peace (project title: "Law, Transitional Justice and Social Repair in Post-war Peru"). In addition to my ethnographic work with survivors and relatives, I conducted research in the archives of the Peruvian CVR, made an archive of judicial and prosecutorial rulings pertaining to my case studies, and conducted formal and informal interviews with judges, prosecutors, attorneys, and CVR officials. I made follow-up visits during each summer until 2012. All research was carried out in Quechua and Spanish, languages in which I have native fluency.

Chapter 1

1. Asociación de Familiares Afectados por la Violencia Política del Distrito de Accomarca (Association of Relatives Affected by Political Violence from the District of Accomarca).

2. *Dar cristiana sepultura* (to give somebody a Christian burial) is the contemporary Peruvian Spanish expression for "proper burial."

3. At the time I met him, in May 2006, Celestino was in his late fifties. Like many other Accomarquinos, he moved to Lima at an early age. Thus, he did not directly witness the

1985 massacre, but his mother was killed, as were many other of his close relatives. Soon after, relatives of the victims living in Lima organized themselves into an association to denounce the killing and pursue justice. The association was reactivated in 2003, when the Peruvian legal authorities reopened criminal investigations in the case. Celestino became president of the association in 2005 and was acknowledged as a very active and effective leader.

4. In postconflict Peru the term "genocide" is politically charged and its use is highly contentious. While carefully avoiding the term in reference to the violence of the state, the CVR attributed "genocidal" tendencies to the Shining Path. In short, at odds with how some survivors speak of the violence their communities suffered—emphasizing how "killability" was clearly defined by ethnicity, language, and cultural affiliation—the CVR politically qualifies the term to modulate how political violence should be spoken of. Interestingly, a member of the CVR, anthropologist Carlos Iván Degregori, had argued earlier that the war might well be characterized as genocidal. See Degregori et al. (1996).

5. The trial for this case started in November 2010. As for similar cases, the trial was conducted at a special court in Lima. On August 31, 2016, more than thirty years after the facts and a trial lasting nearly six years, the court finally pronounced judgment, sentencing the defendants, among them high-ranking officers, to ten to twenty-five years in prison. For a brief account of the sentence, see "Justice for Accomarca," Council on Hemispheric Affairs, http://www.coha.org/wp-content/uploads/2016/09/AccomarcaPDF-2.pdf (accessed December 29, 2016).

6. Despite its importance, scant academic attention has been paid to the case. But see the ethnography on reconciliation in rural Ayacucho by Theidon (2012).

7. The IML experts completed the exhumation of the remainder of the victims in 2010. However, the full individualization and identification of their remains was still pending at the time of writing (2015).

8. Diane Nelson (2009, 40–41) observes for Guatemala that the beginnings of both a war and postwar period are difficult to pin down because it is always possible to go back in history in search of causal factors for a war, and war flares in different places at different times and with different manifestations, making it difficult to conclusively assert when a war ends in a certain place. We can say something similar about Peru. If, as the CVR suggests, the origins of violence lie not only with the political will of the groups that took up arms against the state, but also with deep structural failures in society, we could trace the historical origins of the latter and establish continuities between previous episodes of violence—frequent rather than exceptional in Peruvian history—and the most recent one (e.g., Heilman 2010.) Also, as in Guatemala, the internal war in Peru flared up in different places at different times and in different forms. Yet here I am following the convention of describing the war and postwar period in terms of global events that marked inflections in the national process of violence.

9. For a succinct and compelling analysis of the first decade of the internal war in Peru, see Poole and Rénique (1992).

10. Around this time, the police also detained MRTA's major leaders. In April 1997, the Fujimori regime completed the defeat of this group when the military stormed the embassy of Japan in Lima, where the guerrillas had taken hundreds of people hostage.

11. For an account of corruption during the authoritarian neoliberal regime of Alberto Fujimori, see Alfonso Quiroz's (2008) monumental history of corruption in Peru that dates back to the country's colonial past.

12. Former CVR commissioner Carlos Iván Degregori (2004, 76) coined the notion "memory of salvation" to conceptualize the Fujimori regime's politics of memory of the internal war.

13. Peru's withdrawal from the jurisdiction of the IACourtHR followed a ruling in which the court ordered a new trial for a terrorism suspect and demanded that the Peruvian state adjust its antiterrorist legislation to internationally accepted standards of due process. *Castillo Petruzzi et al. v. Peru*, Judgment of May 30, 1999. This was the last episode of a two-decade period of troubled relations between Peru and the international system of protection of human rights.

14. Paniagua initially thought that the problem of human rights abuses of the past should be left to the next administration. The human rights community and its allies within the regime managed to overcome Paniagua's reluctance to expand corruption investigations into a much wider search for truth and accountability in human rights. See Root (2012, 43).

15. This sentence inaugurated a postamnesty era in Latin America as other national courts reopened cases of human rights crimes that had been closed by amnesty laws in the 1980s. For more on this, see Burt (2009), Gonzales-Cueva (2006), and Roht-Arriaza (2005).

16. Some perpetrators were subsequently prosecuted and even convicted, including Fujimori himself, who was sentenced in April 2009 on charges of crimes against humanity during his tenure. For more on the Fujimori trial, see Burt (2009) and Youngers and Burt (2009).

17. Inter-American Court of Human Rights. Case of Barrios Altos *v.* Peru. Judgment of March 14, 2001 (Merits), p. 11. http://www.corteidh.or.cr/docs/casos/articulos/seriec_75 _ing.pdf (accessed April 24, 2013).

18. Directiva No. 011-2001-MP-FN, issued September 8, 2001. The Fiscalía de la Nación/Ministerio Público is the Public Prosecutor's Office in Peru. In this book, I make use of the noun Fiscalía to refer to this legal institution. In addition to laying down step-by-step instructions to establish uniform criteria for the investigation of clandestine graves, the Fiscalía's ordinance mandated bureaucratic adjustments that would enhance the institution's capability for this kind of investigation and summoned the participation of experts in forensic archaeology and anthropology. The Fiscalía also ordered that two of its provincial branches specialize in the investigation of human rights violations, forced disappearances, extrajudicial executions, and clandestine mass graves and that prosecutors who worked in former war-torn areas be trained in forensic techniques of investigation of clandestine graves.

19. Rosenblatt (2015) defines it as a "small scientific revolution" and locates its origins in the Argentinean search for the disappeared during the 1980s. He offers a systematic account of how a new subdiscipline has emerged from the various and frequent interventions of forensic scientists in contexts of mass violence and gross human rights violations. This is an instance of the Foucauldian observation that a discipline emerges when its practitioners begin to reflect on the discipline itself and a distinctive style dominates its forms of inquiry and practice. See also Wagner (2008).

20. See, for instance, Naqvi (2006) and Mendez and Bariffi (2012).

21. "Annual Report of the Inter-American Commission on Human Rights 1985–86," OEA/Ser.L/V/II.68 Doc.8 Rev.1, 193, quoted in Mendez and Bariffi (2012).

22. It is beyond the scope of this chapter to engage with a theoretical discussion on the inability of the law to represent mass atrocity. For such a discussion, see Arendt (2006), Felman (2002), and Agamben (1999).

23. Cristina Olazabal, interview, Ayacucho, Peru, February 1, 2006. Olazabal is a dedicated, courageous, and sensitive prosecutor who, at the time of my fieldwork in Ayacucho, was in charge of investigating major cases of human rights crimes committed during the counterinsurgency campaign in the region. During her tenure, powerful political actors whom she had indicted for human rights violations retaliated with legal persecution, harassment, and death threats. See also Rojas-Perez (2010, 2013).

24. On the evolution and expansion of notions of trauma and narrative modes of healing in contemporary international politics, see Fassin and Rechtman (2009).

25. At the time, I was working as a professional human rights activist for the Instituto de Defensa Legal, and I can attest that the truth commission emerged out of negotiations between the Paniagua regime and the Peruvian human rights community, rather than, as is usually the case, out of negotiations between an outgoing and an incoming regime. The truth commission was brought to Paniagua's attention early in the transition but only came into being well after the appointment of a specialized team of prosecutors to investigate the Fujimori regime's pervasive corruption and the 2001 negotiations between the Peruvian state and the Inter-American system of human rights. Mainstream Peruvians initially accepted the appointment of this body of inquiry only because they saw it as part of a broad effort to leave behind Fujimori's legacy of corruption. For more on the creation of the Peruvian truth commission, see Youngers (2003), Gonzales-Cueva (2004, 2006), Degregori (2004), Hayner (2011), and Root (2012).

26. Decreto Supremo No. 065-2001-PCM. In July 2001, Alejandro Toledo (2001–2006) succeeded Paniagua as president. While confirming the appointment of the truth commission, Toledo added the notion of "reconciliation" to its title. The commission was thus named Comisión de la Verdad y Reconciliación (Truth and Reconciliation Commission) and was known as the CVR. Toledo also expanded the commission's composition from seven to twelve members. Decreto Supremo No. 101-2001-PCM. Comisión de la Verdad y Reconciliación, Final Report, "Agreements," http://www.cverdad.org.pe/ingles/lacomis ion/cnormas/ (accessed June 30, 2013).

27. Decreto Supremo No. 065-2001-PCM. The mandate also asked the commission to recommend proposals to dignify victims and for a set of institutional reforms to foster peace among Peruvians, promote national reconciliation, and strengthen the rule of law and the democratic regime.

28. For an insider's analysis of the CVR's work regarding the problem of prosecuting perpetrators of human rights crimes, see Gonzales-Cueva (2004, 2006).

29. It must be noted that the question of clandestine mass graves was just one component in a broader context of tension, distrust, and disagreement that marked relations between the CVR and the Fiscalía throughout the former's existence. For more on this

fraught relationship, which prevented a more productive cooperation, see Gonzales-Cueva (2006).

30. The notion of a "necropolitical hold" on society comes from Robben (2015). For the pertinence of this notion to the Peruvian case, see Chapter 8.

31. In another innovation, the CVR put together a much celebrated photo exhibit of dramatic scenes and characters that became typical in the war. Under the title "Yuyanapaq" ("To Remember," in Quechua), this exhibit was meant to awaken sentiments of compassion and solidarity for those who have suffered the bulk of violence. For a sympathetic appraisal of "Yuyanapaq," see Saona (2014). For some critical renderings, see Poole and Rojas-Pérez (2011), and Murphy (2015).

32. Sarah Wagner (2008, 13) coined the notion of "path of recognition" to describe a similar trajectory of restoration and recognition of victims of the genocide in Srebrenica.

33. The CVR's archive is now held by the Ombudsman Office in its Lima-based Centro de Información para la Memoria Colectiva y los Derechos Humanos.

34. Because some villagers surreptitiously witnessed the killings carried out by the army in an isolated rural area, the relatives could later find their loved ones' remains but did not attempt to move them to the village cemetery. In Chapter 2 I explore the question of why Quechua-speaking peasants did not attempt to move their fallen relatives to cemeteries but instead hurriedly buried them wherever they lay. In Chapter 3 I discuss the crucial question of the surreptitious witness. See Comisión de la Verdad y Reconciliación, "Exhumations in Chuschi Ayacucho," http://www.cverdad.org.pe/ingles/apublicas/exhumaciones/exhum _chuschi.php (accessed May 10, 2013).

35. "Chuschi-Restos en Ataúdes." 2002. Comisión de la Verdad y Reconciliación. Centro de Información para la Memoria Colectiva y los Derechos Humanos (Defensoría del Pueblo) DVD. The CVR also helped to identify the army captain responsible for the massacre of the eight peasants. See Gonzales-Cueva (2006, 83).

36. Bishop José Antunez de Mayolo and Father Gaston Garatea.

37. *Doctores* is the colloquial name given to the forensic experts.

38. See "Chuschi-Restos en Ataúdes."

39. Perhaps in an attempt to make sure that this was achieved, that the violence had indeed been symbolically tamed, just before the release of the coffins one of the commissioners who was a priest asked relatives not to open the caskets. "They are closed for the good of you all," he said as a closing statement for the ceremony.

40. For these exhumations, at the CVR's initiative the Fiscalía appointed a team of three international experts to direct the procedures and train national experts. This decision came on the heels of a crisis in 2002, after the exhumations in Chuschi. Because of a series of disagreements, members of the Peruvian Team of Forensic Anthropology (Equipo Peruano de Antropología Forense, EPAF) resigned from their positions as the CVR's experts. In response, in mid-June 2002 the CVR along with the Fiscalía, the Ombudsman Office, and the human rights community constituted a joint platform of institutional cooperation for the investigation of mass graves. This platform would henceforth coordinate the forensic work and aimed at "contributing to finding the truth, *restituting dignity* to victims and their families and promoting access to justice" (emphasis added). Comisión

de la Verdad y Reconciliación, "Plataforma Conjunta de Trabajo en la Investigación de Fosas Comunes," http://www.cverdad.org.pe/ingles/apublicas/exhumaciones/declaracion .php (accessed June 30, 2013).

41. For a brief history of the infamous military base of Totos and the atrocities committed there, see Uceda (2004).

42. Comisión de la Verdad y Reconciliación, "Exhumations in Totos," http://www .cverdad.org.pe/ingles/apublicas/exhumaciones/exhum_totos.php.

43. The exhumed remains from both cases were moved to Ayacucho, the provincial capital, for laboratory analysis on the IML premises. The experts managed to identify five bodies (four from Ccarpaccasa and one from Sanccaypata), following the standard procedures of biological profiling and recognition of clothing and personal effects. However, only the families of victims at Ccarpaccasa accepted these results. The relatives of the fifth identified victim, buried in Sanccaypata, demanded the results of DNA tests before accepting the conclusions. "Reunión Peritos Forenses-Familiares de Víctimas." August 2002. Comisión de la Verdad y Reconciliación. Centro de Información para la Memoria Colectiva y los Derechos Humanos (Defensoría del Pueblo) DVD.

44. "Reunión Peritos Forenses-Familiares de Víctimas."

45. Abimael Guzmán, the foremost leader of the Shining Path, himself acknowledged that the decision for the attack was made by the party's central committee and that perhaps it went beyond what was planned. However, he ultimately justified it as a "necessary" strike to teach these communities not to rebel against the rule of the party. For Guzmán's writings, see Borja (1989).

46. For instance, these sites had tombstones, and relatives visited the graves on a regular basis.

47. In 1993, a military court sentenced Abimael Guzmán and most of the Shining Path's central committee members to life imprisonment. One of the evidential grounds for this conviction was the massacre of Lucanamarca. However, because the trial lacked basic guarantees of due process, the legality of the sentence was always tainted. At the time of the exhumation in Lucanamarca, following a ruling of the IACourtHR, the Peruvian Constitutional Court was revising the Fujimori regime's antiterrorist legislation to adapt it to international standards of human rights. In 2005, the Peruvian civilian courts retried Guzmán and his followers and sentenced him to life imprisonment in 2007.

48. Video clip 02020301030I. January 2003. Defensoría del Pueblo. Comisión de la Verdad y Reconciliación. Centro de Información para la Memoria Colectiva y los Derechos Humanos (Defensoría del Pueblo) DVD. A discussion of these subaltern constructions of heroism and nationalism is beyond the scope of this chapter. For more on this topic see Del Pino (1996), Degregori et al. (1996), Coronel (1996), and Theidon (2012).

49. This was the first and only time when a Peruvian president offered apologies to Quechua-speaking victims of political violence. Video clip 02020301050I. January 2003 DVD.

50. "Es un deber elemental de toda persona humana lo que hemos hecho con la exhumación de los cuerpos y con esta intervención forense; es el derecho más elemental,

que es el derecho a la vida, es el derecho a que si se perdió la vida, tener por lo menos una cristiana y decente sepultura." Former CVR commissioner, Carlos Ivan Degregori. Video clip 020203010604. January 2003 DVD.

Chapter 2

1. Except in the cases of Benita and César, I use pseudonyms throughout this ethnographic account.

2. See Murra (2002) for the notion of "ecological niches."

3. *Faenas* and *cargos* are social mechanisms through which Andean rural villagers organize communal work as well as distribute responsibilities among as many members as possible.

4. For a description of the kinship system in the region of the Pampas River valley, see Isbell (1977).

5. The term "mobile subjects" comes from Berg (2007).

6. The image of the soul lingering around the body after death is, of course, a classic motif in anthropological representations of death. Robert Hertz (1960) provided a theory of these representations that is often and widely cited. In the late nineteenth century, in his classic book *Primitive Culture* (1871), Edward B. Tylor also referred to these representations to formulate his theory of animism, which for him is the origin of all forms of religion in the world.

7. This set of ideas pertaining to human souls is pervasive in the anthropological literature of death in the Andes. For the Peruvian southern Andes, see Robin (2008, 2005), Allen (1988), Gose (1994), and Ricard Lanatta (2007). For the Ayacucho region, see Ansion (1987). For Bolivia, see Harris (1982).

8. "Diosninchik manas recibinchu chay kiki makillanwam wañukuskanta. Chaymanta *kutichimunsi*" (emphasis added). What I understand here in this seemingly interchangeable use of the notions of *alma* and *animu* in the dialogue is that moral sin brings additional danger to the already dangerous release of *animu* that happens at the moment of biological death.

9. On this notion of collective responsibility for individual transgressions, see Durkheim (1973).

10. In some versions of the myth, *condenados* attain redemption after a long and painful process of expiation of their sins. For how stories about *condenados* were mobilized during the internal war in the Andes to make and unmake violence, see Gonzales (2011) and Theidon (2012). I return to this discussion in Chapter 7.

11. For ideas of autopsy as a postmortem desecration of the body in the southern Peruvian Andes, see Robin (2008).

12. As a local public health official working in the village for more than two decades, Aurelio had intervened in several previous cases of suicide. He told me that before the times of violence, suicide was rare in Accomarca, but following the August 1985 massacre, suicide became more frequent in the village. The vast majority of these cases were related to problems of alcoholism, solitude, and abandonment of elders. Some elders who lost their

relatives in the 1985 massacre were among the cases Aurelio registered in his *posta medica* (rural health post).

13. See Robin (2008), Harris (1982), Ricard Lanatta (2007), and Gose (1994).

14. The *juez de paz* (justice of the peace) is the legal authority in charge of dealing with familial issues and small conflicts. The *gobernador* is the representative of the central government in town. He is not elected but designated by the executive branch. As a representative of the executive, he fulfills the role of political authority in the village in charge of enforcing the law.

15. I should note that there is a legal and political aspect to all death. However, this aspect usually goes silent in "natural" deaths. In ordinary circumstances involving "normal" death, the legal procedures are limited to obtaining a written statement certifying the causes of death. Then, this document is submitted to the Civil Registry Office for the purposes of registration of the new civil status of the dead person and official statistics. Typically, these proceedings involve only the village's *sanitario* and the clerk of the Civil Registry Office.

16. The *fiscal provincial* is the public prosecutor of the province. Typically, provincial authorities avoid traveling to the communities, alleging lack of public resources to finance such trips. Thus, most of the time, the costs of the legal procedures are charged to the people personally involved in each case.

17. This medico-legal autopsy consists of a thorough external examination of the dead body, looking for external signs of disease or trauma. It is performed to confirm the cause of death and does not necessarily entail dissection of the dead body. By contrast, clinical autopsy is performed to find out the cause of death and always entails dissection of the dead body.

18. On paperwork and the temporality of law in the Peruvian legal system, see Poole (2004).

19. After telling me the details of his conversation with the *fiscal*, Jorge went on to say: "Doctor, people in Accomarca do not like to see their *almitas* [dear dead loved ones] cut open. Besides, the costs of the autopsy are burdensome to them. It is almost 200 soles [$70]."

20. Rogelio's surprise is grounded in the pervasive belief in the Andes that a Protestant cannot commit suicide. For him, this discovery would constitute a contradiction of this belief.

21. It is very interesting how in the public conversation of these local state officials, clinical and legal notions such as "depression" and "intention" are crucial for making sense of an event of which the only and primary witness could not speak.

22. Aurelio told me that villagers do not usually attend funerary rites when suicide is involved: "Poca gente va [few people attend the wake]." The Quechua term *waqcha* means poor, but this poverty does not necessarily refer to the lack of money. Rather, it refers to the lack of social relations that are nurtured in the realms of family, kinship, and community. In this sense, *waqcha* is better translated as "orphan," someone who is alone. See Isbell (1978).

23. Villagers in Accomarca told me that mules and horses are also affected by *qayqa* to the point of death. To protect these animals from *qayqa*, villagers burn rubber around them. They say that the pungent odor of the burned rubber scares away *qayqa*. In the southern Peruvian Andes, *qayqa* is also known as *uraña* (Robin 2008, 146).

24. See note 3 for *faena*.

25. I could not find out why they painted the coffin yellow. Usually, coffins are painted grey or black for adults and white for children. I do not know whether it had to do with the problem of suicide.

26. See Robin (2008), Gose (1994), and Harris (1982). There is no direct translation of the Spanish noun *compadre* into English. It can be literally translated as "co-father" ("co-mother," in the case of *comadre*). It is a spiritual bond that emerges among families as a result of the Catholic rituals of baptism, first communion, and marriage, among others. The *compadres* commit themselves to be the spiritual parents of the initiated children. These spiritual parents become godparents of those children.

27. Lucho had not developed his own network of *compadres* yet. In theory, it had to be his godfather, but because the godfather was not in town at the time of Lucho's death, the godmother took charge.

28. The area of funerary rites is one of the most affected by the expansion of Protestantism in Peruvian Andean villages. This is how Ezequiel described for me the changes Protestantism is introducing in Accomarca: "Nowadays, with [the influence of] those evangelicals, many customs have changed. [. . .] Nowadays those evangelicals do not want to carry out a wake for their dead loved ones; they do not want to carry out the ceremony of the fifth day celebration; they do not even, I think, wash their dead loved ones' clothes; they do not even wear *luto* (mourning clothes); [for instance], a [evangelical] brother is there in mourning, lamenting 'Oh I lost my dad,' and you ask him why he is not wearing *luto*, he says: 'Oh, I am [already] brother; I do not wear *luto*.' Before [converting to Protestantism], they would have surely worn *luto*." It is beyond the scope of this chapter to discuss the cultural transformation brought about by the expansion of Protestantism in the Andes in terms of moral responsibility, forms of sociality, and notions of personhood. For some studies, see Gamarra (2000), Del Pino (1996), and Theidon (2012).

29. These ancient ancestors are generally known as gentiles or *machukuna*. See, for instance, Ansion (1987) and Allen (1988).

30. Hertz (1960, 85) lists suicide among the types of death that, because of their violent nature, fall outside normal ritual and are often the object of special rites.

31. Robin (2008, 150) finds similar ideas in rural Cusco: "*malamuerte* is characterized not only by the brutal or unattended circumstances of death (suicide, murder, accident) but also by the post-mortem harms inflicted upon the dead body (autopsies, delay or absence of funerary treatment)."

32. Ramos (2010, 50) notes that these colonial practices of desecration of bodies reflected European penal practices in which the boundary between crime and sin was very faintly drawn: "Transgressions against the authority of the king and against divine authority tended to merge." She mentions the problem of suicide only very briefly to tell us that in Spain, the bodies of suicides used to be burned (2010, 263). A history of suicide in the colonial Andes is still to be written. For a history of suicide in colonial Mexico, see Tortorici (2011) and Lomnitz (2005).

33. Robin (2008), for instance, collected stories in rural Cusco about how the bodies of the *condenados* are to be mutilated before burial in unconsecrated ground as a means of

both preventing the damned souls from finding their way into the afterlife and diminishing their predatory powers against the living. Ansion (1987) collected similar stories in the region of Ayacucho about the way in which the form of burial and treatment of the deceased's bodies indexes their moral exile. For similar tales in rural Ayacucho, see Gonzales (2011) and Theidon (2012).

34. Durkheim observed that the absolutist state appropriates the sense of crime as offense against the collectivity, and therefore as religious transgression, to legitimate the use of coercive power in its own defense. Quoted in Giddens (1986, 5–6).

35. In Chapter 5 I offer a more extended discussion on the question of desecration of bodies carried out by the guerrilla groups and the Peruvian military during the internal war in the Peruvian central southern Andes. See also Gonzales (2011) and Theidon (2012).

36. For an analysis of how certain unprecedented forms of violent death do not leave ghosts behind, which reveals their profoundly traumatic nature and for which traditional defenses are unavailable, see Siegel (1998, 93–98).

37. In Chapter 7 I return to the theme of political ghosts and how they emerge during excavations of clandestine mass graves.

Chapter 3

1. All the names of the legal and forensic personnel are pseudonyms, except for the public prosecutor, who is a public figure. The term *hoyada* is an idiosyncratic derivation of the Spanish noun *hoyo* (hole). It may be translated as "the hollow."

2. See, for instance, Saunders (2002).

3. For earlier reports on the arbitrary detentions and disappearances at Los Cabitos, see, among others, Amnesty International (1983). For the CVR's 2003 report, see Comisión de la Verdad y Reconciliación, Informe Final, vol. VI, ch. I, section 1.2, http://www.cverdad.org.pe/ifinal/index.php (accessed January 25, 2013). In Chapter 4, I offer an account of the patterns of state terror as retold by the mothers of the disappeared during the forensic exhumations at Los Cabitos.

4. This is the small team of three forensic anthropologists I met in early 2006 when I started my fieldwork on exhumations in Ayacucho, Peru.

5. In Latin America, investigative journalism uncovering atrocity and state terror based on the testimony and memories of former members of death squads has become a well-established genre. Perhaps one of the most well-known works is Horacio Verbistsky's 1996 *The Flight (El Vuelo)*, based on the testimony of former naval officer Adolfo Scilingo, detailing the atrocities of the "dirty war" waged by the Argentinean military juntas of the 1970s and early 1980s. In Peru, a similar book titled *Ojo por ojo: la verdadera historia del Grupo Colina*, written by the investigative journalist Umberto Jara (2003), was used as evidence in the trial that resulted in the conviction of former president Alberto Fujimori.

6. The criminal investigation had also adopted the reports submitted by the CVR, which had followed the same legal procedures to collect testimonies from survivors. However, despite the fact that these testimonies spoke of furnaces in Los Cabitos, the CVR did not conduct any in-depth investigation into this specific technology for the massive

disposal of the bodies of terrorism suspects and made just a passing reference to this atrocity in its final report, as if it were something too hyperbolic or fantastic to be believed or talked about.

7. During this time, former commanders of the military base during the counterinsurgency campaign publicly declared that the forensic exploration was uncovering bones of just animals such as cows and dogs—nothing that could be taken seriously as evidence. Clemente Noel Moral, "Puedo Morir en Ayacucho," *Caretas* No. 1859, February 3, 2005.

8. The IML forensic team used the Spanish notion *temporada de excavación* (excavation season) to refer to those periods of time in which they excavated at the site. Depending on the kind of tasks at hand and available resources, each *temporada* typically lasted between two to four weeks of full-time work. When necessary, the Fiscalía extended these *temporadas* for one or two more weeks.

9. I learned of this story during my fieldwork the following year.

10. See, for instance, Suarez-Orozco (1991), who argues that the end of political terror in Argentina brought about a flood of the unspeakable into public discourse. What had been previously denied and forbidden returned in the form of an almost exaggerated need to talk about the atrocities of state terror.

11. During my fieldwork I found among Quechua-speaking people a general unwillingness to be involved in these legal procedures. In her fieldwork in urban Ayacucho conducted during the CVR's tenure, Leinaweaver (2008, 35) also found this general reluctance of people to talk about and remember violence and atrocity in the region. She contrasted this reluctance with the CVR's insistence that people should talk about and reveal the violence of the past. This contrast only reveals how one of the presuppositions of the necrogovernmentality of postconflict is that people are ready to talk about the traumas and atrocities of the past as soon as conditions allow it.

12. On the notion of interpellation, see Althusser (1971).

13. For instance, in the bilingual Andean site of Harvey's study, bilingual "high-frequency" Quechua speakers tend to speak mostly in Spanish when drunk, whereas bilingual "high-frequency" Spanish speakers tend to speak in Quechua.

14. Poole's (2004) notion of how the law swings "between threat and guarantee" for Quechua rural peasants powerfully captures this ambiguity and unpredictability that are historically embedded in the work of the law in the Peruvian Andes.

15. As Harvey (1991, 20) notes, in ordinary contexts in the Andes, *viciosos* are those people who do not drink for socially acceptable reasons but because of addiction. As nonsocial drinkers, they are seen as being sick and therefore not aware of what they are saying. In the Peruvian legal system, the testimony of a drunk person is not valid. The law is sober.

16. In my last visit to Ayacucho in August 2016, one of the mothers explicitly referred to the *borrachito* as a ghost during a tour around La Hoyada in which she was offering an account of the happenings at the excavation site to a group of visitors. She said that the mothers came to believe that the drunken man was actually the ghost of one of the disappeared who helped the forensic experts to find the first fourteen bodies. I return to this theme of the ghosts of the disappeared in Chapter 7.

17. *Awkis* is the term for mountain spirits in the region of Cusco, where Harvey conducted her fieldwork. In Chapter 7 I return to the question of how the ghosts and mountain spirits are seen as intervening in the work of justice at Los Cabitos. This is an additional reason why I decided not to search for the *borrachito* and "humanize" his agency by knowing more about who he was and what his motives and intentions were. I wanted to leave his agency aligned with that of the ghosts of the disappeared as well as the *Apus* or *Wamanis* or *Aukis* (earth-beings), in the region from which they intervene in human affairs according to Andean people.

18. Peruvian pepper (*Schinus molle*) is an evergreen tree native to the Peruvian Andes that grows up to 1.5 meters tall. Locals use it for medicinal purposes and as fodder for their cattle.

19. These *invasiones* did happen in later years. I return to this problem in Chapter 8.

20. Until early 2007, the small forensic anthropology team at Ayacucho worked under very difficult conditions. Not only were they in charge of several concurrent excavations in the region, the material resources available to them were scarce. Thus, they had no choice but to ask victims' relatives to help by providing unskilled workers for the digging. In the case of Los Cabitos, these unskilled workers were usually young unemployed relatives of the disappeared associated with ANFASEP. In addition, the forensic team invited undergraduate archaeology students from the local university to volunteer as research assistants. When I first arrived in Los Cabitos, the leading archaeologist was training a group of these students, and the *forenses* (forensic experts) teased me, saying that another unskilled worker had arrived to help. I took this as a nice welcome and accepted their invitation to join their work with gusto. I had met them during the first forensic archaeology excavation I observed, which took place in the village of Accomarca in early 2006. In February 2007, with funding from the European Union, the IML significantly reinforced the forensic archaeology team in Ayacucho by appointing five more archaeologists and some research assistants. As part of this expansion, in later years the IML built a specialized laboratory in Ayacucho for the identification of victims of the internal war.

21. In the next two years after I left the field (July 2007), with more resources and qualified personnel, the forensic archaeology team was able to find more complete bodies. See below.

22. On the "humanitarian" aspect of the work of forensic archaeology, see Fondebrider (2002) and Rosenblatt (2015).

23. The prosecution filed indictments in early 2009. The charges were for crimes against humanity in the forms of torture and the disappearance of suspects of terrorism in Ayacucho, Peru, in 1983. For this purpose, the prosecution grouped all the recovered human remains under the category of "contextual evidence." This was because the bodies could not be identified and therefore could not be used as evidence of extrajudicial execution. Nor could they be evidence of disappearance because by definition, in this type of crime the body is missing. I return to this question in Chapter 8.

Chapter 4

1. Mama Anki spoke in Spanish, but her last word, *ñiykamuway*, is Quechua. It derives from the word *ñiy* (to say, to tell). According to context, it can acquire an imperative

connotation similar to *rimay* (to respond, to speak up). The suffix *muway* is reflexive. It can be translated as "to me" because it refers the action to the first person singular. Thus, *ñiymuway* would be "say it to me." In this context, however, the word *ñiykamuway* combines the imperative connotation implied in the demand for a response (respond, speak up) with a connotation of begging implied in the suffix *ka-muway*. The particle *ka* introduces this variation.

2. Juana's clause here expresses the cultural idea that excessive grief is dangerous for mourners because suffering debilitates the body and soul; to indulge in consuming grief may create an opportunity for the *pacha* (earth) to take and eat the mourner's soul. For a discussion of excessive grief as a debilitating condition in the Andes, see Stevenson (1977, 304).

3. La Red is the nickname of La Red de Salud Mental y Derechos Humanos de Ayacucho (Network for Mental Health and Human Rights of Ayacucho), a coalition of NGOs and public health institutions organized in the wake of the CVR's final report to provide emotional support to victims of political violence.

4. *Harawi* is a genre of Andean ritual music reserved for moments of mourning. I return to mournful songs in Chapter 6.

5. On the notion of interpellation, see below.

6. As is well known, Althusser (1971, 171) argues that interpellation is the quintessential operation through which individuals are constituted as subjects: "All ideology interpellates concrete individuals as concrete subjects." However, for this operation to come to full circle, recognition is essential. The individual is interpellated (Hey, you there!), but he has to recognize that it is he who has been interpellated. This mechanism of subject-making is "always-already" in place to the point that "individuals are always-already subjects" even before they are born. Naming is the classical example of how this mechanism works: "it is certain in advance that it [the unborn child] will bear its Father's Name, and will therefore have an identity and be irreplaceable" (ibid., 176).

7. The history of this form of humanitarian intervention in postwar Peru deserves a broader treatment than I can offer in this book. Suffice it to say that since the mid-1990s, a group of psychologists associated with the Peruvian human rights community started to offer individual and group therapeutic support to "innocent" people falsely accused of and incarcerated for terrorism. This team reported that by the end of 2001, they had provided treatment to at least one thousand people. As a rule, these psychologists did not offer support to those people they suspected to be members of the guerrilla groups. In 2001, the psychologists formerly associated with the human rights community established their own institutions. They participated actively in the work of the CVR, providing emotional support to victims, witnesses, and CVR staff members. They also participated actively in the forensic exhumations jointly sponsored by the CVR and the prosecutor's office (see Chapter 1). Following the end of the CVR's work, some of these institutions established La Red in Ayacucho. For an initial story of this form of humanitarian intervention, see Youngers (2003, 278–80). For these practitioners' own systematization and theoretical reflection on their participation in the CVR project, see de Burstein et al. (2003).

8. In this regard, LaCapra (1999, 699) writes: "Indeed, in post-traumatic situations in which one relives (or acts out) the past, distinctions tend to collapse, including the crucial

distinction between then and now wherein one is able to remember what happened to one in the past but realize one is living in the here and now with future possibilities."

9. In this respect it is important to note that courts of human rights themselves have categorized the forced disappearance of persons as an "ongoing crime" to uphold the prosecution of perpetrators. See, for instance, Sikkink (2011, 146).

10. In the Peruvian "lexicon of terror" (Feitlowitz 1998), the term *botadero* emerged during the early years of the counterinsurgency campaign in Ayacucho to name those sites on the outskirts of the city where the military dumped the bodies of people they abducted, tortured, and killed. See Amnesty International (1988). I return to this topic in Chapter 5.

11. I am inspired here by Nehemiah Grew's definition in *Cosmologia Sacra* (1701): "A point hath no dimensions, but only a whereness, and is next to nothing."

12. Good (1994) suggests that people living with the uncertainty of chronic illness leave alternate possibilities available by "subjunctivizing" reality—that is, they articulate narratives of suffering that, rather than being close accounts, validate alternative possibilities and alternative appraisals. In one way this is done retrospectively, by looking toward the origins of suffering, and in another way prospectively, by looking toward the possibility of cure or relief of suffering.

13. According to Allen (1988), the difference between ritual uses and ordinary uses of coca is that the former is governed by narrow stipulations pertaining to the ritual and the latter is governed by rules of etiquette, even if the consumption is individual.

14. A small and fragile vehicle that has become a popular means of transportation in urban areas in Peru.

15. As Wax (1972) says, the tent is a familiar and highly charged symbol in anthropology. It is primarily associated with the figure of Bronislaw Malinowski, who established the modern method of fieldwork with the idea that only by "camping right in their villages" could the ethnographer "evoke the real spirit of the natives, the true picture of tribal life" (Malinowski 1922). At the most basic level, the "ethnographer's tent" is the intimate space to which the ethnographer invites his or her "informant" in order to have an ethnographic conversation. I had the opposite experience in my fieldwork among the mothers of the disappeared: rather than the "ethnographer's tent," it was the "informants' tent."

16. For some sociological accounts of the struggle of the mothers of the disappeared in Peru, see Muñoz (1998), Coral (1998), and Tamayo (2003).

17. Kernaghan (2009, 2) suggests that hard folds in time, separating historical eras but also denoting the rise of legal regimes, can be read from the stories people share in their attempts to make sense of the historical experience of conflict.

18. This picture of the forced disappearance of alleged terrorism suspects following their kidnapping from home is typical of urban settings and in the early years of the campaign of state terror. Other modalities, such as the kidnapping of suspects from streets and public spaces such as schools, developed later. In the countryside, the forced disappearance of alleged suspects typically occurred following military incursions in the villages. For more on these modalities, see Comisión de la Verdad y Reconciliación (2004, vol. VI, ch. 1, section 1.2).

19. Defensoría del Pueblo (2002); Comisión de la Verdad y Reconciliación (2004). For earlier official documentation, see, among others, Document ONU E/CN.4/1986/18/

Add. 1, https://documents-dds-ny.un.org/doc/UNDOC/GEN/G86/100/58/PDF/G8610058 .pdf?OpenElement (accessed December 30, 2016). For other sources, see Amnesty International (1988) and Mendez and Chipoco (1988).

20. The most damaging indictment in this respect comes from the CVR's final report. Among other conclusions, the report says that since it was a systematic and generalized practice, tolerated or organized by the state, supported with the resources from the state, with de facto impunity assured implicitly by the state, etc., the practice constituted a "crime against humanity" and that, as such, it was an international crime. The CVR's final report also endorsed the notion that forced disappearance of people is an "ongoing crime" until the body of the victim is found. See Comisión de la Verdad y Reconciliación (2004, vol. VI, ch. 1, section 1.2).

21. For a detailed account of how this killing machine operated in the region between 1983 and 1985, see Uceda's book *Muerte en el Pentagonito* (2004), the first six chapters of which offer a gripping description of the atrocities the Peruvian military committed in Ayacucho. The chapters are based on firsthand accounts of former secret service agents who directly participated in these operations.

22. This scene reveals popular understandings of sovereign power in the Andes that draw from Peru's colonial era, when the Catholic religion provided a grammatical basis for legitimizing the colonial state's claim over life and death. In my fieldwork in the Andean village of Accomarca, I heard people referring to the state as a "second God" several times. I suggest that this formulation resonates with theories of natural law in which the state appears always as a second formation, after nature or God, with godlike powers over life and death. Thus, while the state as a "second God" has sovereign power over life and death, this power is limited by the power of God or primordial life. On the intersection between political theologies, violence, and state formation during colonial times in Peru, see Gose (2008), Estenssoro (2003), and Ramos (2010).

23. For the notions of "terror's talk" and "silencing," see Taussig (1989).

24. See, for instance, the CVR's stringent criticism (Comisión de la Verdad y Reconciliación 2004, vol. VI, ch. 1, section 1.2).

25. In this regard, Déotte (2002, 323) writes: "The law does not necessarily stipulate what anyone is to do ethically, but it always already stipulates that one needs to expose oneself. The exposition of the self is, in effect, the condition of possibility of political action."

Chapter 5

1. Infiernillo is the name of a deep ravine at the outskirts of Ayacucho that became a *botadero* during the early years of the campaign of state terror.

2. "Un caractère borné ou indiscipliné serait lié au nombre d'âmes présentes dans la personne."

3. In her work on violence and memory in the Andean village of Sarhua, Gonzales (2011) also finds the notion of *capricho*. However, in explaining how it is that a community can kill one of its members who came to be perceived as an enemy of the community, she offers a different interpretation of the term than the gender-inflected one I offer here. For Gonzales, *capricho* is an "impelling force arising from accumulated and repressed anger

because of harm done." It is a force associated with irrationality and outburst of emotions. "*Capricho* was associated with the kind of anger that responds not to reason but to power and can lead to violent outbursts, not as means to any preconceived end but just as manifestation of its existence. Like the insistence of a child who wants a sweet and won't let go of the craving until satisfied, the willful and stubborn energy of *capricho* cannot be reversed or controlled until triumph is achieved" (ibid., 131).

4. Hegel (1999, 210) writes: "Antigone, the woman, is pathetically possessed by the interest of family: Creon, the man, by the welfare of the community. Polyneices in war with his own father-city, had fallen before the gate of Thebes, and Creon, the lord thereof, had by means of a public proclamation threatened everyone with death who should give the enemy of this city the rights of burial. Antigone, however, refused to accept this demand, which merely concerned the public weal, and constrained by her pious devotion for her brother, carried out as sister, the sacred duty of internment." For an analysis of how Hegel mobilizes notions of the "political" and "prepolitical" in his reading of Antigone, see Butler (2000).

5. As de la Cadena (1995, 2000) argues, racism and race-thinking continue to inform social relations, hierarchies, and personal identities in Peru, but they do so through a kind of "racism without race" that elides references to biological concepts of race and instead builds upon cultural differentiators such as literacy, formal education, and forms of social and symbolic capital that are in turn racialized. In a study conducted in the 2000s, Tamayo (2003, 110) found that two-thirds of ANFASEP's constituency was composed of Quechua-speaking monolingual women.

6. For other anthropological accounts of the Shining Path's brutal politics of dead bodies, see also Robin (2008, 154–55) and Gonzales (2011). For a compelling account of these practices of the Shining Path in the Peruvian Upper Huallaga valley, see Kernaghan (2014).

7. For a similar formulation in the case of Guatemala, see Nelson (2009, 95).

8. An important body of literature focuses on this gendered response to state violence and terror in Latin America. See, for instance, Stephen (2005), Bejarano (2002), Maier-Hirsch (2001), Arditti (1999), and Schirmer (1993).

9. Mannheim (1988, 256) offers the following definition of *puriy* in opposition to *tiyay*: "*Tiyay* is thus used for sitting, residence, sedimentation in a liquid, or calming one's spirit. *Puriy* is the marked counterpart of *tiyay*. It denotes a kinetic form of existence, one that cancels the notion of 'boundedness' and implies either motion or the interaction of parts. *Puriy* has a semantic range from 'to travel' to 'to function.'"

10. In contrast to this stationary house-centered morality, other scholars emphasize mobility as a defining characteristic of life in these Andean communities. See, for instance, Berg (2015), Cornejo Polar (1995), and Weismantel (2001). In the register of literature, see the work of Arguedas (1978) on peripatetic figures such as the *kimichu* (a pilgrim who walks from town to town bringing with him Catholic images) and Andean migrants to the coast.

11. Hegel (1999) argues that the ethical nature of the family is revealed in the act of burial and of caring for the dead.

12. The idea of "self-referentiality" of the law appears in Agamben (1999) in relation to the trial. I return to this notion below.

13. The usual sense in which *gestionar* is used is *tramitar*, which can be translated precisely as "processing paperwork." Another related sense is "to negotiate." When *gestionar* is successful, it has the sense of "making things happen." De la Cadena (2015, 120) observes how Quechua peasants in Peru are invested in documenting their interactions with the state. She coined the notion of "indigenous archivists" to denote this political practice meant to keep a log of gamonales' [local strong men in charge of state affairs] abuses against indigenous communities. In addition to this practice of documentation, de la Cadena notes, Quechua peasants also keep watch over the efficacy and lawfulness of these documents, which, in turn, usually entails the need to travel to the far away centers of power. The southern Andean peasants among whom de la Cadena conducted fieldwork call this political practice as "queja-purichiy," which she translates as "walking the grievance."

14. Following Das (2007) we can say that these discourses about the place of the Andean Indian woman in the nation draw from broader discursive practices that place the figure of the woman within the domestic sphere, as sexual and reproductive being, as a result of the (implicit) sexual contract that typically underlies the social contract in liberal political formations. See also Brown (1992).

15. Muñoz (1998) describes how, at certain points in the internal war, the mothers were trained in human rights and techniques of organization.

16. Bennett (2010, 100) notes that for Dewey, "conjoint action" is not under the control of any rational plan or deliberate intention: "No efficient cause of the problems it generates can be pinpointed. What is more, there is no action that is not conjoint, that does not, in other words, immediately become enmeshed in a web of connections. For Dewey, any action is always a trans-action, and any act is really but an initiative that gives birth to a cascade of legitimate and bastard progeny."

17. In an irate response to Antigone's refusal to hate the enemies of the city, Creon shouts: "Then go down there and love those friends, if you must love them! But while I am alive, a woman will not rule!" (Sophocles 2003, 76). In Heaney's version, this sentence is formulated as follows: "Go then and love your fill in the underworld. No woman will dictate the law to me" (2004, 34).

18. See below for the translation of this very difficult word.

19. Cf. Mama Anki's cry at the excavation site in Chapter 4. The word *desahuciando* derives from the Spanish verb *desahuciar*, which has two possible translations: to declare someone terminally ill, and to evict someone from somewhere.

20. For the association of flies with human souls in the Andes, see Chapter 6.

21. Cf. Kernaghan's (2009) rendering of the Shining Path's visual politics of dead bodies in the Upper Huallaga valley.

22. I am translating this expression as "I became crazy *because of* my son"; however, it can also be translated as "I am crazy *for* my son." Again, the expression is ambiguous.

23. Cf. Lacan's (1997) analysis of Antigone. See also, Das (2007).

24. See, for instance, Mbembe's (2003) notion of "necropower." I return to this discussion in Chapter 8.

25. In her work in Peru's southern Andes, Harvey (1994) shows how domestic violence is both legitimized and contested along the lines of kin and affinal relationships: "People

distinguish between legitimate kin and other social relation with the term *pariente legitimo*. *Parientes legitimos* are close consanguineal kin, traced through one's own parents or siblings but not through second marriages of a parent nor through one's own or a sibling's spouse. Respect is the only appropriate behavior within the hierarchy of legitimate kin" (ibid., 70). Physical violence is thus seen as "legitimate" when it comes from consanguineal kin. Given that husband and wife are not in fact *parientes legitimos*, the legitimacy of the use of physical force between spouses is, in fact, very commonly contested.

26. I do not mean that this was the case in every situation. In fact, I have also recorded stories of fathers involved in the search for their missing sons, but such involvement was not typical. The experience of fathers of the disappeared in Latin America in general, and Peru in particular, is still a history that needs to be written.

27. For the Argentinean case, see Robben (2004). I must emphasize here that these are stories retold by the relatives of the disappeared (mostly women) at the excavation site. In this sense, it is a gendered retelling of the story from the perspective of ordinary people in extraordinary times. It is not the history of the ordinary in extraordinary times. That history still needs to be written. For this distinction, see Das (2007).

28. For the Argentinean case, see Archetti (1999, 114) and Burucua (2009, 87).

29. I take the idea of the "last word" from Seremetakis (1991).

Chapter 6

1. Arguedas (1964, 266) refers to it also as *wañuy chuspi* (the fly of death).

2. The register in which these relatives made statements about the *chiririnka* was the impersonal mode, which can be translated as "it is said." The notion of *kachsqa* here denotes confirmation through personal experience of phenomena that are spoken of or rumored through the grammatical form of "it is said." Its general form would be, "I can tell that what is said happens is indeed true." For a discussion of the impersonal mode, see Deleuze (1995).

3. This association of flies with the dead is certainly not uniquely Andean. Greenberg and Kunich (2002) show how omnipresent this association was in societies of the Middle East. Huchet and Greenberg (2010, 2851) report that even today, people in parts of rural Egypt believe that flies carry the spirits of departed ancestors. See also the classical study of Hertz (1960) and Kritsky (1985).

4. See, among others, Arguedas (1964), Bastien (1978), Gose (1994), Harris (1982), Ferraro (2008), Robin (2008), and Millones (2010).

5. In the literary register, Peruvian writer and anthropologist José María Arguedas (1978, 205–6) has written of this perimortem apparition in the following terms: "They [the flies] can smell corpses from a great distance and come to hover around them with their melancholic little music." In the scientific register, Huchet and Greenberg (2010, 2852) say the following: "Blowflies do not normally lay eggs on the living, but respond with surprising promptness and remarkable sensitivity to odors of the newly deceased." See also Greenberg (1973).

6. As in other regions of Latin America with histories of colonial Spanish Catholicism, in the Peruvian Andes people celebrate major holidays on November 1 (All Saints' Day) and November 2 (All Souls' Day).

7. Butler (2009, 38) suggests that to be deemed killable entails being deemed ungrievable and, hence, unmournable: "One way of posing the question of who 'we' are in these times of war is by asking whose lives are considered valuable, whose lives are mourned, and whose lives are considered ungrievable. We might think of war as dividing populations into those who are grievable and those who are not. An ungrievable life is one that cannot be mourned because it has never lived, that is, it has never counted as a life at all."

8. See, in this respect, the volume edited by Shimada and Fitzsimmons (2015). This volume gives an account of how archaeologists in the Andes have begun to move beyond an earlier approach that privileged the study of grave contexts based on objects such as ceramics and other artifacts from burials. In this development, archaeologists have started to pay important attention to skeletal remains, particularly through bioarchaeology and other fine-grained analysis of processes involved in the treatment of dead bodies, both before and after internment. The aim of this move, as the editors say, is to adopt a "comprehensive vision of and an integrated approach to the interrelated subjects of death, the dead, the soul, and the living, as well as the living-dead relationship" (ibid., 18).

9. For Moche burial patterns, see also Millaire (2002).

10. In her analysis of these representations, Hocquenghem (1981, 66) concludes that they have pre-Columbian origins: "The ethnographic information, the Huarochirí text and the Moche iconographic scenes indicate a relationship between the flies and the dead, which leads us to think that, for Indians of other regions as well as for the Moche, these insects would be related to the souls and spirits of the dead. This association would have its origins in the observation of the fact that flies are attracted by decomposing bodies, where they lay their eggs from which larvae will emerge. We find this same association in other cultures."

11. The debate on the question of the effect of colonial Catholic evangelization of Andean peoples in Peru, however, is far from exhausted. For historical perspectives, see Estenssoro (2003) and Ramos (2010). For recent anthropological perspectives, see Gose (2008). A full account of this debate is beyond the scope of this chapter.

12. See, among others, Bastien (1978), Custred (1979), Earls and Silverblatt (1978), Gose (1994), Harris (1982), Nuñez del Prado (1972), and Rosing (1994, 1995).

13. *Mondongo* is prepared by boiling grains of dry maize in water, similar to another typical dish called *mote*. Usually, the dish is accompanied by *tamal* (tamale) and *guiso de calabaza* (pumpkin stew). *Mondongo* is typical of the All Saints' Day celebrations in Accomarca. It is served in the early afternoon of November 1 after welcoming the *almas* that return to visit their surviving relatives during these days.

14. For pedagogical purposes, Catherine Allen (1988) compares All Saints' Day with Thanksgiving in the United States.

15. Duviols (1973) suggests that the *mesada* is not Catholic-inspired. Its genealogy goes back to pre-Columbian times, in which people used to celebrate the return of their dead with banquets of food and drink. Nowadays, the growing influence of Protestantism is introducing a variety of changes in the cultural grammar with which these communities organize their rituals and festivities. For more on this, see Del Pino (1996) and Gamarra (2000).

16. *Karichuri* is composed of two words: *kari* (male) and *churi* (offspring). This is how a father refers to his son. *Kariwaway* is how a mothers refers to her son. For a glossary of kinship terms in the region of the Pampas River valley, see Isbell (1977, 97–100).

17. César was enthusiastic about calling me *karichuri*, but Benita was more circumspect.

18. For an extended analysis of these kinship terms in the Pampas River valley, see Isbell (1977, 1978).

19. I first met Emilia in May 2006 during the forensic exhumation of the remains of her parents, who had been killed in the 1985 massacre. I started to visit her frequently and soon developed a friendship with her and her family. She was twelve years old when the carnage took place. She managed to escape and witnessed how the Peruvian military killed her parents and set her family's hut on fire. She is very shy, and although she understands Spanish, she does not speak it. Despite this, as survivor and witness, she has testified before the Spanish-speaking courts and dozens of commissions of inquiry that the Peruvian state has appointed since 1985 to investigate the massacre. Emilia also participates actively in the association that survivors organized to claim legal justice in the case.

20. White flowers that grow in the Andes and are usually used at funerary rites. See Gose (1994).

21. In the southern Peruvian Andes, *t'anta wawas* are given to children on All Saints' Day. Adults also exchange *t'anta wawas* and perform mock rituals of Catholic baptism in which the *t'anta wawas* are eaten, mocking the Catholic symbol of eating the body of Christ. Both Catholicism and cannibalism are mocked. I did not find in Ayacucho the mockery rituals referred to by Bastien (1978) for Bolivia and Harvey (1991) for Cusco.

22. Below I show how in contradistinction to this theoretical perspective, grief and individuality can actually be conduits for reconstituting the social in the aftermath of mass atrocity.

23. One year after the first exhumation in May 2006, the legal authorities returned some of the identified human remains to their relatives (see Chapter 1). However, the relatives could not bury them because their attorney wanted to have these remains at hand in case the courts ordered another forensic examination during the trial.

24. For the notion of *pensamiento* in rural Ayacucho, see Theidon (2004).

25. The musical structure of *huayno* stems from a pentatonic scale with a binary rhythm that allows stanzas of four verses. This is a dialogic structure. For more on this, see Ritter (2002).

26. We also find this connection between excessive grief and going blind in Chapter 2, in the expression *tutapuriylla* (always walking in darkness).

Chapter 7

1. *Pagapu* (*pago a la tierra*, in Spanish) is the name Quechua people of the Peruvian central southern Andes use for the ritual of payment to the earth that is performed throughout the Andean region under different names. See below.

2. Former president Alan García took office for his second term (2006–2011) on July 28, 2006, with a strong message against human rights. Major massacres against civilian populations occurred during his first term, including the massacres of Accomarca (August 1985)

and Cayara (May 1988). Also, more than three hundred suspects of terrorism incarcerated in Lima's jails were extrajudicially executed by the military as part of the García regime's response to a prison mutiny. Victims and survivors feared that with García back in office, criminal investigation into their cases might be closed.

3. *Wamani* is a Quechua word with which *orqos* are invoked. It means "falcon" and "lord." *Wamani* is used primarily by Quechua-speaking people from the central southern Peruvian Andes. In the southern Andes, these beings are known as *apu, apukuna,* or *pachatira* or *tirakuna.* In other regions of the Andes these beings have other names, such as *mallku, aukillo,* and *awki,* among other deferential names. The anthropological literature on these rituals and beings in the Peruvian Andes is extensive. See, among others, Arguedas (1964), Isbell (1978), Delgado (1984), Arroyo (1987), Gose (1994, 2008), Ricard (2007), Robin (2008), Allen (1988), Bastien (1978), and Earls (1969). In her work in the Andean region of Cusco, de la Cadena (2010, 2015) follows southern Quechua peasants' way of addressing the *orqos* as *tirakuna* or *apukuna,* to render these entities as beings in themselves, whose presence within complex relational regimes cannot be adequately rendered with such notions as gods, spirits or deities. Instead of these formulaic notions, de la Cadena offers the notion of "earth-beings," which is much closer to the ontological status that Quechua peasants customarily assign to the *orqos.* As I show below, Quechua peasants in Peru's central-southern Andes address the *orqos* in the same way than their southern counterparts. I thus follow here de la Cadena's notion of "earth-beings" to refer to the *orqos.*

4. There are notable exceptions. During the *yarqay aspiy* (cleaning of irrigation channels) in August, the entire community offers the *pagapu.* Arguedas (1964) offers a fascinating account of one such instance in the Andean village of Puquio, Ayacucho, recorded in the early 1950s. Isbell (1978) offers another interesting account of the same ritual in Chuschi, Ayacucho, during the 1970s. Delgado (1984) confirms that these communal offerings are still taking place nowadays, although from his account it appears that their practice is declining. De la Cadena (2015) also offers a fascinating account of how Quechua peasants of the Peruvian southern Andes typically offered *despachos* [payment to the earth] to recruit the help of the presiding earth-beings of their region in their legal and political struggle against abusive *hacendados* (large landowners).

5. "Lord" (*Señor,* in Spanish) is also used to refer to the Christian god.

6. *Kintu* is an arrangement of three coca leaves that participants of rituals hold with both hands to show reverence for the sacredness of the ceremony.

7. This *mal aire* is similar to the *qayqa,* the malign force unleashed in the moment of death. See Chapter 2 on the notion of *qayqa.*

8. Arguedas (1964, 236) provides the following account: "The mountains and pampas are the Earth's personification. Each of them has his own name. The indigenous people worship the mountains because they embody the Earth's attributes: its generosity, but also its destructive power. 'The *Wamani* is fierce'—one of the indigenous authorities [*alcaldes*] said—'he can suck up our hearts while we are sleeping.' I asked them why the *Wamani* was that fierce. 'It is as fierce as powerful men are when their money is at stake.' The indigenous authority of Chaupi said that the *Wamani* gets very angry if his people do not pay him back what was agreed with him."

9. In translating *munayniyoq* into English I follow Arguedas's translation of it into Spanish: "quien deseaba, en virtud de que lo que se deseaba se hacía" (1964, 232). Alternatively, de la Cadena (2015, 243) translates the notion as "owner of the will," which to my ear sounds more descriptive and somehow loses the imperative force that the Quechua notion embodies.

10. *Wamanis* typically manifest themselves in dreams, apparitions, or both. At times, they also take the form of animals such as condors, pumas, bulls, falcons, or *amarus* (sacred snakes). I return to the topic of dreams later in the chapter.

11. For a review and brief critique of Gose's argument, see Salomon (2010).

12. In this respect, it is important to note that while *Wamanis* are sovereigns of their local jurisdictions, they have an organizational hierarchy akin to provincial governmental structure. They never work alone and always seek the cooperation of their neighbors to intervene and mediate in human affairs (Arguedas 1964, Isbell 1978, Ansion 1987).

13. While some of these mothers might attribute the fate of their missing loved ones to the betrayal of friends, neighbors, or relatives during the campaign of state terror, they know that the ultimate source of the violence and death that have devastated their lives lies outside of their close sphere of relations.

14. See Mueggler (2001) for a fascinating account of how Chinese peasants exorcise lethal and murderous effects of state power in rural China through elaborate rituals that draw on bodily idioms of eating, digesting, and excreting.

15. Citing Argentinean writer Julio Cortazar, Taussig (1989, 9) writes that the tactic of disappearing people "combines the terrible fact of loss with the ever-present hope that the disappeared will tomorrow, the next day . . . reemerge. Hence mothers are reported as saying that they wept tears of joy to find the dead body of their daughter or son, because at least they were sure. But that is the exception. For most it's a dream world, which decidedly puts 'magical realism' in a new light, as when they rush to a site where, in a dream, a friend has seen the disappeared. As Fabiola Lalinde, who last saw her son [. . .] being put onto a track by the Colombian Army [. . .], puts it: 'If the days are difficult, the nights are torture, especially when I dream of [the Spanish is *con*, thus dreaming *with*] Luis Fernando.'"

16. Cecconi (2011) thus argues for the need to expand the category of "history," and particularly the history of war, by including not only what people do and say during the day, but also their night experiences and visions. For the ethical and political dimensions of dreaming, see Mittermaier (2011). For the epistemological value of dreams for history, see Koselleck (2005).

17. "*Tullus kausam* [bones are alive]," said Mama Benita in Accomarca (see Chapter 2). Human bones are conceived of as having agency in themselves. This is particularly the case with ancient human bones. Unmediated contact with them brings about illness and death; conversely, ritualized contact with them brings about healing. As Allen (1982, 185) explains for the southern Peruvian Andes, these pre-Christian ancestors are said to provide for the people's well-being; however, these benevolent ancestors blend conceptually with malevolent beings that can bring death and misfortune.

18. In the Peruvian south-central Andes, some of these evil beings are ordinary human beings who hide immoral behavior during the day and become evil creatures that prey on

other human beings at night. The *uma* (head), for instance, is a promiscuous woman who at night becomes a witch whose head leaves her body to take possession of the body of anyone who has the misfortune to run into her. Another terrifying being is the *qarqacha* (incestuous being), who maintains incestuous relations during the day and is half animal and half human by night, roaming to prey on human beings. See Ansion (1987).

19. In her ethnographic work on dreams in the Andes, Cecconi (2011, 415) also found that sometimes the disappeared delivered information, denounced murderers, or revealed the places of their corpses' burial in dreams. She notes that these dreams are also mentioned in official testimonies gathered by the CVR.

20. The notion of dream-vision comes from Mittermaier (2011).

21. These dreams "with *pensamiento*" resonate with Freudian theories of dreams as hallucinatory projections of inner states or the unconscious. A full discussion of the theory of dreams in the Andes is beyond the scope of this chapter. Nonetheless, let us note that while almost every ethnographer working on violence in the Andes makes reference to dreams, the topic remains underinvestigated in Andean anthropology. One recent exception is Arianna Cecconi's compelling work. For more on her work, see her 2008 doctoral dissertation, "Les Rêves viennent du dehors: Une ethnographie de la nuit sur les Andes péruviennes." For more on the interpretation and semiotics of dreams in the Andes, see the works of anthropologist Bruce Mannheim (1987) and linguist Luis Andrade (2004).

22. Cecconi (2011) has recorded similar stories of mothers and wives saying that they had stopped crying and started to accept their missing relatives' deaths after receiving the visit of their *desaparecidos* in dreams to comfort them and tell them that they were fine.

23. See Taussig (1989) on the distinction between the standard "dreaming of" and the "dreaming with" with which the relatives speak of the visits their missing relatives pay them in dreams.

24. In Chapter 8 I show how the mothers indeed started a move to demand the authorities to declare the former site of mass killing as a site of memory and commemoration.

Chapter 8

1. For a brief history of ANFASEP, see Tamayo (2003) and ANFASEP (2007).

2. Although *campo santo* can be translated as "cemetery," the phrase emphasizes the idea of sacredness. Thus, for my purposes here, I translate it as "sacred field" or "sacred site." Mama Lucila had two sons who were disappeared in the late 1980s. She participated in ANFASEP but eventually quit the organization because of disagreements with the leadership. Nonetheless, she regularly visited the excavation site whenever she heard news of a new season on the local radio.

3. The notion of ownership (*dueño*) here conveys the idea that as a general norm, dead human bodies belong to networks of family and kinship that can take care of and commemorate them.

4. A case in point is "Comandante Centurion," who has reportedly become one of the most important land traffickers in Ayacucho. He organized one of the biggest *invasiones* during my fieldwork. As I had the chance to observe when I visited this settlement, in

their leadership the *jefes ronderos* display military forms of organization and social control. On peasant patrols in Ayacucho, see Del Pino (1996), Coronel (1996), and Degregori et al. (1996).

5. The threat of the *invasiones* never fully disappeared. In May 2014, for instance, a group of families took over a portion of land in the northernmost section of La Hoyada. The legal authorities have been trying to evict them ever since.

6. When introducing this administrative change, the Peruvian judiciary argued that this move was necessary to guarantee the defendants' right to due process. For an assessment, see Defensoría del Pueblo (2013).

7. Let us recall here that the CVR compiled a preliminary list of more than four thousand people disappeared by the security forces during Peru's twenty-year internal war and established that most of these disappearances happened in the region of Ayacucho between 1983 and 1985—one of the worst periods of the Peruvian state's war against the Shining Path in the Peruvian south-central Andes. Luis Bromley, former executive director of the IML, said that the number of victims at Los Cabitos was more than one thousand (*La República*, April 26, 2008). Uceda (2004) says that more than five hundred suspects were killed and clandestinely buried at Los Cabitos.

8. As of the fall of 2016, the legal authorities had not opened a case for the victims disappeared in 1985.

9. Alberto Fujimori was sentenced on April 7, 2009, on charges of crimes against humanity during his tenure. For more on the Fujimori trial, see Burt (2009) and Youngers and Burt (2009).

10. I attended the hearings during the early stages of the trial from late May to August 2011 and again from June to August 2012. During the latter season, the court traveled to Ayacucho to cross-examine survivors of torture and relatives of the disappeared. In contrast to the hearings in Lima, the hearings in Ayacucho were packed with survivors, relatives, and bystanders. As of the fall of 2016, the hearings had not yet concluded and discretely continued to take place in Lima.

11. In this respect, Das and Poole (2004, 13) write: "This refounding happens both through the production of killable bodies, as posited by Agamben [1988], and through the sorts of power embodied by figures such as the policeman or local 'boss.' Like homo sacer, these figures enjoy a certain immunity to law precisely because they are configured as existing outside or prior to the law."

12. See Theidon (2010) for an astute analysis of how the coastal Spanish-speaking ruling elites produce these discourses in Peru.

13. I am following here Foucault's notion of the "object" as it appears in *Discipline and Punish: The Birth of the Prison* (1977) with regards to the object "delinquency."

14. For the use of these Catholic images in contexts of political violence, see Aretxaga (1997).

15. Bergson (1988, 169) writes: "Memory, laden with the whole of the past, responds to the appeal of the present state by two simultaneous movements, one of translation, by which it moves in its entirety to meet experience, thus contracting more or less, though without dividing, with a view to action; the other of rotation upon itself, by which it turns

toward the situation of the moment, presenting to it that side of itself which may prove to be most useful."

16. In this approach I am inspired by the work of Das (2007).

17. See the introduction for a brief consideration of how the CVR used numbers and statistics as a central means for distributing moral and political responsibilities for past atrocities. For an anthropological discussion of how counting and cataloguing have been used in the realm of human rights in Latin America, see Tate (2007) and Nelson (2009).

18. For how the Quechua mothers use the notion of *chunniq* to refer to those spaces of death the military created during the counterinsurgency, see Chapter 6.

19. See, for instance, the discussion of the notion of *tullus kausam* (it is said the bones are alive) in Chapter 2.

20. For the idea that the dead can have political lives because of the meanings the living assign to them, see in particular Verdery (1999).

21. For a discussion of how the materiality of human remains deserves analysis as a phenomenon in itself that has the power to animate politics, see Stepputat (2014). For instance, he writes: "dead bodies and human remains are not only symbolizing aspects of social and political life and acting as blank canvas for the inscription of political agendas. It is not politics that gives meanings to bones, . . . ; rather it is the bones that animate social and political processes such as mourning, othering, marginalization and subversion" (ibid., 26).

22. For the idea of floating energies and affects around bodies, see Gil (1998).

23. Customarily, Roman Catholic rituals start with the statement, "Glory to the Father, and to the Son, and to the Holy Spirit; as it was in the beginning, is now, and will be for ever. Amen."

Afterword

1. Eduardo Vega, cited in "Ley de búsqueda de desaparecidos: sus claves e importancia." *El Comercio,* June 22, 2016, http://elcomercio.pe/politica/gobierno/ley-busqueda -desaparecidos-sus-claves-importancia-noticia-1911229 (accessed July 28, 2016).

2. "Normas Legales," Law No. 30470, June 22, 2016, http://www.elperuano.com.pe /NormasElperuano/2016/06/22/1395654-1.html (accessed July 28, 2106).

3. See, for instance, Anderson's (1983) well-known study on the emergence of the modern nation-state in which he argues that nationalism is built on a fundamental paradox: the need to forget acts of violence central to state formation that can never be forgotten.

References

Agamben, Giorgio. 1998. *Homo Sacer: Sovereign Power and Bare Life.* Stanford, CA: Stanford University Press.

———. 1999. *Remnants of Auschwitz: The Witness and the Archive.* Brooklyn, NY: Zone Books.

Allen, Catherine. 1982. "Body and Soul in Quechua Thought." *Journal of Latin American Lore* 8(2): 179–96.

———. 1988. *The Hold Life Has: Coca and Cultural Identity in an Andean Community.* Washington, DC: Smithsonian Institution Press.

Althusser, Louis. 1971. "Ideology and Ideological State Apparatuses (Notes Towards an Investigation)." In *Lenin and Philosophy and Other Essays,* 127–86. Translated by Ben Brewster. New York: Monthly Review Press.

Amnesty International. 1983. "Peru, Torture and Extrajudicial Executions: Letter of Amnesty International to President Fernando Belaúnde Terry." New York: Amnesty International.

———. 1988. *Peru: Violations of Human Rights in the Emergency Zones.* New York: Amnesty International.

———. 2009. "Peru: The Conviction of Fujimori—A Milestone in the Fight for Justice." https://www.amnesty.org/en/press-releases/2009/04/peru-conviction-fujimori-e28093 -milestone-fight-justice-20090407 (accessed November 13, 2016).

Anderson, Benedict. 1983. *Imagined Communities: Reflections on the Origins and Spread of Nationalism.* London: Verso.

Andrade, Luis. 2004. *Aguas turbias, aguas cristalinas: el mundo de los sueños en los andes sur-centrales.* Lima: Fondo Editorial PUCP.

ANFASEP. 2007. *Hasta cuándo tu silencio: testimonios de dolor y coraje.* Ayacucho, Peru: Asociación Nacional de Familiares de Detenidos y Desaparecidos del Perú.

Ansion, Juan. 1987. *Desde el rincón de los muertos: el pensamiento mítico en Ayacucho.* Lima: GREDES.

Anstett, Elizabeth, and Jean-Marc Dreyfus, eds. 2015. *Human Remains and Identification: Mass Violence, Genocide and the "Forensic Turn."* Manchester: Manchester University Press.

Arce Borja, Luis, ed. 1989. *Guerra popular en el Perú. El pensamiento Gonzalo.* Brussels: Luis Arce Borja.

Archetti, Eduardo. 1999. *Masculinities: Football, Polo and the Tango in Argentina.* Oxford: Berg.

Arditti, Rita. 1999. *Searching for Life: The Grandmothers of the Plaza de Mayo and the Disappeared Children of Argentina.* Berkeley: University of California Press.

Arendt, Hannah. 1968. *The Origins of Totalitarianism.* New York: Harcourt.

———. 2000. *The Portable Hannah Arendt.* Edited with an Introduction by Peter Baehr. New York: Penguin.

———. 2006. *Eichmann in Jerusalem: A Report on the Banality of Evil.* New York: Penguin.

Aretxaga, Begoña. 1997. *Shattering Silence: Women, Nationalism, and Political Subjectivity in Northern Ireland.* Princeton, NJ: Princeton University Press.

Arguedas, José María. 1964. "Puquio, una cultura en proceso de cambio." In *Estudios sobre la cultura actual del Perú,* 221–72. Edited by Luis E. Valcárel et al. Lima: Universidad Nacional Mayor de San Marcos.

———. 1978. *Deep Rivers.* Austin: University of Texas Press.

Aries, Philippe. 1974. *Western Attitudes Toward Death.* Baltimore: Johns Hopkins University Press.

Ariss, Rachel. 2004. "Bring Out Your Dead: Law, Human Remains, and Memory." *Canadian Journal of Law and Society* 19: 33–54.

Arroyo, Sabino. 1987. *Algunos aspectos del culto al tayta wamani.* Lima: Universidad Nacional Mayor de San Marcos.

Asad, Talal. 2003. *Formations of the Secular: Christianity, Islam, Modernity.* Stanford, CA: Stanford University Press.

Austin, J. L. 1957. "A Plea for Excuses: The Presidential Address." *Proceedings of the Aristotelian Society, New Series* 57: 1–30.

Bastien, Joseph W. 1978. *Mountain of the Condor: Metaphor and Ritual in an Andean Ayllu.* St. Paul, MN: West.

Bejarano, Cynthia. 2002. "Las Super Madres de Latino America: Transforming Motherhood by Challenging Violence in Mexico, Argentina, and El Salvador." *Frontiers* 23(1): 126 50.

Bennett, Jane. 2010. *Vibrant Matter: A Political Ecology of Things.* Durham, NC: Duke University Press.

Berg, Ulla Dallum. 2007. "Mediating Self and Community: Membership, Sociality and Communicative Practices in Peruvian Migration to the US." PhD diss., New York University.

———. 2015. *Mobile Selves: Race, Migration and Belonging in Peru and the U.S.* New York: New York University Press.

Bergson, Henri. 1988 [1919]. *Matter and Memory*. New York: Zone Books.

Blau, Soren, and Mark Skinner. 2005. "The Use of Forensic Archaeology in the Investigation of Human Rights Abuse: Unearthing the Past in East Timor." *International Journal of Human Rights* 9(4): 449–63.

Bloch, Maurice. 1982. "Death, Women, and Power." In *Death and the Regeneration of Life*, 211–30. Edited by Maurice Bloch and Jonathan Parry. Cambridge: Cambridge University Press.

Bloch, Maurice, and Jonathan Parry, eds. 1982. *Death and the Regeneration of Life*. Cambridge: Cambridge University Press.

Boesten, Jelke. 2014. *Sexual Violence During War and Peace: Gender, Power, and Post-conflict Justice in Peru*. New York: Palgrave Macmillan.

Bolton, Charlene, and Ralph Bolton. 1976. "Rites of Retribution and Restoration in Canchis." *Journal of Latin American Lore* 15(1): 73–79.

Bourdieu, Pierre. 1987. "The Force of Law: Toward a Sociology of the Juridical Field." *Hastings Journal of Law* 38: 805–53.

Brown, Wendy. 1992. "Finding the Man in the State." *Feminist Studies* 18(1): 734.

Buchli, Victor, and Gavin Lucas. 2001. *Archaeologies of the Contemporary Past*. London: Routledge.

Bueno-Hansen, Pascha. 2015. *Feminist and Human Rights Struggles in Peru: Decolonizing Transitional Justice*. Chicago: University of Illinois Press.

Burnet, Jennie E. 2012. *Genocide Lives in Us:. Women, Memory, and Silence in Rwanda*. Madison: University of Wisconsin Press.

Burt, Jo Marie. 2009. "Guilty as Charged: The Trial of Former Peruvian President Alberto Fujimori." *International Journal of Transitional Justice* 3: 384–405.

Burucua, Constanza. 2009. *Confronting the "Dirty War" in Argentine Cinema, 1983–1993: Memory and Gender in Historical Representations*. Woodbridge, UK: Tamesis.

Butler, Judith. 2000. *Antigone's Claim: Kinship Between Life and Death*. New York: Columbia University Press.

———. 2009. *Frames of War: When Is Life Grievable?* New York: Verso.

Carrescia, Olivia. 2008. *Sacred Soil*. Videorecording. New York: OLC; distributed by Icarus Films.

Caruth, Cathy. 1991. "Unclaimed Experience: Trauma and the Possibility of History." *Yale French Studies* 79: 181–92.

———. 1996. *Unclaimed Experience: Trauma, Narrative and History*. Baltimore: Johns Hopkins University Press.

Cavell, Stanley. 1982. *The Claim of Reason: Wittgenstein, Skepticism, Morality, and Tragedy*. Oxford: Oxford University Press.

———. 1994. *A Pitch of Philosophy: Autobiographical Exercises*. Cambridge, MA: Harvard University Press.

Cecconi, Arianna. 2008. "Les Rêves viennent du dehors: Une ethnographie de la nuit sur les Andes péruviennes." PhD diss. Université de Milano-Bicocca et École des Hautes Études en Sciences Sociales.

———. 2008. Parecía todo un sueño. *Argumentos.* http://revistaargumentos.iep.org.pe/ar ticulos/parecia-todo-un-sueno/.

———. 2011. "Dreams, Memory and War: An Ethnography of Night in the Peruvian Andes." *Journal of Latin American and Caribbean Anthropology* 16(2): 401–24.

Conklin, Beth. 2001. *Consuming Grief: Compassionate Cannibalism in an Amazonian Society.* Austin: University of Texas Press.

Comisión de la Verdad y Reconciliación. 2004. Hatun Willakuy. Versión abreviada del informe final de la Comisión de la Verdad y Reconciliación, Peru. Lima: Comisión de Entrega de la Comisión de la Verdad y Reconciliación.

Coral, Isabel. 1998. "Women in War: Impacts and Responses." In *Shining and the Other Paths: War and Society in Peru, 1980–1995,* 345–74. Edited by Steve Stern. Durham, NC: Duke University Press.

Cornejo Polar, Antonio. 1995. "Condición migrante y representatividad social: el caso de Arguedas." In *Amor y fuego: Jose Maria Arguedas 25 años después,* 3–14. Lima: Centro de Estudios para la Promoción y el Desarrollo.

Coronel, Jose. 1996. "Violencia política y respuestas campesinas en Huanta." In *Las rondas campesinas y la derrota de Sendero Luminoso,* 29–116. Edited by Carlos Ivan Degregori. Lima: Instituto de Estudios Peruanos.

Coxshall, Wendy. 2005. "From the Peruvian Truth and Reconciliation Commission to Ethnography: Narrative, Relatedness, and Silence." *PoLAR: Political and Legal Anthropology Review* 28(2): 203–22.

Crossland, Zoe. 2000. "Buried Lives: Forensic Archaeology and Argentina's Disappeared." *Archaeological Dialogues* 7(2): 146–59.

———. 2002. "Violent Spaces: Conflict over the Reappearance of Argentina's Disappeared." In *Matériel Culture: The Archaeology of Twentieth-Century Conflict,* 115–31. Edited by J. Schofield, W. G. Johnson, and C. M. Beck. London: Routledge.

———. 2009. "Of Clues and Signs: The Dead Body and Its Evidential Traces." *American Anthropologist* 111(1): 69–80.

Crossland, Zoe, and Rosemary Joyce. 2015. *Disturbing Bodies: Anthropological Perspectives on Forensic Archaeology.* Santa Fe, NM: SAR.

Custred, Glynn. 1979. "Symbols and Control in a High Altitude Andean Community." *Anthropos* 74: 379–92.

Das, Veena. 2007. *Life and Words: Violence and the Descent into the Ordinary.* Berkeley, CA: University of California Press.

———. 2010. "The Life of Humans and the Life of Roaming Spirits." In *Rethinking the Human,* 31–45. Edited by Michelle Molina, Donald K. Swearer, and Susan Lloyd McGarry. Cambridge, MA: Center for the Study of World Religions, Harvard Divinity School.

Das, Veena, and Deborah Poole, eds. 2004. *Anthropology in the Margins of the State.* Santa Fe, NM: School of American Research Press; Oxford: James Currey.

De Burstein, Ruth Krystal, Martha Stornaiuolo, and María del Carmen Raffo, eds. 2003. *Desplegando alas, abriendo caminos: sobre las huellas de la violencia.* Lima: Centro de Atención Psicosocial.

Degregori, Carlos Iván. 2004. "Heridas abiertas, derechos esquivos: reflexiones sobre la Comisión de la Verdad y Reconciliación." In *Memorias en conflicto: aspectos de la violencia política contemporánea*, 75–85. Edited by Raynald Belay, Jorge Bracamonte, Carlos Iván Degregori, and Jean Joinville Vacher. Lima: Instituto Francés de Estudios Andinos.

Degregori, Carlos Iván, José Coronel, Ponciano del Pino, and Orin Starn. 1996. *Las rondas campesinas y la derrota de Sendero Luminoso*. Lima: Instituto de Estudios Peruanos.

De la Cadena, Marisol. 1995. "'Women Are More Indian': Gender and Ethnicity in a Community in Cuzco." In *Ethnicity, Markets and Migration in the Andes: At the Crossroads of History and Anthropology*, 329–48. Edited by Brooke Larson and Olivia Harris. Durham, NC: Duke University Press.

———. 2000. *Indigenous Mestizos: The Politics of Race and Culture in Cuzco, Peru, 1919–1991*. Durham, NC: Duke University Press.

———. 2010. "Indigenous Cosmopolitics in the Andes: Conceptual Reflections Beyond 'Politics.'" *Cultural Anthropology* 25(2): 334–70.

———. 2015. *Earth Beings: Ecologies of Practice Across Andean Worlds*. Durham, NC: Duke University Press.

Defensoría del Pueblo. 2002. "La desaparición forzada de personas en el Perú (1980–1996)." *Informe Defensorial* No. 55. Lima: Defensoría del Pueblo.

———. 2013. "A diez años de verdad, justicia y reparación. Avances, retrocesos y desafíos de un proceso inconcluso." *Informe Defensorial* No. 162. Lima: Defensoría del Pueblo.

Deleuze, Gilles. 1988. *Bergsonism*. New York: Zone Books.

———. 1995. *Negotiations. 1972–1990*. New York: Columbia University Press.

Deleuze, Gilles, and Felix Guattari. 1986. *Kafka: Toward a Minor Literature*. Translated by Dana Polan. Minneapolis: University of Minnesota Press.

———. 1987. *A Thousand Plateaus: Capitalism and Schizophrenia*. Minneapolis: University of Minnesota Press.

Delgado Sumar, Hugo. 1984. "Ideología andina: el pagapu en Ayacucho." Thesis, Universidad Nacional de San Cristóbal de Huamanga.

Del Pino, Ponciano. 1996. "Tiempos de guerra y de dioses: ronderos, evangélicos y senderistas en el Valle del Río Apurímac." In *Las rondas campesinas y la derrota de Sendero Luminoso*, 117–88. Edited by Carlos Ivan Degregori. Lima: Instituto de Estudios Peruanos.

Del Pino, Ponciano, and Caroline Yezer. 2013. *Las formas del recuerdo: etnografías de la violencia política en el Perú*. Lima: Instituto de Estudios Peruanos.

Déotte, Jean-Louis. 2004. "Las paradojas del acontecimiento de una desaparición." In *Memorias en conflicto: aspectos de la violencia política contemporánea*, 323–28. Edited by Raynald Belay, Jorge Bracamonte, Carlos Iván Degregori, and Jean Joinville Vacher. Lima: Instituto Francés de Estudios Andinos.

Derrida, Jacques. 1992. "Force of Law: 'The Mystical Foundation of Authority.'" In *Deconstruction and the Possibility of Justice*, 3–67. Edited by Drucilla Cornell, Michael Rosenfeld, and David Gray Carlson. New York: Routledge.

Desjarlais, Robert. 2003. *Sensory Biographies: Lives and Deaths Among Nepal's Yolmo Buddhists*. Berkeley: University of California Press.

Dewey, John. 2012. *The Public and Its Problems: An Essay in Political Inquiry*. University Park: University of Pennsylvania Press.

Dumézil, Georges. 1988. *Mitra-Varuna: An Essay on Two Indo-European Representations of Sovereignty*. New York: Zone Books.

Durkheim, Émile. 1973. "Two Laws of Penal Evolution." *Economy and Society* 2(3): 278–84.

Duviols, Pierre. 1973. "Huari y Llacuz: agricultores y pastores. Un dualismo pre-hispánico de oposición y complementariedad." *Revista del Museo Nacional* 39: 153–91.

Earls, John. 1969. "The Organization of Power in Quechua Mythology." *Journal of the Steward Anthropological Society* 1(1): 63–82.

Earls, John, and Irene Silverblatt. 1978. "La realidad física y social en la cosmología andina." *Actas del XLII Congreso Internacional de Americanistas*. Paris: Tomo, 4: 299–325.

Equipo Peruano de Antropología Forense. n.d. *Desaparición forzada en el Perú. El aporte de la investigación antropológica forense en la obtención de evidencia probatoria y la construcción de un paraguas humanitario*. Lima: Equipo Peruano de Antropología Forense.

Estenssoro, Juan Carlos. 2003. *Del paganismo a la santidad: la incorporación de los indios al Perú del catolicismo, 1532–1750*. Lima: Instituto Francés de Estudios Andinos.

Fassin, Didier. 2011a. "Coming Back to Life: An Anthropological Reassessment of Biopolitics and Governmentality." In *Governmentality: Current Issues and Future Challenges*, 185–200. Edited by Ulrich Bröckling, Susanne Krasmann, and Thomas Lemke. New York: Routledge.

———. 2011b. *Humanitarian Reason: A Moral History of the Present*. Berkeley: University of California Press.

Fassin, Didier, and Richard Rechtman. 2009. *The Empire of Trauma: An Inquiry into the Condition of Victimhood*. Princeton, NJ: Princeton University Press.

Feitlowitz, Marguerite. 1998. *A Lexicon of Terror: Argentina and the Legacies of Torture*. Oxford: Oxford University Press.

Felman, Shoshana. 2002. *The Juridical Unconscious: Trials and Traumas in the Twentieth Century*. Cambridge, MA: Harvard University Press.

Ferrandiz, Francisco, and Antonius C. G. M. Robben, eds. 2015. *Necropolitics: Mass Graves and Exhumations in the Age of Human Rights*. Philadelphia: University of Pennsylvania Press.

Ferraro, Emilia. 2008. "Kneading Life: Women and the Celebration of the Dead in the Ecuadorian Andes." *Journal of the Royal Anthropological Institute (N.S.)* 14: 262–77.

Fondebrider, Luis. 2002. "Reflections on the Scientific Documentation of Human Rights Violations." *International Review of the Red Cross* 84: 885–91.

———. 2015. "Forensic Anthropology and the Investigation of Political Violence: Notes from the Field." In *Disturbing Bodies: Anthropological Perspectives on Forensic Archaeology*, 29–40. Edited by Zoe Crossland and Rosemary Joyce. Santa Fe, NM: SAR.

Foucault, Michel. 1977. *Discipline and Punish: The Birth of the Prison*. New York: Vintage.

———. 1978. *History of Sexuality*. Vol. 1. New York: Pantheon.

———. 2003. *Society Must be Defended*. New York: Picador.

———. 2007. *Security, Territory, Population: Lectures at the College of France, 1977–1978*. New York: Palgrave Macmillan.

———. 2008. *The Birth of Biopolitics: Lectures at the College of France, 1978–1979*. New York: Palgrave Macmillan.

Gamarra, Jeffrey. 2000. "Conflict, Post-conflict, and Religion: Andean Responses to New Religious Movements." *Journal of Southern African Studies* 26(2): 271–87.

Giddens, Anthony. 1986. Introduction. In *Durkheim on Politics and the State*, 1–31. Edited by Anthony Giddens. Stanford, CA: Stanford University Press.

Gil, Jose. 1998. *Metamorphosis of the Body*. Translated by Stephen Muecke. Minneapolis: University of Minnesota Press.

Gillespie, Susan. 2001. "Personhood, Agency and Mortuary Ritual: A Case Study from the Ancient Maya." *Journal of Anthropological Archaeology* 20(1): 73–112.

Ginzburg, Carlo. 1989. *Clues, Myths, and the Historical Method*. Baltimore: Johns Hopkins University Press.

Gonzales, Olga. 2011. *Unveiling Secrets of War in the Peruvian Andes*. Chicago: University of Chicago Press.

Gonzales-Cueva, Eduardo. 2004. "The Contribution of the Peruvian Truth and Reconciliation Commission to Prosecutions." *Criminal Law Forum* 15: 55–66.

———. 2006. "The Peruvian Truth and Reconciliation Commission and the Challenge of Impunity." In *Transitional Justice in the Twenty-First Century: Beyond Truth Versus Justice*, 70–93. Edited by Naomi Roht-Arriaza and Javier Mariezcurrena. Cambridge: Cambridge University Press.

Good, Byron. 1994. *Medicine, Rationality, and Experience: An Anthropological Perspective*. Cambridge: Cambridge University Press.

Gose, Peter. 1994. *Deathly Waters and Hungry Mountains: Agrarian Ritual and Class Formation in an Andean Town*. Toronto: University of Toronto Press.

———. 2008. *Invaders as Ancestors: On the Intercultural Making and Unmaking of Spanish Colonialism in the Andes*. Toronto: University of Toronto Press.

Grandin, Greg. 2005. "The Instruction of Great Catastrophe: Truth Commissions, National History, and State Formation in Argentina, Chile, and Guatemala." *American Historical Review* 110(1): 46–67. Available at http://ahr.oxfordjournals.org/content/110/1/46.full.pdf+html.

Green, Linda. 1999. *Fear as a Way of Life: Mayan Widows in Rural Guatemala*. New York: Columbia University Press.

Greenberg, B. 1973. *Flies and Disease, Vol. 2: Biology and Disease Transmission*. Princeton, NJ: Princeton University Press.

Greenberg, B., and J. C. Kunich. 2002. *Entomology and the Law: Flies as Forensic Indicators*. Cambridge: Cambridge University Press.

Harris, Olivia. 1982. "The Dead and the Devils Among the Bolivian Laymi." In *Death and the Regeneration of Life*, 45–73. Edited by Maurice Bloch and Jonathan Parry. Cambridge: Cambridge University Press.

Harvey, Penelope. 1991. "Drunken Speech and the Construction of Meaning: Bilingual Competence in the Southern Peruvian Andes." *Language in Society* 20: 1–36.

———. 1994. "Gender, Community, and Confrontation: Power Relations in Drunkenness in Ocongate (Southern Peru)." In *Gender, Drinks and Drugs*, 209–33. Edited by Maryon McDonald. Oxford: Berg.

Hayner, Priscilla. 2011. *Unspeakable Truths: Facing the Challenge of Truth Commissions.* New York: Routledge.

Heaney, Seamus. 2004. *The Burial at Thebes: A Version of Sophocles' Antigone.* New York: Farrar, Straus and Giroux.

Hegel, Georg Wilhelm Friedrich. 1999. *The Philosophy of Fine Art.* Bristol, UK: Thoemmes.

Heilman, Jaymie. 2010. *Before the Shining Path: Politics in Rural Ayacucho, 1895–1980.* Stanford, CA: Stanford University Press.

Hertz, Robert. 1960. *Death and the Right Hand.* Glencoe, IL: Free Press.

Hinton Laban, Alexander, ed. 2010. *Transitional Justice:. Global Mechanisms and Local Realities After Genocide and Mass Violence.* New Brunswick, NJ: Rutgers University Press.

Hocquenghem, Anne Marie. 1981. "Les mouches et les mortes dans l'iconographie Mochica." *Nawpa Pacha* 19: 63–66.

Huchet, J. B., and B. Greenberg. 2010. "Flies, Mochicas, and Burial Practices: A Case Study from the Huaca de la Luna, Peru." *Journal of Archaeological Science* 37: 2846–56.

Ignatieff, Michael. 1996. "Articles of Faith." *Index on Censorship* 25(5): 110–22.

Ingold, Tim, and Jo Lee Vergunst, eds. 2008. *Ways of Walking: Ethnography and Practice on Foot.* Burlington, VT: Ashgate.

Isbell, Billie Jean. 1977. "'Those Who Love Me': An Analysis of Andean Kinship and Reciprocity." In *Andean Kinship and Marriage*, 81–105. Edited by Ralph Bolton and Enrique Mayer. Washington, DC: American Anthropological Association.

———. 1978. *To Defend Ourselves: Ecology and Ritual in an Andean Village.* Austin: Institute of Latin American Studies, University of Texas at Austin

Jara, Umberto. 2003. *Ojo por ojo: la verdadera historia del Grupo Colina.* Lima: Grupo Ilhsa.

Joyce, Rosemary. 2015. "Grave Responsibilities: Encountering Human Remains." In *Disturbing Bodies: Anthropological Perspectives on Forensic Archaeology*, 169–84. Edited by Zoe Crossland and Rosemary Joyce. Santa Fe, NM: SAR.

Kernaghan, Richard. 2009. *Coca's Gone: Of Might and Right in the Huallaga Post-boom.* Stanford, CA: Stanford University Press.

———. 2014. "Time as Weather: Corpse-work in the Prehistory of Political Boundaries." In *Governing the Dead: Sovereignty and the Politics of Dead Bodies*, 179–202. Edited by Finn Stepputat. Manchester: Manchester University Press.

Koselleck, Reinhardt. 2005. "Terror and Dream: Methodological Remarks on the Experience of Time in the Third Reich." Chap. 12 in *Futures Past: On the Semantics of Historical Time.* New York: Columbia University Press.

Kritsky, G. 1985. "Tombs, Mummies and Flies." *Bulletin of the Entomological Society of America* 31: 18–19

Kwon, Heonik. 2008. *Ghosts of War in Vietnam.* Cambridge: Cambridge University Press.

Lacan, Jacques. 1997. "The Splendor of Antigone." In *The Ethics of Psychoanalysis: 1959– 1960. The Seminar of Jacques Lacan, Book VII*, 243–56. Edited by Jacques-Allain Miller. Translated by Dennis Porter. New York: Norton.

LaCapra, Dominick. 1999. "Trauma, Absence, Loss." *Critical Inquiry* 25(4): 696–727.

La Serna, Miguel. 2012. *The Corner of the Living: Ayacucho on the Eve of the Shining Path Insurgency.* Chapel Hill: University of North Carolina Press.

Latour, Bruno. 2000. "When Things Strike Back: A Possible Contribution of 'Science Studies' to the Social Sciences." *British Journal of Sociology* 51(1): 107–23.

Leinaweaver, Jessaca B. 2008. *The Circulation of Children: Kinship, Adoption and Morality in Andean Peru.* Durham, NC: Duke University Press.

Lemke, Thomas. 2011. *Foucault, Governmentality and Critique.* Boulder, CO: Paradigm.

Lerner Febres, Salomón. 2003. "Peruvian Commission on Truth and Reconciliation: Presentation of the Final Report." *ReVista, Harvard Review of Latin America,* Fall, http://revista.drclas.harvard.edu/book/peruvian-commission-truth-and-reconciliation.

Levi-Strauss, Claude. 1966. *The Savage Mind.* Chicago: University of Chicago Press.

Lomnitz, Claudio. 2005. *Death and the Idea of Mexico.* Brooklyn, NY: Zone Books.

Maier-Hirsch, Elizabeth. 2001. *Las madres de los desaparecidos: ¿Un nuevo mito materno en América Latina?* Mexico City: Universidad Autónoma Metropolitana and La Jornada Ediciones.

Malinowski, Bronislaw. 1922. *Argonauts of the Western Pacific.* New York: Routledge.

———. 1948. *Magic, Science and Religion, and Other Essays.* Boston: Beacon.

Mannheim, Bruce. 1987. "A Semiotic of Andean Dreams." In *Dreaming: Anthropological and Psychological Interpretations,* 132–53. Edited by B. Tedlock. Cambridge: Cambridge University Press.

———. 1998. "Time, Not the Syllables, Must Be Counted: Quechua Parallelism, Word Meaning and Cultural Analysis." *Michigan Discussions in Anthropology* 13(1): 238–87.

Marks, John. 2003. "Gilles Deleuze: Writing in Terror." *Parallax* 9(1): 114–24.

Mbembe, Achille. 2003. "Necropolitics.: *Public Culture* 15(1): 11–40.

Mendez, Cecilia. 2005. *The Plebeian Republic: The Huanta Rebellion and the Making of the Peruvian State, 1820–1850.* Durham, NC: Duke University Press.

Mendez, Juan, and Carlos Chipoco. 1988. *Tolerating Abuses: Violations of Human Rights in Peru.* Washington, DC: Americas Watch Committee.

Mendez, Juan, and Francisco J. Bariffi. 2012. "Truth, Right to, International Protection." In *Max Planck Encyclopedia of Public International Law.* Institute for Comparative Public Law and International Law. Oxford: Oxford University Press.

Metcalf, Peter, and Richard Huntington. 1991. *Celebrations of Death: The Anthropology of Mortuary Ritual.* New York: Cambridge University Press.

Millaire, Jean-François. 2002. *Moche Burial Patterns: An Investigation into Prehispanic Social Structure.* BAR International Series 1066. Oxford: Archaeopress.

Millones, Luis. 2010. *Después de la muerte: voces del limbo y el infierno en territorio andino.* Lima: Fondo Editorial del Congreso del Perú.

Milton, Cynthia E. 2014. *Art from a Fractured Past: Memory and Truth Telling in Post–Shining Path Peru.* Durham, NC: Duke University Press.

Minow, Martha. 1998. *Between Vengeance and Forgiveness: Facing History After Genocide and Mass Violence.* Boston: Beacon.

Mittermaier, Amira. 2011. *Dreams That Matter: Egyptian Landscapes of the Imagination.* Berkeley: University of California Press.

Mueggler, Eric. 2001. *The Age of Wild Ghosts: Memory, Violence and Place in Southwest China.* Berkeley: University of California Press.

Muñoz, Hortensia. 1998. "Human Rights and Social Referents: The Construction of New Sensibilities." In *Shining and the Other Paths: War and Society in Peru, 1980–1995*, 445–69. Edited by Steve Stern. Durham, NC: Duke University Press.

Murphy, Kaitlin. 2015. "What the Past Will Be: Curating Memory in Peru's Yuyanapaq: Para Recordar." *Human Rights Review* 16: 23–38.

Murra, John. 2002. *El mundo andino, población, medio ambiente y economía.* Lima: Instituto de Estudios Peruanos.

Naqvi, Yasmin. 2006. "The Right to the Truth in International Law: Fact or Fiction?" *International Review of the Red Cross* 88(862): 245–73.

Nelson, Diane. 2009. *Reckoning: The Ends of War in Guatemala.* Durham, NC: Duke University Press.

Nuñez del Prado, Juan. 1970. "El mundo sobrenatural de los Quechuas del sur del Perú a través de la comunidad de Cotobamba." *Allpanchis Phuturinqa* 2: 57–119.

Ost, Francois. 2005. *El tiempo del derecho.* Buenos Aires: Siglo XXI Editores Argentina.

Poole, Deborah. 1987. "Landscapes of Power in a Cattle-Rustling Culture of Southern Andean Peru." *Dialectical Anthropology* 12(4): 367–98.

———, ed. 1994. *Unruly Order: Violence, Power, and Cultural Identity in the High Provinces of Southern Peru.* Boulder, CO: Westview.

———. 1997. *Vision, Race and Modernity: A Visual Economy of the Andean Image World.* Princeton, NJ: Princeton University Press.

———. 2004. "Between Threat and Guarantee: Justice and Community in the Margins of the Peruvian State." In *Anthropology in the Margins of the State*, 35–65. Edited by Veena Das and Deborah Poole. Santa Fe, NM: School of American Research Press.

Poole, Deborah, and Gerardo Rénique. 1992. *Peru: Time of Fear.* London: Latin America Bureau.

Poole, Deborah, and Isaías Rojas-Pérez. 2011. "Memories of Reconciliation: Photography and Memory in Postwar Peru." Hemispheric Institute, E-misférica, 7(2), Winter, http://hemisphericinstitute.org/hemi/en/e-misferica-72/poolerojas (accessed December 30, 2016).

Presner, Tod Samuel. 2007. *Mobile Modernity: Germans, Jews, Trains.* New York: Columbia University Press.

Quiroz, Alfonso. 2008. *Corrupt Circles: A History of Unbound Graft in Peru.* Baltimore: Johns Hopkins University Press.

Ramos, Gabriela. 2010. *Death and Conversion in the Andes: Lima and Cuzco, 1532–1670.* Notre Dame, IN: University of Notre Dame Press.

Renshaw, Layla. 2011. *Exhuming Loss: Memory, Materiality, and Mass Graves of the Spanish Civil War.* Walnut Creek, CA: Left Coast Press.

Ricard Lanatta, Xavier. 2007. *Ladrones de la Sombra.* Cusco: Cera las Casas.

Ritter, Jonathan. 2002. "Ritual and Revolution in the Peruvian Andes." *British Journal of Ethnomusicology* 11(1): 9–42.

Robben, Antonius C. G. M. 2004. "State Terror in the Netherworld: Disappearance and Reburial in Argentina." In *Death, Mourning, and Burial: A Cross-Cultural Reader*, 134–48. Edited by Antonius C. G. M. Robben. Malden, MA: Blackwell.

———, ed. 2004. *Death, Mourning, and Burial: A Cross-Cultural Reader*. Malden, MA: Blackwell.

———. 2015. "Exhumations, Territoriality, and Necropolitics in Chile and Argentina." In *Necropolitics: Mass Graves and Exhumations in the Age of Human Rights*, 53–75. Edited by Francisco Ferrándiz and Antonius Robben. Philadelphia: University of Pennsylvania Press.

Robin, Valerie. 2005. "Caminos a la otra vida: ritos funerarios en los Andes Peruanos meridionales." In *Etnografías del Cuzco*, 47–68. Edited by Antoinette Molinié. Lima: Instituto Francés de Estudios Andinos—Centro de Estudios Regionales Andinos "Bartolomé de Las Casas"—Laboratoire d'ethnologie et de sociologie comparative.

———. 2008. *Miroirs de l'autre vie: pratiques rituelles et discours sur les morts dans les Andes de Cuzco, Péru*. Nanterre: Societé d'Ethnologie.

Roht-Arriaza, Naomi. 2005. *The Pinochet Effect: Transnational Justice in the Age of Human Rights*. Philadelphia: University of Pennsylvania Press.

Rojas-Perez, Isaias. 2008. "Writing the Aftermath: Anthropology and 'Post Conflict.'" In *A Companion to Latin American Anthropology*, 254–75. Edited by Deborah Poole. Malden, MA: Blackwell.

———. 2010. "Fragments of Soul: Law, Transitional Justice and Mourning in Post War Peru." PhD diss., Johns Hopkins University.

———. 2013. "Unfinished Pasts: Law, Transitional Justice and Mourning in Post War Peru." *Humanity* 4(1): 149–70.

Root, Rebecca. 2012. *Transitional Justice in Peru*. New York: Palgrave Macmillan.

Rorty, Richard. 1991. *Objectivity, Relativism, and Truth: Philosophical Papers*. New York: Cambridge University Press.

Rosaldo, Renato. 1993. *Culture and Truth: The Remaking of Social Analysis*. Boston: Beacon.

Rosenblatt, Adam. 2015. *Digging for the Disappeared: Forensic Science After Atrocity*. Stanford, CA: Stanford University Press.

Rosing, Ina. 1994. "La deuda de ofrenda: un concepto central de la religión andina." *Revista Andina* 12: 191–216.

———. 1995. "Paranam Purinam—Going for Rain: 'Mute Anthropology' vs. 'Speaking Anthropology.'" *Anthropos* 90: 69–89.

Sahlins, Marshall. 2013. *What Kinship Is . . . And Is Not*. Chicago: University of Chicago Press.

Salomon, Frank. 2010. Review of *Invaders as Ancestors: On the Intercultural Making and Unmaking of Spanish Colonialism in the Andes*, Peter Gose. *Journal of Latin American Studies* 42(1): 164–65.

———. 1995. "The Beautiful Grandparents. Andean Ancestor Shrines and Mortuary Rituals as Seen Through Colonial Records." *In Tombs for the Living. Andean Mortuary Practices.* Edited by Tom D. Dillehay. Washington, DC: Dumbarton Oaks. 315–54.

Sanford, Victoria. 2003. *Buried Secrets: Truth and Human Rights in Guatemala.* New York: Palgrave Macmillan.

Sant Cassia, Paul. 2005. *Bodies of Evidence: Burial, Memory and the Recovery of Missing Persons in Cyprus.* New York: Berghahn.

Saona, Margarita. 2014. *Memory Matters in Transitional Peru.* New York: Palgrave Macmillan.

Saunders, Rebecca. 2002. "Tell the Truth: The Archaeology of Human Rights Abuses in Guatemala and the Former Yugoslavia." In *Matériel Culture: The Archaeology of Twentieth-Century Conflict,* 103–14. Edited by J. Schofield, C. Beck, and W. G. Johnson. London: Routledge.

Scheper-Hughes, Nancy. 1993. *Death Without Weeping: The Violence of Everyday in Brazil.* Berkeley: University of California Press.

Schirmer, Jennifer. 1993. "The Seeking of Truth and the Gendering of Consciousness: The CoMadres of El Salvador and the CONAVIGUA Widows of Guatemala." In *"Viva": Women and Popular Protest in Latin America,* 30–64. Edited by Sarah Radcliffe and Sallie Westwood. New York: Routledge.

Seery, John Evan. 1996. *Political Theory for Mortals: Shades of Justice, Images of Death.* Ithaca, NY: Cornell University Press.

Seremetakis, Nadia. 1990. "The Ethics of Antiphony: The Social Construction of Pain, Gender and Power in the Southern Peloponnese." *Ethos* 18(4): 481–511.

———. 1991. *The Last Word: Women, Death, and Divination in Inner Mani.* Chicago: University of Chicago Press.

Sharma, Aradhana, and Akhil Gupta, eds. 2006. *The Anthropology of the State: A Reader.* Malden, MA: Blackwell.

Shaw, Rosalind, and Lars Waldorf eds. 2010. *Localizing Transitional Justice: Interventions and Priorities After Mass Violence.* Stanford, CA: Stanford University Press.

Shimada, Izumi, and James L. Fitzsimmons, eds. 2015. *Living with the Dead in the Andes.* Tucson: University of Arizona Press.

Siegel, James. 1998. *A New Criminal Type in Jakarta: Counter-Revolution Today.* Durham, NC: Duke University Press.

Sikkink, Kathryn. 2011. *The Justice Cascade: How Human Rights Prosecutions Are Changing the World.* New York: Norton.

Sophocles. 2003. *Antigone.* Translated by Reginald Gibbons and Charles Segal. New York: Oxford University Press.

Stephen, Lynn. 2005. "Women's Rights Are Human Rights: The Merging of Feminine and Feminist Interests Among El Salvador's Mothers of the Disappeared (CO-MADRES)." *American Ethnologist* 22(4): 807–27.

Stepputat, Finn, ed. 2014. *Governing the Dead: Sovereignty and the Politics of Dead Bodies.* Manchester: Manchester University Press.

Stevenson, Neil. 1977. "Colerina: Reactions to Emotional Stress in the Peruvian Andes." *Social Science and Medicine* 11(5): 303–7.

Suarez-Orozco, Marcelo M. 1991. "The Heritage of Enduring a 'Dirty War': Psychosocial Aspects of Terror in Argentina, 1976–1988." *Journal of Psychohistory and Psychoanalytic Anthropology* 18(4): 469–505.

Tamayo, Ana María. 2003. "Anfasep y la lucha por la memoria de sus desaparecidos (1983–2000)." In *Jamás tan cerca arremetió lo lejos. Memoria y violencia política en el Perú*, 95–134. Edited by Carlos Iván Degregori. Lima: Instituto de Estudios Peruanos.

Tate, Winnifred. 2007. *Counting the Dead: The Culture and Politics of Human Rights Activism in Colombia*. Berkeley: University of California Press.

Taussig, Michael. 1984. "Culture of Terror—Space of Death: Roger Casement's Putumayo Report and the Explanation of Torture." *Comparative Studies in Society and History* 26: 467–97.

———. 1989. "Terror as Usual." *Social Text* 23: 3–20.

———. 1999. *Defacement: Public Secrecy and the Labor of the Negative*. Stanford, CA: Stanford University Press.

———. 2001. "Dying Is an Art, like Everything Else." *Critical Inquiry* 28(1): 305–16.

Taylor, Gerald. 1987. *Ritos y tradiciones de Huarochirí: manuscrito quechua de comienzos del siglo XVII*. Lima: Instituto de Estudios Peruanos.

Teitel, Ruti. 2000. "Transitional Jurisprudence: The Role of Law in Political Transformation." *Yale Law Journal* 106(7): 2009–80.

Theidon, Kimberly. 2000. "How We Learn to Kill Our Brothers: Memory, Morality and Reconciliation in Peru." Bulletin de l'Institut Français d'Études Andines 29(3): 539–54.

———. 2001. "Terror's Talk: Fieldwork and War." *Dialectical Anthropology* 26: 19–35.

———. 2004. *Entre prójimos. El conflicto armado interno y la política de la reconciliación en el Perú*. Lima: Instituto de Estudios Peruanos.

———. 2006. "Justice in Transition: The Micropolitics of Reconciliation in Postwar Peru." *Journal of Conflict Resolution* 50(3): 433–57.

———. 2010. "Histories of Innocence: Postwar Stories in Peru." In *Localizing Transitional Justice: Interventions and Priorities After Mass Violence*, 92–110. Edited by Rosalind Shaw and Lars Waldorf. Stanford, CA: Stanford University Press.

———. 2012. *Intimate Enemies: Violence and Reconciliation*. Philadelphia: University of Pennsylvania Press.

Tortorici, Zeb. 2011. "Reading the (Dead) Body: Histories of Suicide in New Spain." In *Death and Dying in Colonial Spanish America*, 53–77. Edited by Martina Will de Chaparro and Miruna Achim. Tucson: University of Arizona Press.

Tuller, Hugh. 2015. "Identification Versus Prosecution: Is It That Simple, and Where Should the Archaeologist Stand?" In *Disturbing Bodies: Anthropological Perspectives on Forensic Archaeology*, 85–101. Edited by Zoe Crossland and Rosemary Joyce. Santa Fe, NM: SAR.

Tylor, Edward. 1871. *Primitive Culture: Researches into the Development of Mythology, Philosophy, Religion, Art, and Custom*. London: Bradbury, Evans.

Uceda, Ricardo. 2004. *Muerte en el Pentagonito. Los cementerios secretos del ejército peruano*. Bogota: Planeta Colombiana.

Urioste, George, and Frank Salomon, trans. 1991. *The Huarochirí Manuscript: A Testament of Ancient and Colonial Andean Religion*. Austin: University of Texas Press.

Valderrama, Ricardo, and Carmen Escalante. 1980. "Apu Qorpuna: visión del mundo de los muertos en la comunidad de Awkimarka." *Debates en Antropología* 5: 233–64.

Valverde, Mariana. 2003. *Law's Dream of Common Knowledge*. Princeton, NJ: Princeton University Press.

Vatter, Miguel. 2014. "Foucault and Hayek: Republican Law and Liberal Civil Society." In *The Government of Life: Foucault, Biopolitics and Neoliberalism*, 163–84. Edited by Vanessa Lem and Miguel Vatter. New York: Fordham University Press.

Verbistsky, Horacio. 1996. *The Flight: Confessions of an Argentine Dirty Warrior*. New York: New Press.

Verdery, Katherine. 1999. *The Political Lives of Dead Bodies: Reburial and Postsocialist Change*. New York: Columbia University Press.

Wagner, Sarah. 2008. *To Know Where He Lies: DNA Technology and the Search for Sebrenica's Missing*. Berkeley: University of California Press.

Walker, Charles. 2014. *The Tupac Amaru Rebellion*. Cambridge, MA: Harvard University Press.

Wax, M. L. 1972. "Tenting with Malinowski." *American Sociological Review* 37: 1–13.

Weismantel, Mary. 2001. *Cholas and Pishtacos: Stories of Race and Sex in the Andes*. Chicago: Chicago University Press.

Wilson, Richard, ed. 1997. *Human Rights, Culture and Context: Anthropological Perspectives*. Chicago: Pluto Press.

———. 2001. *The Politics of Truth and Reconciliation in South Africa: Legitimizing the Post-Apartheid State*. Cambridge: Cambridge University Press.

———. 2003. "Anthropological Studies of National Reconciliation Processes." *Anthropological Theory* 3(3): 367–87.

Wrobel, Szymon. 2014. "Funeral Policy: The Case of Mourning Populism in Poland." In *Nationalism and the Body Politic: Psychoanalysis and the Rise of Ethnocentrism and Xenophobia*, 65–84. Edited by Lene Auestad. London: Karmac.

Youngers, Coletta. 2003. *Violencia política y sociedad civil en el Perú: historia de la Coordinadora Nacional de Derechos Humanos*. Lima: Instituto de Estudios Peruanos.

Youngers, Coletta, and Jo Marie Burt. 2009. *Human Rights Tribunals in Latin America*. Washington, DC: George Mason University, WOLA, Instituto de Defensa Legal.

Index

Page numbers followed by "f" indicate material in figures and maps.

The authorized representative in the EU for product safety and compliance is:
Mare Nostrum Group
B.V Doelen 72
4831 GR Breda
The Netherlands

www.ingramcontent.com/pod-product-compliance
Lightning Source LLC
Chambersburg PA
CBHW020455270326
41926CB00008B/613